PROJECTIONS 10

PROJECTIONS 10

Hollywood Film-makers on Film-making

edited by Mike Figgis

executive editors
John Boorman and Walter Donohue

faber and faber
LONDON·NEW YORK

First published in 1999
by Faber and Faber Limited
3 Queen Square London WC1N 3AU
Published in the United States by Faber and Faber Inc.
a division of Farrar, Straus and Giroux Inc., New York

Typeset by Faber and Faber Ltd
Printed in England by Clays Ltd, St Ives plc

A CIP record for this book
is available from the British Library

ISBN 0–571–19357–9

10 9 8 7 6 5 4 3 2 1

Contents

Foreword

John Boorman

We asked Mike Figgis to take over this edition of *Projections*. Like many a fine film-maker, he struggles to follow his vision in an increasingly hostile and volatile environment. After bruising encounters with Hollywood, he broke free of the system by shooting *Leaving Las Vegas* on Super 16mm in three weeks. Not only a critical success, it was a surprise hit with the public. Despite its minuscule budget, according to the MGM book-keeper it has yet to show a profit, and the man who made it and deferred his life went unrewarded. Much more money was spent on promoting it than making it. But the way it works in Hollywood is that when you make a hit, it's the next film that pays you. Desperate to be associated with success, they line up to shower you with money. He took on a script by Joe Eszterhas – *One Night Stand*. Until recently this man was the highest paid, most wooed and successful screenwriter in town. His erotic fantasies made millions, but then came a couple of flops and he was suddenly a pariah, reviled as a purveyor of semi-soft porn. Mike rewrote the script, expunging all traces of the man, but the stigma was such that he had great difficulty in casting it. It was a beautiful movie, subtle and tenderly erotic, yet it never quite succeeded in escaping the stigma of its provenance. Fear of failure is so pervasive and so distorting that it colours all judgements.

What follows is an account of a journey Mike took through the Hollywood labyrinth, a series of conversations with people working in the business. It is a remarkable snapshot of how it works and how it malfunctions.

Mike has since turned away from the system once more and made two low-budget, independent movies – *The End of Sexual Innocence* and a version of *Miss Julie*, shot in two weeks.

He is a guerrilla fighter, lean and fast, he pillages his pictures and is gone before they can catch up with him. His quickness of eye and his honesty are manifest in these pages. These are despatches from the front.

Introduction
Mike Figgis

After my first short film, *The House*, was seen on Channel 4, I received a call from David Puttnam, and all seemed rosy as he commissioned *Stormy Monday*. There followed a year in which he never read the treatment, and in fact I never saw him again until quite recently, when I bumped into him at some film function. Meanwhile I went back to part-time teaching and working in theatre and one day, while retrieving discarded sound tapes from a skip in Soho, I bumped into Nigel Stafford Clarke, the producer of *The House*, and after a chat he suggested I take the script of *Stormy Monday* to him. He gave me notes, we went ahead with a script and he got funding from Channel 4 and British Screen. This came to about half of the budget and we needed about $750,000 from an American distributor. Which is what took me to Los Angeles for the first time in my life . . .

Hemdale, flushed with their success on films such as *Platoon*, were picking up cheap British products, and *Stormy Monday* was one of the many that they announced at Cannes in the spring of 1987. Nigel and I set off for New York and Los Angeles to begin casting for the two American parts. We got through New York, but things were tense in LA because we still didn't have anything in writing from Hemdale and it was Nigel's job to get a contract. We arrived in LA and went straight to the Beverly Hills Hotel for a meeting with Kate Capshaw (later to become Mrs Steven Spielberg). I wasn't allowed in without a jacket and so I went back to the car to get one. It was green with a yellow lining; a nice enough jacket. As I came back into the lobby, three men who had witnessed the initial refusal of entry laughed and said (in a friendly manner), 'Is that the best they could do for you?' They thought I'd been given some reject by the staff. Kate was pretty and charming and talked about the script, as they all talk about any script, and then got into her huge Jeep and drove off.

We checked into the Holiday Inn in Santa Monica, and the next morning I experienced my first earthquake. At breakfast I was writing in my notebook and a very chatty waitress pumped me for information about what I did in the entertainment business. When I said I was a director, she shouted very loudly, 'Dolores, come here, this man's a *director!*' Dolores, a pretty Hispanic girl, appeared, blushing, from the kitchen, and was made to parade for me. I was even more embarrassed than she was; probably because I'd described myself as someone I wanted to be but was not yet.

Being with Nigel was like being with an older brother, although in fact he was younger. But it was he who held the money, and we ate together; and he rented the car and drove, so we went out in the car together. On Sunday we went to the beach; two Englishmen, very white and overdressed. Every day he tried to have a meeting with John Daly (the man who put the 'Dale' in Hemdale) and every day he was fobbed off with another excuse. Daly never even came to the phone. After many days of this humiliation we admitted defeat and got on the plane and went home. The film more or less died for a time and, hard up, I went back to teaching.

About a year later, there was a small bite on the line. Sales agent Bill Gavin was at that time one of the movers and shakers in the new British film industry. It was he who had set up the Hemdale fiasco and he persevered and got some interest from a small independent company called Atlantic Releasing. I was on holiday with my family in Devon and would ring up every couple of days from a phone box to see if Nigel had any news. Usually the answer was no, but on one occasion the answer was a cautious yes. I then spoke to Bill and he gave me a number to call in LA and said it was very important that I introduce myself and subtly insinuate myself into Atlantic's awareness.

Because of the eight-hour time difference the best time to call was early evening UK time. So I went to the local b. & b. and asked if I could use their phone in the evening. They agreed reluctantly, and that evening I set off down the hill and arrived at the guest-house just as they were serving supper. The phone was in the dining room; and the guests that week appeared to be deaf, since they were all shouting at each other. And outside all the goats and sheep and animals were making a lot of noise. So I phoned Atlantic and eventually got through to the Senior Vice-President in charge of acquisitions, Bobby Rock. Bobby sounded pretty blasé and underwhelmed by my introduction. As I walked back up the hill I pondered the meaning of life.

Things moved slowly and about three months later, just before Christmas, I set off again for LA, but this time by myself. The budget would not stretch to both of us going. My mission was to be a cool, happening, British director; to impress the Americans enough to give us the dosh.

The following is taken from my notebook . . .

A Walk Down Sunset Boulevard

Nigel's secretary asks me where I'd like to stay in LA. I have never been to LA on my own before. I tell her to book me into a hotel on Sunset Boulevard – yeah, Sunset. Atlantic Releasing's office is on Sunset also. So, armed with a coach-class ticket and £300 for expenses, I set off for LA. It is December 1986.

I wake at four-thirty in the morning and turn on the TV. What seems to be a soft-porn film is just finishing and is followed by a serious American play. You can tell it's a play because it's filmed in a theatre. Nice Girl from a Thornton Wilder-ish town is going out with a Rich Boy but she doesn't love him. He loves her but his parents think she is white trash. Enter Bad Boy. He's the kind of character that is described in the script as exuding animal sexuality. He doesn't but everyone acts as if he does – particularly the Nice Girl. She offers her cherry and he takes it and then bunks off leaving everyone in tatters.

I have breakfast in my room and read the LA papers. Adrenaline is starting to flow in anticipation of my 10 a.m. meeting with the film company. The phone rings and the meeting is shifted to two-thirty in the afternoon. 'Here we go again' flashes through my mind but I sweep away all negative thoughts and try to be constructive as I work on a new script.

But it's hard to concentrate and I think about walking. Everyone has always said, 'Don't think about walking in LA', but I know better. I love walking in New York; I love American architecture; the sun is shining; I have three hours to kill. Why not walk slowly to the meeting?

I look at myself in the mirror, swap the sweater for a jacket, check the address of the film company for the tenth time – 9000 Sunset Boulevard – and step out of my room.

The Filipino doorman is vague. Sure he knows the direction of the 9000 but can't understand why I don't take my car. He cannot absorb the fact that I don't have one. I set off but it takes a while to cross the freeway that surrounds the hotel. So many cars.

This first part is interesting. I'm wearing a bright green jacket (the same one with the yellow lining) and playing the part of the affable Englishman in love with the culture. From time to time I stop and take a photograph of a house. After a while I realize that I have not seen a single pedestrian but it doesn't worry me. Sunset Boulevard at this point has lots of bends and little hills. There are huge, ostentatious houses with private roads; notices state that there is armed-response security and closed-circuit TV. I see a few Mexicans tending gardens, their pick-up trucks loaded with garden machinery.

Suddenly the sidewalk stops and is replaced with grass, which is . . . quite nice, like being in the country and yet not. The grass becomes a discreet footpath and I notice quite a lot of rubbish, mainly beer bottles thrown from cars. A fantasy flashes through my mind that I will find a partially clothed, partially decomposed body that has been dumped from a car but then I realize that cars are not allowed to stop.

I've done a couple of miles by now and it hits me that it is a long way to go yet, but I still have a couple of hours so no problem. At a traffic light a lost woman in a car winds down her window and with a look of relief asks me where . . . The traffic starts to move and over the noise I shout 'no' and then smile as charmingly as possible because shouting seems so rude and I know how she feels. I pass UCLA and suddenly there are lots of young, healthy joggers with Walkmans who don't smile back.

The sidewalk stops and so do I. Immediately ahead is a sharp bend. The hillside rises sheer from the road and there is no possible route there. On the other side of the road is a small turning and a group of kids are selling maps of stars' houses. I realize that my best chance is to cross the street and bum a ride with them or at least get to a phone. It takes me another ten minutes to come to terms with the fact that I cannot get across the street; six lanes of fast-moving traffic have defeated me. Eventually I manage to get halfway across. The kids watch me in a detached manner as I look at my watch and begin to panic. There is a lull in the traffic and the road ahead curves out of sight. I run for it. Behind me I hear the roar of approaching traffic. It's been a while since I've run as fast as this. Cars hoot furiously at me for being in the inside lane, and the handle of a garden implement, leaning over the side of a pick-up, misses my head by inches. I dive into the side of the road amidst the thorns and the dirty ivy, and it occurs to me that I could die here.

A lone taxi approaches and at the last moment I see that it is empty and I jump into the road, waving my arms, and it stops, which strikes me as amazing. As I flop on to the back seat I notice two things: my knees are knocking and my clothes are wet with sweat.

The taxi driver is a woman, very cool and friendly, and after quite a long ride she drop me outside 9000 Sunset Boulevard. The fare is six dollars and fifty cents and, with trembling hands, I give her what I think is a ten-dollar bill. 'Keep the rest,' I say, trying to be grown-up. She gives me a look of immense pity and counts out $93.50 in change.

I now have over an hour to kill so I go into a Sushi bar to clean up and calm down. I drink a beer then, with ten minutes to spare, I stroll into the lobby of the 9000 building. This is a big building with a big lobby, and there is a big notice-board that lists all the names of the companies in the building and where to find them. The name of my film company is not on the board. The lobby receptionist guy is busy with a roll of paper issuing from a printout machine. I give him the name of the film company, Atlantic Releasing, and without looking at me he says, 'Ninth Floor, room 25.'

In the lift I look at my distorted image in a brass plate and try to get myself together. I walk down the ninth-floor corridor towards Suite 25. The door does-n't have a handle, only a hole where the handle should be. I knock and the door swings open. Suite 25 is completely empty: not a stick of furniture; marks on the walls where the art used to be. It is now precisely two-thirty.

Back in the lobby the man is unmoved by my rage. 'Yeah, that's right, they moved to . . . let me see . . .' and he consults a piece of paper, '. . . Washington Boulevard.' I ask if it is far and he gives me a withering look of contempt and we go into one of those 'depends what you mean by far' routines. He won't let me use his phone so I cross the street and get a cab driven by a Russian, new to LA, and he's pissed off that I don't know the way because he certainly doesn't. It takes a while for him to look it up in the Thomas guide but finally we hit the freeway system. Yes, the freeway system.

About twenty-five minutes later, with $30 showing on the meter, we pull up beside a derelict car lot at the address given to me by the psycho from the 9000 building. I feel like crying and killing at the same time but I borrow a quarter from the Russian and dial the film company's number. It rings and then the operator's voice asks me to deposit my 25 cents. 'I have,' I tell her. She tells me again to deposit my 25 cents. 'I have,' I repeat. Now we plumb the depths of insanity as she explains that my 25 cents has not registered and that I should deposit another 25 cents and give her my name and address so that the telephone company can refund the first 25 cents. She is not at all fazed that they would have to send it to England. I borrow another quarter from the Russian and eventually I do get through to the film company and I do get through to my contact whose name is Bobby Rock, and at that moment I understand why Patti Hearst married her bodyguard. I tell him where I am and he chuckles. He then explains that, yes, they have moved but, heck, only a couple of blocks down from the 9000 building, still on Sunset. I calculate that by the time I make it back to Sunset I will be $60 lighter and sixty minutes late.

'Don't rush,' says Bobby, 'the meeting's been postponed until tomorrow.'

Tomorrow turned into a series of tomorrows that would have made a Mexican blush. I moved hotels to a place called the Hyatt on Sunset which was almost next door to the offices of Atlantic. The hotel was pink and was much favoured by rock 'n' roll bands that had yet to succeed or were already failing. But one day I did meet Little Richard in the lift and he said hello in a very cheerful manner. I had no car of course and during the day I would go and sit in Bobby Rock's office . . . waiting for a meeting that never came. On that first afternoon after finally making it to the office I did meet the two bosses, Jonathan Dana and Bill Tennant. BT seemed interesting but gruff and Dana seemed aloof and wore a suit. Rock tried to include me a little in his social life but his then girlfriend was not enthusiastic about my presence on their jaunts and I felt very awkward about the whole thing. A week went by and I got my first taste of Christmas in LA. It is weird and without any European resonance.

I got a second taste of Tennant through the wall of Rock's office as he screamed at four other men about a film they were making in the Philippines. He said, 'I speak three languages, fuck you, fuck me and fuck them.' It became clear from the way people spoke about BT that everyone was frightened of him. Rock told me stories of his fall from grace and his drug addiction and alcoholism. Still no meeting. In the evenings I pounded away on a portable typewriter on a second draft of *Liebestraum*, which I had started after the first failure of *Stormy Monday*. Much of it is about being a stranger in an American town, staying in a strange hotel. I had no money at all to spend and no car and I knew no one.

One day at the office I heard from Bobby that there had been a discussion about the film in which, for reasons I never fathomed, the start date had been shifted. I was angry that this had been done without any kind of consultation with me. So I rang up Tennant and complained and he was furious that I would have the nerve to even question him. He told me rudely that this conversation was going nowhere and I should get off the phone. I cannot remember the dialogue but I carried on talking and he said words to the effect of either shut up or fuck off and I said fuck you and hung up. Rock was shocked and I realized that I had probably screwed up everything. But at the same time as being frightened by what I had just done I was also pleased and felt better inside.

Then the phone rang and it was Tennant's secretary and she asked that I step into his office. I remember that it was a Friday and by now I was wondering how soon I could get on to a plane. I also remember that my knees were again shaking as I arrived at his office and was shown in. He had a miniature basketball court in his office; all executives find it necessary to have a shrunken sport thing going for them. I walked in and he got up and said he was sorry. I was not expecting this. He hugged me and said that he realized I had been treated without respect and that I was absolutely right to complain. He went on to say that although it was no excuse, he was having personal problems himself. He said that they loved the script and me and would be making the film and that from now on everything would be fine . . . which it was . . . more or less.

After the film was released I came back to the Hyatt one more time and then they booked me into the Château Marmont and I have stayed there ever since, whenever I need a hotel. This is much to the puzzlement of my American friends who cannot imagine why anyone would want to stay in a place that has no food, no muzak, very bad service, and never gives you your messages.

When I came to town to make my first American film I moved into the Château for almost a year and became part of the furniture. It was, in retrospect, a very sad year for me.

1   Elisabeth Shue

Mike Figgis: Why did you choose to be an actress? Be honest.

Elisabeth Shue: Really honest? Well, the initial reason I chose to be an actress was to get attention. Then, as you go, you realize how much more you've found that works for you in your life, and why you like being an actress kind of develops.

That is why a lot of people come to Hollywood, isn't it? They're usually good-looking and they want to get attention.

I think everyone would like attention, but to go so far as to become an actress, you have to really, really *need* attention. And maybe there's some wound that you experienced when you were a child that you're trying to compensate for, and eliminate. Now I think I have higher ideals about why I do it. I guess this is self-ish too, but I like to experience all sides of my personality, and express different sides of myself. In that way, I feel that I understand more of who I am. If I play somebody who's totally sexually manipulative, then I can honestly face that side of myself, and put it away. Or if I'm playing somebody who is in pain, then I can somehow process pain that I've experienced in my life. Or if I'm playing some-body who's shy, then I can acknowledge that I'm actually really shy. We're all so controlled, trying to just be whatever we think everyone wants us to be. But as an actor, you get to experience every aspect of yourself. So that's what I like about it now. The attention, I think I still crave, but I hate it now. I disrespect that part of it in myself and in other people. I find it somewhat evil, what it does to people and how it hurts your soul.

So how do you deal with that? Emotionally, it's always going to be a contradiction for you, as long as you're in the business.

In some ways you deny it and you look at that aspect of it as just business. Like you have to go and do the talk shows, and publicize the films, and be recognized in the street and be nice to the fans that care about your work. If you don't deal with that, then you can't do what you like to do. But I find I don't really enjoy any of those things any more.

It's a bit of a lie, isn't it?

Yeah. And you're not sure who that personality is that you have to put out for that part. I get in trouble because I just become myself. And then when you're too much yourself, people tell you you're not enough of a 'saleable personality' or whatever.

That is quite unique to this business, right? The perversity of having to talk about what you just did, all the time, as part of the machine of selling the prod-uct. I think it's a real soul-destroyer.

You're just like a specimen for people to constantly pore over. Every film that comes out, I have to at least make a few magazine covers. And you have to do a very long article, you have to spend almost two days with the reporter, who wants to know everything about you. You get into a conversation and you want to feel really open, but you have to be really careful about what's private and what's not, because you're constantly talking about yourself. You just feel raped, or you feel boring, or you said too much or, 'Oh, God, I probably said something negative about somebody.' I've said things about my mother in print. They've described my brother's death in disgusting ways that aren't true, which is really painful.

So did you then think, 'I just shouldn't have said anything about any of that'?
Yeah, I should've said nothing. But you get bored during the interview process, you get bored reading those articles yourself. So you feel like, 'What's the point? If I'm not honest about myself and I don't really talk about things that matter to me . . .'

I know you're expected to do it. But do you think it makes the slightest bit of difference to the success of the film whether you do or not?
I just know that if you don't, the executives and the business people really get angry. Then you're antagonistic to the business aspect of what it means to be an actress. And then they don't want to pay you your salary. It's almost like you don't get your money unless you do what you're told.

Unless you're a good girl. And that means going out and baring your soul, again. And how many times can you tell those stories, about your inner self, or your brother?
Now I won't talk about him at all.

Are you 'difficult' now?
No, I still open up and feel too comfortable with everybody and get into trouble by talking too much about everything. But I've also come to the conclusion that if I'm going to spend my time doing that, I want to have a good conversation with the person. I'm sick of doing it if it's boring.

Do you see a way that you can avoid that in the future? Do you think you can get big enough, for example?
No, the bigger you get the more you have to do it. If you get paid twenty million dollars a movie versus whatever I get paid – which is piecemeal compared to that – then you really have to go out there. I can still say that I hate talk shows and I get too nervous, which I do. And they let me off, if it's a small picture and they didn't pay me much.

Right – it's in direct relation to the money you get paid. Okay – why are you still in films? We sort of covered it, but I ask you that bluntly.
I ask myself that question a lot. I definitely have fantasies of leaving, all the time. But then I think I'm probably wanting to leave out of fear of it ending, or fear of growing older, or feeling I'd rather leave than be unable to do the kind of work I want to do. I don't want to ever have to face whatever that would feel like. But I still do it because I'm still able to work with people that I respect, and I still play

parts that challenge me. Also I enjoy the gypsy aspect of it, going off and meeting people whom you get to know in a very deep and intimate way. The actual experience still enriches my life. If it didn't, and I was one of those people who lived in their trailer and never talked to people, and was angry and isolated and bitter, I wouldn't continue. But I still like the filming family.

How do you rate film as an art form, compared to literature, painting, theatre?
Well, that's hard – what kind of criteria are you going to use? But because film is accessible to so many people, the other art forms less so, I think film has incredible potential to touch people in ways that the other art forms don't come close to. I mean, there is such an élite crowd of people who go to museums, or have enough money to go to the theatre. A lot of people can't even read a book. But everybody can find seven dollars to go see a film. At the same time, because it's so accessible, it also sometimes isn't as pure . . .

Film works. This factory here can produce wonderful things. But of every hundred movies that it turns out now, how many of them would you say work?
I think they work – on all levels – very, very rarely.

So is that what's wrong with Hollywood?
I can't decide if what's wrong is that certain movies make so much money, so they constantly want to remake those movies and have a formula that sells – in other words, that people are too fearful of losing money because it does cost too much money. But, at the same time, because movies are making so much more money, isn't there more opportunity to make independent films than there was a long time ago? Do you think?

I think so. Things can get through. But I've found that young film-makers coming up, their ambitions are not to make astounding independent films, à la Godard. They might pay lip-service to those films, but really their ambition is to be very famous, and incredibly rich – to be, in a sense, more glamorous than the actors they employ. Nic Cage said to me, of a certain director, 'It's kind of worrying when the director is better-looking than the actors – better dressed and more stylish.' If the money wasn't so good here, would the job be quite as attractive for you?
I think so. When I started out, I know I did not do it for the money. I had no idea you could make money. The first film I did was *The Karate Kid*. I had no idea just how much money that movie made until maybe five years ago, when someone told me. I was paid thirty thousand dollars for my part. I thought, 'My God, that is so much money.' What I love about this business is that it's incredible that you're paid at all to do what you do. But it's dangerous, the more money you make, the feeling you get of wanting to make that much money the next time. And if they won't pay you that money, you wonder, 'Do I really want to work that hard and not get paid?' It starts to become an issue.

We both know that our friend Nicolas is on – we hear – twenty million dollars a picture, right? And only a couple of years ago we were doing *Leaving Las Vegas* for practically nothing. I don't know about you, but I'm still waiting to be paid for that.

Oh, but I wouldn't have had a career without that film.

When I first met you, you were just visiting, like me. We both stayed at the same hotel. Now you live here, you've bought a house. How much has that changed your perception of what you do as an actor?

Well, it hasn't changed it that much because we actually do live in the first house we bought, which is very modest and very small. I know the dangers of living here, and I know that people buy houses just to show off and have people thinking, 'Wow, they've really made it.' That whole side of LA doesn't affect me. What does affect me is the jealousies that it starts to create, that feeling of being in a factory town, of comparing yourself, of never wanting to read the trades. But if you just happen to be in the 7-Eleven and you start paging through the trades and you see who's filming, and what parts they're doing, and 'Why didn't I read that script?' . . . You're talking to your agent every day and you have no other input. You don't even have a subway to go on where you can see other people and think about their stories and what their lives are like. You're just 'Me, me, me'. That's the part I think is really evil. Everyone's isolated and thinking about the business all day long. It kills people's souls.

How do you get over that?

Well, I'm really lucky because I'm married to somebody who has a very deep soul, who is striving for the same kind of life I am, and who's as frustrated as I am with the lack of culture here. We've created a little oasis for ourselves in the middle of it all. Having a baby really helps a lot. And I know that I'm going to move – I'm getting out, it's just a matter of time. In about two years, we're going to move back east. But then again, there's something really easy about life here. You can live in a house and still be in a city. That's hard to do if you want to live in New York.

Should there be a ceiling on earnings for actors? For their own sake?

To save them from themselves? Well, as long as somebody like Tom Cruise or Jim Carrey can bring in the audiences that they do, I think they do deserve a share of the proceeds. I think it would be more fair, though, if everybody got pieces of the movie. A ceiling, I don't know – that seems like it's taking away freedom.

I have a theory that actors get paid the amounts of money they do in order to internally justify the amounts of money that everybody else pays everybody else. It's much easier to talk about what Tom Cruise is earning than to talk about an executive or producer whose name isn't known, who's not in *People* magazine. But every time I've gone in and proposed making a low-budget film, it fills people with horror and panic. Because if I can make a film for three mil-

lion dollars, what the fuck are you paying twenty-five million for? Everybody's on a gravy train here. I've come to the conclusion that actors are the whipping-boys and girls.

It's their fault. If they didn't make so much money, then the movies wouldn't cost so much. But then again – the last film I did was as small as *Leaving Las Vegas* in its scope. And I got paid a really good salary, for me.

Do you want to say how much?

I don't know.

That's part of the deal, isn't it? That you don't talk about it.

Well, unless you make a lot – then everyone talks about it.

I'll make a deal with you. If no one else talks about figures, I won't mention it. But if they do, then we'll be honest.

All right. Well, I made two and a half million dollars, which is – I mean, my God, that could give me security for the rest of my life, because I'm definitely going to save it. I did a commercial film after *Leaving Las Vegas*, where I did get paid my first million dollars, but it didn't turn out to be a good experience. But here I feel good that I got paid to do what I wanted to do. It was a small movie, a twenty-two-million-dollar budget. And I still, for the life of me, cannot figure out where that money went – because all the actors got paid nothing. The director didn't get paid anything. I know the unions cost money. But it must have gone to the executives, nameless people.

I did *Leaving Las Vegas* for a budget of three and a half million, then *One Night Stand* for twenty-five, and now *The Loss of Sexual Innocence* for three and a half again. On *Leaving Las Vegas* I felt we were flying. We shot the movie in – what, four weeks? Then to go back to twelve-week shoots, it just feels like wading through cement.

But, Mike, it's different doing a low-budget film with you. The problem is, not a lot of the more artistic directors are doing low-budget films. So most of the low-budget films I'm offered, there's not a director involved who makes me think, 'I've got to have this experience.' If it was a great part, I would do it in a second. But the parts are not that great. It's just hard to find a good script with a good director, period. It's fucking impossible. And I'm supposedly at the top echelon. The stories that they're telling and the roles they're writing for women just don't really interest me most of the time. Every once in a while there is a great script, and you go, 'Ahhh!' But then you find there's not a good part in it for you.

Why?

Because they're all male-dominated scripts.

Why?

Because that's what sells. That's what is proven to sell.

How important is sex to men in this town, as portrayed by women? And why is it always the same story over and over again? Have you ever thought about this?
Yeah, definitely. The easy answer is that the town is run by men, so they want to see themselves in the movies. They want to see themselves as heroes. They want to see themselves with younger women. They want to see themselves on a spaceship going to Mars. So they're trying to put their own egos into the stories through the actors. And writers are writing commercial scripts with male leads, because they know that's how they will make their money. So it's just a vicious circle.

Most interesting stories are about men and women, right? And most popular stories are love stories in one form or another, as was _Leaving Las Vegas_. Love stories, unless they're gay stories, tend to involve a man and a woman equally, in a complex relationship. So why isn't that reflected in films? When did this jock culture take over and strangle storytelling?
Maybe when the executives or the writers assume that people wanted to escape when they went to films, that they didn't want to have to be challenged emotionally. People saw _Leaving Las Vegas_ and loved it, but it was painful, difficult to watch. 'I wasn't going to go see it, but I did . . .' Then they were so surprised that they could see a film and feel something that deep. That was so shocking.

Moving on – what is the easiest and quickest way for an actress to succeed in Los Angeles?
(_Laughs._) Get on your knees.

Is that true?
No, but I've always been fascinated with how some actresses do become so successful so quickly. For me it was definitely a thirteen-year process. I definitely wasn't on my knees. Maybe it would have got me here much quicker.

The expression 'on your knees' – is that literal or metaphoric?
It's metaphoric. Although it was always something that I heard about when I was younger – 'Beware of the casting couch.' It never happened to me. But I think a lot of women do learn how to seduce, in a way, in order to get certain roles that are beyond their talent.

Has that always been the way?
Yeah. As an actress or an actor, in some ways you are a prostitute, selling yourself and seducing people and hoping they'll hire you. Five times a week you're coming in and putting yourself on display. You have to be a good actor, but there's also a level of seduction – which I didn't get, and I think that's why it took me so long. But that's terrible to say. Maybe it was just that I wasn't very talented for so long that I assumed there was some shady business going on for the other people. But women are definitely more vulnerable in wanting to please, wanting to be liked, wanting to be daddy's little girl . . .

Which goes back to our first question. Why are you an actress? Because you wanted to be liked.

It's also what your quality is. Personalities sell in Hollywood. And one of the things that maybe saved me is that I didn't really know how to do that. I didn't have a personality to sell. Now, Cameron Diaz, I think, is a really beautiful woman – really sweet. Her natural personality, who she is, is really what sells. She's very open, she's very free sexually, and she makes people feel really good about themselves. And that's beautiful because it's real, it is her. But there's a sick side of this business where you come in and create that kind of personality to become successful.

What is the most humiliating thing you had to go through in the process of arriving at who you are?

Definitely that feeling of being metaphorically raped, putting yourself out there in such a raw and open way, and having them mistreat you or disregard you or disrespect you – and not give you the opportunity to express what you need to express, and audition you with respect. It took me so long to be respected. You understand why actors say, 'Fuck you, I'm not reading.' It's because they have so many memories of years of walking in, sitting down with a casting director who can't act. You sit in a cold room reading a script with somebody who couldn't give a shit, who's not giving you anything, and you just feel disrespected. They should hire an actor to read with you. The director should be there if he cares at all. The first time we worked together was the first time I felt respected as an actor, and the first time I did good work in an audition.

Do you want to tell the story about how we met at the Château Marmont Hotel? We'd already met in New York. We then met to read. You said you didn't want to, I persuaded you.

The casting director and I were going in the elevator with you upstairs to go to your room. And I, just for a moment, was just honest. I asked the casting director to leave. I said, 'I'd rather you stay downstairs.' She did. I think she was shocked.

She was very shocked.

I had no power, I was like nobody. But we went up to the room and we spent about two and a half hours. And you're a really good actor, which is very rare for a director. So it was just the two of us reading, and instantly we were connected to the process.

We've talked about why there are so few good roles for women in mainstream American films. What could make things better?

I don't know how you could ever change the blockbuster mentality that is so male-dominated. The actresses that do make a lot of money could use their power more. But they get sucked into the same thing. 'Well, we need you to do another romantic comedy because the last one made money.'

In general, are women portrayed at all realistically?
No, they're never complicated enough. They never have needs. They only represent something to the man. They're only there to reflect on the man.

Have you ever felt guilty about the way you've portrayed a woman?
I felt a little bit guilty about *Cocktail* because I never stood up and fought for who I thought she should be. I felt so insecure that I just did what the director told me to do. It obviously wasn't supposed to be complicated. I was providing a service, I knew that was my job.

Do you have any feelings about how violence is portrayed?
I think it's disgusting when it's cartoon violence. A movie like *Saving Private Ryan*, done in a way that's affecting and raw and honest, at least says something about violence that people can learn from. But I think that the *Die Hard* kind of movie does inspire kids to go out and buy guns and join gangs and feel that macho power that they see in films. It has to have an effect.

I've had to deal with complaints from quite a lot of women, particularly in Britain, over the rape in *Leaving Las Vegas*. I have very mixed feelings about the scene now – because it was so realistic, and because your performance was so strong, it really upset a lot of women. Not that they were angry with it, just that it devastated them.
But I think it upset them in a way that's honest. The power of that scene was in the simplicity and the way you shot it. You never saw one thing. You never made me feel disrespected as an actor, you never made me feel that I was actually being raped. You took care of me in the process and the way you filmed it took care of the character and gave her dignity in a very terrible, terrible situation . . .

I feel that, as a film-maker, you should be prepared to argue and be in a controversial area. I showed the film initially to lots of men, and I said, 'Please be honest, did you get a hard-on in the rape scene?' And they all, without fail, said, 'No, I felt deeply ashamed of being a man.' I took the film round the States, to colleges and so on, and at one screening a girl came out before the end, led by a friend, just sobbing uncontrollably. I went up to ask if she was okay and her friend said, 'Look, it's nothing personal. She was a victim and it was just too much for her to watch.' I think, as film-makers, sometimes we don't know how powerful something is to somebody else. And that shook me, it gave me real food for thought.
I think also if there is going to be violence against a woman, it has to be an integral part of the story, and it obviously was at that moment. My character wanted to be damaged – she was so in pain because Nic's character left her. I always looked at that scene as if I was going in there to instigate violence.

Have you had negative feedback for it?
No. Now, I was upset by the rape scene in *The Accused*. What I found upsetting

but also powerful was the way it was shot. It ran long enough so that I think audience members did get turned on. I know I did. I was freaked out by the fact that I had been turned on by something that was so horrific. And in that moment I understood the horror, the reality of how those moments happen.

The more successful a film is, the more people see it. A lot of guys could rent that and masturbate and have not a second thought about the ramifications. For them it's just a turn-on, a porn movie.
Think of the pictures they have on the Internet now. If you do a nude scene in a film, they can send it out through a computer, and people probably masturbate to a picture of me nude. That's pretty horrific. There's a whole part of this business that I pretend doesn't exist.

There's very little you can do about that. How important is an Oscar? Crass question, but . . .
It means a lot to the little girl inside of you who wanted Daddy to tell you you were good. I definitely felt the good feeling that having a nomination brought, which is you're being respected and patted on the back. But the flip side which confuses you and makes you feel kind of dirty about it is, 'Oh, now you're a bigger deal, you can make more money', which is pathetic and sad. People want an Oscar in order to have a bigger career, and so getting it becomes a business. That's something I didn't realize. People campaign for them. I mean, I realize that at the time MGM was campaigning for me, for all of us. They were putting out advertisements. But we were so in the dark about what they meant.

Do you know how much money was spent on P&A? Twenty-five million.
That's a lot for a small film.

The film cost three and a half million, then twenty-five million promoting it. It made just over thirty million domestic. So it didn't make any money. It's a hit that made no money. Last thing – would you rather have an Oscar for a mainstream film, or a European acting award for a small film?
I'd rather have the European award for a good film.

2   John Calley

Mike Figgis: What do you think is right about Hollywood today?
John Calley: It's hard to find a lot of things that are right. If you're talking about the mainstream, major studios making X number of films a year to drive their revenue requirements – it's become truly crazy. Everybody's flailing around trying to deal with the absurd costs – the consequence of a mistake is terrifying, and there's no dependable formula. There never has been, of course, but I don't think the odds against screwing up got any longer in the interim. So there's this idea of buying an insurance policy – like a writer who gets three million dollars because he's written two successful films out of his last five, or a star who gets twenty million dollars against 20 per cent of the gross, because you think at least you'll get the picture opened. We're in the middle of summer now, it's August 1998 – last weekend the top ten films each grossed five million dollars, which is a significant gross for any film at any time. But some of them must fall by the wayside, because there are four more new ones coming in next week. So films are no longer allowed to mature in the market – their lifespan has been stunted by the nature of the competitive environment.

How long is it that you've been back in the studio business?
Five years. I came back in 1993.

Before that, you took a hiatus.
I took off for thirteen years. I was running Warners, and in 1980 I decided that I wanted to leave. I had no idea what I was like, what my life was all about – it was all just studio-system madness. Running a studio is like an endless trip through a George Lucas meteor-shower – it's all coming at you and you do your best to manage it, and it almost seems like fun. But then you realize that your life is defined by your telephone list, and your relative salary as contrasted to the salaries of your competitors. I was fifty, I'd been in the movie business in one form or another for almost thirty years. I'd just signed up for another seven-year deal and I went to see my attorney, who was also my friend, to do a will. And this is gauche, but as we were running down my list of assets and what we might do with them upon my departure, I realized I didn't have to work any more. And I was electrified by that thought – it had never occurred to me. I was on the conveyor belt, going to work every day – and I thought, 'Why? It isn't fun any more'. So I stopped. I had owned a house on Fisher's Island for some years, just as a vacation place in the summer. I moved there year-round, and I became a bit of a hermit for some years. I became, almost as a matter of discipline, disengaged from my time. I stopped watching television, stopped reading newspapers and listening to the radio, and I tried to keep my phone calls to a minimum. And I loved it.

Did you read books?
Incessantly, but not recent stuff. I read a lot of things that I'd always wanted to read. When I was at Warners it was tough to squeeze in things you wanted to read if they weren't considered possible bases for movies.

Did you manage to squeeze anything in then?
A bit. But it was a world where nobody reads a book if you can't make a movie out of it. One time I was flying to London from Los Angeles, and the person in the seat next to me was a movie producer, whom I knew. We all carry those little travel bags with the things we plan to do on the plane. And I had a book that I'd been desperate to read for months, but hadn't had the time. So I took it out of my bag, and the producer looked at it and said, 'Don't waste your time reading that, it's already been sold to Twentieth Century Fox'. But I did, and I do read. It's critically important to me.

And did you see many movies in your hiatus?
I probably saw about four movies in thirteen years. I had always loved movies. I was that person who would see *The Maltese Falcon* or *Laura* every time they came to New York. I would see *The Seventh Seal* over and over again. But I found my love for movies was corrupted by the fact that I worked in the movie business. It became what I did, and carried with it the nightmarish quality of work.

So after a couple of years on Fisher's Island – how were you feeling?
I kept waiting for the anxiety attack to hit – the withdrawal symptoms. And there were none. For the first time – this sounds corny – but I felt joy. I was standing on the beach in the middle of February in a snowstorm and I had this curious feeling. At first I thought I was having a coronary, and then I realized that I was feeling some sort of joy. So the further I disappeared into that solitary world, the more comfortable I became and the more addictive I found it.

So what in the hell are you doing sitting here now?
I made some changes in my life. A friend came to visit me, we got involved in a relationship, and what had been a very interesting meditative experience on my own soon became merely eccentric. I realized that if I was going to remain in the relationship, I'd better get out of Fisher's Island.

Did you get rid of it?
Sold it. A friend of a friend wanted to see what the island was like, came to visit, and basically we sold the house to him over lunch. Then I got more conventional in my retirement choice, living in north-west Connecticut in one of those mock-farming communities that are like God's waiting room – everybody pretending to be local but not feeling local, and the locals feeling contemptuous of the non-locals who are pretending. I found that I was sleeping more and more, up to eighteen hours a day, having sort of sequential dreams. I'd only worked in the film business twice in the thirteen years I was away. I produced *Postcards from the Edge* with Mike Nichols, who's been my best friend for many years, and my inspiration, and in many ways my saviour. And he and I did a film as producers, *The Remains of the Day*, in 1992 with Merchant-Ivory.

That's a gorgeous film.
In the aftermath of that, I felt that I had a choice to make. I either could come back to the world, or continue to live this mock-country-gentleman life in Washington, Connecticut. Then Mike Ovitz intervened in my life and suggested that I take a job at MGM-UA. I met with Frank Mancuso, and he hired me to run UA, which I was attracted to because it was a non-existent studio. I had the chance to start something from scratch and do it the way I wanted to, without the residue of a prior administration. I had always had the sense that one could make a very small studio be a very pleasant place to work. So I did it with two executives, basically, then expanded to three. And we made a very few movies. We were lucky enough to release your thrilling *Leaving Las Vegas* and, in many ways, it saved our lives. It was one of the three successful films that we had, along with *The Birdcage* and the Bond movie *Goldeneye*.

What were the main differences you noticed when you came back? Or, essentially, does it never change?
No, no. It changes radically. During my hiatus, it became much more businesslike, and much less fun. It was while I was gone that Mike Ovitz appeared. I have some admiration for Mike, I like him personally, he's been a lovely supporter of mine. But his extraordinary gifts as an agent resulted in something that, thank God, seems to be fragmenting. I came back to a world in which fundamental decisions about the pictures we made were not being made at the studio. They were being made by CAA, driven by Mike, because he had become so controlling of the talent pool. If Mike wanted you to make it, he'd call and say, 'I want you, Dustin,' and 'Barry Levinson, you'd better direct it.' If you didn't make it, you were not going to be at the top of that 'Get-a-look-at-it' list. So major decisions were being made by people who had no responsibility for the ultimate result of the decision. They'd be gone by the time the picture came out, for better or for worse, and it was your problem. When Ovitz got out of the agency business, that started to come apart, and I think that's a good thing. It is not to say that leverage no longer exists, it certainly does – but not to the extent where it was heading to.

But I'd say the main difference was this – when I left, studios were sort of controlled by one-man bands, a Steve Ross or a Charlie Bludhorn. Or a descendant of Jack Warner or Harry Cohn. I worked in the studio system when those men who actually owned the business were also running the studios and understood the business. Darryl Zanuck knew how to make movies. Harry Cohn had been doing it for many years. Warner was astonishingly bizarre, but nonetheless he was betting his own money. When I came back, I was working for Crédit Lyonnaise, which had foreclosed on Peretti, an international swindler who had somehow obtained the rights to MGM. A Japanese company owned Universal. Warners was by that time in the hands of Time Inc., although Terry Semel and Bob Daly, who had succeeded Ted Ashley and Frank Wells and I, were still in the jobs. Fox was owned by a kind of conglomerate, certainly dominated by Rupert

Murdoch, a brilliant, gifted man but not a film guy necessarily. He was buying it as part of a mosaic of companies that he felt interacted well.

The point is that the parental entity that owned the studios were not film people. If ownership of the movie business is vastly removed from the process of movie-making, that creates an astonishing number of aberrations.

So the emphasis changed. Development got insanely out of hand, because it was a realm in which one could operate in a businesslike manner. You could project what your development expenses would be, and you could stick to them, and that seemed rational to the owner. You could say, 'We're going to spend a hundred million bucks on development this year.' If you spent thirty-two million in the first quarter, they'd start to look at you funny, like you were incompetent. But by the end of the second quarter, you could be under budget. And you could finish the year maybe twelve million dollars under budget, and they'd think you were a wonderful manager for that reason. But the fact is, you might have developed nothing of value. It was very hard for the new owners to live in a realm where there's no objective reality, just somebody's judgement of somebody else's judgement.

I think of film-making as a process where someone has given you some money that you are then corporately responsible for; and I think of it as suitcases full of crinkled paper – real stuff that you can buy stuff with. But I get the impression in the studio system, no one really seems to see money; they see the product of money, and they have a nice lifestyle. But the two-hundred-million-dollar budgets and so on – it seems almost like the money doesn't exist any more. There are just figures.

Well, it's very hard to imagine two hundred million dollars sitting on your coffee table, and then have it leave incrementally to complete this movie. It's much scarier than thinking of millions coming in, millions going out, this tidal flow of money; and hopefully at the end of the year your tide will be higher than what it was at the start. I think Sean Connery was, at one point in his life, paid a million dollars flat for a Bond movie, and he sure did deserve it. And as I understand the story, he had a million dollars in sterling put on a table in a vault at Barclay's Bank in London and brought his family down from Scotland to actually see a million dollars.

I do get the sense that people don't know what the money is any more. It must affect corporate responsibility, the way that they're handling it.

It also is reflected in directorial responsibility. People don't feel that they're spending money, they feel they're measuring their power. Films that used to be shot in forty days now take eighty if you're lucky. Limitless money is spent on effects. It's completely out of hand, it's terrifying.

Is it possible to stop it?

I think there might be a change if something cataclysmic happens, if there is a terrible year and massive loss all over the place. Last year Sony had the largest grossing year of any company in the history of the film business. We did over a billion two domestic box office, and we did that by releasing very expensive movies that did very well. It's hard to come back from that brink, except in the face of tragic failure. But I think the possibilities for change are technological. I think about the potential of digital video recording of material, so that you can release films on tape in a much more enlightened way, through satellite to receivers on flat screens in theatres. On *Godzilla*, which we just released, we spent over fourteen million dollars on prints, on cans of film. And that then has to be managed by the industry in terms of security, making sure piracy is minimized, to the tune of ten million dollars a year. So the average studio making big movies is spending a hundred million dollars a year on prints alone. That's crazy. An enlightened evolution where one can tape and transmit electronically could take over half a billion dollars a year out of the expenses.

Are you in any way sentimentally attached to celluloid?
Sure. I mean, I grew up with it. And I was the production manager on live television shows that are no more, but I'm still able to watch television, which is mostly on videotape, without a great deal of psychic pain. I think upcoming audiences will be used to what the new format is – an electronic screen, highly defined, and a much higher quality image because the tape projection won't suffer the diminution of quality that the film does as it's cycled from place to place.

We tend to forget that, don't we?
Yeah, we always see it as well as it can be seen, but go down the line to the second or third run where often the projectionist couldn't care less about what's on the screen. It's usually a little out-of-focus, sound is weak, lumen levels are down. I could imagine digital having some positive effect on cost. But as long as it's a competitive universe, and I don't see that changing, the prices will go up. There are six or eight stars that can demand huge sums of money, and there are six studios ready to pay them because they think that they guarantee openings. I don't know how that stops.

I'm really interested in making a very commercial film that would economically perform really well for the studio, but I would also like to make it for virtually nothing. I just think certain executives would be less interested in that – because the system has got out of control, not just with stars at the top but all the way down the pyramid.
Look, here's the issue. If we all decided that there would be genuine ownership of rights and sharing of profits, but that it was contingent upon success – all of it could change. If the big star or the big director said, 'Look, I will do the picture for a stipend, but I want 5, 10, 12 per cent of the real receipts', costs would come down astonishingly. But that doesn't serve the interest of the agents or the business managers. They don't want 10 per cent of what Tom Cruise or Tom Hanks or Mel Gibson might make. They want 10 per cent of twenty million dollars right now, because that's how they live – 'Get your money in front. Get these big fees.' The

deals that are written are so onerous now, if you have a net profit participation in a movie it's almost impossible to make profits – not because the studios are stealing money, but because the artist signs a contract that is designed to make it very difficult for profits to ever accumulate. So everybody's salary goes up. You hear of studio executives that have made three hundred and fifty million dollars on their stock options. And that leads the creative artist to say, 'Well, what about me? How come this guy who doesn't do anything that goes up on a screen and gets people to spend their money – why should he get that kind of money and I get nothing except the hope that I'll be successful?' So they want theirs in front too. Everybody is at the trough and it's very hard to reverse that because the people that are deciding how the industry is structured are the people that are earning huge sums of money as a result of its present structure. Unless you can imagine a world of such high purpose and benevolence, in which people say the greater good is served by all of us reducing our salaries and making this a more rational world, unless you believe that's possible – and I don't – then we're doomed to this.

How do you bring about changes?
I will lay it at the feet of digitalization again, which may seem like it's my one-stop answer to everything. What the majors have now is adroit distribution, that's the critical mass that we control. But we're recording this on a small digital camera. You set it all up yourself. When the process is simplified, so that commercially acceptable levels of taping can occur that can be transmitted one-stop to a commercial outlet, the whole thing will fragment. I don't think it will be necessary for a brilliant person to come to me to ask for sixty million dollars to do a movie. I think he can buy fifty dollars' worth of tape, rent a camera like that [*points at my Sony DVC*], get some talented people together and make a film. And if I'm not smart enough to see that his film, when finished, is brilliant, he can take it to a distribution centre that transmits these signals out to receptors who will bid on it.

I love what you're saying. I do quite a lot of work with students and would-be directors and I come as the guy who shot on Super 16, made a low-budget movie that made money – theoretically, did everything that you'd think a film student would want to do. But it's very hard, particularly in America, to get the remotest interest in 16 mm. They find that, from a snobbish élitist point of view, to be a step down. And the thing that, sadly, I have discovered with a large percentage of wannabe film-makers is they just want to be rich men.
Well, I don't think there's a morality to it. I think you can choose your poison. But take the acting profession. There are, as we both know, remarkable actors wandering around – they're gifted artists, they want to be engaged, they've developed their craft to an intensely high level. And they end up living in Los Angeles, doing situation comedy walk-ons – two lines, utterly innocuous. It leads to one conclusion for me, which is that there are two levels. There's the practice of performing, or film-making, which gives one pleasure as an artist, so that the process

is an end in itself. Then there is the issue of career. You come here and struggle to get your agent, and decide that you'll do almost anything to stay alive in Hollywood, simply in the hope that you'll score, get the series lead, go on to feature films. Then you've made a different choice, and you're not a film-maker *per se*.

The last time we spoke, you told me a great quote about basket making . . .
Oh, that was a line of Tom Stoppard's. Tom said, 'If you have skill and no imagination, it can nonetheless result in very attractive and interesting things like wickerwork and picnic baskets – usable, pleasant. On the other hand, if you've got a great deal of imagination and you have no skill, what results is modern art.' I think he's right. I also wanted to quote David Lean on the paradox of it. I was with him when he said this, but I can't remember it exactly. He either said that 'The movie business is an art masquerading as a business', or he may have said, 'It's a business masquerading as an art.' Both are true. It is a high-stakes business. And when you look around at the aberration of people making twenty million dollars for fourteen weeks' work, or the director making a hundred and twenty million dollars if he has the right gross deal on the right picture – directors have made that much on pictures that I've been involved in.

What do you think about film? I just gave a talk at a university proposing that film was grossly over-valued as a cultural pastime, that the depth of literature is something that we should be really concerned about. I said, 'Ask yourself, how do you feel after you've watched TV for a couple of hours, or come out of a movie, compared to the moment when you've finished a book?' I worry about literature – because I think that up to the late nineteenth century, early twentieth century, literature had a big role in the way we thought, how our thought evolved.
In the development of the species.

And the potential for fineness.
Something we don't offer in the movie business, and certainly not in television, is the opportunity for the full use of imagination. When I read a book that has a powerful effect upon me, I create a world that's detonated by this experience of reading. And I'm engaged in a way that I'm never engaged when I go to the movies. When I see Anthony Hopkins, who I think is brilliant, play the butler in *Remains of the Day*, he is inescapably that image thereafter. But I had a much better time reading the novel than I did seeing the picture – and I'm proud of the picture.

There's another level of film-making, isn't there. Let's just go over the directors you worked with in the sixties and seventies. A lot of Europeans, right?
Kubrick I worked with. There were things with Fellini, with Bergman – picture never came to fruition, but we went through it. Truffaut . . .

Was your interest always with the Europeans?
No, not necessarily. I just loved good film-making and was attracted by their

work. I did two films with Visconti and was crazy about him – *The Damned* and *Death in Venice*. And I was crazy about Lindsay Anderson, did *O, Lucky Man!* with him. It didn't work commercially, but I'm thrilled about it, and in some ways compare it to *A Clockwork Orange*, which was a thrilling experience I had working with Stanley. I did three or four pictures with Stanley. But another thing I notice is that as an art evolves, more and more of it becomes derived. Stanley went to the head of one of the major companies after he had done *Spartacus* and they were keen about him, and he had this dream of doing *2001*. They read it quickly and called him in and said, 'Listen, here's a bit of advice, kid. Don't ever consider doing a science fiction movie for over a million bucks. It just doesn't work.' So people were inventing things in those days. You can go back to Todd Browning and the Germans and see remarkable horror films. But I think that the work Billy Friedkin did with *The Exorcist* when I was at Warners was terribly important in that it elevated the horror movie form. He treated it seriously, got terrific artists, made a real movie and it was a gigantic success. But I think that, as it goes along, the originality that Stanley brought to things, that John Ford brought to things, are now third and fourth generation. I used to kid around about *The Searchers*. There's a generation of young film-makers, all of whom make *The Searchers* as their first commercial film, they just call it something else. Then they name their first-born male child Ethan. It's become the world of the remake.

I love Quentin Tarantino. He's smart, I like talking to him, and I do think he's original. There's a thin line between theft and homage, though.

It's not for nothing that he worked in a video store. He's got remarkable energy, he's very gifted. But the thing is – this is down memory lane, but there was a cultural difference with some of the film-makers in the late fifties, sixties and seventies. They were immensely interesting human beings. David Lean was an extraordinarily interesting guy. And Stanley is a remarkable man, engaged in a very complex life. Kazan, who I had the pleasure of working with on one film, was a remarkably interesting man. Even fringe people who would not be of the absolutely highest level of film achievement were fun lunches or dinners – they had a life. There was just a world of intense creativity that you felt that you were a part of – it was more than just highly evolved technique. I think that we've become incredibly insular now. Where do you find the support to live a life that is not utterly Hollywood-centric? It's very hard if you're living here. You become a citizen of the business. After leaving Warners, I tried to stay here for about a month. It was clear to me that it was utterly impossible. I remember going to sort of a farewell party held for me. A young actress came over to me, and she said, 'Are you John Calley?' I heard myself saying, not as a wisecrack, 'I was.' And I realized that I had identified myself to myself as this person that ran a movie studio. Divorced from that, I had no idea who I was. So I embarked upon a hunt for that person, to see who he might be.

3 Paul Mazursky

Mike Figgis: You're an admirer of Kusturica's *Underground*. Do you ever see anything coming out of American cinema that's as powerful as that?
Paul Mazursky: Not lately. I thought it was fantastic, overwhelming. One can only imagine what would happen if Kusturica made a movie like that with financing that wanted to interfere. I don't think the studios would make that kind of movie anyway. It's surreal, crazy, wild. I haven't seen anything like it in American cinema. He's a wonderful director, I think. I don't really know him, I had lunch with him once. He wouldn't shorten *Underground*, and he couldn't get a release here.

I think that they were asking for too much money when they wanted to sell it.
Yeah. He won the top prize at Cannes – it didn't help at all. It was over three hours, I thought it was a little long.

I didn't mind.
You know, we talk about how bad things are now if you're operating within the system, because there seem to be six executives where there used to be one. One way or the other, everything I've made is within the system. I made films for major studios like Fox and Columbia and Universal. I didn't have final cut, but I never really had interference. You'd have an intelligent conversation or two. Some of the executives were very smart, some not. But you took it for granted that in the end it would be your choice. That changed somewhere in the last seven or eight years.

Can you pinpoint it?
When the synergy thing happened – when the studios went 'We also merchandise, and we sell Batman toys, and we have a world market and we have video and cable'. They put all that synergy together, they're not worried about how much the picture cost, because they get the money back in many ways. But that makes them homogenize the thing to a degree that mostly it loses its soul. I don't want to romanticize the good old days as if everything was fabulous. But it was better for the director, there's no question about it. Every now and then, a film-maker comes along, and it validates that the talent is there. But have they lost the ability to just do it, and not worry about getting a deal with New Line or whoever? I was there for the first Sundance Festival, I presented the award to Soderbergh. That place is completely different now . . . What we do has become a business. And while it is part of a business because it costs money, it's really about the gut. The pictures that most influenced me, even by Hollywood directors – they dealt with their instincts, their gut. I'm not asking all pictures to be like Fellini and De Sica and all those neo-realists who I love so much – but where are the William Wyler pictures? Where are the William Wellmans, the John Fords, even the Hitchcocks? It's something else out there now. I don't see a way to beat it, by the way – except not to do it.

Each generation has specific goals. How radically do you think the amounts of money now involved in film-making have changed the goals of people described as film-makers?

Well, clearly it's changed it drastically because the price that half a dozen actors get now is more than five movies that I made. If a guy is getting fifteen or twenty million dollars, it's clear that the studio has done a certain amount of research. They're hoping they can achieve something. And they'll let you know one way or the other whether they think you're achieving it. I haven't had many problems personally. But there seems to be a climate of greed and mistrust in the air, everyone's got these horror stories. Last night I heard Norman Jewison say that being a director is like waiting. You're waiting for a script, you're waiting for a deal, you're waiting for an actor to commit, you're waiting for the caterer, you're waiting for the sun, or the rain. And then when you're finished, you think, 'Okay, my waiting's over.' But now begins the waiting for what they really think about the picture. I just made this movie for HBO about Walter Winchell, and there was a certain amount of post-stress. Opinions. Some of their things I didn't mind, I actually shot an additional scene or two and it was okay. But some of them were almost vulgar in their insane insistence on trying to change a line reading or a cut.

What's on your mind when that happens?

I get angry. I think they're crazy, they're meddling. When you leave the room you don't know what they really think. When the door closes, I want to be in the room, I want to hear what's really going on, I want to have the Linda Tripp tapes! You get a little paranoid. You could leave the room and it's, 'What the fuck is wrong with him? Why doesn't he listen?' It was a little different in the old days. When I did pictures for Alan Ladd, it was really just Alan Ladd. He probably spoke to Gareth Wigan, his right-hand guy – and that's it. There were no other opinions. Now, there's a lot of people making points – maybe not with every director. You know, Mike, they're not going to tell Stanley Kubrick that he doesn't have two years to make the movie – they're just not. I don't know what they tell Marty Scorsese. But most people, they're going to get in there a little bit. It's their money.

It's not their money. It doesn't come out of their pockets.

No, no, but they're responsible for the money. They're making calls on things – 'Okay, let's green-light it. Cage gets twenty. This guy gets five, the other gets nine.' It's forty above before you even turn the thing. They budget it at eighty and they have to know it's going to be at least a hundred. And then the prints and ads, they're into a hundred and a quarter. You'd think they'd be worried. The studios are making fewer pictures, but the ones they're making are more expensive. So they want to make pictures that can grab the brass ring, that can make the big, big number. So if you go into them with a small, intimate story . . . I hate the word 'small', by the way. People say, 'Oh, it's a small movie. It sounds so interesting.' *La Strada* was not small.

But I've been going out with this one project now for four or five years. *Pictures of Fiddleman* – about this painter, Jewish-American, who fails badly in New York and ends up in Rome. It's very funny, dark at times – a picaresque adventure. I had Nic Cage for three months, about three years ago – before this big stuff happened with him. And before we could consummate the whole thing, he had to take a picture to make some money. And that picture led to – boom-de-boom-de-boom. So I lost him. The Europeans would give me half the money, but the Americans all thought, you know, 'It's arty, we can't make money with this. Even if you win Cannes, we have to put up seven, eight million dollars with prints and ads. It would have to make thirty. Pictures like that don't make thirty.' That kind of talk. You can't argue with that. When you say to them, 'Yeah, but you just made a movie for ninety which only made eleven', they don't care. They speak differently now, too. They use expressions like 'the arc of the character'. Those are funny things.

I remember sitting around a boardroom table, listening to a twenty-eight-year-old ex-agent now-executive giving me notes on 'character arc'. And my having sort of a vision of the person within me coming out, leaning across the table, grabbing him by the tie, head-butting him, breaking his nose. Do you ever have that?
I've had it a lot. Sometimes I'm very rude. I never actually walked out, I have to admit. I go, 'Well, let me think about that.' You just can't believe you're hearing it. It's like the best training to be an executive is to be in 'development', whatever that means. Have you ever seen the development reports on any of your projects? I've seen a couple on mine. I don't know how I got 'em, but I did. And some reader, probably fresh out of college, comments on what they think of the script, its commercial prospects and so on. It can be devastating.

How do you deal with that now? Given that it's not going to go away, that system. And you still want to make your kind of films.
You never know what's here to stay. But I always felt that Orwell's *1984* came true around 1975. Big Brother had already come in. And now we're all on the Internet of big business commerce. We're tiny little creatures. You can't let it get you down, you just have to keep pushing at what you do. You've found some interesting ways to battle it by trying to make these pictures cheaper. And I envy you. I have not been able to quite do that myself. How do I deal with this? I get very frustrated. I sometimes feel like I'm nuts. Why bother? I've made seventeen movies, some very good pictures. But they're over. I can't live on, oh, *Enemies, A Love Story*. I'm very glad I made it, I loved doing it. It's just now I'm interested in telling whatever stories are around.

Was the Winchell film for HBO your project?
No, I didn't write it. You're just getting your chops in.

Director for hire?
Director for hire, sure. Of course they say, 'We won't bother you.' And then you start casting, and you've agreed on maybe three parts. You talk to them, and suddenly you get some comments about the fourth and fifth parts. I say, 'No, no, I want to use so-and-so.' 'Well, we'd really appreciate it if . . .' They do a lot of that. You learn to live with it or you won't do anything, frankly.

You know, these readers, these executives – they're not evil, they're not villains. But it's like they've been cloned. They seem to be kind of Middle-American-Nice. They went to Barnard or Sarah Lawrence. They say, 'We think the arc of the character is wonderful. We just wondered – in that scene, is there any way you could put an ADR line over that shot, which would say X-Y-Z?' I say, 'No, the guy's mouth is right in the shot, you can't do that.' 'I was just asking.' I deliberately didn't shoot certain things because of that.

What do you mean, you 'deliberately didn't'?
You don't have much time to get a lot of coverage. You know, if I were covering the scene you and me are in now, sitting here – I'd get some kind of wide shot that sees both of us. I might even get the camera. But that's it. Then I've got to go shoot another scene in the corridor. So it protects you in a way. I had the pleasure of knowing Vittorio de Sica a little. He used to cut in camera, so that no one would interfere with the movie. And they cut the thing together in two or three days. Buñuel did the same. Single takes.

But there's a new breed of younger directors who think nothing of shooting with seven cameras. I mean, I'd love to have two. I heard a story the other day about a straightforward dialogue scene which was covered with thirty-four set-ups. I said, 'How many ways can you shoot dialogue?' And then you realize it's entirely designed to facilitate choice in the editing room, rather than performance on the floor.
One cannot deny the influence of MTV – which maybe I'm responsible for, because I wrote the pilot for *The Monkees*, which Bob Rafelson's company produced. Yeah – 'Hey, hey, we're the Monkees.' That started this whole trend. MTV is the training ground for a lot of people who now make movies. And MTV is based on endless close-ups and moving shots, cutting them together.

The great news about that is that you now have an audience that is completely pissed off with blink editing.
I don't know. You think they are?

I do. So when you give them a dynamic single take, they're mesmerized, because to them it looks really fucking fresh.
I like long takes, personally. I like the behaviour of the actors when they relax and forget that they're acting. I think the hardest thing to do is to throw out your own prejudices. Don't be rigid, stay with the thing itself. It may take you down some

road you didn't even know about. Because until you shoot it, it's really just an idea on paper.

Let's talk about your working with Sven Nykvist. I'd like you to talk about 'the creeping zoom'.
Sven did *Willy and Phil*. I met him in New York, he and Mia Farrow were sort of going together. And Mia had kind of saved his life. Sven's son killed himself, and Sven got a job shooting *Hurricane* with Mia. She got him out of this funk, as much as a person could. So I met Sven at Mia's mother's – at Maureen O'Sullivan's apartment. Of course, I was in awe of him. But he was very down-to-earth. He operated probably 50 per cent of the picture. And he wanted to make slight adjustments during the take, which he couldn't tell me about until the take happened. They would involve 'the creeping zoom', at which he was a master. He would do the slightest pan and the slightest move at the same time, so that in a barely perceptible way, you'd get a tiny little bit closer. It was poetic – quite miraculous. And it violates what most operators are taught about making it crisp, clean, no movement – unless you've told them you want movement. There's a lot of rules and regulations they all go by. They always report to you – 'There's this tiny bump, it's almost imperceptible, boss,' – when they call me 'boss' I know I'm in trouble – 'but I just want to report it, so you know when you see the dailies . . .'

But you'd rather work with someone who has an instinct . . .?
I would like to. He doesn't have to be an older cameraman. Maybe some of these young guys are that way.

I think they are. I just think they're not often asked to be instinctive.
You know what I think would be a very good idea? Often you don't have the cameraman long enough. Fool around, and let 'em shoot the rehearsals on video. Discuss it as if it's dailies, say, 'You know, why don't you . . .?' You might get that language going.

I had the opposite experience on a film. I shot the rehearsals on video, and I felt I wasn't getting the camera move I wanted. I was back with 35 mm after working on 16, and I was really annoyed by the limitation of 35, the lack of fluidity. I had just bought my video camera and I had a little Steadicam thing for it. So I said, 'I want the camera to go under this table, then up again.' I shot it, camera in one hand and a portable monitor in the other, and I said, 'Look at the monitor, this is what I want.' But it can really piss people off – because you've demonstrated that it's possible.
I think the thing though is to keep yourself open. So that if the cameraman says, 'That's great, but could we also try . . .?', it's a sketch. With a new cameraman, a new relationship, it takes a month to get close. Then the picture's almost over. Close, in the real way that he's fucking around the same as you are, trying things.

Everyone's so worried about the dailies, no one wants to make a mistake in a business which is very technical. But sometimes, if mistakes are good – they're not mistakes. And usually you can do something over again if it's a *really* big problem.

I'm going to ask you a couple of specific short questions. How often do you go to the movies?
About once a week. I alternate between going to a normal theatre and going to the Academy, or the Writers' Guild. I prefer the seating in the Academy, very comfortable. And they have great projection – it's wonderful to see your own picture up there. But I like going with real audiences. They prepare you for the reception of your own film. They don't sit in stunned silence – they make noise, they get up and go to the bathroom, they eat. They can drive you crazy – particularly at a preview. But I mean, after the preview – go to see the picture. I'm sure you've done it.

Never. Do you rent videos?
Yes, a little bit. It's not the same. You don't give yourself up to it in the same way, because the phone will ring, and you go off it . . . I must have sent a hundred people to see *Nights of Cabiria* which played here in a new print. And all of them said, 'It's the best picture we've seen in years.' Very simple-looking picture, none of the tricks. And a couple of out-of-focus moments, by the way.

What percentage of the films you see in a year would be non-American?
It used to be more than half. But it used to be that every eighteen months or so there'd be a Fellini, a Truffaut, a De Sica, a Kurosawa, a Godard, a Fassbinder. What's the great one? *Rocco and his Brothers* – what's his name? The big guy, does a lot of opera, he's dead now. You'd get about twenty of those movies a year. We couldn't produce that many great movies in this country – not in the last fifteen, twenty years. But we do things that they want. And Europe now wants English-speaking movies, if they can get them. With American stars. They want hits, they want *Saving Private Ryan*. And they don't know how to do it themselves – not in a way that will sell internationally.

Do you think films affect people – really?
I think they do – because when I hear people talking, even about television, they seem genuinely animated in a way that they don't seem to be about much else. 'Did you see that?' 'I never laughed so much in my life!' I think the really interesting question is, 'Are the movies a reflection of the culture or do the movies influence the culture?' I think they reflect the culture. I think the culture has become more brain-dead. It would seem to me that people don't read nearly as much. I think that's a serious problem.

Why?
Because the ideas that come from great books – not just novels but poetry and drama, whatever – you can fill your mind with your own images. A movie does it for you. Of course, when you see extraordinary movies it's okay –

Why? What's unique about an extraordinary movie?

It gives you – I don't know what the Greek word is – a kind of ecstasy. It's larger than your own experience, it takes you out of yourself, it moves you. Steven did it in the beginning of *Saving Private Ryan*. Twenty-five minutes that just took you – you were right in there. Very rare. *Nights of Cabiria*, there's a scene at the end where this pathetic little hooker has been subjected to a second beating and robbery. She's really down and out, it's over and she's walking in this park. And it's starting to get early morning. Some teenagers are singing and carousing, and she's in despair, weeping. She sees them and they're so full of life and youth and joy. And she just looks at them and makes that face . . . That took me into another place.

Prioritize the following four things – film, literature, painting, theatre – in terms of how important they are to the culture.

Whenever a sixteen-year-old tells me they're desperately interested in cinema, my advice is always, 'Don't go to film school. Study fine arts, learn about literature, drama, history. Then find a way to go make some shorts, and you'll learn about cinema.' I didn't start out wanting to be a film director.

Mike Figgis: I thought your film was fantastic.
Paul Thomas Anderson: Thank you.

One of the best films I've seen in a long time, just the whole way you made it. So, is it something you'd been with for a long time?
Long, long time. When I was seventeen I wrote a short film called 'The Dirk Diggler Story', and shot it on videotape. I was a big fan of *Zelig* and *Spinal Tap* and it was that format, fictional documentary. Also I was seventeen, so I was completely immersed in watching porno, in a horny-young-boy way but also in a film-maker's way. I wanted to make movies and here were these terrible movies, but I also got off on them, they were so goofy and bad. Plus I lived in the San Fernando Valley, which is the capital of porn production. So it was always peripherally around me. There were warehouses near where I went to high school, some of them had signage, then there'd be one that didn't, but it had a ton of expensive cars parked out front. So you're thinking, 'What the fuck is going on inside of that one with no sign?' It's because they were making porno movies. So the story obviously stuck with me for nine or ten years. I was twenty-five or twenty-six when I made *Boogie Nights*.

That's your first feature?
Actually, my second. *Hard Eight* was my first one, I wrote and directed it.

Is that a good film?
It's a great film.

How would I see that now?
You can see it on tape or laser disc, or I just did a retransfer for a DVD, which I'm excited about. It was financed by people whose roots were in bad television, *Baywatch*-type stuff, and they decided to try and get into movies. Clearly they hadn't read the script. I delivered the movie and they were really confused. All I could do was point to the script and say, 'This is what I shot, this is what you paid for, this is what you agreed to.' And this argument would always come up – 'Well, the script is not the movie, and the movie's not the script.' I had the most horrendous, terrible time in the editing process. I fought, and I was fired off of it, then eventually got it back. So now the movie is my movie, it's out there – with the exception that the title was 'Sidney', and it was changed to *Hard Eight*.

I just had a similar situation. I spent two and a half years on one movie, *Mr Jones*. Now they've actually asked me to re-cut it, do a director's cut.
Oh, great.

And I've discovered the footage all still exists, they don't throw anything away. So I think I'm going to do it. At first I thought, 'Fuck it, I don't know if I want to revisit all of that.' Then I was lying in bed thinking about certain scenes. I remembered shooting them, thinking, 'This is good.' So I thought, 'No, life is about closure, and I would like to finish this.'

You'll feel great. I had to spend all my own money to finish *Hard Eight* after I got it back. But I did it, and now I'm happy. It came out last February and died an instant death, because it was always a bastard child for this company. They'd had so much trouble trying to get me to make their cuts. They were saying, 'We don't like the movie, we don't like you, we don't even care that Sam Jackson and Gwyneth Paltrow are in it. We're not going to do anything for it.' It got amazing reviews, almost as good as *Boogie Nights*, but it played for about a weekend and then it was gone. Now, a lot of people have found it on video because of the success of *Boogie Nights* – frustrating that it's on video, but that's fine. And the company that paid for it, Rysher Entertainment, went out of business – which is wonderful. The greatest part about the day they went out of business was that *Daily Variety* published a chart of Rysher's film history, what the movies cost and what they made. And at the very bottom, the lowest-grossing movie in Rysher history was my movie. So I was so happy that I aided their downfall in some way. 'My movie made ten thousand dollars and it cost you guys two million.'

So why are you especially excited by the DVD release?
My cut came out in the theatres, and that's what was put on video. But they brightened it up, because that's the tradition, 'It's got to be brighter.' And they did it behind my back. Then when I got my laser disc at my local video store it was like, 'This is my cut but it sure doesn't look like the movie I made.' So Columbia Tri-Star Home Video had the rights, and I convinced them, they were kind enough, to sink a couple of extra bucks into it and release it properly on DVD, with some commentary and extra scenes – to really preserve it properly. It wasn't good enough for me that my cut was preserved when the colour was all wrong.

When *Leaving Las Vegas* came out on laser disc – director's cut, wide screen, blah blah – some real film buff from Birmingham, England, called me and said, 'You know the frame line is right across the eyes?' I'd never seen it, didn't know it was out. But they'd got it out in time for Christmas. So I went out and bought one. It was Super 16, and they'd done a wide-screen version where they'd just literally and arbitrarily sliced through it. They hadn't racked it, it was just a complete mess. I couldn't believe what I saw. So I got the negative out and forced them to do it again. But people had already bought it. You have no control, unless you're Kubrick and you watch every frame . . .
I watched every frame in the process of *Boogie Nights* towards the end. But I think I drove a lot of people nuts, like 'Why do you have to sit here all day?' 'Because it will be wrong otherwise.' It's not distrusting people, it's just that things get handed down in an assembly-line nature, it goes from one lab to another, one transfer house to another, and honestly, it's just that mistakes get made on order forms because people don't pay attention. There's no conspiracy – although generally if it comes across someone's desk, they want it brighter. It's just about keeping on top of basic POs – okay, this has got to be blue and it's green. I've only

made two movies but I can't imagine being able to make as many as I'd like to make, because it takes so much time.

And there's a certain point when maybe you have to let go. Because if obsessively controlling the detail of a film stops you making the film ... well, there's nothing quite as close to watching paint dry as film-making.
Or watching paint not dry.

Exactly. What was the time-span on *Boogie Nights*?
We started shooting in July of 1996. We shot until October and then edited until October 1997. We finished everything a week before it came out – we waited till the last minute.

And your first movie?
I shot that in twenty-eight days, then I had three weeks to cut it. But then came the mêlée with Rysher, which lasted a year, essentially. I thought the movie had been taken away from me, and the only way I could deal with that was to go make another movie. So I started prepping *Boogie Nights*, but in the middle of that I essentially stole back my work print elements on *Sidney*.

How did you do that?
I had a dupe work print made. I submitted it to Cannes, and they invited it to come into Un Certain Regard – a big deal. So I called Rysher and I said, 'Listen, I know you guys own it. But I took my dupe work print, I submitted to Cannes, and it's in. It's a big mistake if you guys don't give me some money and let me finish the movie.' And they said, 'No, we don't care.' What was great is that we ended up going to Cannes, and Rysher had made their flyers promoting the products they were unveiling at the Festival. And my movie was nowhere to be found on their product list. It's like, 'You guys have a movie in the Official Selection . . .' Of course, I didn't want to go into the Grand Palais with my dupe work print, so I had said to Rysher, 'Let me have the original negative elements.' But they'd already cut negative on their version, so I couldn't just match up my dupe work print to the negative.

That would cut into your shots . . .
Exactly. I had to go to alternate takes, which weren't always as good. There were three or four very long Steadicam shots and, of course, they cut right into the middle of those.

Can you splice back in now?
You can, but pretty much always you'll lose a frame. I had to do it. I had to go through the whole movie and lose a frame at the head and tail on either side of each shot, pretty much. It made for a great study in what one frame is. Because a lot of times you cruise along, taking your frames off, and you think, 'I don't miss them.' Then you get to one, and you find that one frame makes all the difference.

It's insane. You don't want to believe it. But in one or two scenes, there's a slight rhythm change that will always stick with me. It was the best I could do.

You know how films are speeded up for cable? Scorsese pointed this out. Say the cable schedule slot is two hours and twenty-two minutes. And maybe the movie is running two hours and thirty-two. They get a calculator out and say, 'What speed would this have to run at in order to fit in the slot?' Then they use a harmonizer to take the voice back down to the original key, so we don't notice. But everything is speeded up.
Oh, shit. Maybe there is a conspiracy.

The conspiracy is capitalism because there's no cohesive system.
There you go.

One thing about *Leaving Las Vegas* that pissed off the technical community was the 16 mm. Because everyone's invested in lightweight 35 mm. The last thing they want to hear is Super 16. 'Fuck off, Super 16, we don't want to know, we don't have the cameras, we don't have labs set up for that.'
But single-handedly you made that a viable format. You convinced everyone else. Super 16 has taken off now, in terms of the potential for independent movies to possibly break out.

If there's a problem with budget and schedule, that's the way to go, without a doubt. Stocks are good enough now to blow up from Super 16.
No director has final cut, projectionists have final cut. Theatres are so fucked. This THX is the biggest scam going. THX doesn't mean anything, it means that George Lucas gets a cheque to say that some theatre is now THX-approved. It sounds good, but it's bullshit. Not to mention the projectors. You spend all this time, you want the film to look right. A few months after *Boogie Nights* came out, my girlfriend and I were walking by a theatre on the 3rd Street Promenade in Santa Monica. I said, 'Let's look in.' It was a Fuji print and it just looked terrible. The scope, the ratio were fucked up.

That's because New Line have a Fuji deal.
Yes. But now I got rid of that.

Did you?
Oh, yes, I said there's no way I'm making a movie with you guys again unless you get all Kodak prints. So they signed off, which is good. At the same time, I was thinking, when I was watching my movie on 3rd Street, 'If I can't enjoy anything about this bad Fuji print, and this bad mono soundtrack, have I done my job?' This movie should still come off, the story should still work. So do I want to be the guy who's got a Kodak print that's precise and perfect, and that's the only way it can work? Or do I want to be the guy who says, 'Yeah, I know it looks like shit and it sounds like shit, but you liked it, didn't you'?

My first American movie was *Internal Affairs*. Years later I'm in Cuba doing a commercial, and I'm at the airport waiting to meet a plane, because my crew's coming in. It's delayed, so I'm hanging outside and a guy tells me, 'The drivers will be in that little hut there if you need them.' So I'm standing by the hut and I hear Andy Garcia's voice and I think, 'That's *Internal Affairs*.' I go in and they're all watching a little black-and-white telly, a broadcast of a bootleg print of *Internal Affairs*. It looks terrible. I'm stunned and I start to say to the guys, 'You know, that's –', and they go, 'Shut up, we're watching this movie.'

But in that case it's probably a better feeling even than going to the Hollywood première at Grauman's Chinese.

Were you happy with *Boogie Nights*?
Yes. There's probably a couple of things I'd like to have done differently, but it's not like I didn't stick to my plan that I had. The first assembly of the movie was three hours and fifteen minutes. And I took about a half-hour out of it, it's now two hours thirty-seven. But the *Boogie Nights* that's out there is the director's cut.

The scene with the firecrackers – was that always written in?
Yes.

That's impressive. I enjoyed the scene more than most things I've seen in cinema, just because it's such a funny idea.
Well, the idea comes from two places. It's a distant piece of background action in a movie called *Putney Swope*, directed by my idol Robert Downey Senior. I called Bob up and said, 'This is the greatest fucking thing, I want to take it and run it through a whole scene, make it foreground action. And I want to say that it's my idea.' He said, 'Great.' Also, my dad was in early television in Cleveland in the mid-sixties, he was the horror talk-show host. He would introduce bad horror films like *Beast from 50,000 Fathoms*. And he was one of the first guys to chroma-key himself inside the movie and comment on how bad the dialogue was and so on. He would constantly blow stuff up with firecrackers, take little skulls and throw firecrackers at them. So it's a combination of those two father figures with firecrackers. There it is in the movie.

What experience did you have with actors prior to making movies? Have you acted?
No, but it's always been my favourite thing in movies. I love the pizazz and the cool camera stuff and that's why I'm a director, but I'm just an actor-freak fan. My first experience with actors really was on the short film that I made. Philip Baker Hall who's in *Boogie Nights* and *Hard Eight*, he was in it. He was the first real actor that I met, and he introduced me to how to look at acting and how to write for acting. For my first movie I had Gwyneth Paltrow and Sam Jackson and John Reilly and Philip Baker Hall. You can't get into it any better than that.

No, you can't. I've had such a crush on John C. Reilly. I met him on *Internal Affairs*. And for some reason he couldn't do the part I wanted him to do. His voice is just brilliant. I was so pleased he was in your movie.

He's the main man of *Hard Eight*. John is my best friend. A listing of the people whom I see the most and who are my friends would be all actors. So I get sick of agents and directors saying, 'Oh, actors are crazy, all the great ones, we love them, but they're crazy.'

There's such a clear division now between film-makers who like toys for boys, and that rarer breed who are actors' directors and who are story-driven. One of the things I loved about your film was there's a real gentleness about it, which I found really moving. Because I'm so fed up with the way films are going. I really don't like movies any more.

I don't know, I want to be with you there, but I'm scared to say that, because I feel like I'm bad-mouthing the cause. Even though I know in my back pocket that there's shit out there – yes, it sucks – I almost want to keep it to myself, because I don't want anyone to see our collective cards. But, yes, we're fucking up like crazy, and I wish it wasn't going on. The action genre, that little club, is fucking up lately. I love those movies, and I want them to succeed, I want to see good action-adventure films. I wanted *Godzilla* to be wonderful, I love monster movies.

That department is a committee film-making process. That's like the sacrifice that cinema has made. Okay, you guys, you can have that genre because that's money and everything.

I think it's unfortunate because there is an intelligent Godzilla movie to be made, an intelligent action-adventure film. But that genre's getting killed by committee. I've wanted for a long time to make a real romantic comedy in the most traditional way. I mean, I'd fuck it up in an untraditional way, but I'd dive into it thinking it was traditional.

I want to do a smart thriller. I love the genre. You can do what you like, you can make a surreal film – because once you're in the genre, people don't care what you bring in with it, as long as the dynamics work. All those genres, the horror film, the monster movie, they're great. Are you going to do one?

Absolutely. I've got a million ideas and scripts I've tossed around and played with. I write my own stuff.

I've found (and you may find) that the limitation of being a 'slash', as we're called – a writer-director – is that you're tied to the project you're tied to. But if you've got a quick brain, you might have six of those ideas, and it maybe takes eight years to realize them. That's a little bit depressing. I'm desperately trying to find writers now, so I don't have to commit myself to every script. I can oversee. I'm trying to come up with a script factory, where we have script meetings, talk about it, come back a week later with a couple of scenes, and

divide them up, so there's maybe three of us writing together. It's an experiment, but I can't carry on being the assigned writer.

What about television? Have you ever –

I think television and video and disposable non-sacred formats are wonderful for storytelling.

I've been thinking about this for a while, and then *The New York Times Magazine* asked me and a bunch of other people to write about what our dream TV shows would be, if we could create them. I gravitated instantly to the variety show. Look at *Boogie Nights*, there are so many actors in it. I'm saying the variety show could be the perfect place where actors and directors could go – so that, say, John Reilly doesn't have to do *Armageddon* to support his family. He can just come to the show for three or four months. And Bill Macy can do the same, or Heather Graham – like a pit-stop for great actors who want to keep their wheels turning, get paid a little bit of money, and not have to go sell their souls in crap. I think you'd have enough interest from some really talented actors.

I love ensemble. I think that's healthy. The problem with film is it's on the altar and it takes a long time and it slows us down. And creative people are fast and tend to fire things out quickly.

What's the fastest you ever made a movie?

The last one was a four-week shoot. Three, four months editing.

See, that's pretty good.

So satisfying. I want to ask you about the porn industry. You said earlier that you got fascinated as a willing participant, as a teenager. What do you think about the way they're made? Could they be better?

Oh yes, God, there's so much to talk about here. Porno movies could and should be a genre. There's a whole series of John Holmes movies about 'Johnny Wad' – it was a character he created, a suave, sophisticated detective, a bit James Bond, a bit Sam Spade. The Brock Landers stuff that Dirk Diggler creates was modelled after that. These were essentially murder mysteries, but they were also fuck films. So you wanted to watch him solve the case or defuse the ticking bomb just as much as you wanted to see him fuck the beautiful girl.

Were they well made?

Well, they pull it off because they're actually sexy. They were on film and certainly it helps that the girls are at least natural. My hormones go towards, 'Oh, she's pretty. And, no, she doesn't have enormous fake tits. There's a little zit on her butt, she's got a little tummy. It's natural.' The same thing with the guys – the guys are not appealing in porno today. They're like fucking robots, chiselled to perfection. There's nothing you can relate to, it's like watching space aliens. The Johnny Wad stuff pulled it off because it didn't take itself too seriously. And John Holmes was quite an actor, really natural. The main thing about them is that a lot of the sex doesn't happen for the camera. Most porn actors now complain that every position in porno is completely uncomfortable. Seventies porno was much more 'Let the camera figure it out'. It was a bit more hand-held, and trying to get into the spot where you got the good juicy close-ups. Somehow it comes out more sexy and natural. Nowadays they're in contortions that are clearly guided towards the camera. It doesn't come off in any way. And the goal of a porno movie should be to give you a boner.

What else? I mean, my experience of porn movies is being in Hamburg, in some generic concrete block of a hotel, away from people you love, alone in a bedroom. And there's a porn channel and you find yourself watching it. You end up with such a feeling of loneliness and desolation, and at that point, it's almost as if we have a duty here as film-makers. Somebody should be making better stuff that doesn't leave you quite so devastated.
Well, I think some of that devastation comes from just watching the sadness in a lot of the performers' faces nowadays. You instantly think, 'Who are they? How did they get there? How can I help?' And it's almost like they're looking into the lens going, 'Save me.' It's funny because, late sixties, early seventies, this sort of porn was fashionable and okay to see in the theatre, it was a date movie. *Deep Throat* was the highest-grossing independent film of all time. *Behind the Green Door* was happening. But *Midnight Cowboy* was also happening. Had it not been for video, I think more porn movies would have come closer to legitimate, traditional narrative stuff.

It kind of did in other world cinemas – like *Ai No Corrida* in Japan, in France, and in Spain, such as in what Pedro Almodóvar does.
Totally. Or even in *Betty Blue*. One example I've used before – not to be salacious or anything – but how interesting it would have been to see Forrest Gump and the Robin Wright character making that baby that we see in the end. How does Forrest Gump have sex? And it's not trying to give you a boner, to show you Tom Hanks and Robin Wright, in bed. What could be more –

Human.
Right. What could be more of a revelation of a character than watching them have sex? That says a lot about someone, how they touch another person in bed.

I have a theory. Because the way that porn treats the sexual act influences TV and mainstream cinema, it's almost as if actors imitate porn movies when they do sex scenes – which is then what young women and men watch, and they think, 'Oh, that's how sex is.' So real people end up impersonating porn. You think, 'Hang on, this is all wrong.'
Totally. I wrote a scene in *Boogie Nights* for Don Cheadle's character Buck and his wife Jessie. They're lying in bed, they decide to have sex, they suggest to each other, 'Maybe we can try to do this, like, real.' But Don fucks up a little bit

because he starts to say, 'Baby, oh baby, yeah' – and then he catches himself, and then she starts doing it. It's a funny, small, tender scene where you watch these two people who are so caught up –

You didn't shoot it?
No. We rehearsed it and it was great, but I knew it would never be in the movie.

Why? I think that's very strong.
I thought it was taken care of in other places – porno people trying to be real people. But it is funny, I've been in a situation with a girl and suddenly you think, 'Where did this Elizabeth Berkeley *Showgirls*-sex thing come from? Do you think this flopping around that you're doing is making me excited?' I think porno movies have trained a lot of young people how to have sex, unfortunately – especially the new ones. I think it would help if they were shot on film, I really do. It's more expensive, it requires more of a plan. And I think they fail to plan. Video is a blessing and a curse. It's created an assembly-line mentality. If the concept is that you're making a movie for a consumer – well, the consumer is at home with a fast-forward button. This guy wants to fucking see some dick and some pussy and he wants to see it now. And he's going to fast-forward past all this other shit.

I don't know about the economics, but there's a huge market comprised of captive audiences in hotel rooms, where you can't fast-forward.
Now they have these different systems of Pay-Per-View. There's one where you can click the button and get two or three minutes free, so you can preview it. Within those two or three minutes, you'd better see some fucking or else they're going to go to Pay-Per-View channel two, and if they see fucking, they're going to stay right there. That's why a lot of the Pay-Per-View stuff now is basically highlights. They usually stay away from stories and just do best-of stuff, so you know you've got a constant-fuck thing going.

I think if I had the balls I'd make one. Just to try it.
But I think you have had the balls to put sex scenes in your movies that are explicit. You've injected a bit of porno – in the best possible way – into some of your films.

5   Jodie Foster

Mike Figgis: How would you describe what you do?

Jodie Foster: God, I never know how to describe it. I don't think I do a different job as a director than I do as an actress, or as a producer. For me it's all about creating this reality out of nothing – so that an audience member can sit inside of it and be completely surrounded, and forget who he is and where he came from, and only be with the people on screen.

But why would we do that? How can we rationalize doing that?

You know, for me, going to see movies is a primal thing – maybe because I've been seeing films since before I can remember, and it's always been a part of my life. But it's something that I need to do. I'll be on location, having a great time all week – and then I have to go see a movie on the weekend, so that I can cry. It can be the stupidest movie in the world – just so that I can cry for a good solid hour and a half. I can release myself emotionally as a spectator in an audience in a way that I can't do in my own life, I think.

Do you think that's any different from the function of theatre a hundred years ago?

Unfortunately, theatre just hasn't fulfilled the same thing in my life.

Because cinema is better at it?

I think the experience of going to a movie is so completely different from sitting in a theatre – and maybe you have to have a suit on, and you're sitting next to somebody that you don't really know very well, but you have to be nice to –

But movie-going can be like that too.

I think you have the experience of being alone, watching a movie. You can dress any way you want, it doesn't cost fifty dollars. And you feel much more at one with those faces on the screen. You forget where you are.

Yes, but that's a technical thing. The sound is bigger, it's more real.

Definitely. And because of that, it can touch more people in a much more elementary way than theatre does. Theatre somehow goes to your head first – it sort of gets translated through the senses, and then eventually gets to your emotions. And, for me, film works the other way around. It starts from your gut first, and goes out the other way.

I did theatre for fifteen years. And I saw a lot of European theatre, and ninety-eight per cent of what you said I agree with. But the two per cent that I can remember – they were possibly greater experiences for me than film-going experiences.

With theatre I think it has to be a *great* play, a great experience. Maybe it's once every year or two years that you sit down and you pay the fifty dollars and you actually see something that you hadn't expected, that took you to another place. That's happened to me a few times in my life.

I've never had an experience like that in the fifty-dollar venues. But I've had great experiences in small rooms, where there's no proscenium arch, and an actor can speak naturally, without projection. It's usually been a bunch of mad Polish people, and it's been extraordinary. But free of theatrical convention. And I agree, intellectually you're thrown on to the writing in a certain way. Whereas in cinema, when it's good . . . Let's talk about cinema – is it good right now?

Well, there's always been many tiers. There's the conventional Hollywood stuff that lots of people go see, which is a little contrived – you've seen it before and there is an audience for it. Then there are other layers, there always will be – it just depends on how many people want to go see the smaller, more unique films.

The balance between those various 'layers' – how do you think it compares now with how it was, say, twenty years ago?

It feels like there are too many movies being made, in all arenas – the independents as well as the grander studio films that are more expensive. I certainly can't keep up with it. And, unfortunately, the moment that you have that much quantity, your quality goes way down. You can only make so many great films – it takes hard work and a lot of inspiration, and you just can't have that inspiration twenty times a year.

So we're talking about a market that is saturated on all levels – arthouse movies, mainstream movies. Do you ever feel there's a danger that if ten great films happened to come out at the same time –

Would anybody notice? I don't know. The 'entertainment industry' now has a much wider sense – the news has become entertainment, we have so many more different outlets, everywhere we look there's Pay-Per-View . . . I think audiences' expectations of films have changed a lot too.

A century ago, theatre was such a special thing – a kind of community activity, a ritual of social behaviour. I have the sense now that the entertainment industry which we're involved in is so big that it's out of proportion to the cultural need for it. And that worries me. Let's accept that we both love cinema, and we demonstrate that by staying in the game and making films. But do you think cinema is over-valued now?

Actually, I think it's the opposite problem, which is that there's so much of it coming at us constantly – it's like a food that you get one hundred and fifty times a day. Even if you liked it at the beginning of the day, by the end of the day you've seen enough of it to not really have that much respect for it. And everywhere you go, you can always see another film.

What about the rituals that the community has come up with for revering film – the Oscars, the Golden Globes, the critics' awards?

Unfortunately, there's so many of those accolades – once again, always propelled financially by what's best for the studios or the film-makers. The more award shows you have, the less special they become. The more movies you have, the less special the experience of going to the movies is. The great thing about the seventies was that the actors you liked most only liked to work once very two years – because they felt that they couldn't give their all more than that. It became almost like a fashion. So you really looked forward to seeing a Robert De Niro movie or a Dustin Hoffman film or an Al Pacino movie. I mean, now you have five Robert De Niro movies a year.

I went to one last night – it's opening this Friday. The budget's your usual fifty-plus. And for the studio in question, everything will be riding on this Robert De Niro movie this weekend.
The great thing about the seventies, which I really think is our golden age in America for films, is that they were so interested, all of those actors, in making movies for the right reasons – in having a true and emotional reason for making them. Budget size didn't really matter. It was the content of the story that mattered the most, and that's why those films are so good – why they still stand out.

What's spoiling it? Money? Is it because Hollywood is such a blatantly capitalistic organization? Or is that naive? Has it always been that way?
I guess it always has. But then it hasn't always been a global marketplace as much as it is now. I get this weird feeling that Hollywood has kind of gone the way of religion. There's the local priest that you know is passionate, and is doing it for the right reasons. And then there's that guy on TV at three o'clock in the morning, creating these great performances and milking everybody for their dough. When you think of what 'religion' means, the local priest is the guy you think of. But I'm starting to feel that when America thinks of who an actor is, they think of this greedy guy who makes way too much money, making films that are emotionless and kind of substandard. And it sort of ruins it for everybody else.

What can we do about that?
Oh gosh, I think you just have to hope that you make movies for the right reasons, and that someday you'll become fashionable again. It's like miniskirts.

I want to talk to you about the difference between actors and actresses, the way they're treated and the way they're paid. You always figure on the earnings lists as an actress who commands a certain income. How hard is that for you? Are you aware that you have to maintain a certain market value?
Well, sure, I think about it a lot. I try to be a good businessperson. You want to keep working. And the idea is to be as valuable as possible, but to also make the best movies that you can think of. Once I got a lot of accolades for making movies that I cared about, I thought, 'Well, why change my strategy? Why don't I just keep doing this? This seems to be the right path.'

Did you have a plan? Were you lucky?
Well, I had a plan and I was also lucky. Also I'd been doing it for a lot longer than

most people my age. I guess, because I started when I was three years old, I got to have a long time to come up with a plan. I wasn't one of those young actors who graduates from college and says, 'Now I've got to get up there and make as many movies as I can.' For me it was much more about wanting to be involved in films that I could be proud of. It didn't matter whether I was acting or directing or writing –

As long as it was one of those three or four.
Well, no – I have fantasies of being a caterer on a film, or a technician. It's a really active fantasy of mine, because I just love being on movie sets. I like the night shoots where you talk to everybody and you complain about the food. I like the rapport between people. I like being on location and having this common goal. But I don't always like the responsibility of being the top banana on the movie. So sometimes I would love to do a movie where I was a second assistant camera person – loading the magazines, cleaning the lenses, saying, 'Hey, what's this movie about anyway? Anybody read the script?'

'Does anybody know what they're doing?' . . . Do you understand how a film works? Technically?
Yeah, I think I understand that better than I understand the other aspects of it.

And is that just through being around and watching? Or did you actively say, 'I want to know how that camera works'?
The technical stuff is what I was obsessed with when I was a kid.

Really?
The acting didn't really interest me at all. But that's what I was paid to do, so that's what I did. I spent a lot of time asking questions. I think most child actors feel that way – they want to concretize the experience, because acting seems so nebulous and strange.

Do you care more about acting now than you did then?
I guess I do. Back then, I think I had a remnant of my mom's feelings. She would say to me, 'Acting's not a very important thing. When you grow up you'll probably be a doctor or a lawyer.' She was preparing me for failure, for the fact that usually at fourteen or fifteen most child actors' careers are over. She didn't want me to be lost. And she knew that I was interested in school and other things, and wanted me to go on that way. So I think I immediately got this idea that actors were dumb, and that it was a dissatisfying life and not something you did as a grown-up.

Do you think a lot of people think acting is silly?
A lot of male actors secretly feel very demeaned by it – because they feel like it's a girl's job.

That's the Mickey Rourke Club, isn't it?
Yeah – it's thinking about emotions, talking about emotions . . .

And preening yourself and looking pretty and caring about your appearance.
That's right. You go in with the guarantee that in some ways you'll be exploited for your looks. That's much harder on male actors than it is on the women. Frankly, it's part of women's culture – to know that their face and their body are part of who they are, their appearance has everything to do with their relationships with the world. And I think guys aren't really used to that.

Yes – 'I know I look good but I'm not really comfortable with this, okay?' A lot of younger male actors seem to have that kind of bearing and attitude.
Yes, it's funny. Sometimes, when I try to cast young men between the ages of eighteen and twenty-five, I find it very difficult – because every guy that walks in has the stubble and the trench coat and the tough look. I'll be looking for somebody who's light and full of joy, and naive but accepting of that – somebody who enjoys being young. But you find young male actors want to be brooding and act like they take the world terribly seriously. That's part of being young emotionally.

How did you find making the transition from being a child actor to being an adult actor?
It was a rough time. I think I had it luckier than most because I went away to college, so there was a whole period where people didn't really see me. And when I came back, it was with a movie that was very, very different from what I was seen in previously. But psychologically – coming back to the film business and saying, 'Okay, now I have to try and get a job, and I have to go out with all these young actors, and when somebody says 'Turn around', you turn around – that whole casting scene, which I had never really been aware of as a young actor . . . I mean, I like testing for roles now, because I like to know that I can play the part and I'd like the director to know that I'm the right person for the part. And the best way to do that is to get in a room and read. But when I was nineteen or twenty it really wasn't about ability, it was about image – once again.

Did you just observe that? Or was it ever graphically pointed out to you?
Oh, it was definitely pointed out to me. There were a lot of parts that I knew I wasn't pretty enough for, or I wasn't their version of 'sexy' enough for. *The Accused* is a good example. I really wanted that part –

Why?
I was drawn to it for a number of reasons – mostly unconscious, of course. I thought it was a role that I could sink my teeth into – a woman who was completely unlike me, but like people I had known in my life . . . So, I think the producers had a foregone conclusion about me, that I wasn't 'sexy enough'. And that means, 'Who do you want to rape? Do you want to rape somebody that looks like this? Or somebody that looks like that?' There's really something kind of creepy

about that. Of course, rape is about power, it's not necessarily about how some-body looks. And the producers were making a movie about the worst-case sce-nario – somebody who was tough and also questionable.

I'm going to jump in a lot because you're raising so many issues. Were you aware of the feminist issues that would occur to women who saw the film?
Oh yes, absolutely. That was my last year in college, I was very aware of those issues. And that's why I wanted to tackle the movie – because I thought that its point of view was really the correct point of view. I remember there was a screen test and I really wanted to be involved, but the producers said that I couldn't take part in it, because they felt that I wasn't attractive enough.

They literally said that?
I think they said something like, 'Well, isn't she really overweight?' And an agent said to me, 'Just show up in this guy's office, show him you're attractive and you're not overweight, and then we can go get you the screen test.' So I did it. I felt kind of like a shmuck, but I figured, 'Whatever – because once I get the part, then I'll be able to show people it was for all the right reasons.'

It's this thing of there being two levels of acting, always – one just to get the gig, then the gig itself.
I guess that's true. So then I did a screen test and the producers hated it. They said, 'She's not vulnerable enough, there's something very tough about her body language and the way she smokes' – all that kind of stuff. So the director came to me and said, 'Look, I really want you. Why don't you come in and read for them again and play it a certain way? And then, when we do the movie, you can have your way back.' Which is exactly what I did. I think the second test that I gave was the worst performance I've ever given in my entire life. And they loved it, and they hired me.

If I can ask, what did you do that you thought they wanted that was so horrible?
Well, I think it wasn't so much that it was horrible – it made it safe for them. I think they liked the idea of a victim who has a little weakness, rather than the idea that any of us could be victims at any time. I really wanted to make that point – that it was about somebody who was unlucky enough to be in the wrong place at the wrong time.

When the film finally came out . . .
Everybody, producers included, gave me a big kiss and said, 'What a great job you did.' That's why I don't bear any regrets or grudges about this kind of thing. It's always a big leap of faith to cast somebody or to hire somebody as a director; you're always putting your throat on the line.

You were specifically playing a rape victim. I seem to see a lot of films about women in vulnerable situations where they are victims.

It's a terrible thing. At least half of the scripts that I read, the women's stories, their lives are never central. They're always the mother or the sister of the person in peril, so that the male actor can show his heroism.

So then I want to know why this happens – because it's not always been that way. I mean, nineteenth-century European literature is not that way. Brilliant characterizations of women exist there. In films, too. It seems to be a fairly recent phenomenon whereby women have really taken a dip in the storytelling. I'd like to say things are changing in the right direction. I think that for a long time people believed that women's stories weren't inherently interesting to the public. Or that the public, in some ways, was male, and they couldn't relate to a woman as the central character – the hero – of a movie.

And younger women also wanted to see men, so they won both ways.
That's right.

Who was making these decisions?
I don't know. The only thing that I know about the film industry is that it's very averse to risk, until the day when somebody bucks the system and comes up with an idea that other people haven't thought of. And then pretty soon everybody else is copying that, and that becomes the convention. When you have millions of dollars on the line, you want to put your bet on the easiest risk. And so far the easiest risk has always been male, white, rich adventures. Immediately, when you go to minorities, women or anti-heroes, you find yourself in the independent realm, quickly.

So what makes you think it's getting better – other than optimism?
Oh, well, I'm sure optimism has a lot to do . . . But I think Hollywood is becoming much more conscious about their effect on the world.

Because of economics, the global market? Or because of goodness?
I think they're reading their own press. I think Hollywood really wants to do better. They'd love to be able to figure out how to be more liberal – how to bring blacks and Hispanics and Native Americans into the process. I always say this, it's the last bastion – but there are so few women directors, especially union DGA directors. And the reason is because directing is psychologically just a very different realm. When you're a producer and you're giving a first-time director his shot – a guy walks in the room and you say, 'I don't know anything about you, I don't know if you're going to be my worst nightmare or my best dream. But for some reason I feel akin to you, I like you, and here's five million dollars.' People don't do that with women. They'd rather do that with a white guy.

There's nothing much to be done about that, is there?
Well, no – except that the more pioneer women who are lucky enough to get the opportunity to make films, the more it changes. It just happens slowly.

But there's no reason, other than that, why women couldn't direct as well and as often as men, is there?
I don't think there's any reason except that – for all sorts of subtle reasons – there are fewer opportunities for women in the film business.

What resistance have you had?
Oh, I'm lucky, I've had very little resistance because I came in as an actor. A lot of the women who have had opportunities to direct came in as something else – a script supervisor, a producer, a writer. In my case it made a lot of sense for them to bank on me for my first movie because I acted in it for a quarter of my fee, and I brought in other talent at a minimal fee. So they already had a movie that financially was without risk.

And you worked it out – that was the way to go?
Right. Also I came in with, say, twenty years of experience with guys. Eric Pleskow was running Orion at the time – he had already made three movies with me. He knew I'm the kind of person who gets there at eight o'clock in the morning and does what they say they're going to do and brings everything in on time. And so I became, in some ways, the prodigal daughter. I guess I got in through paternalism.

To take a slightly different tack – do you think if more women came in with a different attitude, there would be more female directors?
No, I don't. In order for the establishment to accept you, they have to know you. I think that if they don't come into contact with women, then they don't have any reason to give them any opportunities. When I was making movies, aged seven or eight, I didn't see another woman on the set. Occasionally there would be a make-up woman, a script supervisor. Otherwise, they were all guys – except for the woman who was playing my mother.

You're not a believer in conspiracies?
No, not really.

So there's a rational explanation – it's economics, or a social thing?
Yes – almost every decision that's made in Hollywood today is driven by money.

Let me put it a different way. Hollywood has this heady blend of hedonism and money, and sex as a commodity. That seems to be a very volatile mix, a mix that can corrupt. And often there is a kind of a smell of the decadent about the place, in certain pockets.
Well, like anywhere else in the world, there's a little bit of everything. Yes, I think there's a side of Hollywood that's extremely decadent. There's a lot of money, a lot of temptation, the power structure is all about who's hot today – so it breeds that kind of backbiting.

But now it's also organized itself so well. It's harder to get away with stuff now, because there's too many gossip channels and so on, that pounce all the time.

Innuendo becomes fact very, very quickly. You must have felt somehow pressured by some of that.

It's an incredibly small town. The world is changing and information has become entertainment. Now the news is supposed to be as entertaining as going to the cinema. So the news has to have a logo and funny graphics, and a soundtrack and all that stuff. I bet you, if you sat down and plugged somebody in, you'd find out that people are receiving entertainment fifty per cent of their day, whether they were watching television or walking down the street looking up at billboards, or listening to the radio. The thing about this onslaught of entertainment is that, of course, it takes more blood now to really make people shiver, it takes bigger explosions, it takes more scandal, it absolutely has to be incest and fratricide to get people really going.

Do you go to the cinema? To public shows?

Yes. I usually can't handle the screenings. I'd rather go see a movie in a regular theatre than to have to put on make-up and be photographed. I just never feel like doing that

How often do you go?

Well, since my son was born, I haven't been for months. But usually I try to go at least once or twice a week.

Of the films you see, what percentage would be in a foreign language?

Well, unfortunately, in America we don't have enough foreign films to go see them very often. When I was younger I would say it was probably fifty-fifty. But now I see mostly American movies. You have to keep up, and there are so many coming out.

I'm in a dumb question mode for a moment – but how important to you is the whole phenomenon of the Oscars?

Well, objectively you know they're not important, because we all know who votes for the Oscars. But having won a couple of them – it's a big moment. Somebody yells your name and you go to the podium and it's like a dream. It's the dream that anybody in the film industry has.

I agree with you, by the way, and I was immensely disappointed when my name wasn't called. Why is it so important?

Oh, everybody wants to win. And they want that to be acknowledged by billions of people.

Would you rather win an Oscar or the acting prize at Cannes?

I'd rather win an Oscar. You kiddin' me?

Let me put it another way – would you rather be nominated for an Oscar, or win the first prize for acting at Cannes?

Oh, I'd rather win the prize at Cannes.

Why? Is winning more important?

Winning is just a bigger moment. I would be lying if I was to say, 'Oh, winning doesn't really matter.' It's just a big damn deal. I still get really heated about the Oscars, no matter how much I know about the industry. Every year I turn it on, I order the Chinese food in, and the person wins who I don't believe should have won. And I storm around and have a twenty-minute tirade about why they shouldn't have won. I don't know why I care about it so much. I'm sure it's just because it's some tradition of acceptance.

But also you are a part of this community, you know the people well. In London, the Sunday newspapers write about British actors 'taking Hollywood by storm', as if Hollywood is some kind of real place. But it's an industry. So I see why you get upset about who won.

Very often the *New York Times* runs these pieces on Hollywood, and you know that the people who write them live in New York. They really don't know anything about the industry. And they write about these phenomena sweeping Hollywood, as if there was some golden book that everybody could open up and say, 'Oh yes, British actors this year – we all agree, don't we? All the studios agree, we've all got together and come up with this idea.' It just doesn't work that way.

Internationally, 'Hollywood' seems to mean whatever people want it to. But the more you think about it – you are just a group of people who live in Los Angeles and make films, aren't you?

That's right. Having grown up in Los Angeles – in Hollywood, in the film business – I get really mad at people who see Hollywood as this sort of powerful icon that just makes Steven Spielberg movies and nothing else. But I also get really mad at people who over-revere it. It is a combination of those two things, but it's not just one.

I came here quite late, about ten years ago. I already had a career. And then I had a hard time on one movie, I came back from it, and I became a bit of a hero, and people would talk about the system as being like a conspiracy that I'd taken on. I said, 'No, no, I had a fight with Ray Stark and I lost. It wasn't that complicated.' But the studio system is spoken about as being almost like the Gestapo or the SS in full flood.

I've never had a problem with a studio, never had one of those vendettas. The closest I've ever come was to hate one producer, who I vow to hate for the rest of my life – that kind of thing. But other than that, I've just never had any of those sob stories. Partly because I think, to survive here, you need to be polite . . . I kind of believe that you get back what you give. This sounds like somebody's grandmother, like a Hallmark card. But it's really worked for me. Eventually, in this town, this industry, there comes a moment when you're not on top. You're at the bottom going, 'Gee, could you help me out? Could you maybe send me a movie that would be good for me? Could you give me this supporting part?' And you're going to have to depend on your relationships with a lot of people, as to whether they put out their hand and help you back up again. I've seen it happen over and over again, where my career has gone like this – and then these father figures have said to me, 'You know, Jodie, I knew you when you were five, when you were ten. You're a good girl, you were always on time, you've always done what you said you were going to do. Here, let me help you out.' And I know that if I'd been an asshole, they would have said, 'Yeah – stay there and rot.' But I thoroughly anticipate that that will happen again.

I asked a talent manager about this. 'How do you come to terms with working sometimes with a person whom you know to be not a very good or sociable or pleasant individual?' Because we do see actors behaving appallingly. Within a year, they become very big and high-priced, and they seem to fall apart. Have you observed the phenomenon?
Yes, but it can be true of producers and directors as well as actors.

Oh, sure.
Yes – that's where I feel like there's this emotionally adolescent character amongst actors. They don't think long-term, they think short-term.

Do you feel sorry for them when it happens?
No, I just feel like in ten years they'll turn around and realize what they've done. I have to thank my mom. When I was five or six, she had all these things, about being absolutely on time for what it was on the call sheet; revering the director as the visionary of the movie. 'You're here to do a job, you're here to serve your director. Obviously you're supposed to give your opinions, but finally it's his film.' All of those lessons, I wish I could turn around and give them to young actors as well. But I don't know a lot of actors. I don't know why, I just don't.

You don't look for those friendships within the business?
Not with actors. I have a lot of friends who are technicians, but not actors.

You almost made the sign of the cross there. What's the deal with actors?
I don't know if it's an old wound of mine, or some throwback to my upbringing. Or maybe it's just a personality difference. In general I don't have a lot in common with them.

Do you not trust them?
I think they're flaky. It's like being out on a date with a guy, and for three hours he talks about himself – that's like going out with an actor. They're very self-absorbed – as I am. But I guess I look for people who are a little different from myself. Off-screen, actors are very bad listeners, I find.

I find that directing is like being a shrink a lot of the time. I've walked on to film sets with my life in tatters, but I've had to go into nurse mode and say, 'Oh,

God, your boyfriend didn't ring? That's awful – that bastard.' Without feeling bad about it. And then at the end of the day I suddenly felt, 'Nobody asked me how I was.' And I felt miserable.

You have to like that relationship. I don't mind it, professionally. But I don't tend to have actor friends – except for Mel Gibson, who is different from any other actor I know.

Why Mel?

He's the funniest guy in the world – just a barrel of laughs. But there's something very private about him. I suppose there's a kinship we have, because he's a likeable guy, and feels this need to be liked. And he's very polite, he shakes hands, and he sends flowers and thank-you notes and all of that. But there is a darker side to him, a seething side – because he's such a good boy on the outside. Which is something I think I feel as well. I have to be good – that's why I'm so exhausted at the end of the day. You have to please other people's visions for a good twelve hours.

You mean not just on the take, but around the take.

Yes. The cameraman wants me there, the lighting guy wants me there, the director wants this out of me. And you have to continually try to manicure yourself. So that you please everybody, but you also stay central to what you were trying to say. And that's just much more exhausting than anything else – much more so than directing.

What about directing?

I love it. I like the stress of directing. I enjoy making decisions. Saying 'A', 'B', 'Yes', 'No', 'Full crane' . . .

Did you love the fact that when you came to directing you already knew so much about it?

But I wasn't sure that I did.

How was the first day?

Oh, it was a nightmare. It was one of those days when it poured down rain, like a monsoon. We were meant to be doing exteriors, because for interiors I would have to act, and I had tried to make sure that on the first day of shooting I wouldn't have to be acting. But immediately we go to interiors, and I have to act. And there's no air-conditioning, it's one of those humid months, so I'm dripping sweat with curlers in my hair and half my clothes on while I'm looking through the eyepiece . . .

Did you have to agree to act in it in order to get it made?

Yes. It wouldn't have been my choice otherwise. At the time you don't think you're sacrificing anything. You get everything done, you wear all the different hats, you have no time at all, not even to think about the next shot – especially as a woman, because you have make-up and hair, so that pretty much eats up any down time you have. You're the only person who says which shots to print. And how do you know which ones are better? You don't. You have the video monitor but, frankly, I don't think you can rely on that at all. So what you find is that you continually short-change yourself – because you're the one you think doesn't need any attention. Mel found this as well – that he was continually making sacrifices for everyone else, and then he got to the end of the day and he didn't like his performance, or didn't have the time for his performance. Once you get into the cutting room, you realize you don't ever want to act and direct at the same time.

Would you consider doing it again?
I'd consider doing a small part, or a character that was in half the movie, but not the whole film.

A couple of short questions: pieces of music that have touched you?
Oh boy . . . You mean, like songs?

Anything you like that involves music – a soundtrack, whatever.
You know, the Joni Mitchell *Blue* album I still play over and over again.

Me too. I think it's one of the best albums ever made.
Let's Get It On – I play it over and over again. Well, those two popped right out, didn't they?

That would do me. Some literature?
Song of Solomon, Toni Morrison. I wrote my senior essay on it when I was in college, and it's kind of followed me as the years have gone on. Raymond Carver short stories. A book I read that's out of print called *The Crying Heart Tattoo* – it's really romantic.

6   Mel Gibson

Mike Figgis: Why did you choose to go into film? What took you down that route?

Mel Gibson: I've got about four hundred reasons and I'm trying to think if there was one that spawned all the rest. A love of films, for a start. I was just drawn to stories, to being told a story.

When you were eighteen, in Australia, what were your options in terms of what you might do with your life?

Well, I had no idea. I had finished high school, and really hated it. I did average but I passed. I had an opportunity of going to university; I could have gone into journalism; I could have got some manual labouring job to earn some quick bread. The other option open to me was auditioning for a drama school, which I did.

Were there any theatrics in your family?

No. My mother was artistic, she could draw just about anything. Both my parents could carry a tune, and they listened to really beautiful music and appreciated good literature. And my father's mother had been an opera singer and studied under Dame Nellie Melba – she actually came to the United States and did concert tours, she married here.

Are you musical?

I don't play any instruments. I sing in the shower, but I try not to inflict it on people.

So for whatever the multiplicity of reasons, you ended up going towards theatre . . .

Yes. And I really had no conception of what it was. I was just lost at a crossroads for exactly what to do, and I found that acting interested me more than the other things. And I began to do all the things they asked of me – it was a fairly rigorous first year. Later on I began to really appreciate it for what it was – just the joy, the pleasure one gets from being able to tell a story in some form. And I found that I actually had kind of a talent for it.

Had you been aware of that when you were at school? Were you a good story-teller? A joker?

Yeah, I could tell jokes and make up stories and convince people of things that weren't true. Kind of a good liar. I'm not as good a liar now as I was then. Now I try and put it into a framework where I can call it a profession.

It's called acting.

Yeah, lying convincingly. There's a whole school that says that you shouldn't lie when you're acting, but I disagree. The art of it is to lie and get away with it.

Is that a Method/anti-Method issue?

Yes. I can't say that I have a method. It constantly shifts and changes, and I think that's a good thing. I was educated in a very British way of stagecraft and technique. They're all in favour of your actually feeling an emotion and playing it. But they know you're not going to be able to summon that every time. And if you could, you would die young. So you have to be able to at least fake it well. And that, to me, makes a lot of sense.

A lot of our younger actors are sort of third- or fourth-generation Method-ists, aren't they? I was interested by David Mamet's recent book on acting. He basically said, 'I just want the actor to say what I've written accurately, within a certain mode of behaviour. I don't need them to reinterpret the syntax. I don't need them to put "I guess" in between a phrase and so on.' You're a director. How do you deal with actors in that way?
Well, you choose the ones who you want to be with, for a start. I never make them read – I doubt that you do either.

No, I don't like it. I get embarrassed. And when they cry in a reading, you think, 'Oh, God, you want to leave, you feel you shouldn't be here.'
Well, it seems like you're doing something terribly wrong, you feel as if you're committing a crime, it's kind of slimy. Watching someone going through the act of prostituting themselves is . . . There's something almost unbearable about it.

All the actresses I've spoken to, all without prompting, come up with the same thing of how detestable is the casting process. Not the old casting couch thing, just the business of being expected to emote and look sexy in front of a bunch of strangers, and read with someone who's not an actor.
It's not fair. And you find out nothing from it, except the fact of 'Hey, they can read'. You can get 'em in, and somebody might do a slap-up job for that day, but that's what they've aimed at that day. You have to be able to figure out whether they're going to be any good for three months while you're working with them. And the best way to do that is to get them in the room, sit them down, tell them, 'I don't want you to read anything', and they relax a little. Then you say, 'I'm not making anybody read', so they don't feel like they're an outcast. I was fortunate, I only ever had to read one time as an actor, when I was just starting out. I was really bad at it, I just couldn't do it. That's really weird, isn't it.

You're lucky.
I was. What happened, the guy gave me this script, it was like two full pages of soliloquy, not well written either. And he said, 'Can you memorize this in ten minutes, then come back and do it?'. And I said, 'Just give me a little hint about who this guy is', so they gave me a thumbnail and I thought, 'Okay.' I went into the next room and I tried to comprehend it as best I could. I came back, they turned a video camera on me, and I just sat there and tried to do it. I started from the page then just broke off and improvised a whole thing around it – which is all you could do in ten minutes.

And you got the job?
Yeah. I was so far away from the technical parameters that are a given in audition processes that I thought it was hopeless anyway. So I figured, 'Fuck it', I threw the pages away and I was relaxed.

Which is, of course, by far the best way to go into any kind of meeting – don't give a fuck.
Absolutely. The best way to find out whether or not this actor or actress will suit your requirement is to have them relax. Then you can talk about the fucking weather, anything, and you'll know in fifteen minutes whether they can do it.

For the most part anyone who's coming for a gig has done some acting, technically has some ability. First time I did a casting session in America, Christopher Walken terrified me.
Me too.

They told me he was flying in from God-knows-where . . .
But he didn't need a plane, right?

I said, 'Have you had a chance to read the script?' He looked at me and he said, 'Do you like my face?' And I said, 'Yes.' He said, 'That's fucking great, because if you don't, get De Niro. Fuck you, I'm outta here.' And he stood up and walked out. He was flying on a different level to me, but he was right. 'Do you like me?' That's it.
He came to see me on the rooftop of the Peninsula Hotel in New York. He was wearing black, and he floated in, sideways, through a crowd of people – it was like one of those old vampire movies where they don't walk but they glide. He was a dancer, you know, so he's very graceful. He sat down next to me and I just started talking about the Middle Ages. He's a very smart guy and he began to talk tortures – and we swapped stories, because I'd just read this book on the subject. I was trying to recall some of the heinous things I'd read, and he kept trying to top me. And he was getting scary. My assistant left, he couldn't stand it any more – the air had turned cold. And I wanted to leave, because I knew that I didn't want to work with him. I turned around at one point, to avoid his steady gaze, and I was looking at a building with a huge illuminated '666' on top, in red. And he started smiling and I thought, 'Oh no, Chris Walken is the anti-Christ.' I bade him farewell, said, 'I'll call you . . .'

There's a school, isn't there, of his peers – Mickey Rourke and others. A few years back, Mickey said something which at the time I thought was stupid but which I now realize has pinned something about their attitude. He said that, for a man, being an actor is a shameful thing. It's women's work. I think Mickey is a trend-setter for a lot of other actors, in terms of their macho attitude towards women and the way they like to be portrayed on screen. This obsession with being a tough guy and wearing black and looking cool.
Looking mean.

Very mean. Without naming names, there are about four actors, all of whom are very famous, who seem to smash a lot of crockery on film. The minute I see them and crockery in the same shot, I think, 'Oh dear, poor old props guy, there's going to be stuff getting smashed.' And they snarl at the camera, 'Don't fuck with me, you fuck.'

My brother and I used to have a routine we called 'The New York School of Acting'. And we just used to say, 'Hey, you fuck.' 'You fuckin' call me a fuck, you fuck?'. On and on like that – fuck, fuck, fuck – and then we started slapping each other. I know what you mean, it's the School of Self-Torture, which I don't understand. There's enough torture in life without having to inflict it for no good reason.

But there are certain trends that seem to float together. Like, why are there no decent parts for women? And why are women just completely underused in storytelling within this system known as Hollywood? Any thoughts on that?

Well, I think that storytelling has always been kind of a male medium, from the start. Women just think differently to us. And that's a good thing. There are things about the way women think and the way they look at things that we cannot possibly understand. But I think the male of the species is more adept at the telling of a story. That's why, you go to any bar – it's not women telling jokes, it's guys. Women are notoriously bad joke-tellers – most of them. Some of them have the capacity for it. But generally I think men are better at that. And if most of the storytellers around are men, it's very hard to find a good story about a woman.

But even if we go back to, say, the forties and fifties – although the odds were still in favour of men, just in terms of the number of roles, there were some very powerful actresses who were taken just as seriously as men, certainly in terms of box office.

Yeah, like Joan Crawford. But she would display a male point of view, she was very masculine on screen.

If you look at the movies that are being made right now, the scripts floating around – they're woefully short of interesting female parts. Women pop up, endorse the men, take their clothes off if they're in good enough shape, and leave. Ally Sheedy told me that women's roles began to decline when actresses starting taking their clothes off, and it then became a given. So a lack of respect set in.

There may be something to that. There's a successful producer I know, I will not mention names. But his take on this matter is very brief. He says, 'Women on film? Either naked or dead. Both is better.' And it's like, 'Whoa! The man has got a spiritual malady for a start.' The scary thing is, I think a lot of people think that, to some degree. And you find that the woman's role in a film becomes some sort of appendage to the man. So I can see why they're not too fulfilled.

Even if you accept your premise that men have traditionally been the storytellers, if you look at nineteenth-century literature – maybe the golden age of lit-

erature – it was about men and women. *Anna Karenina* is one of the greatest stories ever told. Stories don't get any better than that, in my opinion.
They don't. I tried to tackle it at one point. But she was a woman written by a man.

Now your films aren't full of sex and naked bodies. They are very human sorts of stories. You're kind of old-fashioned, aren't you?
In a way. At times, they're exploitative in their nature. And that's okay with me – you want to get out there and do good business. And in a sense, people want to be exploited a little bit when they go and see a film. I know I do.

You live here in Hollywood, right? You're part of the system now?
Most of the time, yeah, I integrated.

Obviously the system is pretty much based on money?
It is completely based on money. To a degree, I think the way I hook into the system is based on money.

You're a rare bird. We still think of you as an actor, that's your personality out there. I'm driving to meet you today, there's a huge billboard just down the road, and there you are – Mel Gibson. But in fact, that's just a part of what you do now. When somebody told me how many movies you've produced, I was stunned. You turn over, don't you?
Quite a few. We're pretty prolific for a perceived 'vanity' company. I think a lot of people start film companies and don't really do anything with them. But we get into the act – not always successfully either. We've made some horrible little pictures. And we've made some good ones too. So there's a pride in that, I enjoy doing it.

You've got a good team, haven't you?
Yes, there's a lot of people here with good heads on their shoulders. Nobody's immune from making a mistake, that's for sure. We make plenty of them. We call 'em school fees. Every time we get ripped off, it costs, oh, two to four million . . .

Is your judgement on projects pretty much financially based?
Not solely. I think that there's an art in marrying the two, and if you can satisfy both requirements, then you are successful. It doesn't mean you're not successful if you don't meet one of the two – you're just successful within this industry.

What would you say was the good news about Hollywood right now? Being very actively in the middle of it – what's right about it?
The best thing about it is that I grew up, and I guess you grew up, in another industry. And I succumbed to the charm of film – I love storytelling, and I love everything about it, even the crappy things about it I kind of like. And it's almost like religion: if you're Jewish you go to Jerusalem; if you're Catholic you go visit the Vatican; Muslim, you go visit Mecca. And, I mean, Mecca for film-makers is this industry here. It's the chief watering-hole. It's where everyone comes to measure up.

Somebody once told me my problem was I didn't understand the social contract here. I now understand what that means. Do you?

I think I do. You can't get mad. You can't let it get you, because you have to make a deal, and it's almost unspoken, that you are going to be fucked over at some point by people who you may have done something nice for. And it may happen that by circumstance, or even very purposefully, you fuck someone over yourself, maybe to get even. But that shouldn't get in the way of you being able to sit down and have fun with them. Am I on the right track?

Absolutely.

I have felt the knife go in. I've sat there and felt the knife slip firmly in between my shoulder blades, shoved through the other side, through my heart. And I've felt the whole thing and thought, 'Ahhh . . . just wait till next week.' You can't build a resentment about it. You have to let it go, you have to still try and love those people. Because it's not personal. Otherwise you'll eat yourself alive here. And I think it takes that kind of cockroach resilience to survive in this town.

Jeff Berg was my agent at the time when I was in a big fight with Ray Stark, that I clearly was going to lose from the get-go. But I couldn't let go. Two and a quarter years, one movie. And Jeff said to a mutual friend, 'Mike's problem is he doesn't understand the social contract – which is, "Don't take it personally, shut up, stop making fucking trouble."' Mike Medavoy said to me at the time, 'You've got to realize it's not the movie you're making now that's important – it's the next one.' By the time I got wrung out by the studio, he said, 'Have you seen the trailer we've cut for your movie?' I said, 'No.' He said, 'Take a look at it and you'll get an idea of the movie you're supposed to be making.'

It is bizarre, though, isn't it? You come in, you're fresh from the farm, still got shit on your shoes. And people are charmed by that, by the fresh approach you bring to it. They'll stroke the shit out of you, and that's kind of good for you too. But it doesn't take very long before it gets to you. You can't get away from certain attitudes and certain modes of behaviour that this town and this industry dictate. And no matter how strong you are when you come in off the farm with those convictions and a certain line of attack – you are going to be affected by this place. You're going to be diverted.

I've tried to explain to film-makers who are up and coming, who have ideals. They all want to come here, same reason you and I came here. And I say, 'Do you know how difficult it is to say no to four million dollars? If you had an idea of doing an arthouse movie next, and then you had the good or bad fortune to have a hit – can you imagine trying to get off that chocolate-covered boat?'. I think it's almost impossible.

I was in my mid-twenties the first time I really came over here. And I had a whole bunch of weird, paranoid suspicions about what the hell was going on, because there was a lot of stuff I couldn't understand. And nobody was really bothering to explain it to me. I thought, 'Surely this whole place can't be like the weird town, you know, where the stranger wanders into the bar and all the people suddenly shut up. Or they tell you, 'Don't go to the house on the hill . . .' I thought, 'No, no, that's insane, that couldn't be the reason why so-and-so was acting like that – could it?' And then later you find out you were on track with a lot of this stuff. Some of your worst nightmares were real at the time.

I've been away from LA for two years, the longest break I've had since I started making movies. So when I came back I went to a Paramount première of *Snake Eyes* for Nic Cage. Then he got his star on Hollywood Boulevard, and I made a speech with Sherry Lansing. I felt like an anthropologist, like Margaret Mead in Borneo. Every time I came to LA I would get an urge in the first week to make a documentary. By the second week it was gone, because the place is beyond parody. And the shit that you see overseas about Hollywood is such a lie. Always the same stock shots of the Hollywood sign, and the puff pieces about actors in which everybody's just very thrilled to be wherever they are. The English Sunday papers are constantly telling us that Britain is again 'taking over Hollywood', and they'll name four actors that you've vaguely heard of. And presumably those actors read that shit and then are terribly disappointed a year later when they haven't got a job.

I used to be terribly uncomfortable with that stuff. But eventually you start to swim upstream with the rest of the salmon, and if you stay here long enough, you realize it for what it is, and you're not afraid of it any more. So you just walk through it and do the silly puff pieces and be as charming as you possibly can. You can even fool yourself that you're enjoying it. And then you get on with what you tried to get on with in the first place.

Do you think it's easier for you because you're an outsider who came in?
I think so. But who isn't an outsider coming into this?

Yes, but you come in with a particular culture and a sort of toughness. And you've got a family, haven't you? Whereas I think most people come in to get laid.
On some level.

On some level. And they also want to get rich, which is the same thing. Get rich and get laid on a level that is beyond their genetic right.
Okay, I understand what you're saying.

I'm doing Kenneth Turan next week. He's agreed to an interview. And everyone says he's a really interesting guy.
He is. I mean, if you read his things, he makes a point and he backs it up. And he hates my shit. Hates it, always. I get slashed by him. And I know it's going to happen and I don't care any more.

7 Kenneth Turan

Mike Figgis: The nature of this conversation is a little unusual, because it's not often that directors and critics sit and talk. Probably a good thing, because the temptation would be to get into a lot of that . . . stuff. But you have a very specific viewpoint of what people call Hollywood. How would you describe what you do for a living?
Kenneth Turan: I think the simplest way to put it is that I look at films and I provide a point of view on them, for people who are trying to figure out if they want to see the movie or not. I really feel that what I do relates to my readers. I don't do it in a vacuum, I don't do it for the film-makers.

This is an industry based on a series of processes, like any industry. Joe does this, Jill does that, and so on, and finally people pay money either to see a movie or rent a video. What is your process when it comes to watching a film? Technically speaking, what do you actually do?
When I get into a theatre, what I want to do more than anything is enjoy the film – believe it or not. It's almost like a mantra – 'Boy, I hope this is good.' I want it to do what it's supposed to do. In other words, if it's a comedy I want to be laughing. I reacted to films that way before I was a critic.

How long have you been a critic?
I've been at the *LA Times* for about seven years. Before that I was a freelance critic in a variety of places, off and on, for probably twenty years – sometimes only writing once a month, in small magazines.

Twenty years you've been reviewing films. What else have you done?
Newspaper reporting. I started with the *Washington Post*, then I worked freelance for a while, and then I came out to California and did magazine journalism. I've written books. But I'm not out of a film-making background, I'm not a would-be film-maker. I come as a viewer. I've never written a screenplay, not even a treatment.

You must be the only person in Los Angeles who hasn't.
I have friends who are screenwriters and I've seen how painful a process it can be. It's an awful way to make a living, there's no point to getting into it unless you're driven to it. And I'm not.

Do you love what you do?
I love films. I still live for the moments when I'm in a theatre and maybe I didn't expect too much, and the film comes on and you think, 'Oh, my God.' Those moments sustain you through the films that just make you kind of sad or weary.

Two questions. One, is your background typical of the profession? Two, how do you move from one form of journalism to another?
It's very odd how critics get jobs, I don't know that there's any one way or path. Fifty years ago, newspapers would take anyone they thought was a likely subject and make them critics, even if they weren't particularly interested in film. Now,

because more people are seriously interested in film, that doesn't happen much any more. I don't know how many films I've seen – thousands. I've read a lot about film, I've thought and talked a lot about it, and I think that level of interest is pretty consistent across the board of the better critics. How they made the transition to actually get the job – everyone will tell you a different story. Certainly, there are many more qualified people for these jobs than there are jobs.

What would a qualification be?
It's not like you pass the bar, but the things I've mentioned – someone who's seen a lot of films, who's read a lot, who writes well. Maybe he's a critic at a smaller place that doesn't pay very well and he's fully qualified to work for the *New York Times*. But if the job isn't there you can't get it.

You're an important conduit in the small bottleneck of a movie's transition from a finished product to its reception by an audience. What really is the qualification then for speaking to that audience?
My job is maybe to do everything that the viewer doesn't have the time or the energy or the lifetime of film viewing to do. To have a thoughtful and informed perspective on a film which, if I write well, I can make accessible to readers of a newspaper, which is a lot of people.

How many newspapers – real ones – are there in Los Angeles?
You have the *Times*. There used to be the *Herald Examiner*, that's gone. You have the *Daily News* in the Valley, which is still part of Los Angeles, threatening to break off. But technically, physically, there's really only one paper at this point in time in Los Angeles.

Now, in America, there are papers that can be bought pretty much nationwide. The *New York Times* would be the leader in that sense. But it would seem that in the strange world of criticism, as perceived by studios and the industry, there are only two newspapers that people bandy over. They say, 'What did the *LA Times* think? What did the *New York Times* think?' There's a legend that if the *New York Times* likes it, the *LA Times* is going to pan it, and vice versa.
I've heard that. I wish they were that well organized. Janet Maslin's a friend of mine, I like her work, and I'm always curious what she has to say. But the truth is, our reviews appear on the same day. I don't know what she thinks until I see her review in print, and I've already written mine.

Of course. So maybe that's just an urban folk tale. And from the point of view of a film-maker, like myself, it is very useful for one's pride to think that it is a reality.
One thing I always say about film criticism is that God doesn't speak to me. I don't know what a good film is, in an absolute sense, no one does. It's all opinion. I think it's informed opinion, but opinion nevertheless.

I don't agree. I think some films are radically bad, and sometimes I watch them and think, 'It would be lovely to be liberal about this, and say, "It's a matter of opinion."' But in my heart I think I don't believe that. And at the same time I do think that there are some films that jump over the middling kind of mush, and are just very good. It's so arrogant to say it, and it's not a thing to bandy around in public. But I do feel that the passion that drives such statements is necessary sometimes – to have a belief in the badness or goodness of something.

I do feel that way when I write. You couldn't write if you didn't. At the same time, I'm always confronted with people who absolutely hated certain films, and thought they were dreadful – films that I really liked. And vice versa. I've found it increasingly difficult to say to people, 'You're just wrong, you're just an idiot.' I found I didn't believe that.

Sometimes I'm so moved by the daring of a film – like in Kieslowski's *Three Colours Red*, the last film in his trilogy, where he had the patience to pay off an image from *Blue* – Juliette Binoche under water – that had actually annoyed me in the first film. I was moved to tears because of his courage. Then I was on a BAFTA jury where *Red* was outvoted as Best Film – the award went to *Four Weddings and a Funeral*. And I was devastated, for weeks, by the inability of my peers to agree with me.

Well, it's frustrating.

But I felt that they were wrong. They were so influenced by other factors, like nationalism, and the desire to applaud a good guy. And sometimes I think, 'You can't do that.' I mean, you must see films where you know, in your head, they're going to basically sink without trace, be tossed out the next day.

You're always worrying that maybe you're going to like a film no one else is going to like, that's going to die not only among the public but among other critics. All you really have are your own taste and your own instincts, you can't go second-guessing and protecting yourself. I've seen films that I've absolutely loved, that I knew would go nowhere, and I got furious letters from viewers who hated them. There's a French-Canadian film, *Leolo*, by Jean-Claude Lazan – it drives a lot of people crazy. But I know that I really love that film.

I haven't seen it. What did you love about it?

It's a very poetic version of the director's childhood. And he had a genuinely awful childhood, but he turned it into something astonishingly artful. I saw it at Cannes, where I'm generally in a bad mood and I want to go home – I don't want to be seeing five films a day for two weeks. But this one just took me away. That's what you live for. I was a big champion of the film, so were Janet Maslin, David Ansen – many critics loved it. But it just didn't go anywhere – it was too strange, too difficult, too unpleasant. It was simultaneously too real and too poetic.

But you gave it a good endorsement, and that would have helped the film-maker quite a lot. When you see a film-maker who's vulnerable in that sense, someone you think speaks with real talent and poetry – are you prepared to jump out of your role as you outlined earlier – as the man who speaks to the potential audience? Do you feel, we should help this person?

That's an adjunct. I don't have a problem with helping people, but I don't feel that it's my main purpose.

How does business function for you? You have an office, you go to work five days a week?

Yes, most of my writing is done in an office, near my home – not at the *Times*. I live a distance from the *Times* and it's just not a good use of my time to go in there. I write about – between two and four films a week. And the review appears on the day the film opens. About eighty per cent of films open on Fridays, and twenty per cent on a Wednesday. A major studio will not open a film on Monday, Tuesday, Thursday, Saturday or Sunday. I don't know why this is, it's one of the great pieces of received wisdom that the distributors seem to live on.

So really you'll write all week. And what are the viewing conditions that you have to put up with?

It varies enormously. The studios or the distributors determine it. But it's always a very nice screen. Sometimes I'm on my own in a small theatre. Sometimes I'm in a thousand-seat theatre full of people. Again, another piece of received wisdom – studios do not believe that a critic will know a film as a comedy unless he's in a room with a thousand people and they're laughing. I can argue it both ways.

I'd be in favour of you always seeing a film with an audience.

I'm not, actually. I just don't react that much off of an audience. Again it might sound contradictory. But I'm not an applause meter. My job is not to say, 'I know that the audience is going to like this.' You can't tell that.

Are you a fan of video?

No. I like a big screen in a dark room.

I've just always found it odd that a medium designed to be projected huge in front of a lot of people is often reviewed as a solo experience. Television reviewers have a much easier job because they watch shows pretty much the way everybody else does. Unless of course they see it with a bunch of other critics at a special screening, which is entirely the wrong way to watch a television programme.

I just think my job is to think about the film. A friend of yours says to you, 'Should I see this film?' And all you can say to him is, 'Well, I saw it in a big room and a lot of people laughed.' They're not really going to think that's satisfactory.

I don't agree. Henry Bean, who wrote *Internal Affairs* – he and I fell out

towards the end of the film. Then, like all studio films, it went through the preview process – this ending, that ending. And at a final screening, Henry was very aloof and not happy. But he's a gorgeous guy. He then rings me up after the release and says, 'I went to see the film in Times Square with a black audience. What an experience!'

But I've seen the system backfire on films, where people fill the theatre up and the audience just sits there. I do like seeing films with an audience, but to me that's not as relevant to what I do as maybe film-makers and studios feel it should be. I'm just trying to focus on the film. I want the film to speak to me. If I'm going to write about it, that linkage has to happen.

Do you have time to see a film more than once?
As a rule I only see a film once, just because I wouldn't have time to sleep if I saw things twice. But if I see a film in a festival and it doesn't come out for six months, I have to see it again because my notes are cold and I don't really remember intensely enough what my reactions were.

What's right about the Hollywood system?
The first thing that comes into my mind is that I think the level of craftsmanship in Hollywood is exceptional – the below-the-line people, the technical people. There are many reasons why the studio films are so popular around the world. But they look good, they're made so well, in a lot of ways. I speak as a critic. I think maybe as a film-maker, you see things that are not done so well.

But the technique is significantly more sophisticated and better than anywhere else in the world?
I think so. And part of the reason is that some of these jobs are done by people whose fathers did the same jobs, and their grandfathers too. It's almost like a guild system, like something from the Middle Ages. Even though this is in some ways the least important thing that Hollywood does.

But, no, one could argue that it's the most important thing they do now. Is it a shame that the technical achievement has become the most identifiably important thing about these movies?
I think so. The level of writing, the level of thought in the films are rarely up to its technical side. Occasionally, Hollywood may think it should do something prestigious, something to get an Oscar, but mainly it's about making money. And increasingly it's about making money around the world. It's a question of 'What can we sell everywhere?' And I think that leads inevitably to a focus on films where language is not important, films that are simplistic, that can be easily subtitled into other languages and easily understood. Given how much money films cost and how studios want to sell them around the world, this mitigates against sophisticated writing. But it hurts film. I don't believe there have to be big dumb movies and small smart movies. I believe that there can be massive popular

movies that are well written. Look at the *Godfather* films, which were hugely popular and I think they are –

As good as it gets, on any level.
Exactly. That's my dream – when I see a Hollywood film that's the kind of thing I'm hoping to see. But in a sense, the emergence of the independent film world has given the studios an excuse to forget about it. 'Yes, those people are doing it now. We don't have to worry about that. We do something else.' I think it started with a very shrewd move by Jeffrey Katzenberg when he was at Disney. As I understand it, he was a prime force in the buying of Miramax, because I think he understood, number one, that there was a market for these kind of films. And, number two, Disney was never going to make them. But he saw that there was money in them, maybe not as much money as *Titanic* made, but certainly respectable money.

I've heard stories about studios threatening to pull advertising from the *LA Times*, because they've been somehow affronted by something that was written – a review, or a news story or feature.
I don't really think about that. It's a strong paper, a lot of readers, a lot of advertising, it's owned by a fairly successful company. And it's traditional for papers like that to resist that kind of pressure. The pressure may exist, they may yell at my editors. But I don't hear about it. So the fact that someone at a studio was personally unhappy has no more effect on me than if a reader in Simi Valley wrote me a very articulate letter about why I'd missed a point in the film.

Do you think there could usefully be a time limit on the job that you have?
Interesting question. I could argue it either way. There's something to be said for experience. Sometimes I write a piece that I know I couldn't have written if I was in my first year on the job – just because it calls on all the years I've been thinking about film, all the time I've spent intensely on it.

I have a theory – a plan, actually. I'm very dissatisfied with criticism right now. It's no longer a Victorian gentleman's élitist pastime; it's big business, with big payoffs, and I think the system is outmoded. I'd like to see a critical magazine devoted to films and books and the arts. And I would like to see a film reviewed in four columns, with photographs, by someone who is informed – an expert on film, who nevertheless isn't carrying the entire weight of representing the film to a vast body of readers. I just want to know what the writer thinks.
I could see how that would be interesting.

I'd buy it.
I think what you want to do is read someone consistently whom you like, for whatever reason, because you want to get a sense of how their mind works. You want to be able to use them to help you decide.

I was talking to Stephen Fry, who was in *Carrington* – lovely actor, very clever guy. And he said, 'I always want to know a little bit more about the taste of the guy who's writing, I want to know what turns him on . . .'

Oh, exactly. But even if someone asks me 'What's your taste?', I couldn't really tell them in a way that would be helpful. The only way you find out is by reading someone consistently.

Well, let me try. I'm not asking for anything definitive, I just want to know a little bit about what you like. So give me five pieces of music . . .

Oh, I'm an opera fan. *Nessun Dorma*, Handel's *Water Music*, the *Tannhäuser* Overture. There are some cello concertos by Haydn that I'm really fond of. I think I like older, more traditional music. I think it's safe to say that as a generalization.

Five pieces of literature.

Literature is easier. I'd almost rather give novelists. Anything by Anthony Trollope, I'm a big Trollope fan. I'm a Jane Austen fan, I'm a Balzac fan, I'm a Raymond Chandler fan. I like Isaac Singer.

Five film directors?

Orson Welles, I'm a big fan of. I like John Ford, I like Hitchcock. Kieslowski was a director I was enormously fond of; I was so sad when he died.

Five actors – male?

Brando, when he's good – there's a reason why he's Brando. Actually I'm a fan of Harrison Ford. There are so many good British actors – Ian McKellen I've seen do some wonderful things. Gielgud is a marvellous actor.

Actresses?

I'm surprised to hear myself say this, but I really like Meryl Streep. There's been so much negative stuff said about her, but she hits it very consistently. Margaret Sullavan had a wonderful quality that you just don't see any more. Katharine Hepburn. And, you know who I like, believe it or not? Louise Brooks. She just has this . . . You just watch her.

What about the under-thirty group?

I like Winona Ryder.

And five films that spring to mind, that have sustained?

Children of Paradise is one of my favourite films. I love *The Earrings of Madam De . . .* , Max Ophüls. I like *Citizen Kane*. I like *Touch of Evil*.

I liked *The Lady from Shanghai*. It's flawed – but then I don't like perfect films.

Yes, there's stuff in there that you go, 'Oh, my God.' I don't know if there *are* perfect films.

8   Jean-Jacques Beneix

Mike Figgis: You're the first director I've spoken to for this project who is not an American, and is not living here all the time. So I'm interested in your point of view of the town, as the outsider. When did you first come?
Jean-Jacques Beneix: I came in 1977. That was a love story, I was dating a great girl, a make-up artist. I had long hair, and when I was at the border, they asked me, 'Who do you know in America?' I said, 'Raquel Welch.' And then I was in trouble.

But were you telling the truth?
Yes, I had just been the assistant director on a movie with her and Jean-Paul Belmondo.

Let's go back a bit. Why did you choose to go into film in the first place?
Oh, probably because it was the geometrical centre of all my incompetences, which is a way to be nice. I wanted to be a director when I was fifteen years old. But then I tried to escape from that, because it looked to me like something dangerous, something bizarre. So I went to medical school, but I had no chance to become a doctor because I had problems with mathematics – I was very, very bad. But I was very good in the other things.

Are you a Parisian?
Yes, born and raised. First generation – my father wasn't, and my mother neither. I went to this medical school in May 1968.

So you got caught up in all of that.
Yes.

A good time?
A great time.

Who were your cinema heroes at that time?
As a kid I was interested in movies – cowboys and Indians, I was into the fights. But I didn't know who the director was, I just went to movies to experience feelings, like any kid. Then later on I started to read *Cahiers du Cinéma*, *Positif*, and then I started to know about the directors. My great heroes were mainly the older French directors like Carné, Duvivier, Autant-Lara. And also the New Wave, Truffaut, Godard. I share the admiration that Godard had for Jean-Pierre Melville. And I had a great shock when I saw *2001 – A Space Odyssey*. That film made me realize how sometimes people can say that a movie was very important in their life.

***2001* was the movie for you.**
Yes, when I saw it I experienced a shock, emotionally. And the minute I came out of the cinema, I wanted to pick up my phone and call people to tell them I experienced something incredible. I didn't know who had made it, I had no idea who Kubrick was.

My movie would have been *Bonnie and Clyde*. That was the first time I saw a film that completely took me somewhere else.
With time and distance, you can understand more. Recently I was asked to talk about some movies for a French TV channel, and among them was *2001*. I hadn't seen it for years, but seeing it again I suddenly realized how strong the picture is. Because, you know, the new approach is that you have always to cut, and be into the action. A guy picks up a glass, and it can take ten shots. In *2001*, what's incredible are the long takes – so powerful.

Have you seen *Armageddon*?
Not yet. I'm not so thrilled to go to see it. But I have to.

Out of interest.
Of course.

Bruce Willis goes into space to blow up this big meteor, so obviously there's an effects-shot where you see the earth from the point of view of space. But it's over so quickly, gone in a moment. And the music is sort of like high energy. And you think, 'What did it cost to create that effect?' You compare it to *2001*, how beautiful Kubrick's choice of music was, and the gorgeous aesthetic way he shot the planet. And I thought, 'It would not hurt you to steal this from Kubrick. You're stealing from everybody else, why don't you steal from somebody good? And slow down a bit?'
But I think Hollywood is afraid that the audience will turn its attention somewhere else.

They'll change channels.
Yes – the zapping. I see the reactions of some people here when they read a script, they see dialogues and say, 'How many pages? Five?' But it's nice sometimes just to listen to actors, without cutting – especially when you have great actors. I think it's a result of the whole system, which is into gratifying people on the short-term and with the bigger return of investment. Then we are not more into art, we are into something else. And something has to happen every minute or every two minutes, like on TV shows. But sometimes I would like to have a long shot just watching a tree, a child, a woman. And I think one of the great fights for a director now is to be strong enough to say, 'I just want to look at that and nothing else' – not just click-click, tonk-tonk.

A film that had a huge influence on me was Alain Resnais's *Providence*. It annoyed me so badly at first, it's a film that you can't get hold of – until the final scene, when you understand. You have to wait an hour and a half to reach this moment of revelation. But it's worth it. I wonder if anybody would have the courage to expect an audience to wait that long now.
The problem is that it's almost no more your choice.

Is it the same in France?

You still have the right to do almost whatever you want, as long as you accept that the movie should be inexpensive and shouldn't challenge the financiers. But the minute you want to have an expensive movie, you have to more or less conform to a certain format. And that's where the fight is – you have to fight the conventions all the time. Sometimes I wonder if I'm too arrogant. I'm not going to change the system, so maybe I have to change myself. But I don't want to change myself.

Are you expensive?

No, I haven't been, but now I feel that I'd like one day to do an expensive movie – not for the pleasure of spending money but to have the vision and the technical means and the actors. But sometimes I think I should go and make little films for two million dollars.

I think I made that decision because I was becoming quite ill trying to deal with the system, and the energy of fighting was replacing the energy of creativity. And I just think we can't win that battle.

That's very true. You should be expending your energy playing the game, being on the court and trying to hit the ball as strongly and accurately as you can. Instead of that you have to fight with the referee. I don't want to appear like the guy who's come here and wants to complain about the system at the same time. But the worst things I've heard about Hollywood, the most violent complaints – I haven't heard them in France or in England, but right here in this community. And sometimes I think, 'My God, if I had said that, they would have deported me.' My feeling now is that the system is a little bit like Detroit in the seventies. They keep making things that are obsolete, in a way.

Big cars.

Big cars. But the audience is so much more fragmented than that, and the possibility of making films for a little niche is bigger than ever. So it's interesting for me to see the inflation of the budget, the inflation of the stars, I think I enjoy watching it. I like it because it's going to collapse. In flames.

Sodom and Gomorrah...

The bonfire of the vanities. At the same time, there are some very interesting people here, who fight to change, to improve. But it's also some kind of Catch-22. And I feel that I'm weak, I'm not clear enough with myself.

But is it possible to be clear here? I'm like an alcoholic, I know that if I don't go to a bar or hang out with other alcoholics, I'll be fine. But if you put me in the bar – yeah, I'll have one drink, and then another. So I'm smart enough to know, don't go to the bar. But I still know the bar exists. It's a funny thing, in the past three nights I've started watching television. I have cable, I think I have fifty channels. And what I wanted to do for this book was to go through all the channels and write very quickly exactly what was on. So I started doing that sort of

thing and within a day I'm completely addicted to channel hopping. And when I turn it off I feel ill – like I've masturbated badly. It's a very strange sensation. There's something about this town – once you cross the line, you lose your mind very quickly. It's impossible to have judgement.

I think that it may be possible, but only with a lot of – I use this old word – virtue. In the Roman sense of the word, of knowing your rules, your morals, your sense of what is moral. And keeping to that.

Being your own policeman.

Yes. But you know what saves me? Books.

I want to talk to you about that later. But do you think that we – the French, the English, the Germans, the Americans – have made too much of a religion out of cinema? Do we value it too much?

It's difficult to be a priest and to talk about destroying the religion, because then you destroy the priest. And it's nice to be one of the priests, especially in countries like France where there is a real care and understanding of cinema, even if recently it's become a little bit less interesting than it was. It looks more like *People* magazine now. But the most insane dream of certain people in movies is to design the ultimate product which is going to please the biggest number of people. And, slowly, what they are doing is designing the audience. That's what frightens me most. Sometimes I'm in the movie theatre and I wonder what I'm doing there, watching people shooting at each other, agonizing in blood. I'm not a moralist, I'm for freedom of expression, but I wonder what an artist is doing when they get involved in that. Do I belong to this world? I feel so bad I have to go back home, back to my *atelier*, and work hard and keep to my own way. I have been weak for some years now, because I was in a personal crisis. Now I'm back with a very strong determination to do what I have to do, and nobody is going to stop me. Or I will go somewhere else.

I have a theory. If you live in Los Angeles, there is no interaction on the street, everybody's in cars. Everybody just goes from their house into a car, and they drive to one place to meet one person. The guy who parks the car, they don't look at him because he's Mexican. So there's very little interaction between people. And since film-makers are involved in this system, they're going to start writing stories that are totally uninfluenced by the street. They're going to produce a kind of pure synthesized sugar – there's going to be no vinegar, no salt, no garlic, nothing. If you keep doing this cycle, the product will get smoother and smoother, like the cream that comes out of a can.

But there will be a backlash, some kind of revolution. I think we have always to bet on some people who will say, 'We want to do something else. We want to see something else.' I know that a lot of kids go to the movies and come out feeling like, 'Where's the beef? What did we eat?' They feel they've bought something they're not happy with. And I bet on the fact that some kind of resentment is slowly building. So we have to work with this.

So then the question – and the problem – is a very simple one. How do you get to that audience?
You have to accept – I don't want to use big words – some kind of poverty and some kind of simplicity. Even here you can still go to some little cinemas, and see films that aren't huge machines. And the audience is there, the place is full. So the problem is more a question of distribution, a question of retailers. Hollywood succeeded in captivating and kidnapping the audience through the theatre system. Now they control it.

It needs a revolution, doesn't it?
Yes, and I would say that the revolution should also be political, in the sense that we should also talk to the stockholders – because they're entitled to figure out what's done with their money. In reality, the profit is smaller and smaller, and the system is in tremendous need of expansion.

One of the things they're doing at Sony is putting a lot of money into the digital revolution, the idea of shooting and projecting digital, and getting a quality image on a large screen – in other words, to get rid of the huge costs in making two thousand prints. It's a revolutionary idea and there must be a huge resistance from the industry. When I tried to shoot on 16 mm here, it made the rental people completely angry. What they have invested in is lightweight 35 mm cameras. They don't give a fuck about the Aaton, they don't want 16 mm cameras making a problem for them.
One part of the New Wave revolution that very few people remember is the technical side. Because the camera was lighter, film-makers got out of the studio, studio production became obsolete, in their eyes. Of course, after time had passed, we discovered that some of the guys they wanted to kill were not that bad. And some of the guys in the New Wave were not that good. But when young kids tell me they want to make movies, I say, 'You can, you can do it. We couldn't. But you have this.' [*Beneix indicates my video camera.*]

But film students can be so snobbish about this. I ask them, 'Why do you want to shoot on 35 mm, what's the big deal?' And it's a stupid question because the big deal is very clear. 'I'd like to earn four million dollars, sleep with Cindy Crawford, have a swimming pool, and a very big Ferrari.' Simple as that. People haven't come to this town to make Godard movies, they've come to get rich and have a lifestyle.
There is the same problem with a lot of people who want to be famous soccer players, or famous *toreros*, though the love of fighting bulls is maybe not so good. But for some, it's a passion, it's an art. For others, the only reason is to get rich. For me, I'm no longer of the age where I was driving around Beverly Hills, looking at the biggest houses and dreaming that I could have a house like that. I don't dream about it any more. I don't give a shit.

Something I discovered about you, which I found extremely surprising, was how long it's been since you made your last film.
I'm surprised myself.

How long is that?
Let's say that the movie that I'm preparing now is made, and will be released in 2001. That will be ten years, almost. I can't believe it.

And it wasn't because no one wanted you to make a film. It's because you somehow didn't want to make a film.
I didn't want to or I couldn't.

Why? What happened?
Let's say it was a bad combination of a mid-life crisis plus some lack of inspiration, some personal questions. And maybe also because the last film I did wasn't as successful as it should have been – *IP-5*, with Yves Montand. It was the number ten movie of its year in France, though we would have liked it to be number two, number one. But I experienced something I wouldn't wish on any director, not even my worst enemy – having an actor who dies during the shooting. Yves Montand died on the last day, we were doing retakes. He and I got along very well, he said, 'I'm going to change my clothes, I'll come back to kiss you, and then we'll meet in fifteen days in the Maldives.' I said, 'I would like to meet you there.' He died. So there was not only the personal mourning but also the fact that the movie was suddenly an orphan. It tells the story of an old man who's dying, and Montand died the same way as in the movie. It kills the movie. People don't want to go to see that. It's interesting to realize that a movie has to be fiction. People want to see the worst thing, a killing, whatever – as long as it's not true. When it comes true you're dead. It has nothing to do with me, nothing to do with the film. Is the film good or bad? I don't know. I did my best. But there were a lot of personal things. My mother died. My best friend died. She was my press agent, we had worked together for fifteen years. So then I just couldn't make any more pictures. Anything I had was bad. Anything I was reading was not interesting, irrelevant. So I did documentaries. It saved my life.

I understand this feeling very well. It was important for you to be dealing with the image.
Oh yes. Always, always.

Do you take photographs?
Oh yes, all the time. But I have a very conflicted and neurotic relation with photographic cameras. I have a collections of them, a Leica, a Nikon. I love having them, I love to touch them. But taking photos is always painful, difficult, because it's never the good photo. So I have to be involved in some kind of an assignment to take pictures. Then I like it. I managed to escape this problem by doing the stills for my movies. I enjoy that, because it's an assignment.

Yes, I did that for my last one. Do you remember Kubrick's wonderful line? He never uses stills, he always takes them from the print. He said, 'If the stills man is getting good photographs, then the cinematographer is in the wrong position.' I think that's very profound.

I like Kubrick's way. I mean, I don't compare myself. But over time I got into a process which was totally neurotic where I wanted to control more and more of the picture. Everything. Of course, film-making is by a team of people, and I have great respect for the people I work with. But it's my picture, it's nobody else's. Maybe sometimes I went a little bit too far – producing, writing, camera, taking stills.

What you say is horribly familiar to me – because I write, do the music, produce, take the stills. But on the last couple, I was lucky to work with a French DP, Benoît Delon. He's young, he's a painter, he's not so obsessive about cinematography, he's just very good. And before that I had Declan Quinn, a young Irish-American guy, very good. But I feel that, technologically, Hollywood has become this horrible place where actors are directed by cinematographers a lot of the time. Sometimes, when there are seven cameras running, actors must have a real schizophrenic problem about which camera they're working for.

One thing I have discovered – caught in a certain type of light, there is only one place to put the camera. And if you put another one down then it doesn't work, and the matching is not good. But now it's some kind of business, you have to have two cameras, three cameras, four cameras. You shoot every angle. What the fuck is this? Just find the good and do it.

My two-camera philosophy is a little different. I would like the second camera to go in the place where you would not expect it to be, given the light. But they shoot the multi-camera way, to make more choices in the editing room, and if you're using four cameras you have to light as if it was television.

Exactly. So many films are the same, the lighting is terrible. You have to have a lot of lights for depth of field, and because people don't like shadows, and because the actors want to see each other . . . And slowly you build up a degeneration of the art of film-making.

When I first started making films, the thing that puzzled me was walking on to the set to shoot a scene that's meant to be in the dark, and finding the place lit up like Christmas Day – so bright. And you'd say, 'It's meant to be in the dark', and the cinematographer would say, 'No, it will look dark, we'll close the iris right down. But we need the depth of field.' And you'd say, 'But how can the actors, who are supposed to be making love in a dark room, possibly have any freedom?'

Yes, you start to think, 'Oh, my God, this is too dark, they are not going to see it on TV, the video will be terrible.' So you build up some kind of neurosis. That's probably another reason why I stopped making movies for a while, because I was in such stress over this need for quality. Sometimes I was just too tough on myself. Sometimes, the interest of a shot is not in the framing or the light, but just in what the guy says. Also, too many choices in the editing room can kill you. The Avid is very nice, but then you can have thousands of possibilities, and you kill yourself. So I think there came a moment where I had to go back to something more simple. Because they ask you, 'How many metres of track do you want?' I say, 'Twenty.' 'Take thirty, forty, it's nothing, it'll just be in the truck and we can take it out whenever.' So one day I said, 'I'm going to do a movie with a tripod, a simple camera, two lens, and it's okay.'

When I did the last one, it was with a tripod and the new Canon zoom, which is very beautiful.
It's great. Simplicity, simplicity . . .

I wanted to talk to you about books, about how important is literature.
I love books, I need books. Physically, I like to touch them, I like the hard cover very much. Sometimes I go into a shop and I buy five books, without knowing what I'm buying. But I need them. I like books on psychology and psychiatry, but also novels. I discovered that there are books that I need to read again and again.

Give me five books.
Ah, difficult. Flaubert's *Éducation Sentimentale* . . . Every time somebody asks me this, there is some kind of a blockage. It will come to me later. There are some detective novels that I love.

Five pieces of music.
Vivaldi's *Four Seasons;* Mozart's *Concerto No. 1* and *Don Giovanni*; Strauss's *The Seasons*. There are so many – Puccini, *La Bohème*.

Five movies.
2001. Les Enfants du Paradis. Dans La Ville Blanche by Alain Tanner, which is a movie very few people know, but for me it's pure beauty. One Fellini movie. One Antonioni movie. *Le Samourai*, Melville – great movie.

Godard?
Yes and no. Sometimes I think he talks better about the movie than he makes the movie. But the minute after I see what he's done, there's a moment of pure intelligence and grace and genius, of how to place the camera. Sometimes you're glancing at the TV or just flipping through tapes and there's a moment of shock where you say, 'What the fuck? Who did that?' And it's Godard.

9   Rosanna Arquette

Mike Figgis: Why did you choose, if indeed you did choose, to go into the film business?

Rosanna Arquette: My parents were in the theatre. My father was an actor, he was in improvisation groups like The Committee and Second City, so I always saw him on stage. I just remember watching the audience's faces, how they were transformed, and I was very moved by that as a kid. Then I did a play when I was seventeen, and a casting director saw me in it, and that was it. I didn't go to school, I went right into it. And I never stopped working.

Tell me more about why, though. What was so great about acting?

I have to say it's in the blood. Because I have a three-and-a-half-year-old who is already right there. She's not watching me do anything, it's just in her blood, she's a performer. We're a family of actors. My father, my grandfather, my great-grandfather.

Is there anybody in your family who didn't go into the profession?

No. All my siblings are actors. And my mother was an actress for years, but she quit and became a therapist for abused women. She was abused as a child, growing up. And she herself was also an abuser when I was growing up. Then she went into therapy for years and worked on herself, and she and I went through amazing therapy together. We cleared all that up. But she was a young kid, she had me when she was nineteen, and she just didn't have the tools. She had a crazy family.

Is she the mother of all of your siblings?

She's our mom, yes. She just passed away last August.

I'm sorry. I heard.

That was heavy. But it was amazing, too, because we were all with her. It was an incredible experience. She always taught creativity to her kids. We had that in our upbringing. There was always music, dance, art, around us.

So aesthetics above everything. Did you read a lot, was that encouraged?

Yes. I started reading at four, so I was really reading well by the time I was six, six and a half.

Really? What kind of stuff?

I had *The Little Prince*. By twelve, thirteen, I was reading Fitzgerald, and slowly going into Hemingway – just the classics when I was young.

Were you read to?

Always. Mother always read to us. I think that's important. And I do that with my daughter Melissa. Because of the computer thing – I'm really trying to keep that away. That, and The Spice Girls.

How important do you think literature is?

Very. I find I don't read as much as I used to, and I'm really trying to change that now. I'm rereading *A Hundred Years of Solitude* because I read it ten years ago. And it's new and different to me now.

But it's frustrating, isn't it? Because a really great book you should read maybe four or five times. It's a problem of time.
That's it.

Do you think films can change people?
Yes.

You think films are important enough to persevere with?
Yes, I do.

Does it sadden you that it kind of means the death of literature?
Does it have to?

It's a contest – you only have so much time in your day. We want to be fed stories, that's part of our ongoing cultural tradition. But I think now people come home from work and watch television, and something happens to the brain. You don't read. You don't want to pick up a book after you've watched a video.
I went up to Northern California, and I don't want the television up there. I started rereading Pynchon's *Gravity's Rainbow*, which is a great book. It's funny you're asking this, because lately I've been feeling so focused in watching movies that I haven't been reading.

What we read are scripts.
Yes. We read scripts.

And what do you think of the scripts that you read?
I'm fairly depressed by most of them. They're shallow and crass – basically not stories that I would want to tell. The good ones are very few and far between. Did you see *Primary Colors*?

Not yet.
Elaine May's screenplay is really amazing, if you really listen to what's there. I think she's a good writer for our time.

I saw two movies that I thought were smart – *Wag the Dog* and *Bulworth*.
Bulworth was great.

Awesome piece of work, a huge joy. Made me smile so much, to see they still write stuff like that, and films like that still can get through. It's not a low-budget, experimental, indie movie, or a hyped-up, overblown studio movie. Just a smart movie, from people who've been around a long time. Beatty's crew are not kids. They're smart, mature adults.
Wag the Dog was a good screenplay. But I haven't had anything so amazing recently. Allison Anders has written a screenplay with Kurt Voss that we're going

to do in a couple of weeks. They did it in three weeks, and there's some really good writing in it. It's an ensemble piece.

Have you always been involved in that kind of thinking, or is it something that's evolved now through necessity?
No. I've always been there, I've been doing independents since the beginning of my career. Before they were hip. I had agents telling me that I needed to move into studio things. But the best work I've been a part of are all small, low-budget movies. They were always more interesting. Studio ones, you get a nice salary, but my heart was always with the independent world. And now it's become its own political thing.

Have you had good experiences with studios?
I did a film with Hal Ashby, the last movie he made, *Eight Million Ways to Die*. They took it away from him, he never got a chance to see his movie.

And, God, it was just so tragic to see this man. We had to go to a deposition, it was like going to court. They were asking if I'd seen his movies that had been less successful movies. I was, like, 'God, have you seen *Being There*? Have you seen *Coming Home*? He's an amazing director.' Hal was such a great guy. I felt like they killed him, I really did. Because he was so hurt, so angry.

Andy Garcia's really strong in that movie. I'd love to see it again.
If you could have seen what Hal would have done, his cut and his music, it would have been a great movie. So that was kind of tragic. I was very bitter and angry in those days. Talked about it a lot.

What effect did that have on your career?
You're supposed to keep your mouth shut and not be honest. I got myself in a lot of trouble for saying when someone is an asshole.

Were you warned to shut up?
After the fact. I was told it was a problem, that I shouldn't have said anything. I stuck up for Hal.

Were you aware that you were slightly digging a hole for yourself?
No.

No. You felt that was the correct thing to do?
To tell the truth? Yes. Now, I know that there are certain things you can say and can't say. But that's not where I come from. I'm still a really honest person, and I still get myself in trouble. I don't have an agent. That's because I didn't like my agents. And they knew it.

What happened next? After it was made clear to you that you should have shut up. How was it made clear to you?
Well, this is a very small business, and everybody plays tennis and has dinners

and schmoozes with one another. And all it takes is someone saying, even if it's untrue – 'I worked with her, she's a pain', or whatever. I think that in the past, I've gotten a bad rap by leaving one agency, going to another. And the agency I left represents a director who's directing a movie that I had a lot of interest in, so that's gone. That's happened to me quite a lot of times.

But you've survived. You're here, you're still working.
I am. I've been doing this for a lot of years.

There are other people we know who are no longer around.
I know. Debra Winger quit the business. And I think it's a tragedy, because she was a great actress.

I think at a certain point, even in a town like this, if you stand by your principles, ultimately you will be respected for it. It's about long life.
You go into it feeling like you're an artist. And to say that now, it sounds so silly. But it's always been very important to me. Always. And then you hire people who are working for you, and suddenly it becomes like you're working for them. And what's going to get them a big percentage?

I remember the first time I saw you in films, and you definitely came across as someone who was going to be a huge star.
I had that top-of-the-A-list moment, my fifteen minutes. Thank you, Andy Warhol.

For example, I couldn't get a meeting with you when I first came into town.
That is a perfect example of what happens all the time. Agencies would keep away people or scripts, and I wouldn't even know about it.

Did you feel as if you were being manipulated? You say you were perceived as being difficult, off-centre.
I was. But my mother was a political activist and a therapist and a great teacher to us. I was a little girl in Chicago, and I remember seeing Martin Luther King in the back of a truck. I have a certain, very leftist, 'Fuck you' system in my being. So it's really hard sometimes to bow down to morons. Not that everybody in this business is a moron.

What percentage of the moronic mindset do you see in the business now? Has it got worse?
For me it feels a lot worse. Call it ninety per cent. And then the few and far between, the artists who are still doing their thing. But it's hard for a woman to get older in this business. Because our faces are our films. I just turned thirty-nine, and I'm proud of it. But it was funny because this was the first birthday when I thought, 'God, I wish they wouldn't print it in *USA Today*.' Because suddenly a woman is not allowed to age in this business. So many people I know are getting surgery – I'm really against that. Look at Jeanne Moreau. I think she looks amazing. Helen Mirren is a beautiful, sexy woman, and she doesn't seem like she's done

anything. But the concept of beauty in Hollywood has changed, it's like you have to be this perfect thing. I did a movie that never saw the light of day that Sondra Locke directed. I had a bathroom scene with a seventeen-year-old. And my agent at the time said to me, 'Do yourself a favour. Don't show your tits any more.'

Male or female?
Male. Mid-thirties. I said, 'You know what? I bet you've never seen a real tit in your life.' I had just finished breast-feeding, and it was very uninhibited. My character was just an older woman, the scene wasn't trying to be sexy or anything. But, God, I have that etched in my psyche for ever – how hurtful that was, what a horrible thing to say.

Were you devastated?
No, I just thought it was creepy, horrible. I felt really violated.

Was it on the phone or to your face?
To my face.

What else did he say about the film?
He didn't like it.

Did he say you were good in it?
No. But I haven't had that kind of support recently. One of the reasons I don't have an agent right now is that I have a film that just got into Toronto. Martin Scorsese just saw it and loves it and is backing it. A lot of people who I respect really like this movie. And supposedly I have a good performance in it – I play Angelina Jolie's junkie mother. But the people representing me at the time just didn't like it, didn't want anybody to see me in it – they said I looked old and ugly in it. I said, 'I'm not supposed to look good here, that's the whole point.' I wasn't afraid of that. And I had thought they should be proud of me. I got the opposite – 'No one wants to see you like this.' Well, P.S., it's getting a very prestigious screening in Toronto, so we'll see what happens with it.

How's your ego?
My ego? Well, I'm a Leo, and we're very prideful. I have been, in the last few years, really beaten up and hurt and taking it like I'm shit. But I also have a support group, people who really believe in me. And I need that, or else I feel really insecure. Now I'm feeling really excited about getting older, in terms of work, because I'd like to move into the area where it's okay to play my age. I've given birth, I have a child. For me my work is better than it's ever been. I have much more to offer than when I was in my twenties. So it's just too bad that I feel like I'm in my prime, ready to rock, and they want twenty-year-olds.

I think the problem is – is anyone writing good parts for thirty-nine-year-old women?
Few and far between. I mean, where's Meryl? Where's Meryl Streep? She's play-

ing The Mom. I always want to see her because I love her so much, and she's a great actress.

How often do you go and see films?
Not like I used to. I used to go to the movies three, four times a week. Now I'm going once a month, maybe. There just hasn't been anything that I've really wanted to see. Though I want to see *High Art*. I hear it's great. And my friend Ally Sheedy's in it. We're doing Allison Anders's movie together.

Do you rent videos?
I do. I have collections of movies. But when the Academy-nominated movies come on tape, I really try to see them on a movie screen.

Why do you persevere with the Academy movies?
Well, I don't really vote, though I'm a member, I can. Of course, I did vote for my brother-in-law [*Nicolas Cage*].

Thank you. So, do you feel that you're part of the system here, or do you feel apart from it?
I feel very apart from it. But that's okay. I'll tell you a little humiliating story. The other day I was supposed to meet a director, Sam Raimi, for a part in a Kevin Costner film. It's about a baseball player, but it's a love story, and it's well written. The role is for a woman my age. Now they didn't have a pass for me at the studio gate, so I had to park and walk fifteen minutes in 102 degrees. I was melting in it. Then I had to wait for about fifty minutes. And I knew going in that I didn't have a chance in hell on this movie.

Why?
I knew they'd want someone they perceive as a big movie star. But I wanted to meet the director and do a good reading. I have this great acting coach called Julie Ariola, and now when I read it's not just about getting the part, I approach the work as an exercise. That's what I was going in with. Now the casting director came and got me after fifty minutes, shut the door, sat me down in front of a camera – and there was nobody else there, no director. I was shocked. But she said, 'The director can't be here, we just want to put you on film.' And there was this green fluorescent lighting, and I said that I didn't feel comfortable just going on tape right then. I thought I'd do a disservice to myself. If the director was there, I could at least connect with another human in the room. She said, 'Well, I'm sorry this happened, I feel bad, but they really want a movie star.' So I just sat there, thinking, 'Okay, I'm no longer a movie star. Okay.' It was the day before the first anniversary of my mother's death, so I was feeling emotional anyway. I was praying not to burst into tears. So I said, 'Well, I'm really sorry to waste your time, and I understand that.' She says, 'They might offer it to your sister.' I said they'd be lucky to get her, but that would be great. And I left. And I walked another fifteen minutes in the heat, black mascara running.

What were you wearing?

I think I was wearing a skirt about knee-length, and swallow heels. Funky chic.

You'd thought about it?

Oh yeah, I dress as the character, absolutely. And I had the words memorized. The casting director was very sweet, it wasn't her fault. It was just the way the system is now. She said, 'We want a movie star, but I wanted to put you on tape just in case they want somebody like you.' I know I'm not A-list, whatever that means. But I'm a good actress. I'm just not what the studio system wants today. My manager said I should have gone on tape. But it just wasn't the right circumstance.

So whose idea was it for you to go in in the first place?

It was probably my manager pushing to get me in a meeting for a Kevin Costner movie. I don't know. But it was hard. And I'm sure that's a story that a lot of actresses have gone through. It did make me cry, it made me feel really shitty.

Well, it is entirely consistent with what every actress has told me, unprompted. It always comes down to the casting session, and the rage at often not being allowed to talk to the person who's going to make the film. And having to read with someone who's not an actor.

Oh, that's the worst part. You know, you have so many students out there, who would love nothing more than to sit in a room and read with actors and actresses. That would be a great thing to do.

I'm often appalled by the standard of material I'm shown of actors. Out of focus, appallingly lit, not a proper microphone – and I'm supposed to judge an actor's work by this? But it's an area of ignorance that no one's bothered to address. And all it would take would be the Screen Actors Guild (SAG) or someone just to say, 'Look, here's the deal. Would someone second this motion, please? I'm not being a Bolshevik, I would just like some lighting, and I would like to read with someone who is an actor, and of the gender of the character.'

And please don't read in this monotone that you can't connect with. It's all about connection, about hooking in. Without that, I don't know how anybody gets a job. Patricia and I were just talking about this. Neither of us have ever gotten a job from an audition. She was saying, 'I am just the worst auditioner.' I said, 'I am the worst auditioner.'

Do you have good friends in the business?

I've been in this business twenty-four years, and I have some really close, good friends. And then I have a lot of fair-weather friends that have come and gone, depending on the barometer of my career.

Are you troubled by that or are you philosophical?

Very philosophical. They're just acquaintances, you know. Then I have a handful of solid, deep friendships that are for ever. And then my family.

We're close. Everybody was very rocked when my mother died. And so some of us are a little drifting. I'm the eldest, so I'm trying to reel everybody back in.

You're pleased for Patricia?
Oh, my God, yeah. She's got the role in Marty's movie with Nic. I think it'll be fantastic. I'm really happy for her. Of all the young actresses out there, she rules. We would like to work together some day, I hope we get to do that. But I'm also starting to think that I would really like to direct.

Have you directed before?
No, but I have this idea, it's like 'Searching for Debra Winger'. I'd interview actresses, about what they're doing and why they became actresses.

I think there are far more good actresses around than there are good actors. You can mobilize that in some way. People are more interested in documentaries now than they are in features, because they get them on telly. *Cops* is better than any rerun of a cop movie. Real ER is better than *ER*. And, for a thousand dollars, you could buy the equipment to make your documentary. For another five thousand dollars you could edit it. I encourage you to do that. Okay, now I want to ask you – what was it like working with Tommy Lee Jones on *The Executioner's Song*?
We got along great. He taught me how to shoot a gun.

I'll bet.
We had a scene where I had my two kids in the back of a car. And I think at the time he was still drinking, which I don't think he is any more. He had just got married, his little wife Kimberly was really great. And from what I heard, he had actually thrown her out of a car the night before.

Yes, that's what he told me.
And he recreated it in this scene. But we had these two little kids, they weren't actors, playing my children. They were terrified. And he really kicked us out. I mean, I was a sport about it, went with the flow. It was very realistic, and it looked good in the movie. But I was concerned about the kids. Tommy was in his character one hundred per cent on the set. But I spent a lot of time with the real Nicole, and with Gary Gilmore's therapist too. And the shrink said to me that Gary was almost Christlike, really enigmatic, not scary at all. Tommy's interpretation is a fantastic performance, but it was a different interpretation from the man.

He's very devil-like, isn't he? His gestures are so powerfully dramatic. On *Stormy Monday*, he would say to me, 'Where's your cutting point here?' And I'd go, 'I don't know, I've never made a movie before.' He says, 'I'm gonna move my cigar right there, and that'll give you your cut.' I go, 'Oh, thank you.' And of course I get in the cutting room, and he was absolutely right.
Yeah, I remember him saying those exact words on our film.

We've discussed your personal view of what's wrong with Hollywood. So why are you still in films? What's right with Hollywood for you?
I love being an actress, number one. I still feel the need to create, and this is the medium I've chosen to do that. And I do still feel hopeful that people who want to make films that can touch people are still out there, and we can change the world. You know?

How important has money been in your life?
I grew up in a completely non-material family, came into the business at a young age, made a lot of money in my time, enough to buy homes and cars. But I was never extravagant; I was sensible. I own a house in Northern California that is really dear to me. But I don't make the money that I used to at all. And that's hard sometimes – just having to do a shitty television movie to pay mortgage bills.

Was money linked to success in a way? Was that marriage significant?
Money shows where you're at in the business prestige. 'She made so much for that movie.' I had a certain price – which has definitely gone down. You can get me cheap now. I think that it's gotten a little insane now – twenty-five million dollars for a movie is crazy.

Why do actors make twenty-five million?
Well, if a movie makes two hundred million dollars, then I guess they do deserve it, if the movie's being marketed on their name. If I made a million dollars a year I would be so happy, and that's a fuck of a lot of money. Middle America, people don't make that kind of money.

When you first started to make films, in your early twenties, did you have to deal with the clichéd idea of Hollywood as an extended casting couch?
I never had that experience, fortunately. I really lucked out. I think it exists, with a few people, but I never had that.

Have you ever felt guilty about your portrayal of a woman? Have you ever come away from a movie thinking, 'I don't feel good about the way I was asked to portray that woman'?
I just did a Showtime thing where I feel disappointed in my performance. The character was an alcoholic. And I felt I did get her. But somehow it didn't turn out. John Badham directed it, and it was a fantastic script, and I felt really disappointed in my work.

What went wrong, do you think?
I talked to the writer about it, because he had always thought of me as this woman. He was okay, he was happy. But I think in the end, we just didn't have enough time – you know, it had to air 30 August. Other than that – I've played victims sometimes, and I'm not attracted to those kind of roles. I like women who start somewhere and then transform. Most of the roles I've done, the characters have evolved.

That's rare.
Yes. *Desperately Seeking Susan, Baby, It's You* – those women do evolve to a stronger place.

You left Hollywood for a while, didn't you?
I lived with Peter Gabriel for a long time in England, in Bath. We're still good friends. That was a big, long hiatus for love. I still made movies, but I was really focused on making a relationship work. Basically it was about his career, and making sacrifices in my own, which I was really willing to do. But we split up, which was a big thing, and I moved to Paris. I had an apartment in Paris which I loved. I was alone. It was the saddest time and it was the greatest time of my life. I was the quintessential expatriate. And I really would just sit in cafés and write in journals. I lived above the place where – supposedly – Hemingway had breakfast every day. So it was fantastic, and I have really good friends there.

And then when you came back? Big shock?
It was never the same. Never quite came back. I was very vocal in interviews about how I hated Hollywood ten years ago, and I wanted to do art films. I always talked about leaving, about wanting to be in Europe. An agent recently said to me, 'Everybody knows how much you hate Hollywood.' I said, 'I don't hate Hollywood, I live here.' This is where the work supposedly is. And my husband also has to be here. But I could live in Northern California, which I prefer. I don't want to raise my child here. I'd love to be on the East Coast, even Connecticut, for schools and stuff. But my dream is to live in Europe. I really feel good there, I love it. But, you know, Hollywood people are very proud of their town. And if you go against it . . .

My theory is that there is no town to be proud of. What they are fiercely and understandably protective of is the fragility of the place. What's to be proud of? There's nothing permanent here.
Do you ever go to the theatre here? Have you ever gone to the museum here? My friend Angela Harrington is the only person I know who really finds things to do in Los Angeles. I find myself staying in the house and not going out in this city.

Yes. It's not like New York. There are no Frank Sinatra songs about Los Angeles that I recall. Not like Chicago, New York, New Orleans . . .
No. The one song that sticks in my mind about Los Angeles is the Missing Persons' song, 'No One Walks In LA'.

Oh, and 'Hotel California', right? You can check in but you can never leave – yeah. Thank you, Rosanna.
Thank you.

Mike Figgis: Why did you choose to go into film-making, as an actress?
Ally Sheedy: It chose me. Ever since I was a tiny little girl, I was putting on ballets and shows and acting out characters.

What about your family? Are they actors, artists?
No, both my parents came from what I would call abject poverty, and went out and achieved incredible lives for themselves. My father was a marketing director – he's still alive. And my mother is a literary agent in New York. I was born and raised in New York City. There was sort of a credo in my family that whatever it was that you wanted to do, you just had to get out there and do it. So it didn't really occur to me not to be an actor, because that was what I wanted to do.

But why? What attracted you to it?
I think, when I was about six, I saw a movie called *Anne of the Thousand Days*, with Genevieve Bujold. I was an avid reader, I became obsessed with Elizabethan history. And in my imagination I was always becoming different people, and putting on stories and playing all the parts in the story by myself. Also my parents let me see *Cabaret* when I was really young, and I got obsessed with that movie too. There's just something about film – how enormous you can be on screen, and how small and intimate at the same time.

How often do you go to the cinema now?
Not too often, partly because I'm a mom. I'm very picky about what I see because I don't have as much time as I used to.

What do you think of what's being made right now, here?
You mean in studios, or in the independent scene?

In general. I don't think there's a huge gulf between the two.
See, I think there's a big gulf – which is not to say that all of the independent movies are wonderful. But the movies that most interest me seem to be shot outside of the commercial mainstream. I can't remember the last studio movie I went to see. I just look at what seems interesting, and it's almost always an independent. The best movie I saw this year is called *Slam*. It's brilliant – made like a documentary. You can't imagine it being made as a big production, because that would have ruined it.

What do you think is right about the film industry in this town?
Nothing.

Okay. Do you want to enlarge on that?
My opinion is very skewed, because I've actually had a very similar experience to you – which is of having been embraced by it, having been in there when they're telling you you're successful and everyone loves you. And then I've seen the other side, the absolutely horrific experience, when nobody wants to know your name. And then, managing to get out and do something that I feel really great about,

and realizing that I can survive outside of the system – which is a position of strength. Whereas, if we were talking a year ago, I would be talking to you from a position of feeling incredibly rejected and fucked-up. I think the system is an uneasy and unhappy marriage between artistic endeavour and business. The business wins, always – unless you're Warren Beatty and you get to call your own shots. And it seems like the business is being run by people who don't have any creative elements in them. It's not like there is – as horrible a person as he apparently was – a Louis B. Mayer or a David O. Selznick. It's being run by accountants, lawyers and business graduates – people like Mike Ovitz. These are the people who are deciding what's worthwhile and what's not worthwhile. They should be playing the stock market, in my opinion.

Since you started out, actors' salaries have gone through the roof. I believe Nic Cage is asking for twenty-five million now.
It's ridiculous.

Did you make good money?
The most money I ever made was half a million dollars – in 1985, I think – so, yeah, that was quite a lot of money. It was a little movie called *Maid to Order* – a reverse Cinderella.

I loved all your work. I thought you were very funny, and kind of indefinably interesting, which is how film should work. So how tough was it for you to get half a million dollars? How tough for your soul?
For my soul . . . You have to come from my background and understand the importance and non-importance of money. My father was becoming successful when I was very young. My mother, I watched her start a literary agency with one desk and an envelope as a file, and it is now hugely successful. And she went after writers who were black, almost always gay, underground communist lesbian writers, like Sapphire and Audrey Lord. My mom got the first book about a lesbian relationship published by a major publishing house, it was called *Patience and Sarah*. She sold things that nobody could sell. And then suddenly there were people reading them and my mom made money and the agency got bigger. And then there would be a bad year, but you just had to wait and another good year would come along. It went in waves and tides. For me, getting paid half a million dollars at that time meant that I didn't have to work for two years. I could wait to do a movie I really wanted to do, which was called *Heart of Dixie*.

So you always saw that kind of mainstream money-earning ability as a way of subsidizing other stuff?
Yes. But I was very young and naive, and I would use the word 'dumb', actually. I learned early on not to do a favour for somebody and be in their movie just because they had put you in three other movies. Because then it becomes a disaster like *Blue City* and nobody ever calls you. Those same people disappear from

your life. And I wasn't going to make that mistake again, and do stuff that I didn't think was good. But the things I thought were good weren't necessarily going to find an audience, and that never occurred to me. It didn't occur to me that women my age were not going to want to see a picture like *Heart of Dixie* about a woman's awakening during the Civil Rights movement.

Do you think that women your age would have gone to see it had it been marketed in a certain way? See, I was shocked the other way when I made *Leaving Las Vegas*. I didn't give a fuck if anyone saw it, because I wanted to make it. And it didn't cost anything, I wasn't bankrupting anybody, I knew it would get its money back on the European festival circuit. But Cannes didn't want it, Venice didn't want it, nobody wanted it. Then it had a commercial success here, but only because John Calley and MGM spent a fortune, so that it actually got to people who then wanted to go and see it. Without that push nobody would have seen it.
Well, I've had a similar experience with *High Art*. I thought that story needed to be told, I thought it was a beautiful script. I never thought in a million years that anybody was going to see it. But I didn't care, I wanted to play the part. It turned out great, and on its own merit it has done very well. The distributor that picked it up, October – they haven't really spent as much as they could have on ads and so forth. I feel as if the person who's done the most work on publicizing the movie is me – which was the last thing I wanted to do, to get myself out and get interviewed by *Us* magazine. But I know that it has to get advertised somehow for someone to go and see it. That's what I feel the role of studios should be – they should just advertise our movies, and then stay out of the rest of it.

I know that you've had a hard time in recent years.
Terrible.

What prompted that?
First, there was the unleashing of the Brat pack upon the world. Those were the people I did *St Elmo's Fire* and *The Breakfast Club* with – Emilio Estevez, Judd Nelson, Andrew McCarthy, Rob Lowe, Demi Moore, Mare Winningham – though it didn't really affect Mare. A few people were in that group but broke out of it, like Tom Cruise, and Sean Penn, who was always going his own way. But I was right in that cluster. It was a particular genre of movie – young people, in high school or college or just out of college. But then we all starting getting older. And then there was a glut of those movies and nobody wanted to see them any more. And I had a very hard time moving out of that kind of movie. It became like a horrible rock on my head that I was just trying to lift off, and I didn't know who dropped it there. And for a long time I thought, 'This is what I deserve, because I was successful too young. I have to go through this.'

Who were you then? If someone said, 'That's an Ally Sheedy role', what kind of a character is that?

Well, I don't know – that was the problem. I feel like the reason I got stuck was because I'd had this success, but the movies that I was looking to do were a little bit more on the literate side, with darker, more twisted kinds of characters. Not the girl-next-door, happy-go-lucky types, but characters who had some real pain.

Like real people, in other words?
Yes, exactly. But again I'm getting into this age-old conversation that everybody has, about what kind of roles women get offered in movies. And for me at that time, it was the girl-next-door. The only other option was the sex object.

Could they ever be the same person? Could you have a sex-object-next-door?
I think I might have been the sex-object-next-door in *War Games*, but I didn't know that because I was just wearing jeans and a T-shirt. When I was in my twenties it was made very, very clear to me that there was something about my physical appearance and the way I came across on screen that was not selling. And I had to either do something about that – make myself more beautiful, sexy – or I was just going to have to accept my lot.

What were your options, in terms of improving your physical marketability?
I was told to go and get a make-up lesson. And the way I dressed, jeans and a T-shirt? That was inappropriate. I was told to go get a miniskirt and a tight shirt. And if I wasn't going to get my breasts enlarged, at least I should walk around with fake tits, so that I was sexually attractive. I was told point-blank that I had no 'fuckability' quotient – one of the heads of the agency I was working at then said that to me.

How did he put it?
'No one wants to fuck you.'

I want more context.
There is none. I was sitting down trying to figure out why I wasn't considered as a viable alternative for these scripts. How come I couldn't get a meeting with the director? Then it started getting worse – even the casting director wouldn't see me. Why not? 'Well, you know, they think you're really a lightweight actress because you did all those lightweight movies.' I'd say, 'I can do a lot more than that, I just need to get in the door and read.' 'Well, the other problem is that they're looking for something else.' 'What?' 'Someone they want to fuck.' I've heard that over and over again. 'So-and-so wants someone he'd want to fuck. He doesn't want to fuck you, so . . .'

'Thank you for your candour.' How prevalent is that?
Huge. In my opinion, if you wanted to look up the terms 'sexual harassment' or 'sexual discrimination' in an encyclopaedia, you should be able to open that book and see a picture of Hollywood – and there's the definition. Because women are only allowed to be desirable or sexual in very, very narrowly defined terms. Really

it has to do with the white straight guy who loves to look at models in magazines – with what that guy wants to see. So there will be five parts in a movie for men, and one for a woman, maybe two. One's The Mom, and the other is The Girl.

What should The Mom look like?
Well, often you see a great, interesting actor like Joan Plowright or Shelley Winters or Gena Rowlands showing up. And they're not your typical moms, but the Mom part is usually the philosopher or the emotional weight in the movie. And The Girl is usually the sex interest. I'm just talking about the mainstream here. *Jerry Maguire*, one woman's part – it's got to be the girl who looks good with Tom Cruise.

The bait.
The bait. And I'm not the bait.

Did you give it a try? After you'd had the 'No one wants to fuck you' conversation.
Not really, no.

You never bought 'that dress'?
I bought one dress, because the people who were heading Triad at the time said, 'Well, you should give an award out on the Golden Globes and look sexy so people can think about you more in that way.' So I went out and bought this dress, but I was so embarrassed by it because it was strapless. So I went to the laundry person on the corner and asked them to sew some straps on it because I was freaked out. I had friends who were make-up artists, tried to put some make-up on . . . You know, that's not me, that's just stupid. I certainly wasn't going to get my breasts enlarged. And the other part of the equation was, 'It would be good for you to take some meetings with these studio executives, look really sexy, schmooze a little bit, go to parties, make some political connections here.' I didn't do it.

Do you think this is basically a system of prostitution?
Yes, I do. I think you have to prostitute yourself. And if you don't want to, I think you suffer for it. I didn't do it. I have friends who have slept with a lot of people and had relationships with married people who put them in better positions for work. They've gone to parties, met those soulless people –

Carry on with this, but I just want to say – I've asked a lot of actresses this question and most of them say, 'No, no, it's a complete myth.'
Oh, my God, they're liars. I don't believe it. They said it's a myth? Well, they must be married to someone in a good position.

'Sure, maybe it goes on, but I've never seen it.'
Well, that's ridiculous. Or maybe they really never have. I have. Oh, yeah.

And what about your friends? Do they lose your respect, or are you philosophical?
Yes, and I have no friends who are married to men in powerful positions, because there's something really soulless there. A lot of the people that I've met who are in

positions of real power are frightening people. They've had to pay very big prices to get there. Theirs is not the kind of life I would want to live. I think there's another way to do it. But to be a woman, and to have no power, and to look at that and think it's attractive, and make yourself attractive to it and sell yourself to it, and reap whatever rewards there are from that – that is so disgusting to me.

Are you a feminist?
I am.

Were you always a feminist?
From birth. It's ingrained in me. I can't not be feminist, I enjoy it too much.

How many other feminists have you found in the acting community?
I don't know. Women sometimes have a problem labelling themselves as feminists. They have some negative association with the term, which I think is just a media-perpetuated image of bra-burning. But, you know, there's nothing wrong with burning your bra either.

It's like the negative associations of the term 'politically correct'.
Well, it's politically incorrect to say you're a feminist – it's just not hip and cool. But you find yourself saying, 'So you think everyone's equal, but you're not a feminist? And you think everybody should get paid the same amount for their work, but you're still not really a feminist?'

What's the problem with scripts here? Why don't they write parts for women?
I'm sure the argument would be, 'Well, you know, everybody wants to go see Wesley Snipes killing people.' Or whoever it is, in the big action movies.

People say audiences just want to see boys in movies. So how come, in pre-Hollywood times, every culture that was writing stories wrote stories about men and women? Western literature is based on the idea of the romantic novel, if you like. So what happened?
That's right, and in the forties most of the scripts were female-driven. It was Greta Garbo, Barbara Stanwyck, Bette Davis, Joan Crawford, Katharine Hepburn. Now I think our society is incredibly violent. And a movie can't just make twenty million dollars and be considered a success – it has to make two hundred million dollars. So they say, 'We're going to blow up more buildings and make the biggest car wreck, and have more gunfire and special effects' – it's like this 'My dick is bigger than yours' theory, to me. And as it gets bigger and bigger, and it costs more and more money, you have to make more and more money. But the problem is that they do. These movies about war and violence and hatred and division between people, they do appeal to that lowest common denominator.

I don't agree. I think it's a self-fulfilling prophecy a lot of the time.
Godzilla didn't make a lot of money, right? Isn't that supposed to be a big disappointment?

Godzilla didn't make as much as they wanted, but it still made a lot of money, because they spent a huge amount in promoting it. If you can open on two thousand screens and you're prepared to spend sixty million dollars on P & A, you will make money – because by the time word of mouth says 'It stinks', enough people will have gone to check it out.

It's true. It's that old American ethic, the capitalist ethic, which is that we create a desire, we make the market. And then we give 'em the product, and they clamour for more. But it's back to what we were first talking about – what does that have to do with wanting to tell stories, and play characters, and make a movie? Nothing. In Hollywood movies, the story that's told over and over again is the puritan-work-ethic story, about the underdog, who's usually a lowbrow kind of guy. He works hard and throws himself on the line, and sacrifices everything and kills all the bad guys. And in the end he's absolved, he becomes a hero. Then there's also the story about the two brothers who go back to find their father, who was an asshole. But they forgive him, and so complete their spiritual circle and continue with their lives. Those are the two most often told stories. I'm sick of seeing those stories.

What's the female story?
There isn't one. There is no story that I can tell my daughter that is the American female story. Unless I tell her about her grandma, which is a story that's so out of the mainstream – a female story of success, of rising above your conditions and establishing yourself, regardless of what someone may think, making for yourself the definition of what being a woman is. Because there isn't one definition – it keeps changing, nobody's really sure what it is.

Do you think film is important? That it matters a damn, really?
I don't think it's as important as literature, as what's coming out of the mind of a particular writer. Or a painter. I don't think it's as important as that, no.

You'd agree that it's over-valued?
Over-valued, definitely. But that's also because you can make a lot of money in it, and because this society elevates actors to positions of being gods and goddesses. It's not just royalty, it's like Aphrodite.

Watching the Oscars last time, I was thinking, 'It's as if you have a royal wedding every year.' And my next question, which I'm sure you'll find funny, is, 'Would you like an Oscar?'
Would I like one? I don't know.

It is the highest accolade you can get in America.
I know that, but I have a problem with who's giving it.

Okay, say it happens. How do you deal with it?
I don't know. I think it's a Pyrrhic victory. You did the best performance of the year in a movie – according to X, Y and Z. Maybe you did, maybe you didn't. You've got

this gold statue on your table, and what does it mean? That you get paid more money for your next movie? Actually, it seems to me that getting an Oscar is a curse, especially if you're a supporting actress. I've noticed this time and time again, it seems like you immediately go into this dark period where you just can't find anything that's worthy of you, because you're now 'an Oscar-winning actress'. So you can't place any meaning on that. But it's all fun to watch – fun and games . . .

You watch it?
I usually watch if somebody's nominated who I think is wonderful. I watched this year's Best Actress [1998] because I wanted Julie Christie to win it, and I wanted to hear what she would say. But she didn't. Sometimes, someone will say something that I as an actor find incredibly inspiring. So I'll tune in, to hope for a moment of that. But do I watch the whole three hours and the parade of dresses? No.

What do you think of the dresses?
I think it's ridiculous. I tell you something right now – if I ever get nominated, if it ever happened to me, I would wear the same dress that I bought one year to go to the Academy Awards to give out the Best Documentary Oscar. This dress is beautiful, and it's been sitting in the closet since 1985. I spent three thousand dollars of my own money, that I worked to earn, to buy this dress. Nobody sent it to me, designers didn't call me up. And I almost got married in it but I thought, 'No.' I can't imagine going to the Oscars for any reason other than being nominated, and even then I don't know if I would go. But I would wear that dress again, simply because this whole thing of fashion designers showering these people – the only people in the world who can actually afford to buy their dresses – with these free dresses, so that they can walk around and be an ad, makes me nauseous.

Okay. What about age?
I'm thirty-six.

I wasn't asking you for your age, but it's very sweet of you to tell me.
And don't ask me my measurements, 'cause then you'll really get in fucking trouble.

Okay. I mean that's an issue in the community, too, for an actress?
Yes. It's not an issue for me, because I never got bought or sold as being a sex object. But I do know people who are extremely worried about it. And two weeks ago I did hear for the first time ever that I was too old for a part. I was actually too old to play opposite Nicolas Cage in a movie.

And how did that feel? Did you care?
Not really, because I didn't really care that much about the movie. But I have to say that what it made me feel was, 'What? Nicolas Cage? He's older than me!' That was the first time it hit me, that there was this big age discrepancy. It's a little ridiculous when you think about it.

Even if you don't think about it, it's ridiculous.
Sometimes it's appropriate like in *Bulworth*, because Bulworth had to be an older guy looking ridiculous in that club with those kids. And Halle Berry's character had to be this young, lazy, beautiful thing.

And I loved it when he said, 'How old do you think I am?' And she said, 'Sixty.' I thought Warren Beatty handled himself really well, with dignity. That's very rare.
Yes, it was self-mocking too, in a wonderful way.

Talk to me a little bit about the casting process.
It's horrific. There's always a list, that you are either on or not on. If you're not on the list, you're fucked. If you're on the list, you're on for everything else in town. The list has probably got five people on it.

Do you know who's on it right now? Could you hazard a guess?
Well, it would depend on who can play opposite who. To play opposite Nic Cage? Five twenty-year-olds, five twenty-whatever-year-olds.

But who would they be?
I have no idea. Who's the girl in *There's Something About Mary*?

Cameron Diaz.
I'm sure she's on someone's list. But it's awful, it's demeaning, it's humiliating. When I wanted to read for *High Art* – first of all, I had been fired from my agency, so I didn't even have an agent to make the phone calls. I had to call myself.

How did they fire you?
They said they would have no problem if I decided to seek other representation. In fact, they would encourage it. They said this to the manager that I've been working with for about ten years, and he told me. And then I called everybody up and screamed at them.

Were you devastated by that?
Devastated. I couldn't believe it. I thought they were working for me.

How long had you had a relationship with your agent?
I had been there for seven years. Before that, I had left two other agencies and it had been a very painful experience to change agents. I thought, 'I'm not going to do this again, I really need to just stick in one place.' Even though I felt lost there, I didn't want to walk out on them unless I had a really good reason. But then, agents are such a part of the casting process. If you have a powerful agent, you might just be able to get in the door. Some deal-making goes on – 'Well, we'll let you talk to So-and-So if you'll also see this little one who we all think is the one to make into a big star next week.'

I used to get calls saying, 'Could you do me a big favour? Could you see So-and-So, I know he/she's completely wrong for your movie, but would you just take

a meeting?' I'd think, to what end? I don't want to meet an actor I can't encourage. I don't want to lie to actors either. And on two occasions I've agreed, under duress, once with a very famous actress. She was so angry at me, and I was so humiliated. We didn't speak for a long time after, until finally we both came clean. I said, 'I have to explain to you why this meeting took place.' And I found it a terrible situation.

It's humiliating. The casting directors and agents, they always say, 'Oh, don't take it personally.' But they're trading in bodies, not people. So how are you supposed to take it?

So the agency let you know, you rang everybody, you were devastated and you were without an agent. You have a manager still?
Yes, he sticks by me. That's the only way I found to really survive. To be able to find the one or two people who will actually stick with you and believe in you through the whole thing.

Do you now have an agent again?
Yes, the man I'm with right now, Tim Ingle – he called me about *High Art*, because a client of his was going to be in it. He said, 'They can't cast this other role, and you're perfect for it.' He gave me a copy of the script and the phone numbers, so I called. And later, when the movie worked out, I said, 'Yeah, I will sign with you. Because how did you think of me after fifteen years? Maybe you're the one good apple in the barrel of rotten ones.' It was my good fortune that Billy Hopkins and Kerry Barden were casting *High Art*, because they're probably the only two casting directors in New York or LA who would be willing to see me. They're just out to lunch, really – very open and different. So that huge obstacle I had anticipated, of getting the casting director to let me meet the director, that was gone. They said, 'Yeah, fly yourself to New York and he'll see you for it.'

Would you regularly do that? Fly yourself somewhere?
I fly myself all over the place for meetings. And I pay for it, yes.

And is that standard?
Well, no, I think if they really wanted to see an actor, either they would fly out to see you or they would fly you to see them. But in my case it's usually that I'm begging for the meeting.

How much is a round trip to New York?
At, say, forty-eight hours' notice? It's about a thousand dollars.

How do you feel about the accepted casting system, of actors turning up for a meeting with the director and the casting director, and then reading?
It's awful, it doesn't work. Elisabeth Shue was very smart when she asked you if the casting director could get out of the room. The problem is, I find it very difficult to talk to the director about the script, and to work on a scene with the

director, when there's this third person standing there who's got their own opinions. I don't know where the hell they come from, what are their credentials for standing there . . .

Plus, they will have pre-sold you in a certain way.
Either pre-sold me or pre-axed me. 'Well, we're going to see her, you know what I mean, but . . .'

Talk to me about marketing and actors. You remember that scene in *Basic Instinct* where Sharon Stone crosses her legs, and we had been told in advance that she was wearing no underwear. Therefore I think a huge number of people convinced themselves they were seeing something they couldn't actually see. And I found it rather wonderful, actually – to market an entire film upon someone's vagina is really remarkable.
It's pathetic, to me. Actors can decide to make themselves into big, big movie stars by hiring a publicist and putting themselves in magazines, modelling clothes or make-up. And the recognition factor can go way up and they can make themselves into a big, marketable commodity.

So is there a difference between a star and an actor?
I think so. I mean, I don't see Morgan Freeman modelling G-strings in *Cosmo*. I don't think he has to. Or Laurence Fishburne.

Wesley does. He does the Armani shoots and so forth.
Exactly . . . I'm glad we're talking about men here, because it's not just women.

No. In fact, Richard Gere is often credited with putting Armani on the world map when he wore those suits in *American Gigolo*.
Right, but now the designers are famous and rich enough. Armani doesn't need another movie star wearing his clothes. What I'm talking about is actors who put themselves in fashion shoots as some kind of a gimmick.

Have you ever done that?
Never.

If I said to you, 'Look, I'm a photographer, I think you're really great-looking. I've been asked to do a shoot for *Vogue* . . .'
I wouldn't.

You'd say no to me.
Yes. I have been photographed by Bruce Weber once, when he was taking portraits of actors for some European magazine – just their faces. I wanted to meet him because I liked his photographs. And I could wear my own stuff, and no make-up, and that's exactly what I did. It was fine, took five minutes.

Was it a good photograph?
I didn't see it . . . Oh! And I did a thing once, before *The Breakfast Club* came out.

I was about twenty-three. I think it was *Vogue*, they wanted to do a story on me. But they couldn't decide what to do it about, so they had me running on the beach like I was doing an exercise routine. And I thought, 'This is the most incredible waste of my time. And for what?' It ended up with this horrific picture of me in sweat pants, stretching over, featuring my ass. And I cringed and just thought, 'Never again.'

Do you think women's magazines collude quite a lot in a kind of stereotyping of women?

Well, here's a story about *High Art*. I'm asked, all of a sudden, to do a photograph-story for *Interview* magazine and a story in *Us* magazine. And my bottom line was, 'All right, this is a tiny movie that needs some attention.' So I sat down and carefully figured out which stories to do to bring attention to it. I didn't want any of them to be a fashion shoot – I mean, for what? But they didn't only want to talk about the movie, they wanted a picture for the story, with designer X, Y or Z. I showed up for these two shoots wearing my own clothes, and I brought a bag of my own stuff from The Gap or whatever, and I said, 'Why can't I just be photographed in my own clothes?' The bottom line was that, even though it was just a tiny little interview, they had to get a certain number of items of clothes on to somebody famous in the magazine, for whatever reason. The *Us* one ended up being a big feature about a lot of other things, but basically I refused to wear the friggin' Chanel outfit. Why would I do that? I don't dress like that, I can't afford those clothes. To me, doing that kind of stuff is like perpetuating a myth. When I work I want to play real people – people who are ugly, who cry and get herpes on their mouths, and get frustrated and bite their nails and pick their noses and fall apart – all the normal stuff you do in life. The perfection you see in the magazines, that has nothing to do with what I want to do, which is just to act. I mean, it takes an enormous amount of time, two days, to do one of those fashion things, to go out and get yourself all *fapitzed*, as my mother would say. These people, that's what they're choosing to spend their time on instead of working or reading or being with their kids, just living life – which is where I think you really draw what you need to be able to play a part. Like the times when you can't find a parking space . . .

So what happened? With your Gap clothes?

I wore my own stuff. And they didn't use the picture.

Of course. So what's next for you, what are you going to do?

I'm not doing any fashion spreads for anybody, I'll tell you that much. I'm working with Rosanna Arquette on this Allison Anders movie that she's making in three weeks, because she doesn't have any money. Most of it shoots in Topanga Canyon. And then, if she can get her financing together, I think I'm going to do another independent movie called *Graffiti Love*, which is an interracial love story set down in South Central LA. So that means I'll have to come back here again from New York to do that.

How do you feel now about yourself and the business? Have you come to terms with it? Do you think you understand it?
It's taken me a long time but now I feel at least I know where the path is I want to follow. For a while there, I just couldn't figure it out.

You were down about it for a while, weren't you?
Deprived and depressed.

Last time I met you, I guess for *Mr Jones*, we read together, and I was concerned for you because it seemed as if your flame was very low – the opposite of how you are today. You read beautifully, by the way. It was a very sad reading, very melancholic. But I was concerned for your welfare at the time. I didn't know you well enough to say anything, but you hope that people will make it through. There are a lot of victims in this business. How long did that last?
It was a while. I got in some very bad depressions. The things that probably got me out of it were just that somehow my life came together outside of the work. I settled down, and I did meet a person, a good man. And I did get married and became a mom which, for me, has been a very liberating and also grounding experience. But I think what really happened is that somehow I got away from Hollywood, not only by choice but also by the fact that I wasn't desirable here at all. Nobody was sad to see me go.

Was that gradual?
Yes. I felt it happening before it was very obvious that it was happening.

Did you do anything about it at the time or did it just slide on?
Well, I didn't know what to do with the options presented to me: 'Well, you want to turn this around? You're going to have to up your fuckability quotient.' I didn't know how I was supposed to convince anybody that what I was cut out for was more serious roles that had some real depth to them. When the independent film scene kicked in, that was sort of a ray of light.

But you're also a good comedic actress.
I know that I can be very funny. But it has to come out of a situation. I like it when there can be a light touch within something that's actually darker. But I'm not a comedienne, I just don't want to be in light comedies.

I find that all the actors whom I love and admire are all quite funny. Albert Finney can make you smile, even in a very dark hole. Some actors that people think are brilliant, I argue that they're not because I've never smiled at anything they've done. Did you lose your sense of humour at any point?
For a little while I lost it . . . You know what I think really happened? I had a lot of success when I was very young, then a certain amount of time went by, and I feel I've had to grow into myself – which is why I like being thirty-six. I think I'm going to be better in my forties. Even physically – I feel I'm growing into my own

body, I'm comfortable with myself, the way I look. And I feel my range of what I can play has really expanded. I think somewhere along the line being a movie star stopped being important to me, it wasn't something that I wanted. It became something that was degrading, that I couldn't respect. Even when I was younger I don't think it was really what I wanted. I really wanted to be able to act. But there I was in my mid to late twenties in Hollywood, and there isn't any corroboration for your wanting to be anything other than the movie star of the moment. So I started to put together this little list of people, some of whom I'd met, who were actually doing what I was striving for – like Alfre Woodard.

Okay. My next question is, name five actresses you like.
Alfre Woodard, Frances McDormand, Helen Mirren. I love Mare Winningham, love her work. Gena Rowlands.

Actors?
Morgan Freeman, Laurence Fishburne, Albert Finney, Peter Sellers, Richard Burton. They move me.

Give me five pieces of music that hit you in some way.
One is a song called 'Appalachian Lullabye' – there's a band called Shudder, and one of the members wrote this beautiful piece of music. Ballet scores: Tchaikovsky's *Swan Lake*, *Romeo and Juliet*; sections of Stravinsky, especially the ballet *Petrushka*, huge sad sections in there; and sections in Debussy's *Afternoon of a Fawn* – sad, really touching.

Books?
Bastard out of Carolina, and the other book by Dorothy Allison , *Cave Dwellers*. *The Women's Room* by Marilyn French; *The Color Purple*; *The Liars' Club*. I really love Margaret Drabble and Alison Lurie and Alice Hoffman. Mostly women.

Films that have touched you?
Anne of the Thousand Days; Katharine Hepburn's performance in *The Lion in Winter* is really just amazing; Emma Thompson's performance in *Sense and Sensibility*, especially that last scene when she falls apart – it just makes my hair stand on end; *Apocalypse Now*. I love this movie *Slam*, I have to put it in there. I love *Camille Claudel*, where Isabelle Adjani played the sculptress.

Anything on television that you've watched recently?
I don't watch television.

11 Sylvester Stallone

Mike Figgis: Who are your favourite actors?

Sylvester Stallone: I love Peter O'Toole. To me, early on in his career, he was the best, because he just had this extraordinary technique. Even if he didn't feel it, you believed it. *The Lion in Winter* is my favourite film, I've watched it maybe a hundred times. The morality of it, everything about it . . .

When you first had that feeling about O'Toole, where were you in your own career?

I was just floundering in New York. I had basically come to the realization that I was never really going to make it as an actor, and perhaps I should fall back on Plan B. But Plan B didn't really exist, because I had never been very adept at writing. But I got a job as a cinema usher, and I would watch films over and over. Sometimes we'd have a hit there, like *M.A.S.H.*, and then we would have something like *Hello, Goodbye* with Michael Crawford, which no one would go see. But I watched what worked, what didn't work, and then I started to write these screenplays. And the first five or six were really horrible, like 'What I Did Last Summer' screenplays with pretentious titles like 'Cry Full Whisper Empty In The Same Breath' – a little too much Dylan going on there . . . Of course, by then Peter O'Toole had already done *Lawrence of Arabia*, and some very weird stuff like *The Ruling Class*, *Murphy's War*, *Country Dance* with Susannah York – he shoots his ear off in that, it's an incestuous thing. I mean, for a man at his commercial peak, he was making films that had no audience guaranteed – not in America anyway. But he didn't care. I always thought that he had something extraordinary, and I never got off that. And as a young man I was definitely enamoured of Kirk Douglas.

I loved him. I loved *Lonely Are The Brave*.

Oh, it's great. About six months ago, I was asked if I'd remake it. I said, 'Why? It's not broken.'

It's about writing, isn't it – movie-making?

It is. It's all about great storytelling. And then a visual artist puts it all to music, if you will. But I think that the writers of the past obviously were a lot less distracted than today. Hawthorne, Melville – they lived on Walden Pond, they had a little candle and nothing to do, and that was it. So these men really honed their craft, without being pulled in twenty-five different directions. They didn't have agents, that's for sure.

What about the committee system here, that we have to deal with?

It's terrible. I think that quite often the studios, though it's well-intended at times, tend to be the most negative in the nurturing of the artist. They agree to do a project and say, 'Oh, we love the concept.' And then, as the rewrites come in, they begin to scrape away, until it no longer resembles what the director had in mind originally. That's why there's been a stampede, if you will, to the indies. At least some of the director's vision can come out. With the studios, I think that unless you're Spielberg, it's almost impossible for a film to come to fruition the way you interpret it. It's just going to be annihilated. Like Charlton Heston in *Touch of Evil* – you say, why is he there? Well, maybe the studio said, 'We want him here. We're building his career. The movie doesn't get made unless he's in there, and that's the way it is.'

But, even allowing for that – Heston's perhaps not the greatest actor in the history of cinema, but he's not a bad actor. And I felt he was wilfully underdirected in that movie. But, without a doubt, Welles is the star. And when he's not on camera, the camera's the star – and by definition, he is the camera, he's the director. And that amazing long opening shot has created a kind of precedent for brilliant shots. As in *Goodfellas*, when people say, 'Ah, that amazing Steadicam shot Scorsese does.' I was thinking, 'Well, maybe, in a brilliant movie you shouldn't think those things.' The minute you think, 'It's a great shot', I think you've blown something. I wasn't aware of the camera in *Lonely Are The Brave*. It just seemed natural. And, in a way, I think we should strive for seamless, natural film-making, where you just following the characters in the story, and while you're watching it you are in that world.

I totally agree. If you can combine in a film the kinetic, the visual and the auditory in a seamless way – it's an experience. But if you say, 'Okay, the action was great, but God – when they stopped jumping around, the dialogue was terrible' . . . I've only been able to get it right one time, and then only for a couple of moments. It was the last scene in *Rocky* where the fight is over, the music is building, and Adrian is coming towards Rocky. He doesn't even care about the fact that he's gone the distance, now he just wants this one woman who represents his life, his future. And it's – boom! But I've never been able to do that again. It's not easy.

No. If only . . .
'Jesus, the actors were great yesterday, they're not cooking today . . .'

You see the dailies, you feel good about stuff. And then you come to about the third cut, and you think, 'What happened?'
I know – 'Where's that editor? What did you do to my film? Where's the real take?'

You want to kill somebody. It must be somebody's fault.
How much do you hate it? You show the rough cut, and everyone makes a speech. When I directed, I would say, 'Please understand, this is a work in progress. It's not anywhere near finished. So, please, don't get worried.' Five minutes into it – 'This is slow. Why?' It takes a very special individual . . .

They say, 'Can we see something?' And you say, 'It's not really ready, there's stuff missing.' And they say, 'Listen, we know how to watch a movie, this is non-judgemental, we just want to see this . . .'. It never is. That's the beauty of film, because the minute it goes through the gate, you want it to be perfect. My

problem is, I'm often happier with that rough cut than I am with that thing that goes up.

You know, there's something to that. There really is.

You get all the effects in and you smooth it all out, and you smooth a lot of the edge off – which is why I think people go to indie movies, because they quite like the crap . . .

Yeah, it's alive. It's not perfect, but that makes it real. You watch *Panic in the Streets* and you say, 'God, look, they're underneath a real subway, and it's raw and the camera is shaking.' Or *On The Waterfront* – this is not pretty, it's gritty, and that's real steam coming out of the manhole covers. It just elevated the whole thing out of that perfect backlot situation.

Let's talk about money. How difficult is it for you now to realize your vision, given who you are, and the amounts of money that are expected to be earned from one of your movies?

Difficult. I guess I was at the forefront of the giant pay-days. I didn't realize at the time but there's an arrogance that sets in. 'No problem, we'll just do our summer film and our Christmas film.' And the audience began to be repelled by the lack of genuine commitment to making a good film. They said, 'Okay, he's filling slots.' But at the time, especially in the mid-eighties, it was new and wild. Previously, the models of an action movie were *The French Connection*, Steve McQueen in *The Getaway*. But *First Blood* was the beginning of a one-man-army kind of movie, a super-action genre. Rambo took on five or six hundred men, but the film still had some sense of heroics about it, and a morality. And he lived through it, even though in the original book he dies. And right then, we said, 'My God, we haven't had this kind of gladiator in the modern era.' The ensemble piece was the norm. Except for Westerns, where it was always the one man who rode into town.

Sergio Leone's movies kind of pushed that, didn't they? *The Good, The Bad and The Ugly, For A Few Dollars More*, all of those.

Oh, sure. They were visually stunning, for Westerns.

And interesting scores. Morricone's music was a real breakthrough. The biggest influence on me was Morricone.

This man has done – what is it – something absurd, in the thousands . . .

Yes, he's sort of shoving it out a bit. I saw one the other day, was it *Lolita*? I think it was. And I thought, 'He's just taken this from *Once Upon a Time in America*. Though it worked fine, by the way.

I think that we have usually a creative window – let's say, fifteen years? – of real peak. That's about it. Otherwise you're talking genius output. Used to be, you'd have a new Bob Dylan album every six months.

I was thinking about that very thing. Because he did it from eighteen to thirty, let's say. He still does wonderful stuff, but the burning stuff . . .

I speak with many writers. I know that writing is sheer drudgery. In the beginning, you're young, twenty-five – 'Oh, I love writing, I can't wait to hit the desk.' Then you're forty, you're pulling your nails, and that page is jumping up and biting your face, saying, 'I dare you to assault me with some good composition. I dare you.' Then you look in the mirror and you see what used to be your face – drawn, wan, greyish. You know what you're going to look like if you make it to a hundred. And, you know what? Bring me the rewrite. I'm now a rewrite specialist. Writers are insane. But that's the good news. Writers carry a certain psychosis about with them because they listen to voices all day long. And when they're at social gatherings, they're still listening, they're gathering material. They're back with their character, they're not in the moment. Certain writers are so manic – I remember spending about seven hours with Tom Clancy and I think I said, 'You're kidding, no, really?' Even that felt like kind of an intrusion. And the rest was his. Then you have other writers where you need blasting caps to get any sound out of them, they're so withdrawn and melancholy. I'm sure hanging out with Kafka was not exactly a knee-slapper. But if you can supervise writers and not have to sit there yourself, it is quite liberating. And actually I feel a lot more creative working with someone on a story than just trying to hammer it out myself.

I like that balancing. See, I did fifteen years of experimental theatre, touring and all that, it was a four-man and then a five-man group. And we used to lock ourselves in our room for a week to write. And I got really addicted to that process. I love working really hard, but with other people. I don't like me by myself. I'm not that attracted to myself.

It's that kind of sniper mentality. I don't know, this fellow here is not going to have a joyful end. He's such an outcast, so withdrawn. Oh no, especially now, after having a new family, a couple of young kids . . .

How is that?

It's fantastic – quite invigorating.

How old are your kids?

Two years old and two months old. The Fountain of Youth – this is the closest I've found to it. I believe that artists, probably from about twenty to mid-thirties, or forty maximum – that's when you're trying to make your bones –

It's not good for family.

The worst. It's an intrusion. It's difficult to go home at night and explain your movie life. I think Frank Capra put it succinctly when he said that once he would drive on to the Columbia lot, that was the gateway to reality. Driving home was surreal and painful and awkward. And I went, 'Mmm . . .' For directors, especially, to maintain a family existence with any kind of graceful balance is very difficult. Because they literally have two families, that created family and this blood family. That's why with so many directors – 'Hey, he's married eighteen times.' I understand it. The joy of being a director is the nearest to being a god on earth, it really is. You are creating your reality, and you are the infinite power. A director captures it for all time. His universe is up there. Unless he's had too much interference, he's nailed it and he can sit back.

Even if it bombs?
It doesn't matter. Good things bomb, maybe they jumped ahead a bit too far. I usually find that music I'm repelled by – it's because I don't understand it. So the first thing is to condemn it and burn it at the stake, like in a witch-hunt. Well, same thing with these films.

I don't think we really have a broad enough sense of cinema. And I think that's television's fault – they set the standards. The majority of American viewers are trained from television. Films can be a bit unnerving – 'too weird', or whatever. If you look at a lot of comedies made for cinema, they're usually lit like sitcoms on television – like *Friends* or *Three's Company*, ten years back – exactly the same wall of light. I'm so envious of films that have a cinematographer who really paints with lights.

If somebody goes for a piss these days, it's usually a crane shot. You look back at the films you love and think, 'They wouldn't have used a crane unless there was a really strong psychological reason for it.' Now they just want to play with the toys, I think. So I try to discipline myself by cutting out all of that. But I do like the zoom, because there's no camera shake like you get on tracks. Paul Mazursky said that Sven Nykvist was the master of this creeping zoom. And he'd go into a Zen mode, just listening to the dialogue and taking the camera along with it, without knowing where it would end. I love working with DPs who have the balls to do that. Most of them don't. They're frightened of the rushes report, they're frightened of the studio.
Or the time involved. The money aspect today – there's no chance. I've become very nervous about being involved in big blockbuster budgets because it's backfired a few times – the film's done well in the foreign market, but perhaps not domestically. If you cut it in half – let's say you're working on a forty-million-dollar budget, which is still high, but recoupable – it's not embarrassing. It also forces one to be a bit more ingenious and to get back to being hungrier, so you work a bit harder.

It's ironic, isn't it? Your career starts off with a kind of brave success story, right? Now you're one of the most marketable actors in the world, you could really do anything you wanted. But I would imagine there are also layer upon layer of pressures on you to continue being the goose that's laying the golden egg. How do you deal with that?
It's not easy. I was a little worried about *Daylight*. I felt we should bring in a play-

wright to do the dialogue – so everything down there is like in *Das Boot*, all the characters are revealed to be something other than when they were on the surface. Heroes become cowards and cowards become heroes. Well, that didn't quite happen. And halfway through the film, I made a comment that I was tired or finished with action films – which was not a very smart thing to do. That was basically saying, 'I'm finished with my career', because I had been so identified with that genre. And I found there was a kind of reticence from studios about having anything to do with me, because they realized my heart was not in it. The best action film I've done would be *First Blood* because it had a story that stands up today, about alienation. But *Rambo III* was just one big stunt-a-rama, and character be damned. Certain producers literally worked by the stopwatch – three minutes, stunt, three minutes, stunt. It became this sonata of violence. That's why I decided to go into *Copland*, and take this bold leap into stripping myself down – all the muscle, the armour . . .

Did you love doing that?
Yes, but it was very nerve-racking. Because my ace card, my security blanket, was taken away, and I hadn't realized I had become so reliant upon it. When I was doing *The Lords of Flatbush* or even *Rocky*, I wasn't so physically endowed with Olympian proportions. But as the action films continued to come forth with the big pay-days, I started realizing that I was becoming more of an athlete than an actor. I'm really in better shape than fighters. This is ridiculous, what happened?

By now you're on a train, right?
Yes, a downbound train, that has a finite ending. You can only go so far and then you go the way of most stunt-actors. And athletes. You burn out. The entire world perceived me as Rocky / Rambo, period. Most had forgotten I ever wrote and directed. And I understand that. I had forgotten it too.

But you were good at those things.
I felt I was just learning to be good – I loved doing *Paradise Alley*. I really coveted those moments. But now I was cranking 'em out, hitting the slots.

How important was the money?
Money has never been as important as wanting to be at the top of the heap competitively.

And money is a way of measuring that.
Right. I mean, I think more about money now.

Since your career took off, you've been fine for money, presumably. I spoke to Mickey Rourke yesterday about falling off the train and trying to get back on. You were firmly on – however finite the ending was, you were definitely in the pullman front end.
Right. But when I did *Copland* and took no money whatsoever, I thought this was

– I feel so lame in saying it – was kind of like a purification process. People said, 'Oh, you're an idiot, take the money, life is not going to go on for ever . . .'. But to me, going through just doing action films was just not gratifying, and such a waste of money. Lately it's been horrific the way the – quote – 'plastic action films' have done. *Armageddon* is an exception because it was done by a fellow who really gets it. It bombards the senses, but it costs an extraordinary amount of money to just keep that up. If you have some mediocre thing that falls in between, it's like – eighty million dollars . . .!

It's not an actor's medium though.
Oh, not at all. If anything, the actors get in the way. I was duly chastised for some of the dialogue in *Cliffhanger* and I think, 'When you're hanging from a cliff or being chased by an avalanche, there really isn't time to wax poetic.' It's 'Hold on! I'm coming! I'll get there! Watch out! I got your back!'

What about the multi-camera shooting – from an actor's point of view?
I like it – if you feel you're a front-runner kind of actor; in other words, if you nail your takes earlier on, three, four, five times. Some directors want more takes, but it can be lethal – so you're going thirty, forty, fifty takes. And you say, 'Okay, print two.' With multiple cameras, quite often you can nail something that's extraordinary. The lighting isn't always the best, though.

Also, the style of film-making today is much more cutting – it's not as stark.

I miss that.
Me, too. Like, if you were casting *The Godfather* today, who are you going to get? What pool of actors are you going to pull from today? And who are you going to put in Brando's place?

You'd still be going back to those same guys, wouldn't you?
You would and they're not there. If you tried to cast *Serpico* today . . . I believe that films can reflect a period. Every twenty years, cinema redefines itself and there's a whole new kind of actors, a whole new mentality, a whole new kind of film-making. Take the younger guys today, Matt Damon and Brad Pitt or whomever, and say, 'We want you to do *Godfather*' – it wouldn't be fair. But they're perfect for the kind of film-making they're doing today.

Which is preppy, collegiate – sort of the Kennedy clan look.
Exactly. The demarcation between man and woman is not so clear-cut. There's a sort of opaque, nebulous . . . the emphasis is on lighting and beauty . . .

I've been fascinated, looking at this new Matt Damon-Ben Affleck school, and this guy I like, Edward Norton, who was in *Rounders* with Matt Damon. We're talking about third- or fourth-generation family here, of American-style English-speaking acting. They're not in isolation. And it is interesting who they seem to have modelled themselves on.

It really is. Pacino started a certain kind of revved-up New York hyperactive kind of acting, and many actors followed those lines and were very good. Brando set a whole new school of acting in the fifties. It's interesting how we do films that are harmonious with that period of time, and those actors – like the remake of *Cape Fear*. I thought that was dangerous, because the original was of its time and you could get away with the sensuality – there was a simplicity to it. Scorsese added a lot more of those complications that are kind of expected in films of the nineties. And I don't know if the film could hold all that information – if the character wasn't overdeveloped.

Now, if you make a movie, you feel as if you have to have a psychological back-story that a psychiatrist would approve. It never seemed to trouble people in the forties and fifties. It made for a much more direct storytelling, didn't it? Why did you want to make films in the first place? Or act? At what age did that bug hit you, and why?

Well, the first time I really ever wanted to be somewhat of an exhibitionist, I wanted to be in the school play, and I was eight years old. I ended up playing the lower half of Smokie the Bear – this kid sat on my shoulders. I think the play lasted about thirty seconds – 'Be sure to put out your forest fires.' Boom, that was it. Then I tried when I was fifteen years old, in high school in Philadelphia. But that didn't work. So I decided I'd become a horseman. Right after college, I was going to move to Australia and try to raise polo horses. But then, in college, I was walking down the hall and there was a sign that said 'Auditions for *Death of a Salesman*'. I went, 'Hmmm . . .' So I walked in, I hadn't even thought about it, and all of a sudden, I did it. The guy said, 'You've got the part.' I was relaxed because I didn't expect it. That's why I do believe in coincidence. They just happened to have a sign, I just happened to get the part –

That's so corny.

And they just happened to have a man, I'll never forget him, Professor Swanson, who had transferred from Harvard. He had directed a little bit in Off-Off-Broadway and he said, 'You should really consider being a professional.' Well, I was gone. Next year I went to the University of Miami and joined the Ring Theatre, and just the opposite happened. I was met there by a different kind of director – kind of introverted, saw himself as a cross between James Dean and Hamlet. And I was the antithesis of what he considered an actor – too physical, not withdrawn enough, just . . .

Cheerful.

Really cheerful. So I got no parts whatsoever. But, coincidence again – there was a sign outside that said 'Hall for Rent'. A small hall. And that's when I started writing these corny little two-act plays. Then there'd be some good, bizarre plays, like Israel Horowitz's *Rats* or Eugène Ionesco and Harold Pinter. And I started having these one-man shows, culminating with the most horrible moment in my acting career, where my friend and I decided to do an interpretation of Herman Hesse's *Siddhartha*, and all we really had for a costume was a soiled bedsheet. He had the top sheet, I had the bottom sheet – we're trying to play like Hindus. Little did I know, in the back was some tattered, horribly soiled underwear belonging to my friend, which the audience fixated on. That was the end of my live performances for a while. But that's what really started it.

And then when I went to New York I was, quote, 'a type'. I didn't think so. But it's always funny how we perceive ourselves. I was the thuggish type. My voice was deep, and I was always the villain, being beaten up by Woody Allen or Jack Lemmon. I was always being thrashed by somebody. But eventually even that came to an end, and that's when I started to write. I literally painted my windows black, disconnected the phone, I didn't go out with a girl. For two years. That's how fixated I was. I had no money, the place was seventy-one dollars a month. I found this old Afghan Army coat which was basically my bed, I'd sleep in it. Until one day I fell asleep next to a radiator, which was steaming, and the coat shrunk on my back. There went my comfort. So I lived in this shrunken coat and wrote and wrote and wrote.

And, finally, Anthony Quayle started a TV series in Australia called *Touch of Evil*, and one night my director friend John Herzfeld and I said, 'Let's see how many story treatments we can come up with for this new show.' We came up with about seven, and sold five the next day, and that was the beginning of me as a writer. Then John Herzfeld was auditioning for a movie called *The Lords of Flatbush*. We had gotten into a fight about something, we hadn't talked for a year and a half. But he went to this audition and the director said, 'You used to hang around with this big guy, do you know where he is?' He goes, 'No.' 'Oh, that's too bad.' But then John let his conscience be his guide, and he literally slipped a paper under my door saying, 'This guy wants you to come on down and kill them.' And that was the beginning of getting rekindled into acting once again. Eventually, I wrote *Rocky*, just about all the frustrations that I think everybody has in their everyday life.

How much time passed between that period and actually getting *Rocky* made? And how difficult was that?
The Lords of Flatbush came out in 1972 and I thought I was on my way. Three people out of the four in that film did go to Hollywood – Henry Winkler, Susan Blakely, Perry King. I was left behind.

Why?
Again – I was a type. Dark, Italian, swarthy. And these people were just the opposite – blond, blue-eyed. And Henry was much more erudite, he was from Yale and he was not intimidating. So when I came out here, the first thing I did was beg Henry to put me on *Happy Days*. I said, 'I'll be your evil cousin, you can beat me up, but I need a job.' Well, that didn't happen, so I ended up living out in the

Valley. And I had written a screenplay, *Paradise Alley*. A couple of lawyers heard about it and bought the rights for a hundred dollars. A friend of mine had read it – Jimmy Woods, actually. And a guy named Gene Kirkwood took it to Irwin Winkler and Bob Chartoff, who ended up producing *Rocky*. They said, 'We'd like to make this but we heard that the rights have gone to someone else, and we can't work with those two people.' Those lawyers wouldn't come off it. And I went home that night, I was flipping out. Two days later was the Muhammad Ali fight with Chuck Wepner. I identified with Chuck – the guy is going to get murdered and I was feeling the same way, I'm getting hammered. One thing led to another and an idea gelled. I was in this manic state, and I wrote the screenplay – not a good one but good enough – in three days. And I brought it back to them and I said, 'This is the genesis of the idea – just the beginning.'

But basically you did not change the genesis.
You know what changed? Originally Rocky had already retired – he was a leg-breaker, a collector for the Mob. And there was no boxing in the movie. I really had written it as a small movie that could be done for two hundred thousand dollars. And this is why I think sometimes committee is interesting. Because Gene Kirkwood said, 'You know, too bad he doesn't box any more.' So I went back and made him this tawdry kind of boxer and I thought, 'Let me try to make this a redemptive thing.' And I tried to work this Christ symbol, this religious overtone, and it really just came from that aside – 'Too bad he doesn't box any more.' But then, no one wanted to make the movie. They kept changing. 'Can we make the black guy Jamaican?' 'You can't fight the black guy, it's too racist.' We kept going through these rewrites, and when you just start with one character, it's like concentric rings – it changes the whole script. Twenty-six drafts later . . .

Originally, Adrian was Jewish – I wanted everything to be difficult for Rocky. Then she was Irish. Susan Sarandon was supposed to play it, then Carrie Snodgrass – that didn't work. Harvey Keitel was going to play Rocky, that didn't work. Two nights before the movie was going to go, Talia Shire walked in. And I said, 'Guess what? She could be Italian.' Carl Weathers walked in that same night, and he had all this arrogance, he was feeling his oats. I'm in the office with John Avildsen, and Carl and I are reading. He goes, 'You wanna see my body?' He takes his shirt off and he's really built. He says, 'I can box a little bit.' So I get up with him and he's sort of banging me in the forehead. And then he turns to John and goes, 'You know, I could do a lot better if I was with a real actor.' He thought I was the office boy. John says, 'Well, he is Rocky. That's the guy.' Carl goes, 'Huh! Well, I see I won't have any problem with this movie.' I said, 'Hire him, immediately. This is exactly what I want.' So everything just fell into place.

But the biggest problem was they didn't want me. There was a clause in my contract that they could dump me after ten days. It felt like, 'If he snores, fire him.' Luckily John Avildsen shot a few of the dramatic scenes early on, where I'm collecting on the docks. And they accepted it. But I have to say, the producers did something I don't know that I would do, or anyone would do any more – they put their house up for collateral to pay the bond. They went on the line with a total unknown in a film that was guaranteed to make no money. Boxing films just never did well. I was trying to convince them, 'This is not really a boxing film, it's a love story – kind of.' I think the turning point in *Rocky* was the music. It added a nobility that I hadn't even thought of. It went from these trumpets and horns and cacophony, down to a single piano, and it was just brilliant. That was Bill Conti.

You were involved in that?
What I tried to do in the beginning was provide temp tracks, or music I thought was right, like 'Gonna Fly Now', and a Hall and Oates song called 'Grounds For Separation'. Then Bill went off and did great work, completely original, on his own. The movie has certain tag lines. 'I can fight with the best, but I can only go so many rounds.' But I think it came about at a time when anti-heroes were at the forefront. No one was taking a shot. It was 1976, the country's two-hundredth birthday. Everything came about. And here we are twenty or so years later and you have *Good Will Hunting* which is two guys writing a script, refusing to sell it, doing it on their own. But I'm just incredibly grateful. The only problem with *Rocky* is you just don't want to stop making them. Just as I'm ready to put him to bed, I see George Foreman. I go, 'What a great idea . . .'

Maybe. Maybe not.
It's like watching John Glenn go into space. There's something about the battle with . . . I don't have to get old, do I? It seems like our previous generations got to a point, hit forty-five, decided this is the point you drop back and be incredibly mature and go out gracefully. Our generation is kicking and screaming and clawing, and they're not going out so easy. We're not our parents.

Every ten years, as we're ten years older, we kind of change the rules and move the goalposts. And we say, 'You know what? Forty-five is really sexy.'
And they come up with the chemicals now . . . Kicking and screaming. We're not going gently into the good night – no way. As long as there are guys like George Foreman around who give me inspiration, you know, that gives validity to that concept. Hmmm, why not?

12 Jerry Bruckheimer

Mike Figgis: So why did you decide to spend so much of your life making films?
Jerry Bruckheimer: You know what it is? I started as a kid going into a theatre, I'm sitting in that dark room, with my hand in my popcorn and my soda next to me, and it was really a safe haven for me. Those enormous figures on the screen, the romance – it took me to another place, I loved being there, I wanted to be a part of the magic. I always say we're in the transportation business. We transport you from one place to another. I always dreamt about being part of it. And I think it's fortunate that I'm here making movies, because I grew up in Detroit, which is not exactly known for having a thriving film community. I came from a lower-middle-class family.

Any kind of show business in your family?
No. I'm a first-generation American. My parents came over from Germany during the Depression. My mother had fourteen brothers and sisters, and one of my uncles brought all the kids who survived over to America. So they struggled and did okay. And I had this dream to come to Hollywood – didn't quite have a plan. But after I graduated college I started in the mailroom of a big advertising agency – big for Detroit, small by New York terms. And I worked my way into the television department and started taking out cameras and filming equipment, putting together little commercials and then selling them.

Was film-making what you wanted to do initially?
Well, I had to learn the language of film. As a child, I took still photographs. My uncle bought a lot of cameras and when he got bored with them, he used to hand them down to me. They were Argus 35s, nothing really fancy, but good enough to learn the basics of still photography with.

Did you print?
I printed my own pictures and entered a lot of contests and won a lot of awards – National Scholastic Key Awards, and a Kodak Award. That was in high school. Then I went to the University of Arizona, which had no film department *per se*. I took some photo classes, but that was it. So when I got out I really had no film training, and that's why I got into advertising – to understand the medium. You get to work with good directors and cinematographers.

Had you ever thought you would carry on with photography?
I really didn't think you could make a living. The only photographers I knew just did weddings and confirmations.

Right. Were you interested in other photographers?
Mine was a very quiet home and I wasn't bombarded with a lot of information. We never got magazines, we only got one newspaper, so I didn't realize you could take pictures for magazines, or be a fashion photographer. That wasn't really part of my world. But film was always something I had a focus on. Eventually I had an

opportunity to go from Detroit to New York for a lot less money and work for a big agency there, so I took it and I got to handle the Pepsi-Cola account, which gives you a lot of leeway and a lot of money. So I had the opportunity to play with more cameras, and cut my own commercials. I learned cutting styles, worked with very good editors, and became a craftsman.

Presumably, at the same time you had a head for business?
I think we all have to be aware of business, no matter who we are, directors or whoever. Everybody knows what it costs to do certain things and knows when to draw the line and where to put your money. I think everybody learns that. I'm certainly not a businessman, that's not how I made my mark in Hollywood – it's not that I'm the best guy at working out a budget. I'm the last person to tell you that I'm going to make the picture for exactly what we set out to do. We get very close and we're honest about it, but I've never got it down to the penny, under or over.

It's an expensive business, right?
It's called show*business*. And if you don't treat it as a business, you're in trouble. If you go into a very artistic endeavour, you have to do it for very little money. If you go into a big commercial endeavour – yes, you get a little more money. So you have to give a return on your money. And, knock on wood, I've been very fortunate, the films I've made in the past few years have all given a very good return on the money the studios gave me. But I care about the work more than anything else. I care about the stories we tell and the actors and directors we work with. The key to me is putting together the creative talent, and that's what I'm very good at – recognizing talent, seeing someone's first movie and saying, 'This gentleman is really talented.' I've been able to do that my whole career, going back to Tom Cruise, Eddie Murphy, Will Smith and Martin Lawrence and so on. Tony Scott made *The Hunger* and certainly wasn't on the hot list to be hired at every studio. But I recognized the enormous amount of talent.

At what point did you realize that was your own talent?
As a kid, I was always very good at putting things together, organizing things. I started baseball teams and hockey teams and got sponsors and got the best kids in the neighbourhood to play. I always had the organizational skills to put interesting people together in a venture. And I did the same thing when I started in commercials.

As a kid you often have to try and find a way to survive with other kids. Was that an issue for you?
No, mine was the house other kids came to, and we all hung out. I was always good with people.

Big family?
No, I'm an only child. But I had a lot of relatives because my mother had so many

brothers and sisters, so there were a lot of nieces and nephews. There were always a lot of people around.

How much similarity is there between the life you have now, and what you thought it might be like before you came here?
It looks much more glamorous than it really is. I always knew that what I wanted to do was going to take really hard work, so that never scared me. I enjoy it, I look forward to it, I love the hours, I love the commitment. I think a lot of the glamour disappears once you're here. The events you see on television look so wonderful, but at times I'm thinking, 'Do I really have to go? I'm not sure I want to give up my evening, I'd rather be in the editing room with the director.' So some of it is really a distraction, but it's part of what we have to sell to the public. It's part of selling Hollywood, the myth of Hollywood. It's all about certain premières and gala events and Academy Awards broadcast worldwide and I think it's very effective.

Why?
Because we are in a business that has to draw people to spend money. It's expensive for most families to go out for an evening, even though movies are cheaper than most other entertainment. But it's much easier to rent a video and sit home or watch television. We've got to get them out of the living room and into a theatre. Any way you can sell it, you have to be able to sell it. You have to do something really unique and special. And that's why we have press junkets and why we do whatever we have to do to promote our films. You have to reach a large mass audience – at least for the kind of pictures I've been making up to this point. Because they're so expensive, and you have to get a return on that. And that's the business I've been in for the past ten years.

Why are they so expensive now?
Everything always goes up, it never goes down. Manpower is more expensive, the revenues we bring in are much more, so the actors get paid more and they certainly are worth what they get paid, even though I think the press would argue with me.

The image that people around the world have of Hollywood is a very bizarre one. There's hardly any film-making in the bit we call Hollywood any more. We just conveniently continue to call it Hollywood. How would you describe 'it', this collective industry?
That's a hard one. It's the film-making capital of the world. Even though not all films are made here, they all originate here, most of them. This is where the bank is, this is where the money is, this is where the distributors are. If you want to be successful in this business, you have to spend time here . . . depending on what you do . . . directors can spend less time and can fly in and out, especially if they're in demand. Then the buyer will come to them to lure them to do their movies. It's always been that way. The studios are all here. Years ago they were run out of New York, quite a few of them. At Warner Brothers, the main money

people were in New York. They sent Jack out here to actually try to put together the studio, but it was really run from New York, as was Columbia and a lot of other studios, Paramount and Universal, I think, too. But it's all changed now.

For the better, I would have thought.
I think so, because that was more like the garment business in that you had to go to the banks to secure loans to run your slate of pictures. It's no different than the garment guys who had to go to the banks to secure their fall line or their winter line and had to get loans to manufacture their products, the same thing we would do in Hollywood, at least in the old days. Now they're mostly self-sufficient and use their own money or borrow money from very specific banks, but do it here in Hollywood.

What kind of shape is the business in right now?
Well, they all complain about the cost of movies and how expensive these are, but they've always complained about the cost of movies. If you don't want to spend the money, you shouldn't be in the business. That's just the way it is, to reach as broad an audience as we're reaching. It's a terrible business to be in if you're a money man. But it's no different than the real estate business where you sometimes are a negative cash flow until the property starts to create value for you in time. It's the same thing with these film libraries, you look what the libraries have been selling for, what Universal sold for initially to the Japanese, what Columbia sold for . . . it's all based on the library. And when you see the number of different ways they can promote our movies around the world – from laser disks now to DVD to cable to syndication around the world – it's enormous business and it goes on for ever. And there's always a new medium. There were no video cassettes fifteen, twenty years ago. You never heard of a video cassette. Now people have whole libraries of video cassettes. Movies like *Armageddon* pull the train for a lot of pictures that maybe didn't work. They can sell them and sell them in bunches in syndication.

You mean as a collective deal?
Yes, sure. They package movies in deals and give you one blockbuster, and they pull a bunch of pictures that weren't quite as successful along. One big movie can make a whole year. Look at *Titanic*. It certainly made two studios, on a picture that broke every rule, which I loved. It was the most expensive movie, it didn't have a movie star going into it, and it was over three hours long, and it was on water. So everything that you could do wrong, according to the experts in Hollywood, was done. And yet it's the biggest picture of all time, which is great.

Where did they spend their money? How can you spend two hundred million dollars?
You'd have to ask Jim Cameron that. But any time you go near water, you're looking for trouble because you have to deal with the weather, a lot of unpredictable things. You look at Steven Spielberg's *Jaws*. I remember that he was in trouble when he was making the picture because the picture was going over

budget because he had no control over it. The big man in the sky decides what the weather's going to be, not us. And it certainly can shut you down.

Let's talk a little bit more about the financial situation here, and the amounts of money that are spent. The way you run your business, is that different from the way studios spend money? Are you more aware of financial waste?
You see it all around you, unfortunately, and you try to control it as much as you can. But you also have to look at the big picture and you know you usually have a date to meet, for completing the movie, and you usually spend a lot of money in overtime and a lot of other crazy things that you do to make that date. And we certainly did it on *Armageddon*. We had a very tough post-production schedule only because we had over 250 visual-effects shots.

And you'd already booked your release time.
The theatres are booked. You've got to be there that date. The first of July was our date, and come hell or high water, the prints were pretty wet getting to the theatres. I don't think the prints were released until a week before the opening; so they were making over two or three thousand prints in less than a week's time. We had to ship them and get them to the theatres, so it was very tight. And that's how you can spend more money because you're working people on double and triple shifts. It was all done here in Los Angeles. We were running three shifts; we had three eight-hour shifts going on visual effects, so they were working around the clock.

How important to you are the critics?
Look, everybody wants to be praised for their work. It'd be crazy to say otherwise. I would love to get good reviews. We don't usually. It's just the nature of the kind of pictures that I make.

Why is that?
They feel maybe the pictures are too blatantly commercial, it's something that bothers them, that these pictures are so big, they're adventurous. And it's hard for the critics to hurt them. They try to tell people not to go to some of the pictures, and it doesn't matter because people show up anyway and they really get entertained. You don't do the kind of grosses that our pictures have done without really entertaining people, you know. If I talk to other film-makers, they'll say it's a generation gap, that the kind of films I make with younger directors, the older critics just don't get what they're doing, whereas the kids do . . . I'm sure that's a little part of it, but I think critics would much rather find a movie like *Leaving Las Vegas*, where they can really make an impact by telling people to go see it because chances are they wouldn't because there isn't the budget to advertise those kinds of films; so the critics can really pound their chests and say, 'You have to go see it.' With *Armageddon* they're going to show up whether the critics like it or not.

But it works both ways with me because, if four critics say go and see it, it's a must, you'll find a few different points of view – snobbery, élitism and individuality; then a bunch of critics will say don't go and see it, a very overrated movie.

I think the papers have to realize that they're representing to the public a point of view and it's the paper, it's not the critic himself, it's the *Los Angeles Times* or the *New York Times* or the *Chicago Tribune* that are saying don't go see this movie. The *Los Angeles Times* had a real issue with *Titanic*, and went after it not once but twice.

What was their issue?

They didn't like the picture, period. And it's the biggest movie of all time. I think the editors have to look at themselves and say, wait a second, how did we miss that? How did we take one of the biggest pictures ever made, and in my case, the biggest picture of the summer, and say don't go see this movie? They're out of sync with their readers, something's wrong here.

Of course, finally, for James Cameron and for yourself, it didn't matter. But there must be part of you that is offended.

My wife has always had this theory that you don't send a rock critic to review opera. And I don't think you send a critic who doesn't like popular entertainment to go review popular entertainment. If he's in love with the smaller films, that I love too – that's what he should be reviewing. And when the big pictures come out during the summer and during Christmas, you should have somebody that really embraces that medium and would spend their own money to go see it, just like I would. Based on the record, there's billions of dollars that show these pictures have worked for an audience.

Have you ever made a film where you were going to depend on reviews, where it was going to be more of an issue?

I executive produced a picture called *The Ref*, which was a small little movie made for, I think, eight million dollars. We got some good reviews as it turned out. But it still didn't help. So you never know. I've had pictures that they've said were brilliant and nobody showed up, so it goes both ways.

Do you think that once you start making a certain kind of film, it's hard to then make another kind of film?

Not for a producer. I think a producer can make a lot of different movies because I think it's who he gets in business with and who he hires and who he works with. You make your choices; and you make choices of material. I have a reputation for making a certain type of picture. And I will continue to do that.

What is that picture?

They call them action films but I call them action-adventure films. *The Rock*, *Armageddon*, *Con Air*, *Beverly Hills Cop*, *Top Gun* – they have a certain kind of pizazz, and energy. So the audience, when they see the name sometimes, they'll associate it with that kind of picture, and the press certainly will. Yet I made a picture called *Dangerous Minds* about a schoolteacher, really a small movie that became very successful. So I can do other types of movie, and we're developing films that you would never think I would make. And yet I'm going to make them.

Do you feel more comfortable now that you have a bedrock of financial security? Does that allow you to take more risks?
I'm certainly well paid and I don't have to work any more. But I always made my choices on what I wanted to do, not how much they were going to pay me. It was for love of making movies. I grew up on the films of David Lean and Stanley Kubrick and I still love those movies and watch them over and over again.

Do you think people who write about film tend to over-categorize those of us within this industry – as being this or that kind of film-maker?
Oh, I think there's a natural tendency in any profession to pigeonhole people. It's not only done by the press, it's done by the lawyers and the agents in this town. They say, he's this kind of director, that kind of producer. But by doing that you limit the ability of a lot of the individuals who could do a lot more with the talent they were given than people think they can.

Film students reading this might have certain preconceived ideas about me and about you. Tell me – if, say, we decided to make a film together, how would that process work? How would we go about collaborating?
I'm really hands-on, which is the good news and the bad news. So, with me, you have a partner, certainly in the script process, and in the casting process. Then, once the picture is on its feet and filming, you're the director, you run the show.

Well, what if I fuck up? And I don't know it?
I'll be there to say, 'Hey, I think we're making a mistake here. What do you think we can do to fix it?' I'm on the set every day and we look at dailies, so we'll talk through this stuff.

When we first talk, would you be thinking about what kind of a guy I was?
Well, I look at your movies, and they give me a good sense of who you are and what type of artist you are.

But in that first meeting, would you be looking out for certain tell-tale mannerisms?
Not at all. It comes down to the work. That's what I base everything on. The greatest salesmen in the world are in this town and a lot of them can talk the talk, but very few of them can walk the walk. They can come in here and dazzle me with their personality. Then you look at the work and you say, 'Wait a second here, there's something missing.'

Each guy that you work with, it's a partnership?

Absolutely. We take a lot of time and care in developing the material and making sure it's as good as we can get it. Then, once we get a director aboard, it starts all over again. The only thing I'm very careful about with directors is that we have the same point of view – that he's not making one movie and I'm making another. We have to both know what kind of film we want to go see when we're done.

Would pacing be an issue, for example?
Not at all. It's whether you're making *Leaving Las Vegas* or *Honeymoon in Vegas*. It's which direction you're going to take the characters. And how do you want to end the movie? How do you want the audience to feel when they walk out? What's the style of the film? How do you see it being shot, how are you going to light it?

You're ahead of the game, in a sense, because you've already developed the material.
But then a director will come in with a different point of view and it's much better than ours. And it excites us, to add that layer. And then you bring a writer in, and you get another perspective, another layer. A cast member will have interesting ideas that you'll incorporate into the screenplay. Apparently Warren Beatty has a theory that he always wants three great minds with him when he's making a movie. And he's right. The more smart people you have around you, I think the better your movie is going to be. If you're working with smart, talented people, they will always listen. I've found that the stubborn ones, the ones who don't listen, are usually not that talented.

I completely agree with you. But I find it hard to find 'smart'. How do you manage it?
It is difficult. There are a lot of people who get paid very well. Then you get 'em in a room and you say, 'Wait a second, did this person really write this movie that's on their sheet? Or direct this film?' You think somebody else must have been involved, otherwise it doesn't all make sense. But we all need help. I'm never afraid to force the studio to write a cheque to a writer who I feel can make the picture better, no matter what stage of the movie we are in. I'm the first one to go in there and pound the door down. Even if I have to pay for it myself, which we have done.

So when you're shooting, how active are you? You like to be around on the set?
I like to stop by to make sure there are no problems – that there's nothing they need for tomorrow that's not going to be there, that the work being done is what we all decided to do in the initial stages. A lot of times on set, an actor will have a point of view that the director will disagree with, and sometimes you have to get in there and support whoever you feel has the right point of view, and keep it open.

We pay pretty young actors and actresses a lot of money here. Once they're successful, how tough is it for them to deal with that? And how do you deal with what corruption takes place in their personalities once you endorse them

by saying, 'Here's twenty-five million dollars for twelve weeks' work.'
You try to make careful choices. It's such a small business that, no matter who you're going to work with, somebody else has worked with them before. What a lot of people don't understand in this business is that the news travels pretty quick – especially bad news.

This does happen, doesn't it?
Oh, sure – part of the business. I've been very fortunate because my career has built very slowly, so I didn't get a whole ton of money when I first came to Hollywood. I grew into it.

That's an important thing, isn't it?
Yes. It's difficult, when somebody gets thrown a lot of money and they're very young and they have everybody chasing them. Some of them handle it very well. Tom Cruise is somebody I worked with very early on in his career – he was always serious about the work, always trying to make the movie better. He would call at four in the morning with ideas. He was such a gentleman about the process. And you look at his career and you say, well, I understand what's going on here. He's had such longevity and done such good work and been nominated for Academy Awards and every director wants to work with him because he's a good guy. Will Smith is the same way. What you see on the screen is what you get, a guy who loves to come to work in the morning and is never in a bad mood. There are a ton of actors like that.

People do get very damaged in this business. But it's a bizarre business in that it never makes a huge effort to hide what it is either. It's built on hedonism, finance, insecurity. Do you have any thoughts about that?
You know, the problem you have in Hollywood is that there are all these eyes on you, especially today. You have all these television shows that feed off the dirt of this business and looking for it. You have magazines and newspapers that feed on it. So when you get into the business you have to realize that's what you're getting into, especially as an actor. They're going to look at your life with a microscope, and that's very difficult. I remember, we were filming a picture and we had a big star in the movie; and one of the tabloids was offering money to people at the hotel to give dirt on the actor. And that's how actors have to lead their lives, and that's terrible. I feel very sorry for somebody who gets in that position. They've got money being thrown around to look for their flaws. God knows, we're all flawed, none of us are perfect.

Hollywood has always been a magnet for good-looking young women who come in hoping to become a 'film star' and all of that . . . which makes them very vulnerable to whatever may form them. My point is that they know that that is the system.
Well, I'm not sure that they really know that's the system. What I used to read

about Hollywood certainly didn't mention that part of it. They might see it now on some of the tabloid shows, but I think we're all dreamers and we all think that that's not part of what it is; yet I'm sure it's a big part of it. If you interview a young actress or young actor, or even an older actress, they can tell you, I'm sure, some pretty horrific tales of what they had to go through. But I think you've got to be very careful who you associate with and who you're around. You find a lot of the actors and actresses didn't have that kind of problem because they're tough, they built up a shield and they know who to deal with and how to deal with it.

The ones that survive tend to be a very rare breed of people, don't they.
Yes, you've got to have talent, and the camera's got to like you, and you have got to have something that's unique. A lot of it's a God-given skill, and that skill can be developed even further, which the better actors do. But you see so many kids who come in and read for these parts who are so far from having that talent – not that maybe someday they won't acquire it when they get older – but it's hard as a director, I'm sure. When you see some of these performances you say, oh, my God, how are they going to make a living? I think every actor and actress, and even directors, have to look at themselves and say, 'Can I really do this? Can I be effective at this? Is this something I'm really gifted at? Or can learn to be gifted at?'

How realistic is it for someone, a foreigner, to come to this community and want to make a film for the art of making a film, without any kind of financial knowledge of the structure of film-making?
I think you have to figure that out. There are really enough books and enough articles, enough things written about this town that are honest and let you know what's going on. So I think you have to do your homework when you come into town.

But is this the right place for art?
Of course it is. There's so much money here, there's so much need for product, there are so many channels to distribute the product. They're desperate for people to come in and say, 'I have this vision, I have this idea, it doesn't cost a lot of money.' Miramax built a huge film library reputation and everything based on film-makers with passion, and Harvey and Bob understanding that passion and liking those kinds of films, and made a lot of money doing it. So they took the artist and made him into a commercial venture for themselves. And for the artist too. Of course not all the films become a *Pulp Fiction* or a *Good Will Hunting* but a lot of film-makers got an opportunity to show their vision.

Harvey's a good example. Do you think the studios are getting hipper in that sense?
Harvey's a studio, he's part of a big studio. The studios will always make the kind of films that they make. And they will have the Harveys to make the other kind of films.

And that's just as much a part of what we call Hollywood as Warner Brothers.

Well, sure. A couple of years ago, they were talking about how all the independent movies have taken over Hollywood. They weren't independent movies – they were all distributed by or financed by majors, even though they're called Fine Line or whatever. It's just another division.

It's just branding, isn't it?
That's right, that's all it is.

I'll finish just by asking you some questions about taste. You don't have to think about it, just give me five pieces of music that touch you.
Beethoven's *Fifth* is something that really touches me. Ravel's *Bolero* moves me every time I hear it. Vivaldi's *Four Seasons* I love. With popular music, there are some Billy Joel songs, I can't pick one in particular. Some Beatles songs – *Yesterday*, *Imagine* – have always moved me.

Some films – they can be yours, they can be anybody's.
Lawrence of Arabia, Bridge on the River Kwai, Raging Bull, Paths of Glory.

What about directors? They can be from any era.
David Lean, Kubrick. Billy Wilder did some amazing work. Coppola and Scorsese are film-makers I really admire.

And actors – male?
Clark Gable, Cagney, Bogart. Maybe Gary Cooper.

They're all of a very specific style of acting, right?
I'd rather go into the older actors, because I've worked with so many actors and I don't want to get into the ones that are around now.

Actresses.
Again I'll go back – Carole Lombard, Bette Davis, Olivia De Havilland. Those are just some that I can remember that really kind of move me.

13   Tony Scott

Mike Figgis: So why did you get into film-making?
Tony Scott: Because it was part of the process. I started out as a painter, but in the end I felt I wasn't really fulfilling what I wanted to feel about painting. And then Ridley was doing his diploma film at the Royal College of Art, and I helped him on that.

Was that your first experience with film?
Yes. It was about a boy who goes off to school in West Hartlepool. I was the boy – and that's where we went to school. And I found that my painting started to gravitate into still photography. I started doing big mobiles with photo-silks on them.

Who was influencing you?
Paolozzi was my big influence. Some of my roots went back to Hieronymus Bosch, Breughel, Bacon, this dark religious-persecution stuff.

Were you kind of a photo-realist?
Kind of, but not a true photo-realist, in that I liked what paint did for me. But I suppose I just drifted away, I slowly started to do more and more photography. And then I got hold of a Bolex camera and I made a weird, arty film about a buddy of mine, a painter, running through a post-Holocaust city.

Where are you from?
West Hartlepool is where we grew up. I loved it. It was depressing, but it had enormous character. And I loved the fact that, within fifteen minutes of home, I could be up on the moors. That was like being on another planet. And I was big into climbing, so at weekends I'd go up into Northumberland, the Yorkshire Dales, places like that.

Where did the painting come from? Was it your family?
My dad did a little bit of watercolour about once every two years – he fancied himself there. He did one of Durham Cathedral, I have it on my wall. But I was always following Rid, I was always in admiration of him. He's a brilliant draughtsman. I always wanted to be in the arts, and I kept watching what Rid was doing, and he became my real influence. Then I went to Sunderland Art School for four years, ran the Film Society there – I was the projectionist, I had to book all the fucking films, *and* run the cafeteria. Roman Polanski was my man. I suppose the darkness of Polanski attracted me.

Like *Repulsion, Cul-de-Sac* . . .
And the first one, *Two Men and a Wardrobe. Knife in the Water, Rosemary's Baby, Repulsion*, yeah. So from Sunderland I went to Leeds for a year, and then to the Royal College in London.

At what point did you realize you had to come here to Los Angeles?
For me, my life is my work, so I'm like a gypsy. It was just a natural progression. One day you wake up and say, 'Fuck, I'm based here now.' It wasn't a conscious

decision – 'I'm going to uproot, I have no kids, my marriage is changing.' You just follow your nose. Is it good or bad? It's good as long as you're working. I love what I do.

It's important for you to keep working?
I can't imagine not working. It would be so depressing. I always find that when I finish a film, at first I think, 'Thank God, I'm fucking going to lie in this morning.' That lasts for a morning. Then I get paranoid about what the next project's going to be.

Now you and Ridley are producing things together . . .
Yes. Rid's the empire builder, he really gets a buzz out of it. He can sit with the head of Citibank or go to Wall Street – it's his new passion. He wakes up every morning, reads the *Wall Street Journal*. But I'm still in full stress directing.

How many films have you made now?
This is my tenth. How many have you done?

Nine, I think.
So we're pretty close.

If I'm not working I'm at a loose end. And I don't really care now what the work is, that's the nice thing. I can happily go into a 16 mm film or a studio picture. I've done a lot of documentaries as well, which I've started to love, because it's film-making at its grittiest. And I like carrying the equipment.
I admire that. Sometimes I wish I could do that kind of thing.

How much have you bought into the social scene here, the film-making community?
I haven't. I have a great office, a great house, one at the beach, one in town. And I move from capsule to capsule. I've used the same people for five movies now, I'd say ninety per cent of my crew is the same. And it's not just because I'm trying to be a good guy – it's shorthand. They know what I'm thinking, they can anticipate me, so it's more efficient. And they're all characters, all great at what they do, and I enjoy spending time with them. They know when to have fun, or when to shut up, they know I like a quiet set. And I regard them as family.

I admire you for that. I'm trying to do the same thing. It's taken me a while.
I use the same guys on commercials that I do on film.

You still do a lot of commercials?
Yes.

Sort of bread and butter?
It's not so much that – I get off on them. I enjoy shooting, and I'll try things in commercials that I never get a chance to try in film. For instance, Marlboro is brilliant. I get to shoot in the most beautiful parts of the Rockies and I get to try

new helicopters, new mounts, new bits of equipment, certain ideas, like this or that rain effect. I'll take stuff from commercials to film and vice versa.

Where do they get shown?
Marlboro is shown all over the world except for the US. But now they've taken out the cigarettes. It's just, 'This little story came to you from Marlboro . . .' Brand identity. I'm lucky, too, because I'm established. I did these GM commercials, the spots weren't very good on the page, but I was interested in doing this movie *Enemy of the State*. So I said, 'Why not make the commercials about surveillance?' And I got to try all these effects and then use them in the movie.

I love the movie trailer, by the way.
Yes, it's good. It misrepresents the film a little bit because it suggests an all-out action movie, whereas it's really more character-based.

I really admire your style of film-making. I think you're the head of your genre. I think a lot of people have lost the plot when it comes to making action movies.
It's hard. Every time, it gets harder to bring your own stamp to that kind of film. You know, action's been done to death.

How do you deal with scripts?
Well, for instance, *True Romance* was the best, the most complete. When it landed on my desk, the only thing that had to be changed was the ending – because that was Quentin in his heyday. I loved *True Romance*, it was my favourite. But part of the process I have with Jerry Bruckheimer is that I find the script's never quite there when I get it. Then I find there's something that interests me, something I want to do with it. So he and I get into a development period. *Crimson Tide* is a classic example. I was interested in the submarine genre, I loved *Das Boot*, and I'd never done anything like that. The idea of *Crimson Tide* was good, but the characters were no good. So we brought Quentin in – I had just finished with *True Romance*.

That was all amicable then, you and Quentin? It seemed to get blown up.
That was silly. The only thing I changed was the end and I shot his end as well. I think he loved the movie. And he came back to work on *Crimson*. Do you know he totally rewrote every piece of dialogue in *Crimson*, and all those characters? He said, 'I love the story, I hate the characters.' I said, 'That's why you're here.' And he just brought those characters to life.

He's a good writer, isn't he?
He's great. It's not just words out of the mouth, he always looks for a hook in each character, an idea behind each character – like Denzel riding horses, which seems outrageous, but he does it with such confidence. Gene Hackman's role was modelled on someone he knew, a friend of his father's.

I wasn't surprised, but I was disappointed in the predictable critical treatment

of Quentin on his third movie. I thought *Jackie Brown* was a good film, and I thought it was very bold of him not to do 'Pulp II' or 'Dogs III', but to do a very gentle movie, a love story. I thought, 'There's a truly original film-maker.' But critics laid into him in such a big way, they seemed disappointed.

I think Quentin's brilliant. Writers are our lifeblood. And how many good ones can just pick up a script and say, 'I'll make this work'?

Basically the whole system is based on money here, isn't it.

Yes.

And you're lucky, in a sense – it's you and Ridley. I think it helps that you've got family.

And Jake, Luke and Jordan – the three kids – they're all directing.

Yes, you've got your little empire. But a lot of the younger English directors who come here seem to get shafted pretty quickly by the system and get very confused by the amount of money that you can earn. Did you have a problem with it? Did it turn your head?

No. You know, when I came here, Mike, I made a great living in commercials. And sometimes I wake up and go, 'I've made a million commercials in ten years, I only wanted to be in it for two.' Or 'I've just done two movies that I shouldn't have done.' But there's this wave of euphoria that carries you along when you're successful. And I've never done anything for a career move – I've always done it because I followed my nose. In two instances, I got my arm twisted to do movies. But even in those movies, I still found my hook, the hook to make me want to go to work every day.

Why did you do those movies? Was it a financial consideration?

No, it was to do with friends and relationships, and because there was nothing to do out of passion right then. So I just wanted to keep on that roll. But I could have done better, in terms of my choices.

All right, the last thing is where I just throw some quick questions at you. Give me five pieces of music that move you.

A thing called *Lakmé* by Delibes, which goes way back for me. It's a piece I had in my bottom drawer when I did my first film, *The Hunger*. Now it's been fucking used to death. I'm almost reluctant to actually say it. I used it in a British Airways commercial myself. In fact, I was flying back from seeing my mum last weekend, and it was playing on British Airways. I thought, 'It's a far cry from where it began' . . . God, I'm terrible at these.

It doesn't matter if it's something you just heard this week, something you heard on the radio this morning.

Actually, last night I was using *Closer to God*, this Trent Reznor track. And then, oh, God – I love Bowie. Do you have music playing at home when you're at home?

Yes. I just couldn't live without it.
I'm just always so focused on my work. I say, 'Well, what music is right for what I'm doing now?' So I'm always digging and researching. Like these Trent Reznor tracks, they're all to do with anger and heroin, but I can take that element of the music and put it into the paranoia of what *Enemy of the State* is about. I'm trying to think who else. I love the Stones. How many is that, four?

Yes, but that'll do. It gives me an idea. Some literature? Anything that has stayed with you?
Again, Mike, I'm a workhorse, I've read so little in my life. I've always been a doer – painting, climbing, filming. In the end, my day is always full. Even if I go away, take time off, I'm always doing macho things like diving, climbing, skiing. If I'm not moving all day long, I feel as if my heart's going to stop.

What about movies? Five movies that influenced you.
Repulsion, Knife in the Water, Bladerunner, Good Will Hunting. Did you like that?

Mm-hm.
I thought Matt Damon was great in that . . . I'm bad at these Q&As. If you gave me time, I'd sit here and labour over it for a day.

That'll do. If I asked you for directors – clearly it would be Polanski, right?
Polanski; Coppola; my brother, he's always been a big influence; Scorsese; and Bertolucci. I don't think there are any surprises in those guys, but they're all great.

Actors that you admire?
De Niro, Hackman, Duvall. Those three guys, they're in a league of their own. They all do an enormous amount of homework. Most actors talk about their preparation but they never do it. I think these guys are still very insecure about what they do, so that's why they do it. I did one movie with De Niro, which missed, unfortunately – because I fucked it up.

Did you?
Yeah. I made a choice with De Niro at the beginning, to try and do a character which was a little different from the characters he'd done in the past. He was sympathetic, a sad, lost soul. And the audience felt sorry for him, they ran with him. So by the time he came to be a threat halfway through the movie, the threat was no longer there. It's funny, when you do a film and you know halfway through that you've made some choice that is wrong.

Yes. A distant bell rings . . .
Have you been there?

Oh, yes.
And you go, 'How the fuck do I reverse out of it?'

And you can't.
You can't.

I remember writing in a journal, 'This is a nightmare entirely of my own making. And I can't blame anybody for this. I wrote it, I'm directing it.' I still like the movie, as it turns out, but there are parts of it where I . . .
This last movie?

No, this was a movie called *Liebestraum*. I actually think it may be the strongest film I've made. Certainly the freakiest. But there were choices that I made that I wish I hadn't . . . now.
When you hear these stories about *Apocalypse Now*, Coppola casting Harvey Keitel and then six weeks later . . .

I couldn't do that – dropping an actor during shooting. Sometimes I feel I'm not really a film director because of that. Sometimes film directors do things and I think, 'Fucking hell!'
I've been lucky, I don't think I've had a bad relationship like that. Anyway, I think I'd feel so badly about the guy I was getting rid of that my guilt would override my fucking decision of saying, 'Get him out and start over.'

Mike Figgis: How would you describe yourself? What do you do for a living?
Mickey Rourke: I'm an actor – now. Again. I'm starting over, in a way.

Tell me about that.
Well, about ten years ago I had my career going in the right direction. Then I started not liking the business and not liking myself. And I was slowly self-destructing, at a pretty fast rate – if that makes sense. I got to the point where I was hanging around with an element I probably shouldn't have been. But I felt comfortable in that element. I felt like I didn't belong in acting – I felt some sort of guilt about being successful at it.

But at that point, when your job description was 'Actor', how would you have described being an actor?
Being an actor is what I now call behaving in a professional manner – being responsible and consistent, not just hour to hour, day by day, or night by night, but all the way through. That was what I found most difficult. Let's say, if a little wrench got thrown in my spokes, I went haywire. And I was very consistent with my anger.

Well, there's 'What is an actor?', and then there's 'What is an actor in Hollywood?' They're not necessarily the same, are they?
No. I guess I was able to be an actor in Hollywood because I had the ability, and I was able to take a meeting. And I know a lot of boys from the old days that were very, very good actors but they couldn't take a meeting. So they never made it past little dark rooms where people study acting.

How do you take those meetings?
Well, you read. You think about what you want. You size the other person up and you figure out what it is *they* want. If they want something they haven't seen before, then they've come to the right place. If they want something that's ordinary, then I'm trouble.

A lot of actors I've spoken to, they talk about how it's almost like two separate gigs – one is getting the job and the other is doing the job. There seems to be a huge gulf between those two.
I used to get a big kick out of getting the job. I enjoy competitiveness. It probably goes back to sports. They were always my thing, I boxed and played baseball. I left acting for five years and went back to boxing for four years – it was something I needed to do. But I look back on it now and it was a very destructive way of acting out for me. It wasn't the healthiest choice I could have made, but . . .

You mean across the board – physically and mentally? Or just physically?
I think all around. Physically it was great for me. Mentally . . . I sustained some injuries over the years that took me some time to heal from. The adrenaline rush, and the countdown, waiting twelve weeks in between each fight to get trained, get

tuned up, get ready, get focused – there was a lot of responsibility there. It's like – if you haven't done your road work and you're not focused, you can't say, 'Let's do another take.' But I like that. And I wanted to test myself one more time again that way, before I turned into a popsicle.

Is there anything in acting that even remotely compares to it?
I guess I could have looked at acting that way early on. I did, that's what drove me. But now I can look at it that way again, because that challenge of going back to work is here again. I have a terrible reputation. For me, getting in the first time was hard. The second time was a motherfucker. The first time didn't scare me because it was about ability. Sure, I could take the occasional meeting, because I realized that they were like sizing something up on the street – dealing with it or not dealing with it, seeing what it likes or doesn't like.

But also in those meetings, often they are looking for a rogue element, too, aren't they? For an individualism?
Well, you know they talk about that rogue element in acting and it's such a lot of bullshit. The only real rebels and the only real rogues are in Angola Penitentiary behind bars, locked up twenty-three hours a day. That tag they use out here that classes somebody as a rebel or a rogue I find a bit preposterous in a way, because it's not true.

If you grow up in any tough neighbourhood and then you come to Hollywood, the concept of toughness here is pretty stupid.
Yeah. But for me, coming up and having to be hard for long stretches of years before this Hollywood thing – you can get desensitized. You can get so hard that it becomes easy. Now, the last two years almost, it's been very, very hard being good.

Because that's not your inclination . . .?
It wasn't my way, no. So it's something I have to continuously work on.

How do you do that?
I go talk to someone professionally a couple of days a week. And I talk to God a lot, more than one would imagine I would. And it's a journey unto itself. It's a very private kind of hell, because it's a hole that I dug.

Let's go back – what did you think being an actor was going to be? And why did you want to act?
I got tired, when I was about nineteen, of the boxing. I'd boxed for four years and was getting ready to turn pro. Then I got a concussion, two of them, so the doctors told me to take some time off. I accidentally got into the acting. Then something clicked, and I started doing it really hard – really did my roadwork, really wanted to learn it. I didn't want to be mediocre. And I really loved it at the time.

I think that's clear from that period of your work – that you did love it. It comes through really strongly. When did that start to go wrong?

Probably about the time I was working with – I don't want to mention any names, but I was working with a director who would yell at me before I even did anything wrong. He was yelling at me on Madison Avenue when he hired me, a month before the movie started.

Why?
He had heard of my reputation. The entourage I had at the time warranted that, I suppose. And he wanted me to know he was the boss and that he wasn't going to take any shit.

How could he have dealt with it better? I know a lot of directors admire your work considerably, but they have in the past been scared of the commitment.
Sure. I don't know. Looking back at the responsibility of that particular project and who else was in it, I don't think there was any other way that director knew how to handle that situation. I admired him a lot, and it hurt my feelings that he'd yell at me for no reason, and he wouldn't say shit to the other person.

Is this a guy who's also a tough guy by reputation?
By reputation as a general on the set, yes. He's a brilliant director. And from what I heard, I guess I did misbehave at the time without even knowing it. So maybe he was right and I was wrong.

Well, it's tricky. Because a lot of the time you want to work with people because they're not just straight actors who turn up at nine o'clock and fuck off at five. And I guess you have to take what comes with that territory, if that's what you want. You once said something which I think kind of nailed it for a lot of male actors in this town, which was – and tell me if I'm misquoting you, I'm picking this up from the press – that there was a problem with men being actors, there was something lacking, because essentially it was women's work . . .
I did say that at one time. But it's something I'd like to rephrase. I shouldn't have said it was 'women's work', because women are much stronger than men. I just think where the work went sort of south for me was that there's a level of mediocrity that the industry settles for that antagonized me.

You touched on something I've observed in a lot of younger male actors, which is an unease at what they're doing, a feeling that there's something unmanly about it.
I think that was one of the reasons I went back and tested myself with fighting. There's nothing like it. You talk to any professional and when you're sitting in that dressing room, that door opens and you hear the roar of the crowd, your stomach is going over and over and over again. Like I said, I don't think it was the right choice. I hurt a lot of people around me, doing it. But I regained the sense of accepting myself being an actor and feeling very, very fortunate that I have an opportunity to do such a profession. I had lost all appreciation of that at the time when I stopped doing it.

How do you feel now? Do you think it's worthy?
I feel great doing it. Yes, I think it's worthy – when it's honest. If you can find enough moments in the day, or in the whole from beginning to end, when it's honest and there's integrity . . . That's what's important.

It's still a pretty bizarre job, isn't it?
Well, for me it's more interesting than being a mechanic. I still get pretty bored doing this. But yet there's something safe about it – about just doing an eight-to-five job.

I remember seeing you in *Body Heat*, being very amazed by your performance there, and then following your career with interest, as everybody did. Sometimes it goes easy for an actor – there is this heat on you, and everybody wants you to succeed.
Yes, it started getting real easy for me, real quick.

You had it all. You were a sexy guy.
Well, you know, believe it or not, the whole sexy thing was a big turn-off for me. Because you want to be taken seriously as an actor, you don't want to be just 'a sexy guy'. I remember one journalist talking to me, actually crying, saying, 'Look what you've done to yourself since I saw you last.' And it made me think for a minute. That's about the time I got out of it. It was getting too hard to just put up the front.

You had an alternative, this very physical, challenging thing you could go to, for better or for worse. But I completely understand why you did that. Most actors don't have that. And because of the effect of that narcissism and the hedonism and the money, the whole trip – if you arrive here as a young person and then suddenly are successful, it seems almost impossible to get through that without some damage.
Yes, whether it tails off into some sort of narcissism or drugs or alcohol – or you turn into, like, waxed fruit, in your performances. Or you become so big that you end up living in a bubble, which happens a lot.

But I find one of the biggest problems here is the writing. I do believe that even a low-budget movie, if it's intelligently thought through, with good performances and good writing – it's probably going to work. Distribution's a problem, but . . .
Right. I just came back from doing a film where the writing was horrendous, the directing was terribly weak. Some of the actors were very, very good – some were very, very bad. The DP was unbelievably great, and we would look at each other every day like, 'We got our hands full.' And everybody was rewriting daily. In the end, though, I have to look at it and be honest, and go, 'It just wasn't on the page.' And no matter how much I would break my balls or the DP would break his balls – we didn't have enough fingers on our hands. There was no juice coming out. It

was poorly written, poorly directed, with inexperience. So there's only so much you can do to salvage something that doesn't have enough to start with – even if you're good, you're responsible, and you're there every day.

So when was the last time you picked up a script and just went, 'This is terrific'?
A young director gave me something several months ago that I felt that way about. I felt, if I could do this movie, this would do for me what the doctor ordered. And he was very enthusiastic about me doing it. Then he took it to a couple of places and they said no to me. He was disappointed, I was disappointed. Now he just made a movie that made millions of dollars.

Really? Did he ever make the other project – the one you liked?
No.

So that's sitting there. That could come back up.
I don't think so. Because sometimes when people make millions of dollars and their movie's a big hit, they don't want to come back to where they were. He didn't. It surprised me. I could have made him a hero, I know I could have.

Let's talk about money. Did you earn a lot of money?
Spent it. Spent all my money.

But it was good money?
Yes, I made good money – for the time, for ten years ago – I guess more than most people make in a lifetime. Spent it foolishly. When you get your hands on money for the first time in your life, you don't keep it in your pocket.

Do you regret that?
I regret it that I was so reckless with it, but that goes along with a lot of other things in my life that I lost along the way through that kind of behaviour.

In your family were there musicians or actors or anything like that?
No.

Where did you get the bug from?
I didn't really have the bug. I didn't know what else to do. After the sports, I was doing other things that weren't very honourable, and I thought, 'Well, I'd better get out of this line of work.'

What did your father do?
I don't know.

Your mother?
She was a nurse.

Lots of brothers and sisters?
Yeah, here and there.

So why the sport? Was that something that everybody did?
You didn't need a lot of money to do sports. And I got into it very early and I really liked it. You see athletes these days who have made it to the pros, and then, after their day's over, after six or seven years of doing it, they're lost as a pineapple for what to do with their life. That's why, after the boxing was finished for me two years ago, I felt very fortunate that I could at least go back to acting with an element in my repertoire I didn't have before, which was a tremendous amount of concentration. I realized, 'How did I get through years of acting with, on a scale of one to ten, let's say a level six of concentration?' In boxing, it had to be there all the time.

What was the first comeback fight like?
Nightmare. It was fourteen years since I had fought in the amateurs, and it was down in Florida. A lot of publicity – they all came to see me get the shit kicked out of me. That's why I trained for twelve weeks like an animal, so I didn't give them that privilege. But that was a lot of the pressure.

And you'd set that up too, right?
Well, no. I'd gone down to Florida just to hang out, and I was sparring in the old Tenth Street gym, not there any more, with some kid from Philadelphia. And some promoter who knew me from the old days, said, 'You've still got a couple of fights left in you.' I said, 'No, Tommy, no.' But it ended up he put up the money for a fight in Fort Lauderdale. I came back to LA to train with Bill Slaten, down in Watts. Then, about five weeks before the fight, I tore my right rotor cuff, and that's a bad injury for anything. And about two weeks before the fight, the promoter and his partners came to LA to talk with me. And I found out one guy put up his house, another had . . . There was no way I could back out of the fight. But I still couldn't throw a right hand. So the University of Miami doctors gave me about twelve injections the day before the fight, and the day of the fight. I still couldn't throw the right. But I kept quiet, I couldn't pull out, because the boys put up all their money.

How many rounds?
It was a six-round fight that I won, on points.

And how was the actual fight?
Dirty. It was scary walking into the ring with twenty thousand people there. I had my robe on, my knees were shaking. It was funny to see Chris Dundee coming in and going, 'What the hell are you doing back here?' I saw Roberto Duran and Nigel Benn, a lot of the guys. Nigel was sitting talking with me for a little while, then he left. And afterwards I said, 'Nigel, where in the hell did you go?' He said, 'Oh, mate, I walked down the hall, I saw the guy you were going to fight, and I had to go out and have a cigarette, I was so nervous.' I was fighting some big tattooed lump who just got out of prison. God bless him, he's passed away now.

What of?

Drugs. Great guy, though. He hit me a good right hand in the first round, he had a beautiful right hand. He was called Steve 'The Hammer' Powell. Bless him.

So you get in the ring. You're waiting for the bell to go, right? Tell me about the first moments. You'd never had a fight like this in your life before. You'd never had this audience, you'd never had this pressure.

It was the audience that was getting to me. And I couldn't really move. My natural move would be to his left, that was where his gun came from. So I had to move to the left and stutter-step to the right to stay away when he threw the right hand. We were fighting with a very thick mat, a slugger's ring, they purposely put in a slow floor. It was like fighting in a phone booth, it was like a twelve-foot ring. He caught me in the first round and I felt –

Did you see stars?

Yeah, it got a little grey there. But I had sparred with really world-class fighters to get in shape, so the club fighters weren't that difficult for me, as long as I did my roadwork. So I got through, I persevered.

Was it clear to you that you'd won?

No. I knew I had out-boxed him and hit him a lot with my left hand, but I had a couple of warnings – elbow against the throat, this and that. I didn't know how many points I had taken away from me.

And so, when you heard the decision, how did you feel?

I wasn't satisfied, because I didn't knock him out and I couldn't throw my right hand. On one level I was okay. On another level I was terribly unhappy with my performance. You know, three times I fought hurt and I shouldn't have fought. I fought in Kansas City once with broken ribs, and I was lucky – I knocked the guy out in the first round. But my trainer had told me, 'If you don't stop him in the first, we're stopping the fight.' But to fight with a hyper-extended elbow, or broken ribs or rotor cuff or a broken hand – there's no excuse when you lose. You can't say anything to the public. Nobody wants to hear it. So you've got to suck it up and accept it. My nose was broken three or four times and my cheekbone was broken once.

Did you worry about your brain?

Well, not until everybody else did.

But that must have been in your mind.

No, it was the fear of losing.

That was stronger? So how many fights did you have?

Eleven. Over three or four years. I won nine, two draws.

You lost none. Fantastic. So why did you stop at that point then?

I stopped because I took a physical examination, and my doctor recommended that it was time to stop. And I took his advice.

At that time were you also thinking about acting?
I'd take a little movie if it was in between a fight.

But was this a cathartic period to you? Did you kind of rethink stuff?
No, I wasn't thinking about anything. It was a very destructive period for me. Like I said, I hurt people around me I had no business hurting. I had a responsibility to myself and someone else that I . . . I don't know where my head was at.

Give me six pieces of music that you really like.
Knockin' on Heaven's Door, Dylan. I like *One*, U2. I like all the music I used to come out to when I fought. I like *Sweet Child of Mine* by Guns 'n Roses. I like *Delilah*, Tom Jones. There's a couple of Kristofferson songs I like.

What about books? Do you read? Did you read? Is it important to you?
I read a lot years ago, for the sake of reading. But I went through years and years where I didn't read anything. I'm just starting again to read now. I don't watch television, so –

Not at all?
Not really. I'll rent old videos, because I don't go to movies. I just don't like to, it's just something that doesn't inspire me, I guess. If there's something that I hear from somebody that I should see, and it's out, I'll wait six months.

But you still like film? It still moves you?
Yeah, it does.

Give me six movies that have touched you.
The last movie I liked a lot was Richard Harris's movie *The Field*. I like *The Deer Hunter* a lot. I like *Treasure of the Sierra Madre* a lot.

And actors?
I loved Errol Flynn. Wouldn't want to have lived his life, though – too painful. Montgomery Clift, Marlon Brando, Richard Harris, Terence Stamp – those are the guys I liked a lot.

Actresses?
I like Loretta Young. Faye Dunaway, Charlotte Rampling.

You worked with those last two, didn't you?
Yes. Had a good experience with both of them.

15   Robert Newman

Mike Figgis: Why did you choose to go into the film business?
Robert Newman: I didn't have family in the film business. But I've always loved movies, from a very early age – all kinds of movies, everything from Dean Martin to Kurosawa. I remember my grandfather taking me to see *The Wild Bunch* when I was ten years old. And I always knew I'd end up doing something in motion pictures. I studied to be a director, basically because I grew up in the seventies. The impact of motion pictures was really being felt incredibly strongly throughout the culture. I grew up in New York, reading the *New York Times*, *The New Yorker*, so the *auteurs* began to really influence me. So early on, I was able to understand that this was a Francis Ford Coppola film, this was a Martin Scorsese, a Sergio Leone, a Bob Fosse – and what that meant. Because I read Andrew Sarris in the *Village Voice*. The fact that the words '*auteur*' and '*genre*' can be written about in relatively broad-based media is because of people like Sarris and Pauline Kael.

So at that point your interest in film was to do with the art form? You wanted to explore that?
It just seemed attractive. When you find something as fascinating as I found films – found and *find* films – you want to be part of it.

Okay. How would you prioritize the following four headings, for you, in terms of art? Literature, painting, theatre, film?
Film, literature, theatre, painting.

Tell me what you think is right with the Hollywood system.
That, in a funny way, there is no system. Clearly, the distribution machine – the ability to create awareness about motion pictures. That's a marketing technique, and that has increased enormously. I've always found that there's some level of receptivity to the new, and the different, and the fresh and interesting and cool. I think there are always going to be enough people in the decision-making process whose motivation is to be part of something of value, that will endure, and be remembered in twenty or thirty years.

It's a form of capitalism, isn't it?
Absolutely.

And therefore what's right with it is what's right with capitalism?
I think for those people who get involved to make money – everything is just a return investment. Whereas that interest in being part of something interesting, cool, ground-breaking, fresh, enduring – for a lot of people, that runs parallel to the desire to make money. I don't believe all decisions are solely based on what is perceived as the highest rate of return to the dollar. I'm not sure that film-making is always the best investment anyway.

No, it's not, is it? So what's wrong with Hollywood?
Costs. I think it's probably the same in any glamour industry. You have a lot of

people who get involved for reasons of the lifestyle. I'm not trying to be judgemental, I can understand why being in the film business would be preferable to working in an investment firm, for some people. But I think there are a lot of people in the industry who have very little knowledge of or love or reverence for film. Whereas I think that, if you *do* have those, then you don't just follow what opened up last week. You have a longer perspective, and different systems for evaluation of what is true talent.

I submit that there's not that much difference between the studio system now and how it was fifty years ago. There are subtle differences that are worth talking about, just to do with economics...
When costs rise to the extent that they have, inevitably the criteria for moving forward with pictures become far more difficult. And when it comes down to it, I don't necessarily hold the investors responsible for being difficult. It's a lot of money they need to decide upon. And I think you have a lot of people – on both sides of the camera – who get used to a certain lifestyle. They say, 'Well, I need my corporate jet, I need forty people, I need my own chefs.' The films end up being bloated, to support that.

All of us who work in the film business get good money. How much of a factor has that become for you? If the money wasn't so good, would it affect your desire to stay in the business?
Not at all. I have two children now, and a wife who likes to stay home and raise them. But I would live in a smaller house and drive a less fancy car if that was the difference for me.

Why?
I love what I do. Sometimes I can't believe they pay me for it. It's a great business when you can get it right, and be effective. I'll give you an example. Sometimes I deal with executives, and I know they really love the directors I represent, and really struggle hard to help get their movies made. But, ultimately, when they are called upon to make decisions, they represent the money. So when they say, 'I think I'd like you to ask the director to give me a video cassette of a different cut of the ending' – they have to make that call. Then I get to do some work. Not that everybody I work with is always fair and reasonable and honest and good. But when push comes to shove, I work for the artist.

So you have a passion for what you do. You also have a direct contact with the artistic side of film-making, because of the way you've set up your client list. That strikes me as being not so typical for Hollywood. Would you say your position is fairly unusual within the system?
Well, I was thirty before I became an agent – which is relatively old for this business. I'd been at Miramax Films for many years, in distribution and marketing and acquisitions and publicity. I had a broad understanding of how films are

financed, how recognition and awareness are created. So when I came to the agency business, that breadth of knowledge was different to that of people who spent their entire career just trying to get someone a job. Plus, reading about films and studying films was always of enormous importance to me. So this was not a decision that I ragged out because I was weighing career options as a college graduate. This is simply what I've always wanted to be doing, in some form.

So how typical do you think that is for other agents, executives – the people who basically make up the pyramid that creates a film in a studio?
I'm not sure what the ratio is. But there are similar levels – of people who are attracted for lifestyle choices and glamour, and people who are genuinely excited by films, and have figured out some other way to be part of it. I'm not alone.

Do you feel it would be better, both for the artistic output and ultimately for the economic structure, if there were some kind of economic ceiling arrived at?
Yes, things are out of control. I would never want to see an arbitrary ceiling. I'd rather see the model closer to the record industry, where you have defined royalties and participations. Most of the people I work with, they don't necessarily want to profit unduly when others are still in a lost position. But it is an emotionally charged situation when they feel they've created something that other people are enriching themselves upon. So I would rather see more true and fair economic participation. For any director to be in a net position with a studio is ridiculous – even a first-time director. I understand the logic of having a low fee. But if someone creates a film that makes millions of dollars, then receives statements that are clearly designed to enrich the studio, with no participation for themselves – that creates an environment where, once people do have any leverage, they will seek to get as much money as possible up front – which carries the vicious circle forward.

So is it a problem of the same old creative accountancy? Has that put things out of control?
No. Marketing costs are incredibly high. Union costs are high. I don't think artists' fees *per se* are what's determining rising film costs. But as someone who represents artists, obviously I'm aware that when someone does get twenty million dollars for a film, everybody else who works on it certainly is not in a mood to cut their price.

I've noticed that people in Europe – maybe even people outside of New York and Los Angeles – have a concept of Hollywood as a kind of well-oiled, cohesive industrial complex. Mostly they're thinking of big-budget things like *Armageddon* and so on. You're connected with big-budget film-making, but also very strongly with low-budget stuff that works within the system. Could you explain a little about just how complex this collective industry is here?
The decisions to make motion pictures are more anarchic than people would

believe. There's less stuff by design than by accident. The true need comes from the distribution machinery – the impetus to create a number of films per year as regular product for theatres, and for television and home video. Studios are locked into a system, and they have their key seasons, summer and Christmas, which make up the bulk of the theatrical attendance in this country. How things get filled on the product side varies wildly. And so I think people are more open to different voices, and different kinds of films. This is a business where enormous amounts of money are spent on what are essentially test models, every time – it's not like supplying Coca-Cola. You spend eighty million dollars, a hundred million dollars – you have no idea. You can do all the pre-market testing in the world. Until the product is made and able to be seen in some format, it's pretty scary anticipating whether or not anyone's going to actually want to buy *tickets* for this.

When I walk into a bookstore in any town, I'm always taken with how many books have just been published. And I'm becoming more and more aware of the kind of shark-like in-fighting that goes on within the publishing business. The music industry is the same. And the film industry is the same too. It seems to me that there's too much product. And there aren't enough venues. Is there any truth in that?
In terms of the amount of films made, the numbers seem to keep escalating, to a small degree. So, are there too many films made? I think part of the problem is that a lot of films are released at the peak seasons. I think films are capable of having huge audiences throughout the year. But there is a glut sometimes, which makes a problem in creating awareness. Exhibitors have built a lot more screens. But there is this whole system of trying to maximize a return investment, creating nationwide awareness, grabbing as many screens as possible for the films that seem to be working. Whether you can get two thousand theatres whenever you want is a different proposition.

How great a part do you think that sex plays in the system of film-making in this town? A lot of time is spent talking about it.
Sex in terms of what?

In terms of the product, actually on screen. And sex as part of, if you like, a system of barter – as a way of ascending within the system.
Well, in terms of motion pictures, I would welcome a greater exploration of adult sexuality – not MTV sex scenes, but I would love to see a *Carnal Knowledge* for the nineties. Otherwise – as you know, I'm married with two kids, and I tend to go home nights. It's a flirty business – my wife is always amazed at the amount of kissing that goes on just at premières. I guess, when you take it to the next step, and people are having dinner and drinking with one another – I think the lines get crossed, in terms of seller–buyer, flirting–not flirting. Because the communication is all personal, trying to excite other people about your ideas, in a very social format . . .

Often, Hollywood is characterized as male-dominated, chauvinistic. And there's a notion that actresses, who tend to be young and attractive, are subject to a form of prostitution – that the quickest way for an actress to climb the ladder is on her knees. How much of a myth do you think that is? Has it always been that way? Is it acceptable?

To me, it's almost like drugs. If you're not involved in any shape or form, you tend not even to notice what is going on in the next room. I would certainly discourage anybody I know from basing their decisions about who to be in business with on who will sleep with them. And I tend to be idealistic, in that I think talent will always find some natural level of recognition. I would certainly discourage anybody from letting themselves be exploited, just because it seemed like the path of least resistance.

But do you think that the system here is fair both to men and women? Or is it more biased in favour of men?

Probably it has been, historically. But now you see many more women heading production companies, being president of production at studios, being chairpersons. And that will probably continue. I think people are forced, by virtue of the competitiveness, to hire the best individual – one who hopefully will keep them employed, and not lose the company. Because of the economics, there's less of a good ol' boy network. I'm not sure anybody can afford to lose money by keeping their best friend in charge of the company.

You see most of the films that come out of this community. In those, do you think women are represented as accurately, or as interestingly as they might be?

I wonder if men are? I never look at it that way. But do women sometimes play the obligatory love interest? Yes. If you look at who gets paid the most on movies, based on the ability to sell tickets – they're still primarily men. So therefore everybody else tends to play a subsidiary or less interesting role on that production.

But you'd like to see a more realistic portrayal of sexuality, 'a *Carnal Knowledge* for the nineties'. We don't seem to be making those kinds of movies. I'll stop beating this dead dog in a moment, but has it got something to do with the structures of studios, the kind of thinking behind why films are green-lit? Why aren't more interesting stories about men and women getting through the net?

I think certain kinds of broad-based storytelling have always been able to captivate a large audience. If you look back at the glory days of the seventies, movies like *Airport* were way outgrossing *Midnight Cowboy* or *Carnal Knowledge*. I think if budgets rise, studios try to make the broadest-based entertainment for those prices. It's economically determined. I'm not sure it's a political agenda as such.

So is it naive to waste time arguing about equality within this entertainment industry? I sometimes feel that a lot of time is wasted talking about it. It's like, 'Should we not be expecting it here? And if we're not, is there room for it in the

smaller end of the industry?' That would be a better use of energy.
I agree with you. 'For my hard-hitting drama about men and women, is it a conspiracy if I'm being deprived of a fifty-million-dollar-budget?' You can have that argument all day long, up and down the lots of Warner or Paramount or Sony. Is one better served trying to readjust the budget and seek a more hospitable home at Miramax, Artisan, New Line, Fine Line? I think sometimes people want to be paid full freight in all forms for defying the system.

Good point. Let's talk about that for a moment. Money corrupts – we would kind of accept that?
It corrupts some – the corruptible.

I would argue that all money corrupts, in some way. Already, with some money, I'm better off than I was – it's a question of whether you say, 'That's enough for me.' You are known for representing directors who initially did low-budget things – but a lot of us have blossomed under your wing, right? Do you notice people coming in, then becoming aware of how much money there is out there, and then getting fucked up?
Money corrupts, fame corrupts, power corrupts. There are people who are arrogant ass-holes who have no money. They just have less of an opportunity to exert their arrogance. But it is who they are. Then there are people who are thoughtful and generous, and they have no money. If they get some – I think it gives them a greater potential to realize that which they are. A lot of the people I work with, they made their decisions at an early stage about what movies they wanted to make, and how they wanted to make them, because that's what they thought was cool and interesting. And always there was someone to dangle a carrot and say, 'Well, if you do this there's another dollar for you.' They tended to resist that. Occasionally, in some cases, their appetite and their willingness to make sacrifices in order to realize stuff – that changes with success. They expect things will be different and now they will be given *carte blanche* to do things their way.

Let's take a young director who's come from England or France – the new kid in town, has made one successful low-budget film, demonstrated some talent. The great thing about this town is that it will immediately offer you a lot of money to come and do that same thing for them, right? That can be a very corrupting thing for a director.
Without question.

How much do you keep an eye on that? How much is that part of your judgement of who you're going to represent?
A lot. I think people who are afraid to say no, who are scared that if they don't say yes to this project that Sony's offering, then they'll never get anything again – their desperation to make a film supersedes their desire to make a good film. They grab on to something, they convince themselves that they can make it right.

The money dangled in front of them becomes attractive. And then, when people argue with them, 'Why don't you make it *this* way?', they've lost their compass. They've lost the ability to say, 'I'm not going to allow myself to be talked into making choices that are not mine. By my estimation, I can't make a good film that way. So I'll say thank you very much, because I am confident in my abilities, and confident I'll find a home someplace else that does allow me that.' People who jump at the first thing, who are swept away because the chairman of the studio is now being nice to them, instead of focusing on the very difficult question of 'How do I make a good film?' – at the end of it they're left with nothing.

Do you offer counselling on this matter?
I think, instinctively, you start to determine pretty early where people's desires are, what their motivations are. And, for whatever reason, very early on, I'm able to see eye to eye with people – understand what it is they want to be doing, and whether or not I'm going to be able to be helpful in the process.

This is kind of a dopey question but, given that Los Angeles is a unique city, specifically designed around a freeway system, where people just do not walk – how do you think this affects the way films are made here and the way stories are written?
Interesting . . . Well, I'm a native New Yorker, where you're on the street and you run up against every stratum of society. Whereas in Los Angeles you're in your nice foreign car, you identify with the specific *milieu* of people of your class. Does that impact the way you make decisions or the way you perceive life? It probably plays a part.

I had sort of a theory. I believe that the car does allow people a degree of protection within their culture that is unique – an incredibly comfortable existence, completely sheltered from poverty or cultural deprivation or whatever. The car on the freeway gives an experience very much akin to the way a film is projected – we have a wonderful stereo system, we have a widescreen windshield, we can take all our phone calls in the car . . . And if that impacts the way films are written and made here – that very unreal world of stress-free niceness and softness – then we are offering a diet of escapism that is immensely attractive to the very deprived world that we avoid. That was the only unfortunate conclusion I came to.
I think there's probably a degree of truth in that. But to me Los Angeles is like the New York Stock Exchange; it's where the money changes hands. But ultimately there's a wheat field growing in Chicago, and pork bellies, they're the real industries that do the creating. To me, directors are the creators. They're trying to create a story they'll maybe be working on for a year and a half. Now, every day on the Stock Exchange, there are all sorts of attendant changes in the motion picture business, which is fine – which is why agents and studio heads live here. But for the creators, what opened that week and what the number one film is in *Variety* – these momen-

tary blips are distracting. I don't know if that's what they should be focused upon. So, I'm not sure that for creators to live here is necessarily the most –

I think creators live in their minds. Quite frankly, jail is probably the best place for a writer – put him in isolation and his imagination will blossom and be so fertile. What really worries me about this town is the middle men and junior executives within the studio system, who take responsibility for script development, and the sort of soft erosion that takes place in storytelling through all the script conferences and committee stages. If the people who make up the majority of voices – which are predominantly cowardly, because committees are by nature cowardly – are people living in this cocoon environment, who are not in themselves especially creative – I think that has had a catastrophic effect on the way stories are told within Hollywood. I've thought about this a lot, and that's my conclusion. The evils are not necessarily within the capitalist studio system, or the agent system –
Thank you.

Is this an ageless community, do you find? Has it always been youth-dominated?
Well, once you got television, you lost an older, married audience – or it vastly eroded. The people who buy movie tickets now are predominantly younger people, younger single people. And obviously there is a desire to keep in touch with the audience.

Do you think film has an impact on the lives of ordinary people?
Sometimes. It's always hard to say to what extent. Take the Beatles – what did they do? Did more people take LSD? Did more people grow their hair? Hard to say. I sometimes think the changes are subtler than that, in terms of how people define themselves, what they think is cool or interesting, what their role models become. But, yes, I think it does shake people up.

How important are the critics here?
Important for certain kinds of films. For other kinds of films, irrelevant.

The people you represent, the kind of films that we make, if I can be so collective – how important for us are the critics within America?
Very. For *There's Something About Mary*, it's great to have great reviews, but if people believe they're going to laugh, then that's its own attraction. For a drama perceived as being stronger, more challenging – if it's flagged off, it's certainly not helpful. For actors and actresses – look at how many of them have got great reviews out of your films. It doesn't matter that they haven't all grossed two hundred million dollars. The people who have taken part in them have seen their work lionized, extolled. And that becomes incredibly important in your business, to continue to attract money and actors. That jive with your perception?

Sure. And to continue on that riff – collectively, the critics of, let's say, the *New York Times*, *LA Times*, Siskel and Ebert, *Time*, *Newsweek*, *Rolling Stone* – how would you characterize them? Pretty good, average, not good enough?

It's a long way from the heyday. There are some great writers out there, and people that I tend to agree with. The political agendas I find less interesting, I think it becomes unnatural to view things through a prism, a predetermined political agenda of right or wrong. I don't want to beat up on political correctness, but I do see that – a good action film gets flagged off because of violence or whatever. I do think sometimes when I see obvious agendas and the work is solely filtered through that, that's not impressive. But I think most people who write about film aren't getting rich. I think most of them do wish to see good movies. I would put the track record of the New York film critics up against the Academy of Motion Pictures over a thirty-year span, in terms of what films we'll look back on and remember as being worthwhile and significant. So I think they tend to do a good job. I tend to be in a better mood when people I work with get amazing reviews.

We tend to like the critics who like us. Let's detach from that for a moment. Is there any way of improving the level of criticism, in a way that would be of more use to (a) the audience and (b) the film-maker? For example, limiting the amount of time a critic could be a film critic, given that it's got such a built-in wear-and-tear factor?

The thing I miss – when I was younger, critics would not print reviews until the day after a film opened, almost in recognition of theatre, like opening nights. You didn't go into a film with as much awareness of somebody else's point of view. I think a lot of the sense of surprise and discovery has been taken away. That's not simply because of critics, it's the success of the marketing machinery in trumpeting the product for so long, which plays into how films are released. So there's no point in complaining about it, it's the nature of the distribution machine. But, for someone who first and foremost loves films, it's sort of a drag. Pauline Kael would write four-page reviews of a film. And the only people who would read something like that were people who really cared, who engaged. They wanted more than just a consumer review, they wanted to really examine a film and explore all the issues and problems and accomplishments within it. I'm not sure – maybe the work itself doesn't have the cultural relevance it did twenty-five years ago – different times. And audiences view films as another entertainment option in the multiplex, as opposed to something of true relevance and importance, as maybe people once thought of them.

Mike Figgis: Why did you choose to go into films?
Salma Hayek: Because when I was about seven, I saw a film called *Willy Wonka and the Chocolate Factory*. And in this film there was a river made of chocolate, and the flowers were candy, and you could drink a soda and fly, then burp yourself down. I thought, 'There is a place in the world where you can create any kind of world you would like to live in. I can live in the sixteenth century, or the year 2000' – which seemed so far away back then. So I found that this is how to cheat humanity, in a way. You can live many lives instead of just one and experience many different things, and I became fascinated by that possibility.

When you had this particular fantasy, where were you?
Coatzacoalcos, Veracruz, a little place in the south of Mexico.

Did you see a lot of film?
We had one movie theatre that I can remember. And I could only go on Sundays, when they showed a matinée for kids. It was completely packed. Some of the films were Mexican, and some of them were subtitled, things like *Tarzan*.

But cinema had a different resonance for you there than it would for someone your age here in Los Angeles.
Yes, because it was an effort to go. It was a ritual. And it was very special. We didn't have that many things to do there.

What kind of a family were you in?
My father is an entrepreneur. He constructed and maintained the oilfields in the south of Mexico, where about eighty per cent of the oil came from.

Did you have any kind of showbiz in your family?
No. But my mom was an opera lover – she's quite eccentric. Not a lot of people even knew about opera, but she had this hobby of discovering voices. We'd go to a restaurant and a waiter would start talking, and she'd go, 'Oh, you're a baritone. Do you sing?' And he'd go, 'A little bit', then she'd say, 'Do this.'

Can you sing, or play an instrument?
No. Trust me, she tried. But she was always discovering this in everybody else. She would adopt all these people and give them scholarships. One girl went to the Metropolitan School ten years later, thanks in part to my mother really being behind her.

So how did you make the transition from a fantasy of 'This would be lovely', to realizing that you could become a film actress? How old were you?
Well, in my teens I was too embarrassed to say it was what I wanted to do, because it wasn't hip among the people I hung out with. Everybody had different aspirations, and they were going to college.

A lot of actresses have told me that they decided to become film actresses when they were teenagers. Most of them are beautiful. And presumably as a teenager you were already quite beautiful. How much did that affect your decision to act in films?

Well, when I first wanted to do films at the age of eight or nine, I was just a very skinny sort of a tomboy. It wasn't as if I realized I was good-looking and said, 'Okay, let's make something out of it.' In fact, I probably wanted to do the opposite. So that when I did realize I was good-looking, I was doubly embarrassed about acting and I thought, 'I'm going to be a politician' – because it's sort of less obvious. Most of my friends wanted to get married and have kids, and mostly that's what they did. But I said, 'I'm going to study international relations and be a diplomat.'

You had a good education?

Fairly good. I skipped a couple of years in school and went to college in Mexico City, aged sixteen – got good grades. But because I was pretty, I would get picked out of a classroom. 'Would you like to be in this commercial?' 'Look, we're doing this short film . . .' And I made it into my head that it was destiny calling me. I'm sitting here in this classroom, trying to make a decent living, and destiny is telling me, 'What the heck are you doing here?' Then someone needed a really young girl for some low-budget B movie. Somebody saw me in school, I was tested and I did a good job. But then I had to be naked in the film. I said no. But it was very painful to say no, because that's what I wanted to do. I had to overcome a lot of things, this nudity and kissing a stranger. And coming from a Catholic family, there was a point where I wouldn't even swear. So, secretly, I started taking acting classes.

Say I'm from Mars, I don't know what films are, I don't know what acting is, Tell me what you do for a living. Describe what that is.

I represent fragments of life. I detach myself from my everyday life and create someone else's life. And it's not real life but you make it real for that moment. You become someone else, because you are in the environment in which that person would be living. You still retain some of yourself. But you also find something there that you didn't know about yourself, that this person enables you to know.

What do you get out of it?

You get the satisfaction of that journey to something that you didn't know.

And are you bold? Will you go anywhere?

Yes. I think so.

What are the areas in those journeys that worry you the most? From a point of view of vanity, or of being a Catholic girl or whatever?

It doesn't worry me. It's painful and scary to detach yourself from the things that make you comfortable. But that's one of the most interesting things about the process. Letting go of that is also freeing, once you've done it.

Are you confident with your body, for example, now?
Yes. There are some things that I wish were different.

So, generally, you don't think, 'Where's the camera? Ooh, I don't like my bottom, I don't like my shoulders', and so on?
No, Mike. This is something else that we have to talk about. I'll explain something to you. I have like a double personality. I believe that we have a feminine and a masculine side. My masculine side, my memory of a man is my father, and he's a fearless businessman. My feminine side, which in my memory is my mom, she's a true artist. And it's necessary to have that combination in this business. It's like two people living inside of you.

A marriage.
But it's a great marriage because the man in me, most of the time, protects that creative female side. Sometimes you have to be extremely strong and fearless. But to be a true artist, you have to remain very, very vulnerable. So you must be schizophrenic and have this double personality to survive in this business at the level we're talking about. And I have it. So I do films sometimes that do not require a lot of the artist – films that I know I get because of the way I look. When I'm doing those parts I'm aware of where the camera is, how my body looks. I'm very good at knowing how to make the best of what I have as a businesswoman.

Do you always put yourself first? Or – you say sometimes you have to 'let go' – is that a complete letting go, where the businesswoman can take a hike?
It can't be. If I'm doing a film with Barry Sonnenfeld, I do as I'm told. I love to make the director happy. I know I have to lose four pounds for this because I know I'm going to be wearing this skirt. Once we get to the set I try my best to convince them to do this instead of that, to my eye. But with a director like Barry, who has a vision of a style of comedy, you have to just do what you're told. I don't fight that. But it's good to discuss a lot before, when I'm creating the character – to ask all the questions and have all the friction, so that you can really discover this character. If the businesswoman comes in there in the middle of it, then you can't really have a journey, you don't go anywhere. So she has to stay away.

You live here now, right? You're now pretty much a member of this system they call Hollywood – that is, a collection of people making money in the same way. And you seem to observe it quite carefully. What do you think is good or right about Hollywood right now?
Mike, I don't think I can decide what's good or right about Hollywood. It's more of a matter of fact – it is what it is, and we're in it.

Okay, let me elaborate. You said you wanted to act in films because at an early age you were affected, entranced by the idea of this fantasy. I'm sure you didn't come here to get rich.
No.

But the fact is, now you probably are quite rich. And you're in a system where that element is very strong. It's capitalism, in other words, that we are involved in. Now, I think there are good things in capitalism, and there are other things that upset me quite a lot.

For me, it's not so much about the money, it's about the power. You say, 'Well, now you're a part of Hollywood.' But I really felt as if Hollywood made a very big effort not to let me in. Because I'm Mexican. You're English, but English is what they look up to. Mexican is what they look down on. I mean, look at the immigration laws, the people that have it the hardest are Mexicans. It was very, very hard. First of all, they have a very specific image for Mexicans that I didn't quite fit. Mexicans are gang members, on welfare with kids since they were fifteen, and they wear make-up and they're tacky and cheesy. They think we're uneducated and unsophisticated and have no sense of style.

Do you find that ironic?

Very – because I think America has the worst education imaginable. I mean, just for example, I was watching the Jay Leno show when he was running round asking people, 'How many planets are in the galaxy?' And people would say, 'A hundred?' And the two people out of the fifty that knew there are nine – they couldn't name them.

Have you done the Jay Leno show?

Yes. Actually I'm doing it today again.

It fascinates me. Because every actress that's on there seems duty bound to wear a very short skirt, and to flirt with him as if he's funny and fascinating and a very sexy guy. And he always manages to say something quite smutty to them, about nudity or whatever.

The first time I went there, I had done *Desperado*, quite a sexy film. They call you to do a pre-interview, and the show's producers said, 'You know, because you're so sexy, we would really like it if you wore a really short skirt, showed some cleavage, whatever.'

It's great to hear this.

I was shocked. But then I said, 'Oh, okay.' I wanted to get on the show. But I showed up in a man's suit. I didn't have any money at the time and Hugo Boss was the only designer who would sponsor me, because I had a friend who worked there. Jay Leno made a comment like, 'We saw you in the movie and you were so sexy, now you're dressed like a man.' And I said, 'Yeah, but underneath this suit I'm wearing the most fantastic lingerie.' And then he was very, very happy.

So you played him, in other words.

Of course. I always play him, Mike. I always play them all. You have to.

Does that give you problems?

It gives me pleasure.

Why?

Because they think they're so smart. But I look at these very important executives, big men with big titles. And I see nothing but fear in their eyes.

Fear of losing their jobs. Fear of ridicule. Fear of trying anything different. In order to create something magnificent you have to be brave, adventurous. That's what their jobs are about. But most of them are terrified of exactly that.

What do they think of women? This a generalization, I know.

Most of the women's parts on offer just reflect the image that men have of us. And it's very hard to understand our nature – we're quite complex, as you well know. There are men writing parts for women who are afraid of women, or dislike women, or just plain don't understand them.

Ally Sheedy was praising the strong women's roles of the forties and fifties. And I asked her, what was the point where this suddenly took a dip and we started making films about boys for boys. She thinks it was the moment that women not only started to, but were *expected* to take their clothes off in films. The respect for women in films dipped and the way women were written for changed also.

But you know why, Mike – because it worked. Women taking their clothes off brought a lot of people into the theatre. And it is a business, sadly enough. I've been in a few action movies, I am an expert on being the chick. I think it's beginning to change, by the way. But male-oriented films have just made more money.

Okay, a stupid question. Why don't women in this town get together more? Why is there no sisterhood? What is it that stops them from forming a group and saying, 'Enough'?

Maybe we're more competitive. Maybe we are our worst enemies. My father has a story about Mexicans that I think could work for women. A guy is selling two buckets of crabs, one with a cover, one without. Somebody asks, 'What's in that bucket?' 'Crabs.' 'And what's in the other?' 'Also crabs.' 'Why does one have a top and not the other?' 'Well, the uncovered crabs are Mexican crabs, and the others are Japanese crabs.' 'What's the difference?' 'The Japanese crabs try to give each other a hand to get out, so I have to cover them. But the Mexicans, when one tries to get out, another one pulls him down, because he wants to be the first.' And I think that probably works a little bit with women too.

I agree. In this business, you're taught to be competitive. You're taught as soon as you come in, if you don't take the opportunity no one else will do it for you. Do you think that very element is something that is exploited within you?

No. Because I've gone through so much as a woman, that makes me feel connected and bonded with other women who have probably gone through similar things. But there's competition between women because there are only so many good men. And in a way, there are only so many good parts in the film industry. And because we've been traumatized by our men being unfaithful with other women, we tend to be suspicious of each other.

Do you have a manager?
No. I did. I have an agent, I have a lawyer.

We all have these people trailing around after us. When you started out, how much influence did your agents, your managers, all these people have on you?
None. I had a very strong influence on them. They wanted to do things one way, like they always did. And I made them understand that I wasn't like the other clients. We had to fight a battle that had not been won for many, many years. And therefore it could not be fought with the same strategy.

How did they take that?
Badly, until I started being right so many times. But at the start they just said, 'Oh, she's crazy, that doesn't work in this town.' And I said, 'Precisely.'

You came in with some kind of clarity about what you wanted. Is that common?
Mike, I think I came with some clarity about who I was. That's not so common. I think that if you don't know who you are, you are not as strong to come into this madness.

Why does it go wrong for so many actors and actresses here?
Oh, I feel a little uncomfortable talking about other actors because it depends on the individual so much. I think there are two basic schools: actors who want to pursue their art and nothing else – because otherwise they feel belittled or insulted. That's where they get their strength, that's how they can survive the madness – by staying true to their principles. Then there are actors who want big stardom and commercial success, that's where they feel comfortable and where they think they can survive. But they're both fragile positions – you're vulnerable in the second position because if something doesn't work then you don't know who you are any more. But you're vulnerable in the first position too, because we all seek art as an expression because we want to be heard, and if nobody hears you, you're left feeling, 'Nobody understands what I'm doing.'

Is it possible to be in this town and not be badly affected by the money?
I can only tell you about my relationship with money, I don't know how it falls on other people. I don't make a lot of money.

Really? Didn't you once talk about how much money you make?
No, no. It's a joke, because you get caught up into 'Who makes more than who?' and it's tacky and embarrassing. That your salary is printed in a magazine and everybody knows – it's just cheesy and cheap – no class. I don't want to talk about how much I make. I can tell you that I'm underpaid.

Relative to whom? To Julia Roberts, or to a coal miner, or . . .?
Oh no, no. You can't do that. You cannot measure yourself according to someone else. I am underpaid according to my level of popularity and the amount of
people that I bring into the theatres. They don't want to acknowledge that. I came
into this business as a complete unknown to the American market, but the thirty-
two million Spanish-speaking people in this country knew exactly who I was, and
they paid their $7.50. None of the films I've had an important part in have
bombed. They all opened. Surprise, surprise, my co-star's next film bombs. But
nobody gives me credit for that.

That doesn't surprise me, I think you're a star.
I don't understand it, but two years ago *Variety* took a poll of the most popular
movie people on the Internet, and I was the most popular woman – above Julia
Roberts. The guys were Mel Gibson, Tom Cruise. So that was a shock for me too.

That's amazing.
I did a film called *Fools Rush In*, a seventeen-million-dollar film. It opened ten
million, it made forty million domestically. And Columbia thought my co-star
would open it – he's wonderful and has a TV show that is very, very popular. But
the truth was – and Columbia know this – that the Latin areas were very, very
high. And still I make very little money. But you know what? I'm fine with that.
I'm a businesswoman. I do commercials, I have an MCI campaign in Mexico,
and I live well. It's about the power.

**Listen. I made a film that cost nothing and made a lot of money, and I still
haven't seen any of that money. But then I got a really good deal on my next
film. So, in one sense, I'm happy. But another part of me, my businessman,
goes, 'That's not right. Somebody's made a lot of money out of this.' If someone's making money from you, you should be acknowledged for what you've
done, and it's a form of racism that you're not.**
So now I'm producing a film. It's about a very strong woman. And I've been
working on it for two years, I've had to fight so hard, but I have a back end that is
quite good.

A real back end? You might actually make some money from it?
Yes. But it cost a year of negotiations. So I'm dealing with it. I want to be respected.
I have worked hard for it.

Are you an ambassador for your own culture?
I don't want to take that flag; it's too poetic. I want to say I'm a selfish woman
who has suffered what they have suffered. I am looking after my own interest,
but it would give me a tremendous amount of joy to know that, by accom-
plishing anything for myself . . . I just hope I become something they can be
inspired by.

Name me five films – not the best five films ever made, but five films that come to your mind that you think are beautiful.
The Conformist, Nights of Cabiria, The Graduate, A Streetcar Named Desire, Toto The Hero.

Five directors?
Martin Scorsese, Fellini. I like Buñuel, I like Pedro Almodóvar.

Give me five pieces of music. It can be something you just heard on the radio that's cool . . .
D'jour de a moni – very sad. I like *Rigoletto*. *Un Poco Max.* I like *Veracruz* – this is my state, where I come from. I love *The Gypsy Kings*. 'I'll Be Seeing You' by Noël Coward. I love Billie Holiday.

Five books. They can all be Spanish. They can be plays, poetry . . .
I like *Romeo and Juliet*. *Macbeth*. *Summer and Smoke*. I like a book I read a year ago called *High Fidelity*. There's a book by a Lebanese poet, I don't know in English, the title is *The Crazy Man*.

What's the stupidest thing anyone ever said to you in Hollywood?
There are so many. Probably this – I was up for a film, the director Walter Hill really wanted me, it was set on a spaceship. The studio said, 'A Mexican in space?'

What do you think about the system of auditioning – reading, sometimes with the casting director . . .?
I think someone can give a wonderful audition but not be able to carry a film. And then sometimes, someone can give a terrible audition because of the circumstances, but they would have done something wonderful in the picture. But it's only natural for a director to want an idea of what the actor is capable of doing.

Is there anything we can do to give the actor a better opportunity? Maybe a couple of rules for casting directors to stick with?
If they let you read with an actor instead of the casting director, it always helps. No offence to casting directors, but, Jesus Christ – you're acting to this person who's just reading, and staring at you to see what the hell you're doing. They're not really there with you. How can you do anything in that situation?

And what about going on tape?
Mike, I love the camera. I have no inhibitions.

17   Julie Yorn

Mike Figgis: First, Julie, how would you describe what you do?
Julie Yorn: I'm a talent manager, which is to say that I represent actors, actresses, writers, directors.

And what do you do for them?
In some ways I function like an agent – guiding their careers, finding the best work opportunities. But because I work with a very specific number of clients, I have more time and, one could say, more of a mandate to create those opportunities.

Is the role of the manager a new phenomenon, or has it always been around?
I think management really started with comedians and musicians, primarily. In those areas, agents are really in charge of booking – they get gigs for their clients, and they make sure people get paid. Whereas managers are about really partnering the clients, helping them choose their material and create their images.

So Judy Garland would have had a manager . . .
And Jackie Gleason in his day. People who started as stand-up comics in the Catskills – that's where managers started too.

And they lived happily there in that swamp for quite a long time.
Yes. In terms of actors and certainly film-makers, it was a very uncommon thing to have a manager, until the last ten years.

People say that Mike Ovitz was a significant figure in Hollywood history because, in his time, the agency became a different beast. Was it at the same moment when the manager became significant?
I think so. With the growth of CAA and the centralization of power in Hollywood in the mid to late eighties, managers became an alternative for artists who felt they weren't getting the personalized attention they once got.

How did that come about, the Ovitz phenomenon? Previously, there were certain high-powered agents in relation to high-powered actors. Barbra Streisand's agent was a powerful woman, and so on.
But there was a much more level playing field, before the various mergers and the creation of CAA. There were more agencies, smaller agencies, which were able to represent important clients. CAA started a trend of trying to take the power back from the studios and put more of it in the hands of the talent and their representatives.

I always got the impression it was more in the hands of the representative. The actor often ends up as a pawn in a big political chess game between the agency and the studio.
That's true. I try to figure out a way to bridge that gap a little bit. As a representative you can have power, through packaging a project and creating something, much in the way a studio has that power. The goal is to empower your client to be a partner in the process. That's what CAA was able to do in the eighties, and because of that, talent also has a lot of power.

But one of the problems in Hollywood now is that a lot of actors feel that they are merely commodities. And if they're lucky, they're an expensive one, and if they're not, they're a disposable one. I would hear actresses say, 'I'm just the sixth blonde at CAA' or 'I can't even get a job at CAA because they've already got twelve blondes aged between thirty and thirty-six.' Presumably this is where you came in then?

Exactly. You found that artists were insecure about being represented by smaller agencies, understandably so, because they felt they were missing opportunities by not being in a protective environment that was really making everything happen. So people flocked to CAA where they felt they wouldn't be left out in the cold. And inevitably there was just this certain number of agents representing a certain number of artists, and that system imploded in a sense. Because inevitably only one-third of that list is getting the proper attention, depending on their 'heat' at that moment. Then you had probably a big group of established artists making seven-figure fees but not getting their calls returned by their agents in the same day. If you're not getting your calls returned, I can guarantee you that no one is sitting there for hours during the day thinking about planning the course of your career.

You've touched on the insecurity of actors. Now we have a system where an actor may be paying three people fairly large sums of money just to feel that he has an equal opportunity. Isn't that a bit of a mess?

It's a huge mess. Most actors do have to keep a couple of people on the payroll to make sure that they're in the game. It's an incredibly competitive time – fewer movies are being made, fewer movies are successful . . .

So the bottom line is, in order to succeed as an actor coming into this business, you should be prepared to take on a manager and an agent.

I think so.

Now, a big agency is a billion-dollar corporation representing so much talent – directors, actors, writers. Why doesn't the corporation just take care of business, and why don't agents and managers become one and the same? I mean, you're a highly respected manager. What is an agent doing for your client that you're not doing?

Well, an agent – through the resources of the agency they're at – can know as early as possible about what opportunities are available, and can try to make sure that an actor meets a director at the right time. But ideally, at the same time, an agent is also thinking in the long term, and plotting the course of that actor's career. And ideally a manager is not just sitting behind their desk plotting that same course, but is also out there making opportunities. I suppose it's about having a bigger, stronger team. Because few actors can afford the illusion that great opportunities come to them on a platter – there are three or four of them in this town at any one time who have that luxury. The rest have to look in the nooks and crannies for where the opportunities are.

There is another difference. Legally an agent cannot be involved in the production of a film, but a manager can. Is that an attraction to you personally, the fact that you can also produce?

Definitely. It allows you to be very creative. The tragedy is when managers start serving their own agendas over their clients' agendas.

There's a situation right now, a lawsuit between Garry Shandling and Brillstein-Grey, isn't there? Can you talk a little about that? Because it's to do with 'double-dipping' and I don't think people outside of Hollywood will understand.

Well, ethically, as a manager, double-dipping is a complete no-no. That means that if you are producing a client's project and taking a fee as producer, you're certainly not taking a commission on the client at the same time. That would be unethical. The attraction for your client should be that you're partners – you get a fee, and they're absolved of the commission.

In fact, that sounds like a very healthy relationship, because you're both embarking on an equal-risk situation.

In principle it is. I've had that relationship with my clients, and it's been incredibly healthy thus far. In the Brillstein-Grey instance, not knowing too much about it and not knowing the principals that well, I can only say that it seems like, after years of a very healthy relationship between manager and client, something happened that embittered one towards the other. I suppose Garry Shandling could take the position that Brad Grey benefited from his talent of creating a show, and that he used it to further his own business interests and those of his company. The flip side of that is that perhaps Garry Shandling is a brilliant artist, but not so savvy a businessman.

Isn't that the oldest problem in the book between artists and managers?

Exactly. They can function incredibly well together, but when one says, 'Who's more important than the other', it gets complicated. Because it's hard to say.

There is the phenomenon of actors who come in as fledglings, take on management, and obviously they have an agent. Then they become successful, start thinking that they no longer need a manager, and jump ship. That happens fairly regularly, doesn't it.

That's a universal trait in human nature. It happens in marriages. People change, success goes to their heads a little, perhaps they feel that they didn't really need that person. In a healthy relationship I suppose one would say, 'This person not only contributed, but continues to contribute.' But as people's businesses get more complicated, there is a possibility that they outgrow their representative.

So how would you deal with that?

I hope that I could rise to the occasion involved with any client that had the great fortune to grow at that rate. I think it's the inevitable pitfall of being a representative. In the end, I think there's no such thing as loyalty, really.

It's a service business. You have to keep performing for the client or it doesn't make sense for the client. And I wouldn't recommend to a client to keep paying somebody a certain percentage of their income if it wasn't continuing to contribute to their career in a meaningful way.

When you first meet a prospective client, it must cross your mind, as it would in any relationship, whether this person is a lifer or a short-timer – meaning, 'Is this someone who could be really big for five years because they're what Hollywood wants right now? Or is this someone who might not come to fruition for another five or ten years?' I know that you nurtured Sam Jackson for a long time, and he was a very respected actor, but not the huge success he is now. But how do you or your peers deal with the morality of making those choices? Because I've heard so much about the damage that happens to some actors as they start to fail, at a very early age, like athletes.
That's why I'm not in the sports business. It's too tragic. For me, it's not good business to take on a client, and really put the time into building both the career and a mutually trusting relationship, if I don't think there's longevity there. Sam Jackson's a perfect example. I looked at him and I thought, 'This is a fantastic actor, this guy will have a thirty-year career if he does it right.' He was already in his mid-forties.

Sometimes actors go a little nuts, decide that they are Brando or Streep and they should be treated that way. Success goes to their heads, they start behaving badly. That's something that maybe you don't spot in the first week. But you must start to spot it as it goes along.
If you feel as if you're putting your energy into something that's going to be unfruitful in the end, I suppose you withdraw a little bit emotionally. I like to have a really open relationship with clients, so I don't have a problem telling somebody they need help – like, 'You need to figure something out about your behaviour if you don't want to damage your career', or 'You had better put that money in the bank and figure out other business interests, because you may not have this over the long haul.'

You've said that to people?
Yes.

Christ, that's difficult.
Yes. But I've always been right. It's so rare that somebody is able to have a consistently successful acting career that really affords them a nice life. There are lists that float around, and to stay on those lists over the long term is an incredible challenge. This is a business where, as an actor, your success is truly dependent on the public's appetite for you at any given time. And if they lose their appetite, no one's going to hire you to work.

In terms of appetite, it now seems that, if you want to be a leading actress, you have to be a 'babe', whether you like it or not. The way marketing is now, the way the media is exploited, the way magazine covers are used – actresses, whatever

their brain power, are expected basically to be sex objects, and to grin and bear it. It always has been that way, probably.

I think the past five years represents a hugely vulgar dip back down into a sexism that I find disappointing. But that's the reality, right?
Yes, that's what Hollywood always has been, since the forties studio system and the starlets. You're in front of the camera, that's what you are.

As a woman, does that piss you off?
Yes. But as a realist – you are on the screen to help people escape. You provide an image.

Sure, but the quality of that image is negotiable, right?
That's true.

I'm appalled by the level of writing now, and the portrayal of women in particular. There are so few roles for women, and in what there is, the banality of the writing is awesome. Now it's not your job to deal with that, but you do have to provide actresses for those roles. What's your own feeling about the way women are portrayed?
Well, I think it's cyclical, it's about what genres are successful at any given moment. As you know, when something is successful, then it opens the floodgate for forty knock-offs. So I think this could change at any given time. But it is devastating how few good roles there are for women.

What's your percentage of female to male clients?
Equal.

Therefore, the output must be unequal?
It is. It's much harder for women, especially if they're selective in any way, to work as often as men. And the pay standards are completely unequal.

Really?
Oh, there's a huge disparity in the way women and men are paid – at the other ends of the business too.

Without naming names, what's the top fee you could expect one of your female clients to earn, and the top you could expect a male, say, twenty-five to thirty years old?
To get a woman actor into seven figures now is quite an accomplishment, in my experience. And across the board, I think I could write a pretty finite list of women who are earning at that level.

I hear Nic Cage is now earning over twenty million. What's the ceiling on the earnings at the moment for the male actors?
I think all those top male stars have been hovering in the twenty million category. How can they go north of that?

And the top of the females are hovering at about a million?
No, the top female salary ever paid, I think, has been twelve, or twelve and a half. Julia Roberts just got it. *My Best Friend's Wedding* was a big hit, that re-established her. And Sandy Bullock can still open a movie.

Salma Hayek said that, according to her own research, she's a really big star. She has a huge Latino audience that will go and see any movie she's in. But because she's a Mexican woman, she's down the list.
I'm sure it's a fight for her to get the movies she wants, despite the fact that she's on magazine covers and has a huge profile. At the same time – this is controversial, but I think her being Mexican actually opens the door in certain ways, because there are only two actresses they want to employ for certain roles.

That would be her and . . .?
Jennifer Lopez, I guess. In racist Hollywood terms, oftentimes if you have a black lead actor, you'll put in a Hispanic actress opposite him. In *One Night Stand*, I'm sure it was more acceptable to some people that Wesley Snipes was married to an Asian actress.

Not the black community – they hated it. Black women were really pissed at both Wesley and Denzel, because Denzel also kissed a white woman in another film around the same time.
You can't please everybody.

No. I don't want to make black movies or white movies, I just want to make movies. So you just have to accept that you're going to get slagged off by somebody. The subject of sexism and of sexual harassment has come up quite a lot in my conversations with actresses. Some of them say it doesn't really exist, it's an anachronism. Others are very angry about it and say the ones who don't see it must be blind.
I would agree with that notion.

Is it as rampant as some people claim?
Absolutely.

How tough is it for an actress to get through this system without coming up against it, being in some way humiliated by it?
I think some women are more aware of when they're being objectified. And others just aren't aware, even while it's happening. I'm completely immune to it at this point because I accept it as a reality.

Did it shock you when you came into the business?
No, but I grew up with a different self-aware perspective. This was in Manhattan. Both my parents were intellectuals, academics – both feminists, and with a highly informed perspective about what exists out there. So it's never been that shock-

ing or horrifying to me, and it's helped that I'm in a position where I represent women and I can help them deal with it.

Is that one of your functions then, dealing with that very problem?
It's an inevitable function and something that I think that I'm much more aware of than male representatives. Actresses are often upset about having been mistreated. I try to equip them with strength and perspective about it, and help them remember why they're in it. And if they're not comfortable with it, maybe they shouldn't be in the profession they're in.

Do you also advise them on how to avoid these sorts of situations?
I suppose one could be so principled that you take a stand and you don't work with a certain group of people. But there are compromises. If a job makes sense for you and helps you to go forward towards your own goals. You're basically taking the power back. You're saying, I'm not going to let these people have the power. I get that the role I'm playing here, to all intents and purposes, I'm the beautiful painting in this movie. But this I think will help to boost my profile and my power base, so that I can make other, more interesting, choices.

This comes up a lot, this idea that a little pain now will save a little pain later on. Actresses say, 'I took a job knowing that I was going to have a hard time. But I did it because, if I want to continue as an actress, this is a fence that I have to get over.' Then you enter the problem of denial a lot.
Right. I think it's a fine line. There's obviously material that is exploitative to women, and it's absolutely unacceptable for actresses to come off of their principles that much. But there's also a way for a beautiful woman to use her beauty and her sexuality, that will potentially garner the public's interest, if it's used in a way that's not exploitative and will help her celebrity and her power, and open up more doors. I only represent adults, on principle. And if people are adults, they have to take personal responsibility.

So where's the line, Julie? What's the thing in a script where you say, 'I don't compromise on this one with my client. This is unacceptable'?
Well, oftentimes I can find something offensive that they don't. I often find things more violent and uncomfortable than some clients of mine. It's a partnership, but ultimately the client is boss. So if the client feels really strongly that this is acceptable material . . .

I think there's been a gradual erosion of principles within storytelling in the industry. You suddenly think, 'My God, what we're making now would have been so unacceptable five years ago, in many ways.' I've had many strong and angry debates about There's Something About Mary. I found it unacceptable, morally, a very sad lurch into a trough of shit.
Really. See, I don't agree with that.

Most people don't. But I found it so offensive, it almost brought me to tears, to see America sending this to the rest of the world, as an acceptable way to be talking about the disabled, women, all those things that were used as basis for humour. And I think, certainly, five or ten years ago, you wouldn't even have got it off the drawing board.

A lot of very broad comedies got made in the past. I actually don't agree with that. I think the differentiation is when it's done smartly, and I think there was a lot that was so smart about that movie, ultimately, in its comedy.

Let me put it to you another way. Do you think film is important? To our culture, to the development of the culture.

Definitely. I think it has an incredible influence.

And therefore, as an important person within this culture, within this town, which has ramifications right across the world, do you take a moral responsibility for what the output is? Do you see yourself as part of the system or outside of the system?

I see myself as outside of the system, but I have to function as part of the system in order to accomplish other things. It's a means to an end. I hope that doesn't sound complacent. The good news is, I do think there's room for expression, and people are making wonderful personal films with distinct points of view . . .

Oh, so do I. The fact that *Bulworth, Wag the Dog* and *Primary Colors* got released this year, politically very biting satires – I think it's a remarkable thing that Hollywood can also produce those kinds of films as well, whether you liked them or not. They are not entertainment only, although they're entertaining films. I think the system functions really well.

But I think, as an individual you have to work within the system and say, 'I don't make this kind of movie, so although I work in the same business that does, that doesn't mean that I take responsibility for that other movie.' And also, as a representative, you have clients who need to work, who need to be paid, and are oftentimes probably going to work with a product that you don't totally believe in or support. I think where I get more sensitive to it is in terms of violence, that's where my personal concern lies. Did you see *Saving Private Ryan*?

I did.

I don't know if I loved everything in it. I think *Full Metal Jacket* is probably a better film. But I think it is a really important film because what I became aware of so acutely in the first twenty minutes of that movie was just how incredibly desensitized to violence we all are. And it was a painful experience. My stepfather was in the war, he got shot in the head. This is an experience I had never lived. And I was so proud actually to be a part of the business the night that I saw the film. The next night I saw something deeply stupid and I thought, I can't believe millions of dollars were spent on this. It's like any business in that regard. But I do think that, to the extent that –

as an individual – you can be involved in things that do make a positive impact, or at least an expression that you're proud of, that's the goal . . . if that makes sense.

Completely, yes.
But it really did raise my level of concern about violence in other movies. And also I think it's boring already, the gratuitous violence, and I don't think people care any more. I guess the concern would lie more with television; I think it's frightening, a lot of the stuff I see on television.

Frightening in what way?
I think the real-life things are just the most disgusting, vile things. Peter Guber was saying, you have to guard the portals of your brain. He said he doesn't turn on the local news. He watches the six-thirty national news, but he doesn't turn on the local news at night because it's such infectious, disgusting stuff to let into your life at that hour . . . before you go to bed –

Very quickly, off the top of your head – give me five pieces of music that you really like.
I love the new Hole album. The Verve. I saw a special on James Taylor last night, he blew me away. My brother-in-law Pete Yorn, his new album. A fifth? I'll go for my classic favourite, Bob Dylan.

Five books.
I'm reading *The Dark Side of Camelot*, Seymour Hersh, which is fascinating. On vacation I just read *The Art of War* which totally relates to my business. In terms of my need for junk, I read Joyce Maynard's book about her affair with J. D. Salinger. Fitzgerald – *The Great Gatsby, Tender is the Night*.

Five films that you thought were profound. Just as an indication of your taste really.
A Clockwork Orange always springs to mind. I love Audrey Hepburn's movies. *The Godfather*, and *Part II*. *Goodfellas*. *Searching for Bobby Fisher*, one of my favourites. *The Graduate*.

I'm not going to ask you about actors and actresses because you're bound to be prejudiced.
Really? You're not going to ask me about actors and actresses?

No, because I couldn't expect the truth from you. It would have to be Sam Jackson, Saffron Burrows, Minnie Driver –
You're kidding me, that's not fair. I was going to take my own clients out of it.

Were you? Is that possible?
Sure. I like Barbara Stanwyck. Sean Penn, he's always great.

He's not one of yours, is he?
No, I just love him.

Mike Figgis: Why did you choose to go into film?

Ming-Na Wen: *The Joy Luck Club* was my first big film. Before that I was doing mostly stage work. But I always had a fantasy of being on the big screen. I loved films when I was growing up. They were my escape.

A lot of people love films and don't necessarily want to be in them. Why did you want to put yourself in that position where you're going to be sixty feet across and watched by lots of other people, pretending to be somebody you're not?

I never thought about that. I just wanted to be part of a medium that I loved. And once I was acting, it just seemed like a natural transition into doing films. Actually, it's always a surprise to me when I appear on the big screen. I'm only learning to realize that's the end result.

At least in theatre you have the contact with the audience. There's a certain intimacy. That's gone once you get on to a big screen.

On *Joy Luck Club*, I had no expectations, but to me it was very much an intimate experience, where a group of us got together and tried to create a different world. And, unlike the stage, you actually get to be on a set that feels like somebody's apartment, somebody's home. Or you can be on the streets, and really live out the world of your character. That's what I love about film – you have the intimacy of that ensemble feeling, like in theatre. But at the same time you're really in the moment when you're on the set.

Do you keep in contact with people you've worked with?

I try. Sometimes actors and other people just want to move on when they're done with the job. And it used to hurt me when that happened.

Because you took it more seriously?

Yes. When you're involved in such an intimate creative process, and you hang out together, and you laugh, and drink, and really develop a friendship – for me, it's very odd when it ends.

How do you deal with that? It feels as if there are two choices – you either develop a hardened cynicism or you decide, 'That's life.'

I now expect it, as opposed to being surprised by it – I assume that a majority of people will never return my phone call again. I guess that's cynicism – because you're anticipating that people will shut the door and no longer want to connect. And that's a loss of a certain innocence.

So you're on a film and everyone's really friendly, and then suddenly . . . when it first happened, were you also inclined to take it personally in the sense that you're an Asian-American actress?

In the beginning, there might have been a subconscious thing there. I grew up in a very white neighbourhood, and being Asian was always something I had to deal with in my childhood.

Of course, it's the same for everybody, it isn't an ethnic problem.
No, I realized that. I think the real problem of being an Asian-American actress is trying to get into that family in the first place – as opposed to worrying when people don't want to keep in contact.

Why are you still in film? Does it still work for you?
Yeah, I still love it. Unfortunately, there aren't many opportunities. I always feel that no matter what I do, it's back to square one when the project is done, and that's very frustrating.

Yet you're highly recognized. You've worked in TV, film, theatre. You've been on the cover of magazines and so on. What does it take to change the situation whereby you have to start from scratch every time?
I think you have to be in one of those blockbusters. It's about economics a lot of times, rather than talent. Sometimes it's about personality – you know, if someone important suddenly latches on to you and creates a publicity fervour around you, you can be the flavour of the month – it might even last six months, a year.

But even then, you've still got to reinvent yourself?
Yes. I'm hoping that hard work will eventually lead to recognition, where people hire you because they know your work. But I haven't experienced that yet, and I've been doing it for ten years. What's even more frustrating is when someone who's never acted before is hired on the spot, and you're still waiting for your call-back. You just have to be Zen about it and say, 'It's fate. If you're meant to get the job, you will. If not, just move on.'

What's your opposition? Who's going for the same parts as you?
My agents and my managers are always being creative and trying to get casting directors to see me for parts that are not specifically written for Asians. So once I get in the door, I'm competing with a lot of beautiful blondes and brunettes. And either I really stand out, or I'm told, 'Well, they're really not going to go in that direction.' I'm a direction, see – like a one-way street sign. Either you want to go on down, or you take the left turn.

Then, of course, my Asian-American peers are the rest of my competition.

So, obviously, very often you're going for Asian-American parts?
It's half and half. What really troubles me a lot of the time is that you go in for these Asian-specific parts, and you meet these – I'm sorry – these white guys, sitting there professing to be experts on whether you can portray a Japanese or a Korean. 'Well, you're Chinese, Ming-Na.' So I won't get hired for a job because some white dude thinks I can't portray Japanese. That drives me insane. Meanwhile you have Sean Connery being able to play a Spaniard or a Greek, anything he wants – and all with the same accent!

How about Anthony Hopkins?

Perfect example. *The Mask of Zorro*, everybody around him is speaking with a Spanish accent, or attempting one – except him. And he's Zorro!

Why do you think Connery and Hopkins are allowed to keep their own voices?
Because, for some reason, the English accent translates into any ethnic group you want. Maybe I should adopt an English accent. Then I can play Japanese.

Did you get angry, sitting there in that situation?
Yes. And sometimes I voice it, which really helps me to get the job more, I think. Maybe I'm dropping a little seed of something that will make them think. Here's another wonderful situation: I was up for another movie, just a silly movie, but I was going to go in, I was studying the character. All of a sudden my agent calls, saying, 'Oh, Ming, they've decided that this character' – let's call her Anna – 'is going to be the sister of one of the other characters' – let's call her, I don't know – Hooters. 'So could you read Vanessa? It's a smaller part, by the way.' I go, 'Okay, sure. But I like Anna better, she's much more interesting.' 'Oh, well, but now they're thinking Hooters is her sister.' And in the back of my mind I'm thinking, 'Oh? Hence I cannot play Anna because Asian women don't have sisters?'

Then they would have to cast two of you . . .
Two of us? Oh, my God! So that's another barrier that's constantly put up. Why can't the director or the casting person think, 'Oh, she's right for the part. So maybe we can hire two Asians.' Stuff like that really profoundly disturbs me. And they don't even realize it – that's the problem.

You think it's racist?
It's the lack of ability to be creative or think beyond the little white suburbia they grew up in – and which I grew up in. So I'm still tackling this problem of trying to fit in to white suburbia, but now it's in my profession.

Do you think the people you meet who are making movies are clever?
Clever in the sense that a lot of them are good salesmen. If you have the ability to do the talk, do the walk, make yourself seem as if you're more important than you are, and know more than you do, then you're being clever. You have the ability to sell a product, sell yourself, sell a script.

How about in the creative sense?
No. Everybody's always trying really hard to recreate the last blockbuster hit. Then they claim it as if it's something new.

What about TV? You've done a lot of it, and the TV here seems smarter to me than the movies – certainly in terms of the writing.
I think because there are so many TV projects going all at once, you can take more risks and try out new ideas – although it is getting as expensive.

Are you happy in that medium?

Right now I do miss being part of a sitcom series – that family thing again.

On *One Night Stand* I was very impressed by your ability to improvise, which I guessed had been honed in TV.
Television makes you think on your feet, especially sitcoms. Sitcom television is like repertory theatre for me. You get a script on Monday, you've got to slap it all together by Friday. It is so incredibly fast.

And exciting?
Yes, and frustrating. A lot of times you know it really doesn't work, it really isn't funny, but you still have to pretend and put your whole heart in it. I think the real problem is there are so many channels and so many stations, but there just aren't enough writers.

Do films affect people?
Certain ones, yes; I believe that. They have great influence.

Violence in films? Does that affect people?
Oh, yes, absolutely. I think it numbs you.

Therefore, are we morally culpable for what we do in the film industry?
You're always morally culpable, whatever you produce. Whether it's how you raise a child, or how you deal with other people, whether you do it with courtesy or with meanness – I think you're always culpable. As a film-maker, you want to affect people. Otherwise why are we doing it? We always label it – 'Oh, well, we just want to entertain.' But to entertain is also to affect somebody, make them feel a certain way, think a certain way.

Shakespeare was an entertainer – a highbrow entertainer. I think our problem now is that we're dumbed-down, we're in a lowbrow trough of significant proportions.
And it's global now, too.

I can't make Hollywood take the responsibility for the world crisis, or for El Niño and global warming, but I do feel they're part of the problem. When you make a film, do you accept that you're part of the system here?
Sure. It would be hypocritical to say, 'I'm making films here but I'm not Hollywood.'

Well, a lot of us will do.
My pay cheques come from Disney or Warner. But I think you can make choices as an individual, whatever clout you have or don't have. There are times when reality hits and you have to pay the rent, but if you have the luxury to make choices, I think it does wonders if you make the right ones.

Again, on a moral issue, you say that Hollywood involves many forms of pros-

titution, either literal or metaphorical.
To me, prostituting yourself means lowering or denying your sense of self-esteem, or your morals, and just selling yourself – saying, 'I want the fame, I want the money, I want the power. So I'm willing to prostitute myself for it.' Some people are really good at that. And they have big homes and drive fancy cars to show it.

Where were you brought up?
Pittsburgh.

So how long have you been here?
Four years.

Were you naive when you arrived?
Very naive. But in a way that was good, because I always got the reaction of, 'Oh, you're so refreshing. You're from New York? You have that New York energy.' Plus, they don't have a preconceived idea about who you are. But then you live here for four years, and you start thinking that you need to adopt these qualities and mannerisms just in order to feel as if you fit in.

So do you feel part of this family here now?
Never.

Why not? What stops you? Is it the auditions?
Yeah. I keep forgetting how things are. I was away doing a play for seven months. I came back and I realized I'd forgotten the lingo, how this town is. I forgot that for every twenty auditions I go out on, nineteen of them are rejections and maybe one is a hopeful. So it was jarring, the first month. I got very depressed.

Do you come up against elements of sexism?
Oh, yes. Your agent calls and says, 'Hey, Ming, go in and make sure you wear something sexy. Wear a short skirt.'

What does that make you feel?
Like an ass. You think, 'This character is a secretary. She sits behind a desk. Does she require a short skirt?' So sexism like that still exists.

If that happens, do you wear the short skirt?
Yeah.

So you turn up. Are you then uncomfortable?
Well, it's weird when – as happened to me at one audition – I was asked to wear a short skirt, I went in, and there was a room full of women. The casting director, the director, the writers – all women. And they wanted to see me in a short skirt.

And what are you supposed to do then, be bright and sexy and chirpy?
Of course. You never feel you can go in as yourself. Maybe that's where I'm making a mistake now – maybe I feel I have to go in being somebody else.

I think it is a mistake. I know that often the actors who impress me are the ones who have an attitude of 'I don't need you.' I think, 'Wow, there's an independence there.' What are the things that have made you really angry in terms of how you've been treated in the casting process?

When you come into an audition room, and you've worked and you've prepared, and they don't give you the time of day. Because they've already made their judgement: 'This isn't what we're looking for.' At least give the person the courtesy of your full and undivided attention.

So even if you don't get the job, you feel as if you did something.

At least you feel you weren't wasting your time. I don't think casting people or directors realize that we don't just show up. We work on the material, a whole day of energy is expended, and for what? Or they can go in the other direction, where you get the false reception – 'So great to see you!' Then you do the scene and you ask, 'Do you want me to do it again differently?' And you get a really big smile – 'No! You did that better than I could ever have directed you!' 'Oh? Then do I get the job?' That just makes your skin crawl. You think, 'Why am I subjecting myself to this foolishness?'

Why are you?

I think there's a part of me that keeps hoping I will find that great person who I do want to work with. When you work with people who make you a better artist, it's like a drug, that's what you want – that connection, that high, that sense of creating with somebody.

How are you financially?

I've been very fortunate. And I'm not the type of person to go and buy a big mansion as soon as I get my first big job. I tuck it away.

I think we can't underestimate how big an issue money is in the town.

Oh, I think it's the first and foremost. Before art, before anything, is money.

If the money wasn't so good, would you stay here?

That's a tough question to ask me.

Let's say it's a fifty per cent cut we're talking about. Not negotiable.

I have it in my head that unless you project an image that you are worth X amount of dollars, then the people in this business believe that you are willing to take a lesser amount. You're not worth as much as the person who feels that they're worth more.

Do you think there should be a ceiling on earnings?

No.

Okay. How great a part does sex play in the structure of Hollywood?

One hundred per cent.

Really?

All right, maybe ninety-nine.

I'm surprised at that answer. I always think of it as being a bit of a non-sexual place, even though everything appears to be sexual.

I think it's all about sexiness. If it's not physicality, it's power. It's about your connections, or the car you drive, or the designer outfit you're wearing. To me that's all sexuality – the package, the image, all of that.

Those are external sexual signals, if you like. Do they match up with the level of internal sexual drive in people?

Sexuality is what turns you on. And because those things do turn a lot of these people on, they are sexual. That's what drives them.

Your physical appearance – is it something you would consider changing in order to compete?

You mean surgery? I don't look down on people who do it. Except when they go in excess, then it's a little scary. I've definitely contemplated it. There's a little bag under my left eye that I've always hated. And if a little snip here is going to get rid of it, for a couple of thousand dollars, I would do it. I'm just scared – I hate surgery. I know friends who have had boob jobs left and right, hoping they'll get more work.

Did they?

No.

What do you think about a culture where female breasts have been cosmetically enhanced to such an extent that they're like two round melons –

And hard and fake – ecchh!

But without nipples. Suddenly this year's fashions are transparent, so women are having to buy stick-on nipples. That's a fashion accessory you can buy, because the little nipple bump is now fashionable.

Let me check, do I have mine on? No, it's not cold enough in this room. Yes, it's messed up. I did a play about women in China with bound feet. And after the play we would invite questions, and people would be expressing horror, saying, 'Why would these women endure a thousand years of having bound feet?' And we were saying, 'Well, equate it to women who now have these huge breast implants. It's a fashion thing.'

Despite the medical warnings.

Despite the pain, despite the money, everything – they still go and do it. And maybe a thousand years from now, people will look back and say, 'Why did women do that to their breasts?' But is it the fault of men or is it the fault of women?

Good question. Do you want to answer that?

I think it's both.

Do you think women are sufficiently represented within the film community?
To an extent, yes. More so now than before.

Then why are most scripts written for men, without female parts in it that are real?
I think the marketing experts feel that the majority of movie-goers are young teenage girls, and hence Leonardo DiCaprio is like God in this business. And they don't believe that these same young girls will also want to spend their money to go see an image of themselves – let alone of older women.

So it's only women who go and see movies now?
Well, they're saying that the mass that are going back to see *Titanic* ten or twelve times are mostly young girls. Before, when it was all action movies, the marketing experts of Hollywood thought the majority was made up of teenage boys.

So girls want to see boys and boys want to see boys.
Everybody wants to see boys. Hence, all the scripts are written for boys, with girls portrayed only as girlfriends who tag along.

Give me a quick answer – what's the easiest and quickest way to succeed in Los Angeles?
To become a sex symbol.

Should sex be portrayed in films? And, if so, how real should it be?
Well, having done only one sex scene, with this director Mike Figgis, I would have to say that if the material works for you, it's okay.

How often do you go to the movies?
About once or twice a week.

What have you seen in the past month or so that you thought was strong?
Yesterday I finally got to see *The Ice Storm*. I didn't know what to expect because the trailer made it look almost like *The Big Chill*. And it wasn't that at all. It was very strong; great acting in it, very subtle.

Have you seen *Saving Private Ryan*?
Yes. It was a great film in the sense that the way it was shot was just tremendous, but I thought the story was weak. *Good Will Hunting* – I enjoyed that a lot.

A great film?
No, but it told a good story. And sometimes I miss that in films.

19 Nastassja Kinski

Mike Figgis: How would you describe your job?
Nastassja Kinski: My job is to make the people around me happy. I feel my job is to be honest; to learn every day and be better every day, and to prepare myself for everything – for a movie, for life. When I was little I was always alone, I was an only child and a pain in the ass. I really wanted to have a family. Before I had my kids, my family were my friends. Then when I was twelve, I started doing movies, and movie sets were my family.

Someone says, 'I want you to be in my movie' and they give you a script. What do you do when you get the script?
When I read it I look at the whole story, because that's what a movie is. If it's fascinating, beautiful, sad, true, and I can be in it, then I really don't mind what part I play. I think that comes from my childhood. I always wanted to be part of something. I wanted to please. That doesn't mean I lose my personality to do that – because it has to come from the heart. But what gives me the most satisfaction is when I'm working with people I love, and I can make them happy. Maybe that sounds dumb . . .

No. Elisabeth Shue said a similar thing. But, say you're given a character who's a very strange woman, completely different to yourself. How do you go about becoming that character?
Usually I try to find parallels with the experiences that I've had; parallels in the intensity of that feeling. There's usually something you can compare, that connects to you.

What are most of them like, the scripts that you read?
Some are dark and scary just to be dark and scary. I don't mind 'dark and scary' when it has a real source and a real meaning – if you're making *The Killing Fields*, you have to show all the violence. But I read scripts that are just violent for no reason, and I don't like or respond to that.

Film tends to celebrate good-looking people. Most of the stars we can think of are very good-looking, and usually they start when they're very young. Men, of course, can go on being leading actors in their sixties. But Hollywood is very tough on women and their age.
True. But if a woman is smart and creative and fully herself, nobody can take that away, not even Hollywood. That'll always stay – certainly in her private life, but also on screen. Sometimes I think women give in, even subconsciously. You get to a certain age, you think, 'This is the job.' But then there are women who don't give in. They retain a certain joy inside of themselves, as well as a joy in their work – also a joy in not giving in, but just continually reviving, like a flower in water. It takes courage, it's a gutsy thing to hold on to. But whenever I see that in people I like, it's like a light, and I study them closely because that's what I want to accomplish.

Who do you admire in that way?
Elizabeth Taylor is a fighter, she's an incredible person. She truly is a wonderful example of revival, like a phoenix. And she gets down because she's sensitive, she feels everything, but she has that joy inside of herself. Also, Gena Rowlands . . .

Gena Rowlands seems so inspiring to people.
Also a dear friend of mine, Shirley Knight.

Why did you want to be an actor? Where did that come from?
In the beginning it just happened because somebody said, 'Hey, what's your name? You want to be in a movie?' And it was a Wim Wenders movie, my first.

How old were you?
I was twelve. Then it kept happening to me – though I'm sure on a subconscious level I also chose it. And I feel it definitely saved my life, in more ways than one.

Why?
I look back at my life then, and what the other side of the coin would have been, and I feel how lucky I was to encounter certain people and have the chance to get away from where I was – to make my own life, build it up from scratch. It's thanks to the people who believed in me and helped me – like Wim, like Roman Polanski, like Francis Coppola. Those years for me – between, say, twelve and twenty – were really important because it was like catching up on the childhood I hadn't really had. And I was able to look up to people, whereas I had nobody like that in my younger years. I watched people being strong and courageous, sticking together. And I became a part of it. It made me believe in everything again. I could restart my life, like a newborn child. So I drank it up.

Once your career took off, you worked a lot. You were incredibly busy as an actress, weren't you?
Yes, but I didn't quite do my preparation. It happened like, 'Oh, do this and this and this.' And at the same time I was busy growing up and falling in love and then wanting a family. My private life was the most important thing to me. So I can't say I took my career for granted, but I wish I had done more work on it.

Do you feel you had an education?
I had some, I didn't go very far. I wish I had gone to college. I wish somebody had said, 'This is you, this is your spine, nobody can take this away from you, feel proud for the rest of your life.' But I didn't have that. I'm trying to catch up with my education, reading books at night, taking courses, because I'm still missing it and I still want it. But the main thing I'm talking about is how important it is to grow up with real love, with adults who really respect you as a little person, and teach you that you are a wonderful person.

Did that happen to you?

No. I was just exteriorized, Mike. I guess I was pretty – pretty and cute, whatever they said I was – and no one looked past that to the person inside.

How did that feel, to be treated that way?
It felt lonely, it felt dark, it felt cold. It's a wonderful thing, a fantasy thing, to dress up and put on make-up and exteriorize and make yourself into other people; because then you're not in touch with yourself. But you look at other people – other kids, other parents, other families – and you see in them the value that you don't see in yourself, because it was given to them, but not to you. You also see the ones that don't have it. And I just didn't know how to get that feeling of value for myself.

A beautiful woman can walk into a room and devastate every man in there, because of the way she looks. That's a huge power to have, and it's not something that's even in her control. I'm sure that happened to you then. I go out for dinner with you, and I see it happen now. But now you know how to deal with it. How on earth did you deal with that power when you were twenty-two years old?
I had been used to it since I was a very little girl – like trillions of other women. And it was annoying that I was used to it. Also I was saddened if men didn't look at me inside. I was used to that, too. But along the way there *were* people who looked at me inside, and wondered who I was, and believed that I could do something more.

Did that happen?
Yes.

What about the opposite?
The opposite brings you way back down to that dark place – the place where you feel you can't get it right; where you're no good; where you don't fit in; where you're not worthy to be with these people, and do these things. That's the place I remember from my youth. When I came out of it, it was like sunshine. And that's why I want sunshine now. I'm not in denial of the other side of life. But like they say in America: 'Been there, done that, bought the T-shirt.' I was there so long. Now, with my family, my children, I know what to say and how to be there for them, because I know best. What I love most about, let's say, the American philosophy, is that it doesn't matter if you fail here, you can still get up and try again. The most important things to my son are either a girl or a basketball game. We'll be in the car, stuck in traffic on our way to a game and he'll say, 'We're never gonna make it, I'm gonna fail.' I tell him, 'Look, you can see it that way, and make yourself crazy, and arrive already upset and drained. That way, you'll dribble the ball and fall over. Or – you can think, 'Okay, whatever. Maybe we'll be late, maybe not. But we'll make it. And then I'm going to give my damnedest best, everything I've got.' That way, you give yourself a chance to really succeed.

Do you think that we make too much fuss about films, that we almost make film-making like a religion?

I know that films are expensive and I know that many people in the world lack food and shelter, lack education for kids, lack so many things. Even the smallest film costs a lot of money. Even when you say, 'Oh, that film was just a few hundred thousand dollars', that's a lot of money. So there is a big responsibility there, and we should make a fuss over films – they should be made as well as they can be, and made for a purpose.

People start so young, they become stars and are paid a lot of money. It must be hard for them to survive into a mature adulthood without a lot of damage to the ego and the sense of their own importance. So is it healthy for a young man or woman to be paid twenty million dollars?

Probably not. But those young people have all the responsibility of making films work. Millions of people buy tickets just to see them. Why shouldn't they be rewarded really highly? Because they give of themselves completely.

Now I'm going to ask you about things that you like. Answer these really quickly. Give me five pieces of music.

I love the Beethoven piece we used in *One Night Stand*. What was it?

It was the Grosse Fugue, a string quartet.

I grew up listening to classical music, which my mom listened to. It made me sad when I was little because I associated it with certain things. But I have it deep inside of me, and the memory of certain pieces of music – Rachmaninov, Tchaikovsky, Mozart, Beethoven, Schubert, Schumann – I have in me always. Also, Stevie Wonder is a love of mine.

Five books.

All of Dostoevsky; Gogol. Russian literature is really what I love and once I started reading I connected to it so deeply. Goethe – *The Suffering of Young Werther* has always been extraordinary to me. I love reading Krishnamurti.

I heard him on the radio last week, when I couldn't sleep. He was talking about reincarnation.

Oh, yes, he was always someone I wanted to meet. When you really feel strongly that you need to meet someone, you have to do everything possible to do it. Because life is so short and unpredictable, and suddenly you can't meet them any more. Same thing with saying things to people that you want to say. 'One day I'll tell her, one day I'll tell him.' When you feel it strongly, that's when you need to do it.

Five actors – quickly.

Leonardo DiCaprio, Sidney Poitier, John Travolta, Nicolas Cage, Mike Myers.

Five actresses?

Marilyn Monroe . . . [*The tape runs out.*]

Mike Figgis: Being heartbroken – is that part of the deal of being here?
Brooke Shields: I think it's part of the deal of being in the business. I know that, for me, there's a sense of heartbreak all the time. Maybe it's because when I was younger, that was all I knew – every period of my life was regarded as, 'Oh, the time when I filmed this or that movie.'

How old were you when you made your first film?
I was nine. It was a really low-budget horror movie, done in Patterson, New Jersey. I played a young girl who gets murdered, burned and put inside a deacon's bench. They had to take the morgue pictures of my character, so they did all the make-up on me. But there weren't any mirrors around, so I didn't get to see it. Then finally they showed me my face in this cracked mirror, and it looked like pizza had been smacked on my face. I mean, it was all bubbly and pus-y and horrible. I started to cry and the tears went down inside the make-up, and the make-up artist is saying, 'Don't cry, don't cry!'

But you were genuinely upset?
I was. And yet, something else took a precedence over the true emotions.

Which is what? Ambition?
Well, no. Desire for approval, and to be liked. I mean, that was what it started off as – you wanted everybody to like you.

But didn't everybody like you before that anyway?
Yes, but you didn't want to do anything to mess it up. I remember feeling, 'Oh, I don't want to ruin this person's hard work.' I don't think I knew what I was learning then, but that was the beginning of this avid desire to make every movie complete.

Did you know you were pretty?
I was told I was pretty but I –

No. Did you know that you were?
No. The thought of looking at myself and regarding myself as anything just didn't . . . I wanted to be fun, I wanted people to want to play with me and want to be around me. Not necessarily tell me I was pretty. Because the 'pretty' quality was something I felt I could do in a picture – I could put it on.

But you were in a weird position. Because you were like Miss America, weren't you?
I was like America's sweetheart.

Were you aware that you were carrying that image?
I felt a certain pressure, but I think it's always hindsight. I think that as long as you don't know any alternative, if you're just continuing on a certain path, then you don't realize what you're perpetuating. It's just where you are.

I would imagine you were also protected, from a very young age – since you were successful so early? Especially after *Pretty Baby*.

That's why I feel that the industry is sort of a series of heartbreaks. Because to fully immerse yourself in a film – that is so all-encompassing. And people who aren't in the business, they can't really understand it, or appreciate it. It's not just about becoming your character as much as you can. There's this *alter ego*, this other self that gets an opportunity to live, and is supported everywhere you turn. *Pretty Baby* was made when I was eleven, and so I was displaced, in another city, another place, for three or four months. And it was as if that was my only existence.

Was there enough support for you to be comfortable emotionally? So that you didn't have to feel tragic about it?

I only felt tragic, I think, after it was over. Every time a film ends, I feel as if a very distinctive part of myself has been taken away. And I'm not really good at saying goodbye to anything. So there's this sort of – mourning process. I ended up writing my thesis on it – on Louis Malle and the film. Because it's not just movie-making; I mean, the things that went on, on *Pretty Baby*. Girls were getting pregnant, people were fighting with Paramount, and then this sort of Mafia contingent in New Orleans were rigging people's cars. And it was so ugly – break-ins to our hotel rooms, and stuff written on the walls. 'This is to let you know what we can do.' I mean, there was no protection. And I was a minor. My mother and I were very, very close and I swore I would never do another film, it was so frightening to me. And yet it was your entire life. And the only thing that I could do to sort of emancipate myself emotionally afterwards was – I remember getting my hair cut. I had never had a haircut before. And I came out with sort of a bob, and I felt that I had freed myself.

On that set, you were aware of the corruption? Even at that age?

Something felt ugly about it. One night, I was actually taken and put into a stairwell, and this one individual said to me, 'You might not see your mother again. She was in a terrible car accident. You have to stay here for a while.' And you know, I had trusted this man. I thank God that just prior to that, my welfare worker, this French teacher who was sort of assigned to me, had got a phone call. And I was made aware that the brakes had been cut on my mother's car. She was coming to get me and the car went out of control, and she was *instantly* put in jail.

Was she hurt?

No, she had just a little bump on her head.

So what was the warning about?

That morning she had called the Labour Board and said, 'Are kids allowed to work fourteen-, sixteen-hour days?' I was eleven, and I wasn't getting the schooling in. If there was something that could be done, my mom wanted to do it. And I guess they took it as a big threat, because they were doing something illegally.

Luckily she had had a dime in her pocket, and she called a local woman and said, 'Can you bail me out? This is ridiculous.' I mean, in *seconds*, the police were there.

Why did that individual say those things to you about your mother?
I think they wanted to be able to control me. There was this idea of 'If we can separate you from your mother . . .' I mean, this sounds – you'd think I'm making this up –

I don't. Not even remotely.
You know, movie-making was different then. It really was. There was a weird sense of 'anything goes'. Especially in a place like New Orleans. And labour laws for minors were very different.

***Pretty Baby* takes place entirely in a whorehouse. And, of course, your character is an innocent in that environment. Did you understand what the film was about?**
I did. I had a romantic vision of the film, though. Because, you know, I'm from New York, so I knew 42nd Street prostitutes.

At that age?
Oh, God, yes. I was a single kid in New York, I was a wild child with my mom. I was working since I was a baby.

Was your mom connected to film in some way?
No. All of her friends were hairdressers or make-up artists or photographers. One of her photographer friends needed a baby, so I got involved in child modelling because of that. Then I joined an agency, then I went on an audition for *Pretty Baby*. That's sort of how it all started. It was a great time in New York – theatre, really creative people. But the decadence . . . You know, I also saw the sordid side. You saw this solitary existence of prostitutes in New York, and there was pity for them, there was a sadness.

But you knew the facts of life at that age?
Oh yes, from when I was really young. I mean, my mom was always like, 'This is it, this is the score. Got any questions? You want to get stoned, I'll get you the best stuff. But if you want it, do me the favour of letting me be there with you, so that nothing can happen that's wrong.' And if that was reverse psychology, then it was brilliant. But I just think it was less attractive to me.

So you were never really an innocent?
I don't think I ever was. I really don't.

That's kind of weird, isn't it? Because you then became the kind of spokesperson for innocence – the young girl who somehow seems to epitomize innocence, virginity, cleanliness, and all these kinds of things.

That's such a paradox that it baffles me. How could I have been this always provocative child, and then . . .?

But you're aware of that uniform you're wearing. And, to an extent, that's why you're being paid.
Oh, for sure. But it's so bizarre. It has so little to do with anything that you really believe or feel or think.

When I first met you and we went to dinner and talked, I was fascinated – because you're such a cool, completely aware person, on every level.
Well, thank you. I don't have anything to lose at this point. It's sort of that I've been around for so long. I'm not jaded, because I still feel like I've just begun. But there was an arrested development that occurred. And I think it was because I was so protected and buffered, and I played into it. Because it was directly proportionate to reward. I just kept the machine going. Because I hadn't the craving inside to make it any different.

You were making good money.
Yes, but it had nothing to do with money.

I don't quite buy that. Because you have a lifestyle to maintain, presumably you have bills to pay, probably other people to look after. Plus managers and agents and publicists.
But, see, I had been sequestered from all of that. The money wasn't the motivation, from my perspective, because I didn't know what it was. Didn't ask questions, didn't care.

So, what if you wanted to buy something? You rang up your accountant and said, 'Is it okay?'
No, I'd just basically say to my mother, 'I want this. What do you think?' And it would miraculously sort of show up. I was a latent bloomer, it wasn't until I was in my late twenties – I'm ashamed to say – that I started to say, 'Wait a minute, something's not right.' I wasn't doing the movies I wanted to do. And I didn't know why. It was because there was an image of me being perpetuated. And yet it was a confused image.

Were you able to have anything like a real relationship in this period?
I feel they were all tempered. I think I tempered them. I look back now and I realize I'm only starting to understand. There was like this preservation of me, of my image, and then I didn't even realize the lack of freedom. I had tumultuous relationships, but they were sort of from a rebellious standpoint. It wasn't a case of, 'I'm really going to go live in this, and see what it reveals in me.' It was, 'I'm going to get away with this. I'm going to date so-and-so who's a total roaring alcoholic.' You know? 'I'm just going to play that role for a while.'

Be a devil.
Yes. But I was always the devil that had the little heaven to go back to. Home. You know, I always had that safe haven, that safety net. I would go into these relationships for a few months. But nothing took precedence over my mother, or the home, or the 'good girl' thing.

When you went out and partied and said, 'I'm now in love with Joe or Pete or whoever' – were you ever able to really let go of yourself? Or did you become hyper-aware of your image when you were with another person?
Oh, hyper-aware.

Like being in a movie . . . I don't want to get into too personal an area, but I have a theory that one of the things that making films does to us is that it completely fucks us up for any kind of relationship. Because we're always in this bloody movie . . .
I know exactly where you're going. I've been accused of that, I have to say. I've been so craving of true emotional resonance, and I've been in the movies for so long, and seen this. When I was really young, the minute the director said, 'Cut', I would make a face, or do something that would completely affirm that I was not the character. And the director would get really mad, or other actors would get very disconcerted. But I was so adamant at first – that the experience was more important to me than the character. It's only been in recent years that I'm unable to jump in and out – that there's such a connection between the person I am and the person I'm playing. The switch-off is so much more difficult. And that's what wreaks havoc in my personal life. Because no matter how much I can say, 'Oh, it's just a movie', the fabric of who I am has been altered.

Give me six pieces of music that have moved you. Don't think too much about it. I don't care if you heard it yesterday. And it doesn't have to be Beethoven.
There's this song called *Beautiful Goodbye* by Amanda Palmer. There's one called *Beautiful In My Eyes* by Joshua Kattison. Marc Cohn wrote a song called *True Companion*. The soundtrack from *Rent*, there's a song called *Take Me for What I Am*.

Give me six pieces of literature that have touched you.
Conversations with God was recent. *Angle of Repose* is a book I'm reading right now. Any Baudelaire, really. I was a French Lit. major. I love Proust. *À la recherche du temps perdu* has been the one book for me, because it deals with this concept of sensation, which I'm fascinated by. We all want to go back and recapture the past, and yet the essence of that is sensation. Why do taste and smell evoke the past so vividly? I think movies can do that. I mean, smell will probably be the next thing put in films.

If you can evoke smell in literature without smelling it, you should be able to do it in film, shouldn't you? It has more chances than literature.

But the making of a film – you want to believe it's not reality, in a certain sense. You want to say to yourself, 'No, that's not my life.' But I did a film this summer, and I am irrevocably changed. I can't quite shake it, and I don't really want to. I was playing Gena Rowlands's daughter. And the cast was phenomenal. We all lived in one house, we were with each other twenty-four hours a day, and we were doing night shoots. We would sleep a few hours in the morning, then work on the script, then shoot nights. And we were plucked away from our lives as we know them.

That a problem?
It was a very big problem. It was the best time I've ever had in my life. I've never been freer. No agents, no parents, no publicists, no assistants, no friends, no nothing. I was in upstate New York by myself. I thought, any chance I had, I would run into the city. But I didn't leave once, in two months.

Films allow – they perpetuate and support completely different sensibilities, and you go into them and you live in them, and you have to be really strong to be able to come out of them and admit the changes.

I come from a place where there was always such turbulence around me that I was always the one who was adamant to stay still and balanced, to be the one who monitored. And as I got older, that became very uncomfortable to me. So that now I'm addicted to the extremes in emotions, I'm able to tap that. And I can't justify not going forward, otherwise I might go back.

Has something happened to you with your own emotional life that's made you have to make a choice about this?
Yes. It stemmed from being in a certain environment and working with people, and feeling a part of myself that I've never felt before, feeling a sense of freedom. And then having it be supported in the actual work that we were doing. To be able to hold my own, and feel discomfort, but loving that – knowing that I'm at least alive. There was a sense of sexuality, a sense of fear, that was very real.

What do you mean by a sense of sexuality?
The part that I played, she's sort of a whisky-drinking, smoking, you know . . . And you think, 'Oh sure, that's it. Like – do a nude layout and it's going to make all the difference in the world!' That's not it. There was an essence to this person. Her sexual nature was something that I had never really understood in a character. I understood it only sort of nominally as a person. But the tapping into it as a character really awakened it as a person for me. You sort of realize a great deal about yourself just by being in a film, because all the props are there. Do you know what I mean?

There's no conspiracy here, we know that. But did you feel that somehow events conspired in such a way as to deny you that possibility as an actress up until now?
I definitely think so. But when you're not ready for something I don't think it really comes to you – as much as you think you desire it. I don't think that I

would have been emotionally prepared or willing, as much as my intellect would have wanted me to be.

Okay – you're a highly intellectually evolved person. It was always important to you to have an education. And without in any way disparaging the profession – that puts you in a fairly rarefied category amongst actors. It's a youth-oriented thing here. We love eighteen-year-olds with perfect bodies, great teeth, great hair. Now you had all that, still do. But you still got an education. What about other actresses?
What happens to them? I don't know. It's been my defence mechanism – a retreat, a place to go that's my own. Because all the rest seems rather temporary to me. But when I see other actresses who don't necessarily have that, I can't really be judgemental. And maybe there's something that I slightly envy about them too. Maybe I think just a little bit too much. And maybe that hinders me. Maybe there's a more raw, animalistic way, with less filters. You know, I go to that place because I know it, and I know you can't fuck with me there.

You wouldn't swap, would you?
No. And I think it's served me very well. I think it's protected me from becoming a tragedy. It allows me to see. It separates the men from the boys instantly for me.

On your journey, did you ever do what my friend Robert Downey Jr and others have done – did you ever go into substance abuse or anything like that?
No. I think it was because I grew up in an alcoholic family, and I really saw the ugliness of it. And I became sort of the co-dependent at such an early age. I do know that I'm an addictive personality. It's in my genes. But I somehow have this internal mechanism, and maybe that's where ambition comes in. I don't want anything to get the better of me and control me so that I can't go win at the game. However, I look at some people, like Robert, who I think is a genius. And I think it must be hell living in his head, because there's just too much information.

Do you think the industry, intellectually or emotionally, can support someone like Robert? Is there enough to do? I think one of Robert's big problems is that he's bored.
Yes. I think there's such an accepted level . . . Why is it such a rarity when you see something brilliant? It's just such a shame.

Give me six films that you love. And they can be yours.
Pretty Baby is definitely one that I love. *Shadowlands. Big Night.*

Lacombe Lucien?
Yes, I loved it. I wouldn't say it was one of my favourite films, but structurally I loved picking it apart.

Do you think film is overrated – culturally, intellectually?
No. I'm too much of a fan.

I gave a lecture recently, saying film is overrated. And I ended up saying, 'Ask yourself the question, when you've finished a great book, and when you've finished watching a film, usually on TV or on video, compare your emotional state. How do you feel?'

Well, I think literature you're able to carry with you, because it's tangible. I mean, you underline, you fold down, you go back to it, you quote. And I think film is much more transient. It's like a love affair.

We need both, don't we?

Definitely. There's a balance that needs to be struck. And I think that that is where the irony is too. I couldn't live without making movies. Because I don't trust that my life has enough for me to experience.

That's because you are a little bit the victim of being a film-maker, right? You got turned on early and you're a junkie now. You need the fix.

There's no turning back. I need it to live . . . Where I find I'm conflicted is, you know, 'Do films have to have a message?' I don't necessarily think so.

I'm just writing a script, and there are lots of plot points to work out. But a revelation came to me and I said, 'You know what, don't worry about plot. Character is plot. Just work on the characters.'

In the film I'm doing in a few weeks, there is no script.

There's just a character?

And I'm pretty terrified about it. Because I have been schooled to ask, 'What are the words? What do I have to do? Let's figure this out . . .' You know, I was curious about why you wanted to talk to me.

Well, we first met about ten years ago now, and you came and read for me. And I wasn't expecting you to read as well as you did. I was also kind of surprised that you would even consider coming in for that part, because it was quite a sexual film and the character revealed a very dark side to herself. And I could see that as an actress you were frustrated and you wanted to be considered for those kinds of parts. I can see by some of the choices that you've made since that you really want to break out of what people think you are. Unlike most actors, you and Jodie Foster came in as children. So you have a completely different perspective on the industry. You seem to have had a bypass operation on the starry-eyed bit – because you were never outside, looking in.

We just had kids working on the television show, and unfortunately the first two kids we had, they had to recast. And I was sitting there listening to the way they were talking about these children. They'd auditioned well, but when it came time to do it in front of producers and people, I guess they were not strong enough, they were sort of too sweet. But I was listening to them saying this, and I thought, 'I wonder how they spoke about me when I was a child.' For me, there never seemed to be any discrepancy between the audition and the actual film-making –

it just got more intense. And I wondered if I was trying to look back and give myself a little more credit – 'Well, I must have had something.' But you need a certain resilience in this profession. And the two kids who then came in, they knew more than we did. They were off-book, unlike the rest of us. They came in as professionals.

It kind of horrifies me, to be honest, when I see them so adult.
It's a bit terrifying to see the precocity of it. But every now and then you get to see an honest performance, and just a real earnest desire.

What always concerns me is the bit in between the performance, when they're hanging out on the set, at the craft service table, and they're talking about deals. It's like looking at very old people at that point.
I haven't seen that, luckily. I haven't really heard the ugliness in it. I was never really around a lot of the other kids, because I was always cast alone. I was always sort of the only child.

The child star, in fact. So you never did that ensemble madness.
I was always the only one in the commercial or the only one in the movie or the only one surrounded by all adults – who sort of went out of their way to be child-like.

When you modelled, you didn't do catwalk, did you? You didn't do that anorexic seventeen-year-old thing?
No, I missed the anorexia stage. I never did the sort of no-food, cigarette-smoking, anorexic . . . I was always the kid. In fact, I always missed out on a lot of the fun group things because I was always the only one. And when I was still a kid, they said I didn't look 'all-American'. They said I looked European or something.

When did you become all-American then?
Maybe it got solidified around *The Blue Lagoon*, when I was somewhere in high school. When products started to become associated with my name: hair-dryers and shampoos and . . .

Often you don't realize there's been a transition until you look back on something. Were you aware that it was?
It was easier to get caught up into the activity and not fully understand the magnitude of it. I knew I was a part of something quite amazing when we were doing the Calvin Klein commercials. Because they were extremely unique and there was something very hip about them. We were going to be the first people that had a minute-long commercial in a movie theatre. And at the last minute they banned it. They just said, you can't have advertising in cinema, it's unacceptable. But I thought it was cool. It was this discussion about genes and biology and . . .

Was it as explicit as the still campaign?
More so. I mean, you saw me as this kind of schoolmarm-kid, sort of sophisti-

cated, saying, 'In order to begin the study of life we must first understand the function of the genetic code. Genes are fundamental in determining the characteristics . . .' And as I went on, I was slowly taking down my hair and unbuttoning my blouse just a bit. And then at the end, of course, I was in a sort of typical Calvin pose – and then the slogan, 'Survival of the fittest'. At the time I was in high school, and I had biology exams. The first question was, 'What is a gene?' And of course I just copied down the lines I had memorized. I said, 'Well . . .' And I got an A. But you know you're a part of something big when your picture is on the side of buses, and billboards in Times Square.

There's something maniacally egotistic about it as well.
Well, it was so filtered through Calvin and Avedon, they were even bigger stars than I was. They were so maniacal about it themselves that I really did feel like this vehicle. But I enjoyed that whole campaign because it felt cool to me. What I didn't enjoy happened very quickly after that. First of all, Calvin didn't want to continue with the campaign because people were going in and asking for my jeans rather than his jeans. He got all bent out of shape, I guess his feelings were hurt.

Why didn't he offer you a line? Wouldn't that have been the smart thing to do?
His partner, who had basically done all the manufacturing, and put up the money for his campaign, did offer that. And we were going to do a very smart, cool, boutique line. Just about a week before everything was done, the man died. I guess his son took over, but then it started to become . . . there was something sort of cheesy about it. It had a catalogue feel rather than something that was hip. But I would have never dreamt of contesting it because it was what I did. And I got to bring my friends in on it, so all my friends got to be the models. And we got to go on a city-to-city tour, and take the plane, and have the food we wanted. My friends thought it was cool, so I vicariously lived through their, 'Wow, we got free jeans, we got free jackets, this is so great.'

Who got you into all of this? How did it happen?
My mom – it didn't really stem from her. But the offers would always come to her.

The offers just started coming? Just because you were a great-looking teenage girl?
Yes. I was this sort of celebrated teenager that everybody knew.

I've observed in people who are attractive – it's as if, often, being attractive has got nothing to do with you. And then some people often abuse the fact that they are superficially attractive for a period of time. Because good-looking people get away with about a hundred times more than people who are not good-looking. You can appear to be quite a nice person in the period of being a stunning-looking nineteen-year-old. And as long as you don't punch people out or tell them to fuck off, you can really get away with a lot. But inside – it just seems to create such problems in people.

I would have liked to have learned a little bit of that abuse probably, because I think it would have made me more confident or something. But I just never did. I mean, I started to avoid looking in the mirror, because I never saw what anybody else saw. I always thought my face was sort of too round. All I could think would be, 'How would the man who's going to fall in love with me see me?' But I would get very claustrophobic with the thought that I couldn't actually see myself. I could only see a picture of myself. Because you only see your reflection, no matter what you do.

Do you think one should be able to gaze at oneself?
Yes. I think you should be able to get to know yourself on a very physical level. And there's this distance I've always felt from myself physically. But I loved being in sort of provocative things – again I bring up *Vogue* or *Bazaar*. It was thrilling. The excitement was that you could tap into something in yourself that was only yours. And you could give it back. You could play with it. And it was always very provocative, the stuff I enjoyed. I think that seemed much more familiar to me, to be in those types of photographs, than it did to be America's sweetheart.

Did you feel they were phoney?
Yes. I mean, I stood for what I believed in – the morals and values and stuff. Had you asked me honestly I would have answered, 'Yeah, I haven't had a serious boyfriend. No, I'm not into drugs.' That was really the way I did want to live. I really did want to go to a good school.

Who did you work with? Did you work with Helmut Newton?
All of them. I mean everybody from Scavulla and Avedon to Marches and Horst. Everybody. It's interesting – I said to Horst, 'Please, please, give me those eyelashes. I want the reflection of the eyelashes.' They were all out there. It was great. You would be in Paris doing these photo shoots from five in the afternoon to five in the morning. But I could look at those pictures and think it was a part of me. And yet I felt, if I looked at myself, everybody would be saying, 'Oh, look at her looking at herself. The ego of it. The narcissism.'

Describe the character you play in your new film.
I'm playing Gena Rowlands' daughter. She's an angry, sort of B-movie actress from New York. Shock value is sort of her M.O. She visits her mother over a weekend and brings home her gorgeous chocolate boyfriend who happens to be married. And she tries to do everything to shake her mother out of this complacency and sort of artistic snobbishness. She's always trying to get a rise out of her mother. She's defiant.

The part presumably spoke to you.
There was nothing neat and clean about this girl. She has humour about her but she's really just as unhappy as everybody else. And she's about telling it like it is – pretension is something she has no place for. I appreciated that in her. Like I said,

we were all living in one household for the shoot. And only a movie can create that sense that you're living a real life with real emotions, but you still have a place to be, you still get a call sheet . . . That's why I'm obsessed with movies.

One of the things I always notice is, when I finish a movie, a week later you go, 'Where's the call sheet? How do I know what I'm going to do today?' It's great when it's organized. You get to impersonate life, it's cathartic. But it creates huge problems in relationships, doesn't it?
Devastating problems. I used to hear the statistics, and I'd say, 'No, come on, they just have to know. They just have to do what I do.' Where you say, 'No, it's not my life, *this* is my life. And I'm going to play.' That was what I found on movie sets – your obsession was the electrician's birthday in a week's time – what were we going to do about it? There was this all-encompassing thing. And I used to think, 'I don't know how people fall in love on movies.'

Now you understand.
Completely. You spend all this time with these people and it's confusing to you, no matter what you've gone through. I would call home and say, 'Oh, God, so-and-so made me cry today, and I couldn't believe it. I'm so hurt.' And my husband could not understand how I could let a transient person register that deeply with me. But then I never go into something without it being a hundred per cent. And so I give my emotions to people.

All right, is it possible to have a relationship and be a film actor?
Well, I do my best. Obviously, there are certain lines you don't cross.

Okay, you could be cast in a movie where the story dictates that you fall in love with someone, you go to bed with them, you make love with them. Say part of your partner's job was to pretend to make love to women – how would you deal with it?
It's a sickening concept. It really is. Because touching flesh is undeniably touching flesh. For me, romantic scenes are the most uncomfortable. You've got people standing around watching you. The sheet has to be a certain way, or this has to be put on that, you know. I find it odd – and slightly humorous, to be quite honest. But it is my job to make it look as real as possible.

Forget how uncomfortable it is for you on set – that's of no interest to me if I'm your husband or your boyfriend, and I go and see you with another man, fifty feet across at the Cinerama Dome. Apparently, I've done this to actors – destroyed their relationships.
So they tell you. But, I mean, there are people that are better kissers than other people. I've kissed people I've really enjoyed kissing; I've kissed other people I just wanted to gag. You can say that to another actor because they'll understand. It's really hard to translate that to your husband. Basically, all he's thinking is, 'My wife's lips have touched another person's body . . .' I would prefer him to be

less disturbed. Not to love me less, just to be less disturbed by it. Because I have to work harder to forget that disturbance in his mind, so it doesn't inhibit me.

Have you ever come across a couple in the business who have managed to find a good place, a good compromise?
It seems that Ed Harris and Amy Madigan have done a pretty good job. And I think it takes two incredibly strong people. However, they're both actors.

It's kind of a neglected area in the film business, because only in the past fifteen to twenty years have actors pretended to screw each other quite so explicitly on camera. And it's taken for granted now. But there's no counselling, as it were. We go into it blind, and it wreaks absolute havoc. I wonder if directors should take more responsibility. Because they tend to say, 'Okay, you two kids, why don't you just fool around and I'll let the cameras roll.' And the actors are left agonizingly for whole takes, having to do stuff with hardly any direction. I often feel that actors go too far – they feel they have to almost fuck each other, you know. And men feel this huge macho pressure, they're much more uncomfortable than women. It's almost as if that's where they need direction more than in any other scene.
The problem is, it's very often looked at as montage. It's being intimate with someone but also wanting not to be totally embarrassed with what the world is going to see.

I think the director's job at that point is to make damn sure that you look great. And I always try and do that. Because that can be awfully embarrassing afterwards.
Then there's the other element, which is really to deal with the actors on the level. In this movie I just did, I really appreciated something the director did. I had this big scene with a guy. We were rehearsing a week before filming. And the director said, 'All right, now just kiss each other. Figure it all out, and just do it right this second.' And until then the two of us had been like, 'How is this going to happen? Left or right? How are your lips going to be on mine?' Now there was humour and immediacy in it – 'Run the lines, let's kiss, let's straddle each other.' And then, when it came time to film, he really made every effort to do it all in one take, and have the set completely cleared. That was the level of care that we needed to have. But I still had to drink two major shots of Scotch before I did it.

The freedom movie-making gives, to create realities and play with them – does that retard us? And, if so, is that a problem? Is it necessary for us to grow up with responsibilities and to take them seriously and abide by them?
Problem is, I think actors are perpetual kids. I mean, when I have children, I want them to understand the fun and the experience and the opportunity that films provide, but I don't need them to get into the emotional trauma, unless they truly want to be actors – then I'll support them a hundred per cent. I see some people that are truly brilliant, and yet they're so tormented in their life. Do you have to

be that tormented to be good? I don't think so. Because they are just movies. At some point they end. Whether you're making *Lolita* or whatever – no matter how all-consuming it is, it's not a licence to just fuck around.

Having started so early, I would assume that you've missed a lot of the unpleasantness of being an actress – the harassment and what seems to be a series of fairly degrading processes they have to go through.
I feel as if I did. And it's interesting – by working in television and being on a successful show, there's a sense of power to that, which again bypasses a lot of the prejudices and gender-specific power.

I've talked to a lot of actresses and they seem to form into two groups. Either they say the chauvinism just doesn't happen, or they say, 'You're out of your mind. This industry is so rife with sexism and exploitation of women.'
I've heard it, and I've seen young actresses change and lose a sense of innocence. For me, I think so much really had to do with the opportunity of going to university. I think the exploitation exists. I don't know if it's rife. I just never saw it. When I started I was just like everybody's little pet. Even on the sets, they just wanted to protect me. The grips on *Blue Lagoon* were just avid about wanting to make sure I was okay.

It's a big town, with so many roads in. And on each road there seems to be a different toll booth. Some people just arrive in the limos, and people are born within the city limits, so they never have the problem. But it's as if there are traps all around the city.
I really don't know what I would do now if I were to step on one of those land mines. I don't know if I wouldn't just say, 'You've got to be kidding me. You think you're going to intimidate me with that? Come on, that's not going to work on me.' It might work on a seventeen-year-old who walks in there. But I've either heard it spoken about enough, or I'm just too resolved in my intellect, or the fact is, I've been around a really long time.

21   Robert Downey Junior

Mike Figgis: Why did you want to be an actor? Why did you choose to go into films?

Robert Downey Junior: I was seven or eight, in the first grade, and we were doing this play in the classroom. I stood in the hallway, then I made my entrance into the classroom, and I think I said, 'Yield the castle now, Lady Roxanne.' And people liked the fact that I had the confidence to say that. It just worked, I felt confident.

Outside of that, were you not so confident?

No.

Physically, what were you like?

I was a little . . . undersized. I don't know if I was looking for approval so much as looking for a connection. But it's a strange place to feel connected – with a bunch of relative strangers, doing something false.

Pretending to be somebody you weren't.

Yes.

And then continuing to do that as an adult.

Mm-hmm.

I find that very perverse. You do it, I do it – I encourage people to do it as realistically as possible. But sometimes I stop and think about it, and it's strange. But anyway, from the age of seven, you were active as an actor?

Sure. Also, my dad was a film-maker, so it was cheaper to have me play parts. I think with other kids you'd have to stop after so many hours.

Was he pleased that you had become an actor?

I think he was indifferent. My dad says anybody can act, and few can direct, and nobody can write. On a scale of one to ten, being an actor was about the least honourable of those three.

I don't agree. I think anyone can direct; there's always enough support around. But I guess what he meant was 'direct well'.

Right. I think 'well' would come after each of those.

I don't think anybody can act well. I'm sure you know that.

I think there should be a time-limit on how long you can be just an actor.

Does it trouble you that that's what your job title is?

Yes, somewhat. I don't know why. Putting it on a lease application: 'Occupation – actor'. The funny thing is, when, after that, it says 'Employed', you write 'self'. I never employed myself as an actor in my life.

Why doesn't it feel like a real job?

Well, I do think there's something very honourable about it, because it's very humiliating. And you have to be confident that you'll have enough humility to do it well.

Technically you're a good actor.
I'm one of the best, yes.

With some actors, I know they're dying for me to rehearse them. But with you and certain others, I run a mile from rehearsal or any kind of repetition, or even really talking about it. I get a sense that it would so diminish the result, and the only way is to slide into it and then get out again as quickly as possible. I mean, you hope to be able to create some poetry together, but it can only come about by controlled accident – controlled in the sense that we know why we're there. If you were truthful, would you rather not be an actor?
If you woke me up in the middle of the night and said, 'Do you want to do this any more?', I'd say 'No.' And yet I think it's really snotty when actors who have done well, and haven't been chewed up by it all, then say, 'Oh, I really don't have any passion for this any more.' As though it's *déclassé* to say that you love what you do. But it's maybe only working with you, and on a couple of other things in the past ten years, that I felt there was any real merit to what I was doing, whether it was received well or not.

Is Hollywood just completely perverse?
There's a dark benevolence to it. My mom said the last time she saw me with any real humility was when I was seventeen, doing theatre in New York. I was really a busboy then, not an actor. When I came to Los Angeles, everything that I thought I wanted happened for me. And I think that what kept me from really looking at myself, and growing, was my success.

But so many people go into movies, or the music business, where success is synonymous with money and drugs and so forth. And they often describe it as like being on a roller-coaster, swept along on a wave. With you, I don't buy that. Because you have an overview of yourself – I'm sure you had it when you were seven. I can candidly say I worked with you at a point when you were, as far as anybody else was concerned, completely out of your nut. But I always had the impression that you were also sitting outside yourself, completely aware of what you were doing. And if there was a wave, you were watching it.
Yep. I think the further out you go, the better the objectivity you have.

If you'd been more challenged artistically, or if you'd just had to work harder for your rewards, would you have felt better about the whole situation?
No, I did have to work for it, you know. Even when I was doing what I call 'faxing in a performance', it's still work. But there are two separate things – the juggernaut that is external success, and the interior thing of whether you're growing in co-ordination with that.

Then why didn't you?
Just laziness. Success and fame are the best ways to keep people away from you, you can put them between you and other people. And I noticed that other peo-

ple were kind of happy for me, but they didn't really like it because it was like they were losing, in this unconscious not-really-talked-about race. Even people outside the industry, people I went to high school with – success put a great buffer between me and them – and me and myself, in terms of having to deal with it.

How did you relate to other people? Did you behave badly?
I was kind of described as a lovable tornado.

That sounds positive.
Yeah, but a tornado nonetheless . . . I think the openness that might be necessary to be a good actor can be lethal in your real life.

That's true – it's true of musicians too.
I had the whole thing of people saying, 'I'm sorry you're so self-destructive because you've got such a great talent.' As if what someone has to offer is some-how more worthwhile than their pulse, or their personal comfort. And I bought it big-time. I was just thinking today – I got in all this trouble, in jail . . . I stopped growing as Robert when I started becoming successful as an actor and focusing primarily on this or that movie, and diverting my energy from what was going on and what real life lessons were there for me.

But when you were eighteen, that wasn't a consideration in your mind?
No.

Were you having a good time at least?
Oh, yes, it couldn't have been better. I came from New York, I wasn't one of those fellows who grew up in Malibu and their family were in the industry. I'd never had a car, I'd never had the clothes. It's so stupid, but cars, clothes, parties – they were what it was about.

Fair enough. What else are you supposed to do when you're eighteen? But I had in my mind that you'd always been in Malibu. When I first saw you there, you had the look of someone who was painted on the scenery.
Well, that was right before the inevitable decline of recent years. I was bottoming out, but I was living like a king. You told me, 'This is no good for you, you've got to get out of here.' And I was like, 'What the fuck is he talking about? Look at this, look at these tiles, look at this ocean. What's wrong with this?' It all seemed like a finished piece to me.

I thought it was a beautiful place. I was just concerned by the people that were visiting you.
If I moved away, they'd keep coming to this address looking for me, and I wouldn't see them any more.

So – doing all that at eighteen, fine. At the same time, you were educated, right?

No. Well, I think I'm hyper-educated. But not school-wise, no. High school drop-out.

Do you like reading?
Yes.

Do you like watching films?
Sure. Well, not *The Avengers*, but every other one.

Okay, fair enough. But you still like movies. A lot of people I speak to don't any more – particularly people who work in the industry. I can understand that. They get disillusioned, when they pay their money and they don't get what they want. A lot of people are returning to books for stimulation – literature, the word. Did you always read?
Oh, yes, since I was really young.

Were you encouraged to?
No. I think that I was always really drawn to the real *Bodhi Tree* stuff. I think it saved my ass because, in the midst of everything else, regardless of how I behaved, I still felt like I knew what the truth was.

When did you start being a musician?
When I was twelve, in 1977. Where we were living in Woodstock, there was a piano in the living room. Mom and Dad were breaking up, it was there, I went over. I learned a simple scale, and then I realized I could play and I escaped in that. I associate music with a healthy escapism.

I've heard your music and it's really good, I was kind of intrigued by it. You write sophisticated, complex tunes which have what I would say is an advanced harmonic sense in them. You don't just do blues things. So how important is music to you?
I was reading Plato, I think, when he was talking about this perfect society. 'Basically,' he said, 'master the body, and add music.' And I think that's true. I think that music can help you master the body too. I don't know that music has been recognized for what it really is.

Do you want to talk about your jail period?
Sure.

The first time we met, in a restaurant called Kate Mantalini, you turned up, I think, two hours late – with a gun.
Barefoot.

Barefoot and completely speeding. We had what was, for me, an incomprehensible one-hour meeting, and I found myself looking at you and thinking, 'You're fascinating, but there are five hundred reasons why you're not going to

be in this film.' Then, at some point, we started talking about music. I remember driving away and thinking that I'd like you to be in the film, which is what happened. But I could see you were going through a real crisis, and it got worse, and you were arrested a couple of times while we were making the film. Then you were very well-behaved. You never gave me a problem in terms of scheduling, which I thank you for. Then, as we wrapped, you finally got locked up. What was going on?

Well, first up, when I came to meet you at the restaurant, I thought we were going to talk about me playing the lead – which I was perfectly happy with, I was romantic and ready for that assignment. Then, when you said, 'No, I think you should play Charlie', I was dying inside. I went in the bathroom to get high and I looked at myself and I said, 'You know, I may never look more ready to play someone really sick than I do right now.' In years before that, there had always been a sense of 'Robert's in trouble but he doesn't look so bad, so let's not talk about it.' Either that, or 'Let's get into a big discussion about how Robert's got to get it together.' But it really blew my mind that you were one of the first people who seemed to just acknowledge what was going on with me, and honour the fact that I was willing myself into a very bad place, maybe for some higher reason than just death. On the other hand, I wasn't sure if you weren't saying that, you know . . .

That it was okay.

Or rather that I could, for me anyway. I didn't see any direct request to alter my course of action.

That did cross my mind. At one point I came out to see you in Malibu and give you a bit of a talking to. But I also felt that you were on your way somewhere, and I didn't think anybody was going to talk you out of it. You seemed so intelligent. Also I felt it would be good for you to work, hopefully on something with some spirit. There was a lot of passion in that role for me, it was about a friend of mine. But there was a point at the restaurant where I decided to be direct with you and I said, 'Why have you got a gun?' And you went, 'What gun?' I said, 'The one on the floor between our feet.' And you said, 'Oh, I didn't want to leave it in my car.' I said, 'I'm not interested in why it's not in the car, why have you got one anyway?' That showed a sneaky, druggie side of you – your answer was so cleverly evasive. You were addicted?

Yes, I was smoking heroin and coke. The thing is, I don't think that films happen by accident, I think that people do the films they're meant to do. The film I'd done before *One Night Stand* was *Restoration*, which was just a calamity, so I started really plummeting. I saw your film as an opportunity to really explore my dissatisfaction with life, and with being an actor. So I was sort of filmed doing it, you know. But after that I did a couple of things I really didn't like – I did possibly the worst action movie of all time, and that's just not good for the maintenance of a good spiritual condition. You've had a traumatic year, you've been practically suicidal – what do you think would be really healing for you? How about like twelve weeks of running around as Johnny Handgun? I think that if you talk to a spirit guide, they would say, 'That'll kill you.'

Why did you do it?
For the same reason that I did *Air America* ten years before – I thought maybe there was something I was missing, and what I really needed to do was to be in one of those films that I love taking my kid to. It would end up being really depressing. I'd rather wake up in jail for a TB test than to have to wake up another morning knowing I'm going to the set of *US Marshals*.

Really?
Yes. Somehow I finished it, but I felt I was destined to get in trouble for what had happened while I was doing that movie. Then I went to do *In Dreams* with Neil Jordan. The role was dark, he was a serial killer, but I just looked at him as someone who had a really bad childhood. He was very childish, and I could really relate to that. On that, I probably had six of the best weeks I'd had in a couple of years.

In terms of getting up, going to work, being cheerful?
Yes, I felt motivated. But obviously it's not enough. You've said to me about certain actors being paid so much money – sooner or later there'll be a creative downfall by it.

It can't survive. We know we're not really worth that much money.
I remember when Bruce Willis was a bartender at Café Central, and I used to go there – I was a busboy downtown. Now I feel closer to those times than ever – because I'm almost exactly where I was when I was seventeen. I live on my assistant's couch.

How do you feel now?
I feel incredibly grateful to have the freedom to reinvent myself – as opposed to allowing myself to be invented. I mean, it's not like I didn't acquiesce to that happening.

Are you bored still? You were bored the last time we spoke.
Yes, but that's no one's fault but my own.

Have you always been bored?
I think I've been resigned for a long time. I think a lot of it too is to do with being a student of this industry, and of people who have done it their way. I've amassed a little knowledge over the years and I think that humility has not done me a service, in so much as I would go and act any way I wanted, as long as I came back to the crocodile-tear, 'Gee, I'm sorry, I better just follow direction now' routine.

I've never seen you angry. Have you ever lost your temper?

Oh, God, yeah. Last time I lost my temper was when I got into a fight in jail.

Did you win?
Initially – and then I got my clock cleaned. But that's because initially I was scuffling with people my own size. And then a very large shadow was cast over me and the next thing I remember is waking up in a pool of my blood.

You told me something about jail which I found sad – that it didn't seem any different from LA. People were still hustling scripts.
Yes. There was a lieutenant who said he had this script about unicorns, but it wasn't just your usual unicorn script.

I've never read a unicorn script . . .
After I got in the fight I was down in this discipline module, which is like a hole. Three times a day, you see a pair of hands and some food come in – it's pretty awful. One day it opens and there was this lieutenant, with some deputy he'd brought by to meet me. I hadn't had a shower in five days, I was sleeping in my clothes, my hair was all fucked up. But that Hollywood big-shot entertainer thing came in, and I thought 'Well, I'd better come to, I have company.' And this guy came in and said, 'Listen, I know you don't have a lot to read in here. I hope I wouldn't be crossing the line if I brought a script by for you. It's about unicorns. It's not what you think, there's a very human element to it.' And I was just dumbfounded. I said, 'Wow, great.' There were other times, inmates said, 'We should do a movie about this.' I've heard this from other people too – actors, directors, writers, in some mundane situation like driving school. 'Man, we should do a film about this, where we're all in driving school together. It'd be fucking great.' Just the last thing you need.

How long were you there?
Four months.

And it was okay?
Mm-hm. I mean, you can have a great day in jail, and you can have a lousy day in Beverly Hills.

So what's happening now? You switched agents just before all this happened. When you came out, did you expect to get a job?
I've always expected to get a job. Now it's just more difficult than ever before – even before I got in trouble, and I was complaining about 'Why aren't I king of this town?' Plus now, rightfully so, the insurance companies want to take the production companies for a ride – it's justifiable extortion. But nothing's really changed. I think maybe I created all this stuff, so that I could have a period of time to figure out what it is that I really wanted to do to begin with.

How far down that process are you?
Just catching up. I'm setting aside this weekend to really think about it.

What do you want to happen for you?
Well, I think that anything short of a 180-degree, maybe 360-degree change is going to yield the same results – misery, resentment, incarceration, disappointment . . .

Is that happening already?
Yes, because it's like trying to fix a broken hammer with a broken hammer. I realize that, really, since I was seventeen or eighteen, I haven't exactly been in the most realistic mind-set. And if I expect a happy and healthy life and want to continue to be an artist in any way, then I have to recognize that there's nothing to be lost by doing it with a clear head . . .

Do you really think so?
Yes.

I may be wrong, but I don't think of you as damaged or having a problem. I think you know what you're doing. My heroes all seem to have been junkies. That's not because they're junkies, it's just that they're often very brave people who burned fast – because accelerated creativity yields a higher gain. When I was your age I was paranoid about drugs, because I thought creativity had to be a pure experience. It's only now that I've taken onboard the idea that sometimes, as far as creativity is concerned, it's okay not to have an absolutely clear head. You've always seemed to me to have that kind of mind. But I always thought you were lazy, too.
You're absolutely right. And I'm a perfect example of a microcosm of what's going on in this zip-code right now. Because I think laziness is a resignation to inability, and inability is evil.

It's a lazy town. Nobody likes to work hard. And I come from a very old-fashioned work ethic, where you feel guilty if you're not worn out by the end of the day. But your problem is – you can do it. It's no sweat, and it never will be. So I do think you need to go somewhere else – not too far away. But I do think maybe you need to take responsibility.
I believe that will transpire, though I think practically everyone around me will see it as just the latest in a long line of insane ideas.

Yeah, but who gives a fuck?
Yeah – why stop now?

In this town, films are made by mundane committees. There's almost a conspiracy to hold back creativity – because creativity throws a horrible spotlight on the dullness and the mundanity of those committees. So often creativity gets bastardized – as addictive personality or whatever. Sometimes they get it wrong, it's like misdiagnosing schizophrenia as manic-depression. They're close, they look the same – but they're not.
You know the R. D. Laing story about the lady who came in and said she was

really worried her son had become schizophrenic? So the kid came in, and in fact he was properly schizophrenic. And later on, she says, 'Well, the truth is, his father isn't his father. But he doesn't know it.' I can relate to that a lot. Like there's something afoot and, rightly or not, people say, 'Oh, but he doesn't know that.' I didn't come here just to do a couple of junkets a year and keep all the fucking plates spinning. I'm so fearful of letting go of all the things that have contributed to my demise because I'm so comfortable.

Is it the fact that – on a good year, if you don't blot your copybook – you can earn millions of dollars? Hard to say no to, don't you think?
Sure. I also think that if you can get it, then you deserve it.

Obviously, if you don't behave, you won't earn a lot of money, that's a fact. Has your income dropped a lot lately?
Yes.

What's the most you ever earned on a movie?
I think it was in 1994. Two and a quarter million – for six weeks on a movie called *Only You*.

And before and after that, you were in that area?
Mm-hm.

So you've spent a lot of money.
All of it. I've always spent all the money I've made – because I was complacent enough, with no reason to do otherwise.

So you don't really have a lot of assets right now?
None.

What kind of money are you earning now?
Maybe a quarter of what I was – half a million for the latest thing.

And does it pretty much get swallowed up?
Yes. It's just enough to keep all the plates spinning. And that's fucking miserable. Right now I have this idea of doing some paintings and putting a little piece of music to each painting for an exhibit. But how can I survive, following that dream?

Do you feel you're having to go to work right now to pay the housekeeping?
I feel like I have to, but I'm not going to. Because I have to get through that fear of economic insecurity, if I want to live as an artist. I don't think I have been an artist for a long time. I've been on automatic, trying to make the best of it, and it's yielded me a lot of trouble and very little satisfaction. I've done things to anaesthetize myself from the reality – which is that people do write, or direct, or take time to make books or be photographers. And there's a balance that comes with people who take care of their souls, instead of just try to keep a lie running.

For that reason I've always pictured you in Europe – if you wanted to create a base that was a bit quieter, where you could build up those things. And you could – you paint, you do music, you could direct easily, I think. So how much of a challenge is it for you to get off the treadmill? Presumably, your price will creep up again, right? The town is very forgiving, financially. The fact that you're working at all is remarkable.

Well, what nauseates me more than anything is the whole 'Hollywood loves a comeback' thing. Just because I can be embraced again, be the recovered guy and ride that for all it's worth, like everything's different now – why should I play into that? That's just the other side of the same fucking deck.

You shouldn't – I think that's a death. If I saw you on a chat show being self-congratulatory about your evangelism, I'd throw up. I'd worry about you too. I'd think you were being manipulated. Okay, some quick questions to finish – give me five books that you dig.
Emotional Care for the Facially Burned and Disfigured. Seth Speaks. Gore Vidal's *Julian.* The Penguin book on *Etruscan Art.* I've got to say *The Talisman.*

Five pieces of music – any genre.
Erik Satie – how do you say that in French, *Gymnopédies.* Phil Collins, *No Jacket Required.* Elvis Costello, *Imperial Bedroom.* Barry Manilow's *Greatest Hits. The Unforgettable Fire,* U2.

Five movies.
Paths of Glory. King of Hearts. Green Card. Big Night. The Battle of Algiers.

Five actresses.
That's impossible. Hey, who was that French actress, did this movie where she works in a hair salon, she's nuts and she kills all these people at the end? Not Claudette Colbert. Whoever she is – her. Diane Lane.

Why Diane? I agree, but . . .
I don't know. She's just so – she's not full of shit. We worked together on *Chaplin.* Which brings me to Moira Kelly. Kim Novak. Paulette Goddard.

Okay. Actors.
John Malkovich. Chris Walken. The guy who plays the serial killer in *Con Air* – Steve Buscemi. Alan Arkin. Whoever played the sniper in *Saving Private Ryan.* That guy's fucking clean – best thing about the movie.

Five directors.
Stanley Kubrick. For new folks, Keith Gordon. He directed *The Chocolate War.* He was an actor. I would say that's all I got.

Mike Figgis: You're an actor, I guess you've been around theatre and film for all your adult life?

Xander Berkeley: And a lot of my child life . . .

Right. And you live here in Hollywood. What do you think about the quality of the material you're offered in this industry? What level is that at right now?

For me, it's a source of deep frustration, always. I have these ideas about how it could be, and I suppose that's why I wanted to put my money where my mouth is – difficult as that can be – and start to write my own thing – instead of rewriting everybody else's things once I've been hired, which is what I've been doing for years.

What do you mean 'rewrite'?

A lot of times you'll be given a script, but it's still up to you, the actor. Because you find out who your character is along the way, through rehearsal. You bring your individuality to that. And I feel that as long as you're moving the story forward in a way that is germane to the character, rather than trying to hijack a movie moment for yourself, then you're serving the story and the director, and doing your job well by rewriting the lines. A lot of times a writer has no way of dividing his mind into all those different ways that something can be expressed. Great writers have a good sense of it, but it can always be sort of 'tweaked' in the moment. So much dialogue is just like throwing something away, because there's a moment there that really needs to be conveyed through the physical behaviour of the people interacting. And it's about having a sense of what that would be, and being able to just throw it in. A lot of times humour will come into play on a spontaneous level. You try to work with directors who sense that you have a way with words and that you're going to help them.

For the most part, are you lucky in that?

Yes, but ultimately I want to direct, and so my focus has been on trying to work with the best directors there are, even in smaller roles, because I want to learn through osmosis if I can. A lot of times, it just has to do with the chemistry of a director and myself hitting it off in the first place.

What's happened to writing? If we want writing to be the central foundation of the movies – which it has to be, everything comes from the script – what has happened to make it so generic and dull?

Fear, I guess. Fear that somebody's going to lose their money if they take a risk. Fear that an audience won't understand something if it isn't squarely over the head three times in a row.

One problem, it seems to me, is that a lot of the time writers are having to write scripts geared to the reality of getting them produced. I don't want to generalize about producers, there are exceptions galore, but a lot of them are sort of status quo, keepers of the dough. They want to protect the money and the writers are writing for the producers, to make sure they get it. Producers aren't necessarily thinking visually or creatively, they want to see everything spelled out. But there are things driving a story which you would never say, because they're subtext. Even after they've hired more writers to do more polishes, somehow the blatantly obvious stuff is still on the page. So you have to get hold of the script on the day and realize, 'Well, now we're doing this, I don't think we necessarily have to spell out what's going on for the audience. We assume they're intelligent enough to see.'

So it is still possible to change scripts on the day?
Yes. Because film-making is a collaborative process, and if something isn't working, I think it's not only acceptable for actors to change it, it's part of their job requirement, in a way.

So you're saying that the writing process has become a PR exercise, aimed at the selling of a script rather than the performing of it. And the function of intelligent actors is then to partly rewrite that script?
And if the trend continues and goes any further in this direction, we really will have to renegotiate, because I'd like to start getting a little credit, a little bit of money for some of the writing that I offer . . .

I remember the first time we worked together, on *Internal Affairs*. We were doing a scene with you and Richard Gere, and I recall giving you the freedom to be 'badder' and 'badder', to make it funny, unpleasant, whatever. I enjoyed what you were doing.
We'd hit it off in the audition. Then I came in on the day and first I said, 'Mike, these lines are really written for a sixty-five-year-old, broken-nosed thug pederast, I don't know if I can . . .' And you said, 'Oh no, no, I thought we'd just ad lib, have some fun, isn't that what it's all about?' I went, 'Right on!' And you said, 'You could help me out because the film's called *Internal Affairs* and I'm afraid it's become rather an internal affair, so I'm hoping you could maybe bring it out of that in this scene.' I had thought the dangerous thing would be to make that character more of a practical joker, that would be his aegis, that he didn't take this big scary guy seriously. That gave him a threat and danger all of his own.

I always say of De Niro and Pacino that I'm always fearful of the crockery, because you know that at some point they're going to sweep everything on to the floor and say, 'Don't fuck with me.' And people are going to look really frightened. But I just like to remind people that everybody's shit smells the same, that you can be a bad-ass guy and at the same time –
You can have a sense of humour.

Whereas that 'Don't fuck with me' style of writing for men is so masculine it's almost gay.
Yeah. Can't show a single chink in the armour, got to be wearing clad gonads at all times.

Are you treated well as an actor here?
By some people. Not by others.

The casting process, is that okay with you? Is it humiliating?
I'll tell you, I'm getting pretty damn tired of it, Mike. I get a kick out of how tired I am of it, because it makes me a little reckless. You can't help but feel a little strange – I've got Spielberg and Wolfgang Peterson and Mike Figgis offering me jobs without my having to audition. Then there are these totally untested directors, I have no reason to assume they're going to be good –

You should be putting them on test.
Yes. I've done sixty-five films, I have compilation tapes of scenes from lots of different performances. They won't even take the ten minutes to look at that. They just want to bring you in – it may be a total waste of your time. It takes you two hours to read the script thoroughly, it takes at least four hours to work on the material for the audition – because you want to acquaint yourself with it, you don't want to take the time if you're not going to do a good job. But it drives you a little crazy that you're still having to go out there and do this tap-dance. Okay, I'm not a name, I'm not a star. But I think they really should cut you a little break if you're as well established as I am as a supporting player. You don't get accorded that respect.

Who's involved in this lack of respect? Is it the casting director? Is it the director?
Oh, it's just convenience. Human nature is what's involved, it's just that if they can get away with something, they will.

At a certain point you get so fed up with what you're being handed that you take a stand – 'I'm not going to do it.' And perversely, 'No' does seem to be the password to the next realm. People start to take note and consider that you might be worthy of something more.

For years – even before I had a body of work to support it – I went in with this attitude of calculated nonchalance. Without it being unctuous or arrogant, it separated you from the stink of desperation a little bit. Even if it was just an intellectual adjustment you made – 'Well, they don't have the good sense to hire me, it's their loss, isn't it?' This was before I started getting so burnt out and tired of the audition process. But I used to feel, 'This is what I love to do.' And I still get that feeling, I got it last week – this feeling of 'I don't even care if I do the movie, I want to do this character, that's what I want to go and do at the office today.'

Is there really any difference between the independent film world here and the studio world?
You make more money in the studio world. And sometimes you have a lot more creative freedom in the independent world.

I find that most young independent film-makers call themselves 'indie film-makers' but they clearly have their eye on the fast lane.
Yes, their film's an advertisement for their big-budget potential.

I'm going to throw some quick, silly questions. Don't think about it too much, just give me five pieces of music that have touched you.

Boy, oh boy . . . Brian Eno, *Another Green World*. Bach . . . I have such a disparate taste in music. There's some music from the Bulgarian hills that's pretty impressive. Jura Jura, this little Nigerian pop band, about ten or twenty years ago, they still stay in my head. I'm overwhelmed, there are so many things . . .

Okay. Five books.

When I think about the books that changed my life, I tend to think in terms of the sort of esoteric books that I don't like to talk about too much. Those are the ones that are nearest and dearest to my heart, and they're sort of secret.

Okay, that's a good answer. Five films.

The French silent film of *Joan of Arc*. I can't say it's one of my favourites, I just saw it the other night, but it left a tremendous impact.

I just want to get some sense of your taste. I'm asking everybody.

Something in my nature wants to rebel against these questions, because I'm always changing my opinion and my tastes.

Try and make it fast rather than making time to think about it.

Okay – *Blood of a Poet*, *Juliet of the Spirits*, *Cul-de-Sac*.

Okay. Directors that are interesting?

Tarkovsky, Godard, Scorsese, Bergman.

Actors, male.

My mind just goes blank. I can talk about anything and everything, but when it comes to pinning down my favourites of anything, I squirm . . . I like Bruno Ganz.

23   Mike DeLuca

Mike Figgis: Why did you choose to go into the film business?
Mike DeLuca: It probably dates back to the neighbourhood movie theatre – this was Canarsy, in Brooklyn. My father worked a lot of midnight shifts, he wasn't around a lot. My mother worked, so I spent a lot of time with my friends at the movies. I just gravitated towards escapist entertainment and film. Then I started getting into comic books and that gets you into magazines about movies, and then you find out behind-the-scenes stuff, where these stories that you like come from. And eventually I went to NYU Film School.

What course?
It was the undergraduate programme, so mostly it was writing classes. But Film History class was great because this was really before home video, so they would screen prints of anything from Stan Brakhage to *Citizen Kane* and *Touch of Evil*. Then I became an intern at New Line, because the position was available, and I had just seen *Nightmare On Elm Street* and thought it was cool. Then I just ended up staying with this company.

You must be fairly unique in what they call 'Hollywood', in that you've been with this company for how long now?
Since I was nineteen. I've just turned thirty-three, so that would be fourteen years. It is unusual, yes. I think it's a combination of how small the company was when I joined, and how successful it became in a relatively short period. It was an explosion of opportunity – each year they could offer you a bigger job and more responsibility, so I just progressed to where I am now.

The company is doing well today, economically. Again, in a very nervous industry that's quite unusual, because most of the other companies have folded. Who are your competitors now?
I'd have to say the big studios. I think we've met in the middle – we've stepped up a little bit, and they've started to look at the films that traditionally New Line and Miramax and Dimension which is Miramax's genre arm, have been doing. They saw it as a business they shouldn't ignore. So really we're all in competition with each other now.

People are fascinated by the executive machinations of the system here. I am too. And I'm still learning.
When you read the entertainment press, there's so little respect for what they call 'Creative Executives'. Most of the people who have that title are poor kids working for no money; they went to college but they aren't using their education at all. They're struggling to get into the film business, they take home twenty-five scripts a weekend and work through them. But they're the most maligned creature when people talk about what's wrong with the film business. I was trying to think, why is there this vehemence, this hatred?

It may be because some of them are complete ass-holes. As in any industry, there are the real worker bees who work in ensembles, and then there are the big-mouths who –

Ruin it for everybody.

I've worked with you on a reasonably budgeted movie – between twenty and thirty million dollars. That's substantially more than the budget for *Leaving Las Vegas*, which was three and a half. Suppose I pitched you a movie that I'd make for two million dollars, on which you could maybe make three million profit. I'd be pleased with that return, if it was my money. But I think I get very little interest in those sorts of numbers. Is that true?

The big studios are looking to hit home runs all the time, because their overheads are huge and they're in this global pre-packaging distribution business. They don't want to put their time and energy into smaller, riskier films. Miramax and ourselves and the specialized labels like October – we fill that void. I see a lot of studios hurting for product because their slates are empty except for these big, star-driven summer or Christmas movies. There are a lot of interesting movies that they didn't make or won't make, and we feed off that a little bit.

The studios gear up their factories to make two thousand units and suddenly they're only making a thousand. So you see a lot of people looking conspicuously idle, which makes them nervous. Then you get to the other end of the scale and there's a glut of movies coming out every week. So there seems to be a dangerous imbalance now in the industry.

I think there are more people making movies, which accounts for some of the glut. Even if Disney scales back and makes fewer movies in a year, there's Dream-Works now – there seem to be more studios. It takes about five years to get a studio up and running. That's how long it took us to get bigger, after Turner acquired us in 1993. It took me about two years to really fill the pipeline with stuff that could be released in 1995 and 1996.

How did you go about that?

The first thing I did was clean house – look through all the old development projects and see what was never going to get made. Then the smoke clears and you see what you're left with. Then you panic because you realize, even if we do great and make one out of five of these, we're missing fifty or sixty projects that are out there now. Then we went on a buying spree and tried to get our hands on interesting stuff that wouldn't take two years to develop. We worked on a lot of turnaround projects that other studios hadn't got around to making or were missing the point of. And we took our shots with a few of them. *Seven* was one of those.

And that paid off, obviously.

Yes.

Describe what you actually do from Monday to Friday – and, I'm sure, your weekends too. How do you make the business work?

Most of my time is spent on filtering through the scripts and projects the development people tell me are interesting. Can we buy it? Can we develop it? I throw in my two cents and cut out the stuff that I think they're wrong about and support the stuff that I think they're right about.

You have to do a lot of reading.

Yes, I usually take home about twenty scripts a weekend. A lot of it is stuff we own, though – stuff that is about to shoot. The development costs are relatively small compared to the millions that fly out the window once a film starts shooting.

Sure. You can take more risks with scripts, up to the green light.

Yes. Our goal is to have ten or twelve films a year to release; films that come out of our production division. I'm not counting Fine Line or acquisitions.

And amongst those ten films, say, what would be the range of budgets?

I'd say two-thirds of what we do is between five and thirty-five million – either low-budget, or in that mid-range that the studios have decried as unsafe, even though that's the place where all our hits have come from. Then the other third is over thirty-five million, and directly competitive with standard studio fare.

Do you feel a little stretched when you start competing with the blockbusters? Is it like sitting at a card-table with guys who have bigger wallets than you? I'm thinking of films like *Lost In Space*.

Yes, if you're releasing on three thousand screens, people have come to expect certain production values for an action film or a special-effects movie. If the budget is above seventy-five million dollars, then you're out there. We're still good about not needing to go into those summer or Christmas zones just to have a dick-measuring contest. We released *Lost In Space* in April and it was the right thing to do.

With a movie of that size, at the point when the script has been through its various writing stages, how nervous do you get prior to the green light? And what part do you play in that?

I'm the person who provides the forward momentum, keeps the thing moving. I know at the other studios when you have a big star, like a Tom Hanks or a Schwarzenegger, who has a set amount of time in which to do the movie, you know that that start day is a particular day and will not move, because the actor can't move. So you scramble to get the script together. With *Lost In Space*, we knew what the release date was going to be, and it was the best release date, and everything worked backwards from that. So then you have a snowballing nightmare of 'Here's how long it's going to take to complete the special effects. That leaves you this much time to get the script in order.' You do what you can in that time.

Do you think people make mistakes because of that pressure? Not specifically in this company, but in general?

Yes, I think so. The pressure induces a lot of anxiety. I'm not sure it actually causes mistakes, but it doesn't allow you to catch mistakes that are sitting there. You get this 'We'll fix it on the way' mentality.

Film is terrible like that. You can delude yourself always, even at the last stage – 'We can fix it on an Avid.' When you get to the Avid and it ain't fixed, it's almost as if people have already said goodbye to the corpse. 'But we're still going to have this party and release it because we said we would.' By then, you're already so far into the pot, right?

I've always felt that I've known when we've done something that isn't going to fly. I know that when we've got into trouble, it's because a kind of cynicism sets in sometimes. The studios won't admit this, but there's this mentality of 'Well, I would never go see this movie – but *they* might.'

I remember a producer in meetings who kept referring to 'the great unwashed' – he meant anybody outside of LA and New York.

Once you draw that distinction between you and the marketplace, you're just asking for trouble.

What do you think of the marketplace in terms of its ability to read a good movie?

I'm pretty high on the marketplace. I'm an avid movie-goer and I've seen audiences respond to such a broad range of movies. They're a lot more accepting of different or fresh material in films than a lot of the studios give them credit for.

How much nerve do you need – in terms of holding to your faith, given that certain financial figures are going to be staring you in the face?

A lot. You take on the role of cheerleader and team captain. It gets tricky if you use that for films you really don't care that much about – that's when I get into trouble. But when I'm doing it for something I really believe in and want to see happen, then it's effortless – there's no question of anxiety. I take very seriously the amount of money we spend, but I don't let it scare me.

That sum of money you spend – do you ever visualize what it looks like?

No – that's funny. It could be stacks of notes in a bank vault or gold bars at Fort Knox; I have no idea. I'm aware of what we need to do to meet our business-plan, I know when our films go over budget, and I know when our films make money or lose money. But what the money looks like is an abstract concept to me.

And for most of Hollywood, I would imagine.

I think the studios have more anxiety about it. Yet their pockets are so bottomless. And they're so vertically integrated. But our core business really is movie production – we don't have theme parks or a music wing or a publishing wing or a cable wing.

Are you glad?
It's simpler for me that way. We have less of a cushion but we're very focused. Whereas for these corporations, I think movies are almost like a prestigious public-relations component. It's just about having your people on entertainment shows, and winning Oscars. It's a flashy business, and it's always made more sense on that level than as a return-on-investment business. Movies are always going to be a jewel in the crown of any media corporate giant, just because of the sexiness of it.

How much of an issue is that 'sexiness' for people in this town?
It's prevalent. It's a company town, and it's really about making a sexy product that you hope is going to seduce a bunch of people into paying to go see it. In a way, it's like very upscale prostitution.

It appeals to a certain very specific part of the brain, doesn't it?
The pleasure centres. Even if you go to see a movie that's disturbing, there's still an element of entertainment to it, even if it's entertaining the darker side of your personality.

Do you actually believe that films affect people?
That's a big topic. I don't feel as if they affected me. I grew up loving horror films and violent comic books. To me it was just getting a handle on certain kinds of mythology. Having parents who ignore you, having abuse in your background, not being educated – I always feel those things do a lot more harm than any piece of entertainment. I don't think the rest of us should have to give up anything in the arts or entertainment to make up for other problems in society. I think the death penalty has more to do with our violence in society than violent films. I was thinking about this rash of school shootings we've seen. They really got to me, because every time they went into the background of the kid, I recognized qualities in myself at that age. I was an isolated kid, angry and alone a lot of the time, and I always thought that comic books and movies prevented me from going to school and shooting people. But in the reporting of these shootings I noticed a certain line of attack – because Stephen King had written a novella called *Rage*, about a boy who goes to school and shoots his classmates, and the Pearl Jam song 'Jeremy' was based on one of the school shootings, and it supposedly influenced another school shooting. But then you'd hear little snippets about the gun culture in that community – guns in the house, the father and mother who broke up, the mother who told one of the sons, 'I want to kill your father and myself.' Then you'd hear about a kid being beaten up in school every day, being called a faggot in gym class, having his clothes stolen – and the teacher's not paying any attention. Those were the real reasons, but they were getting swept under the carpet, because it makes a bigger headline for the media to blame films or books or music.

Within the media, there's the feeling that the media is more important, positively or negatively.
There was a big debate between John Grisham and Oliver Stone because *Natural Born Killers* apparently inspired two crystal meth addicts to go on a spree, and among the victims were friends of Grisham's. He put forth this notion that if a film is a 'defective product' that causes violence, you can sue the creators. And Oliver Stone argued that it's not a product, it's art. Even though I had a tendency towards Stone, you couldn't just dismiss what Grisham was saying.

No, you can't.
Because these people did watch this movie, they did take a shit-load of drugs, and they weren't exactly the most sound people in the world. But then there's this argument of, 'Even if *Natural Born Killers* hadn't been made, don't you think those kids would have gone on that spree over something else?'

I think they would have been fucked up in some way, yes. But I don't know if they would have gone that far. I know *Internal Affairs* was cited as the defence in a killing in Boston, but it was just an attempt to get the kids off. It turned out to be a gang-related killing. They just happened to have seen *Internal Affairs*, and they claimed that it wound them up. But for a period of time, it was very worrying for a film-maker to think that you might have contributed to the taking of someone's life. That's quite a horrible thing to have to deal with.
I had that experience every time we released a gangster film. Our gangster films have been African-American gangster films. Now, I always thought *Menace II Society* was an art film that was also a gangster film. But gangster movies have always attracted gangsters to the theatres, whether it's Hispanic gangsters or Italian gangsters. So there were a couple of shootings in theatres during the release of *Set It Off*, and a couple of shootings during *Menace II Society*. And it's hard to deal with that stuff, because if you hadn't put the film in the theatre, you knew the incidents wouldn't have happened.

While we were previewing *One Night Stand*, you were also previewing Paul Thomas Anderson's *Boogie Nights*. How did you monitor its progress?
I was very close there. I knew it would need more protection than any other film in the pipeline, because it was a fight to get it made. The budget went up from what I promised them. Originally it was an eight-million-dollar movie with Drew Barrymore and Sam Jackson – then it was fifteen and a half, with Heather Graham and Don Cheadle. And I was coming off 1996 where everything we seemed to do, with the exception of *Set It Off*, really didn't work. Your confidence goes up and down depending on the year you've had. And I hate those test screenings as much as you do, I hate the numbers game.

I don't mind the moment of the screening, that's interesting for all of us.

But I think those numbers are really only telling for films like *Men In Black* or *Godzilla*; films that are just meant to be light entertainment.

Why do you do them then?
It's part of this insecurity where you've got a lot of money invested and they want any sign that it's going to work. Research has become a crutch, but the studios want the research to tell them they made the right decision, and the investment is protected.

What if the research is telling them the opposite?
I think I police these screenings better than a lot of people I know at the studios, because they can really fuck a film up. Audiences are recruited for them with a paragraph at malls, and you get a huge cross-section. Now, normally, you release a film after an ad campaign that acts as a natural filter, so you just get the people who would be interested in 'that kind of movie'. But without the benefit of TV spots or a trailer, you get a lot of people who are unprepared for what they're going to see. And with films that are a little challenging, that will automatically produce low test scores. If people are recruited into seeing *Boogie Nights*, thinking it'll be some campy thing, and what they get is an off-the-wall comedy about the porno business in the seventies, they get really pissed off. We had the same problem with *Seven*, with *One Night Stand* and with *Austin Powers* – we managed to find the five theatres in LA where no one found the film funny. When comedies receive a score in the fifties, that usually sends people back to the drawing board. We were screening the movie for people for whom the last Bond film they saw was *Goldeneye*. They had no idea what Mike Myers was parodying. We should have just screened it out of LA, out of the boondocks.

How did *Boogie Nights* test?
That was an awful experience. That got scores in the twenties, in the thirties. It finally got up to the forties and fifties, because we really tried to recruit an upscale audience.

For the sake of people who don't live here – in an ideal world, what figures would you be looking for?
On the survey, the top two boxes are the 'Excellent' and 'Very Good' ratings. And you're always looking for a combination of anything over eighty in those two boxes. Then there's a 'Definite Recommend' rating and I think the norm is forty-five, but you're always looking for fifty-five to seventy. Sixty-five suggests good word of mouth. I haven't seen numbers like those on any of our movies since *The Wedding Singer* – because if a movie just makes you laugh and feel good, people will rate it 'Good' because they had a good time. But if movies really disturb you or challenge you – especially these recruited audiences who have no idea what they're getting – they react accordingly, they react pissed off.

I've found the stupidest thing about them is the questions themselves. They're designed just for those feel-good movies, as you say. And they don't quantify things like, 'Did it make you feel bad in an interesting way?' I often wonder why the screening questionnaire isn't rewritten specifically –
For each film, yes.

In other words, the executives sit around and say, 'Okay, *Seven*, *Boogie Nights* – they're tricky movies. And because they're both unusual and original, what are the things we want to learn from this screening?'
I've suggested not having questionnaires. We didn't have them for *Wag The Dog*. I suggested that for those challenging movies, we don't do cards, period. Ironically, a lot of film-makers look at me strangely when I suggest that. A lot of them actually want the security of the standard process.

Of late, New Line's been embroiled in two significant disputes, one to do with sexism and another, an ongoing thing, with a director who seems very upset about his movie. This is an English director, Tony Kaye, to whom I will be talking. In his situation, do you think it was a train that was always going to get derailed?
Maybe I was naive, but I didn't think so at the beginning. I loved his work in advertising, I thought he was an incredibly compelling person to sit in front of. And we had been sending him scripts for a while. He liked *American History X*, I was delighted, and he came in. He was very collaborative in the beginning. He worked on the script with the original writer and with Edward Norton, who stars in the film. It had a contrived drug subplot that we all decided should be stripped out. The movie had absolutely no problems during production. He shot a lot of footage –

That's his style.
Yes, but he managed to do it on budget and on schedule. And then we had a screening of his cut, and we thought it was great. People had notes, but he obviously had made a really effective, well-acted, disturbing, poignant movie about hate and redemption – everything we wanted out of the script. Then he had a second-cut screening for us, where we thought he cut back on some stuff. We thought he was truncating certain moments. And it was around that time we started to think the editor we had wasn't the right guy for the job. We'd originally wanted a man named Jerry Greenberg, and eventually got him. We came up with another set of notes, he was cutting away. And then – I guess, in hindsight I shouldn't have done this – but I invited Edward Norton to go into the editing room with us, to expedite the notes process. Edward only had a short period of time before he had to go and do *Rounders*. So I just wanted him to get everything out of his system.

Edward is pretty much a newcomer.
Yes, but he impressed me during pre-production because I thought he made a contribution on the script. It was like what I read about De Niro's contribution

to the script of *Raging Bull*; he really got that character. He endured Tony having two open calls for the part, because Tony thought he could find a non-professional. And Edward was coming off the success of *Primal Fear*, he just wanted to do the movie, he really believed in that character. We all respected that – Tony respected it too, in the beginning. Once we got into the process with the second editor – after Edward had been in the editing room – Tony came back in. Now, I think eventually he'll reveal himself as a film-maker who – like Kubrick, to whom he keeps comparing himself – will tinker in post-production for two years. He really came to a radical new vision of the film, very late in the game. So he collaborated on this last cut of the movie, the one that we're going to release, with the knowledge that he would get to do another cut. First he asked for four weeks, and we said, 'Okay.' Then he asked for eight weeks, and we said, 'Okay.' Then that stretched into ten weeks. Then – now famously – he came in to meet with me here, and he brought a rabbi, a priest and a Tibetan lama.

Was that a joke?
I don't know with Tony. We'd had some contentious meetings, and he told me he thought he and New Line could talk better in the presence of these holy men. I got a kick out of Tony's eccentricity because at least it livens up the day, it's not like the same old crap. So I thought these men had seen Tony's final version, and now they were going to tell me why it was so great, from a holy perspective. But basically the meeting was about Tony saying, 'I haven't done anything in ten weeks. I can't tell you when I'm going to be done and I can't tell you what I'm going to do, but I just want the time I want.' We decided that we couldn't wait any more. I think that message got through, and then Tony kind of revealed to me what he wanted to do to the movie. But he still couldn't say when he would be done. After that, we realized it was over with him, that we were just going to release the last delivered cut of the movie.

In the meantime there's sort of a strange dialogue going on now via full-page ads, white on black letters, which I think cost five grand.
I think Tony expresses himself through these art pieces. Originally – when he thought he wasn't going to get his screening, his chance to do his cut – he ran an ad knocking us, using some abstract quote, if I remember correctly. We didn't get the news to him in time that we were going to reinstate the idea of a new screening. So then he ran a 'Thank you' ad. Then he just got excited about running ads, and started soliciting interest from DiCaprio and Marlon Brando for a Tennessee Williams project. He was just doing it –

As an art form.
As a way of communicating to the town, and to New Line. Then, because I'm an idiot, I thought it would be fun . . . He ran one ad, 'To Michael DeLuca', letting me know that he threw an orange at the screen during the scoring of our version of the movie, because he couldn't watch it. I felt that since he had personally

addressed me for the first time, I needed to respond in some satirical way. So I just ran a nonsensical spoof of his ads, exactly the same way, with my name instead of his. I quoted Dr Seuss – 'I will not eat them, Sam I am, I will not eat green eggs and ham' – and 'I am the Walrus, koo-koo-ka-ju'. But then he calls me and says, 'This is great. Now we're communicating, this is dialogue.' I said, 'This was a one-shot joke. I'm not running any more ads.' And we were cool until he came in and said he was Kubrick, and Warner Brothers weren't bothering Kubrick about *Eyes Wide Shut*, so why were we imposing time constraints on him? That's when it all kind of got . . .

Silly.
Silly. Feelings started to get thinned-out. And we just decided – as much as I hated doing it – that we were going to move ahead.

Have you done that before?
No.

Have you spoken since?
Well, we had a breakfast. I actually had tears in my eyes, because it was so depressing that it had come to this. It's not as if we're going to make a lot of money on a movie like this. It cost ten, we spent another million and a half in post, waiting for his new vision. I just thought it was a good movie to make, with a good message. It was a chance to do something with Edward, it was a chance to do something good for the culture. Tony thought I got emotional because his ideas for the new cut were so good, but I just got overwhelmed. So we've been mis-communicating a little bit recently. But now it's over and I think he'll do what he's going to do until the release of the movie.

Which would be what?
With Tony it could be anything.

Is his name still on the film?
The DGA denied his application to take his name off. They didn't reveal their reasons to us. Maybe they told him.

I've discovered that taking your name off a film is nothing like as easy as a director might like it to be. You have to prove all kinds of things about the way you've been treated. You can throw that threat around but it's quite hard to carry it out.
I'm only speculating, but maybe when a director withdraws his name, they're not supposed to do negative publicity after they are granted that request. They may have found that Tony had already violated that. Anyway we had to give Tony the version we're going to release, and the DGA asked for a copy too. Then Tony had seventy-two hours to respond. Am I going to take my name off or not? The next thing we heard, they had denied his request.

And since then, no communication – other than through the press?
Now it's in the hands of lawyers. He's treating the situation as if we were taking *Boogie Nights* away from Paul or *One Night Stand* away from you. That's a little cheeky because the script was written by someone else, and developed at another studio, Savoy, before it even got to me. Then Tony signed on and said, 'This is the script I want to make.' But I would do another film with him, if it was just as he told me it would be. I wouldn't impose any limits. I'd say, 'Great, here's three, four million dollars. I'll see you at the première.' He's an interesting film-maker and people should work with him. But I don't think he's someone you want to hire for an assignment.

I'm just going to fire some questions at you, to get an idea of your taste. Give me five male actors, whom you like. They can be from any time in cinema history.
Jimmy Stewart, Edward Norton, Robert De Niro, John Wayne, Charlie Chaplin.

Actresses.
Meryl Streep, Rosalind Russell, Ingrid Bergman, Drew Barrymore, Julianne Moore.

Five movies.
That's easy. *Lawrence of Arabia, Raging Bull, Taxi Driver, Citizen Kane, King Kong.*

Five pieces of music, any genre.
Bruce Springsteen's *Live* box set; Pink Floyd, *Wish You Were Here*; anything by the Rolling Stones, *The White Album*. And the first big Nirvana album.

Five books.
The Count of Monte Cristo, Geek Love, The Shining. I haven't read a book in such a long time . . . A new book, *Cold New World* – it's a non-fiction book about delinquent kids today. And *A Tale of Two Cities*.

And, if it comes to mind – what's the stupidest thing you've ever heard in Hollywood?
Remaking *The Island of Dr Moreau* is probably the stupidest thing I've heard of in Hollywood – and I did it. So that's just sitting there.

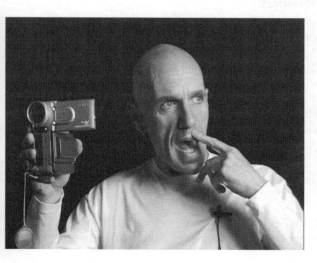

Mike Figgis: *American History X* **was your first film in Hollywood?**
Tony Kaye: It's my first experience of a feature film, which I've been training for, getting ready for, for about thirteen or fourteen years.

And in that period you've been making commercials?
Fortunately, yes. I decided that my best route to what I was going to go for was through the world of advertising. I was involved with that for a lot longer than I planned; I did a lot better at it than I planned, so it kept me there longer. If you're not careful you get paid a lot of money to stay where you are in life. But I always viewed it as an apprenticeship – a limited apprenticeship, in the sense that I was learning technique and style, but not a great deal about content. But I felt I could learn about content from other sources.

What did you do before that?
I tried to be a painter. I sold things on the Bayswater Road. But I couldn't really make a living doing that.

Did you train as a painter? Did you have an art college background?
Yes. Then I went into design – from the Bayswater Road. And then I decided I wanted to pursue film, and I heard about advertising, and I thought, 'Well, I'll take that road.'

How did you deal with the bullshit that's in advertising?
It never really bothered me because it's such an anonymous world. Your name is never associated with the work, because the only name that is associated with an advert is the product that you're advertising. I just fought the battles as hard as I could, went into battle maybe twenty times a year and would win six and lose fourteen.

What does 'win' mean in that context?
It means being happy at the end of the process with what was finished – not that it couldn't be better, but happy in the sense that you were proud to show it to somebody else, as 'I did that' or 'I was part of it'. And every time I was happy, it was very successful, so I thought 'Okay, I think my judgement seems to be sound.'

People used to say about films, and certainly about advertising, something they don't say about writers or painters – which is that it is a matter of opinion what is good or what is bad, or what is success. Do you agree?
No, I believe there is a line – above the line is good, and below the line is bad. There are different types of good and different types of bad, but there is most definitely, definitely a line.

When you fought for something, would you know in your mind that what you were fighting for also happened to be the best thing? That, in other words, it wasn't negotiable?

Well, all I've got is my intuition, and I work totally in accordance with that. So if I'm intuiting that something's not right, then I might not necessarily know myself how to fix it, but I know it's not right. And I also know who are the best people around to fix something.

Would there be certain people you were working with where, if they disagreed with you, you might stop and think?
Oh, I don't care who disagrees with me.

But I mean some people whose judgement you value higher than others'.
In certain areas. If I wanted to get a job as a studio executive, I might well go to somebody like Michael DeLuca and say, 'How would I go about that?' But I wouldn't go to him and ask him how to make a film. I don't need Michael DeLuca to tell me how to make a film because he doesn't know.

He's not a film-maker.
He has no idea. But I would ask him about how to be an executive – not that I see myself wanting to do that job right now. But I might meet somebody who does. I'd say, 'Give this chap a call, he's been quite successful.'

What do you think of Michael DeLuca as a studio executive?
There are some people who you call 'a suit and a haircut'. And I'd say he was 'a T-shirt and a haircut and a pair of motorcycle boots'. I think that he is very clever at creating quite an intimidating persona. He certainly beat me every time I walked into his room. I'm involved in this big battle with them right now and I've been trying to figure out what I do next. Because, to all intents and purposes, I'm dead, the battle's over.

With *American History X*?
As far as they're concerned. Even lawyers I'm employing are telling me it's over. I think I've made a mistake every time I have tried to deal with Michael DeLuca. Everybody's told me that I should be dealing with him, but maybe they've been keeping me away from the real power, which is maybe Bob Shaye or Ted Turner or Joe Levin.

What do you think of Hollywood?
I love it, I absolutely love it.

Have you learned any lessons about surviving here? Is there a code that you need to understand?
The only thing that I'm trying to do now is to proceed with the view of total control. Not that I have to squash everyone I'm working with, so that I don't listen to them. I think I make mistakes that a lot of people have made before me – their work goes downhill because they think that what got them to that point was all their own work, they forget the contributions of everybody else.

When I had my big problems in Hollywood, the word went out that I didn't understand the social contract. Are you aware of it?

Well, my answer to that is I think the industry here has totally lost the plot of what reality is about. And that's manifested in all this crap that it produces. I think if you lose your temper, you have to scream – I don't necessarily think you have to hit anybody, but you have to shout. And if you get really upset, you have to cry, and if it makes you happy to do that publicly, then you should do that. You've got to be totally true to what you believe in, not to what the system tells you to do in order to survive. And as far as I'm concerned, the system has to pay its way to keep in my good books. I don't fucking need them, I really believe that. It's a tragedy, people are not getting the real benefits of life if they have to subdue life to that kind of level just to survive. Certainly, for me personally to produce the best of what's possible for me to produce, I have to be honest to what goes on inside me. [*He begins to cry.*]. I've been fucked over. And it's all very well for these people who fuck me over to say, 'He's done a great job . . .'

Why are you still here, Tony? Do you not feel like going back for a while, until this blows over?

You know, the only thing that's going to get blown over is . . . is their house.

Tell me what's happened, where are you up to now?

The situation is that they are releasing a cut that is not, in my opinion, the proper configuration of what we've got. And I'm not prepared to work on it with them just to coast it in, so I've walked away. I'm trying everything I can to hold up the process and put them in a position where they ask me to come back to continue the work I was doing. They, at this point, have no intention of doing that. They're going full-steam ahead. I think that they're just finding my fight amusing. I guess every now and then I come through with an interesting bit that stops them for a second or so, but then they get back on the track again. And I have to be realistic – I'm working on other things as well, because there is one part of my brain that says, 'You might not get back, you might not be able to finish it.' So I've left a little door for myself.

What's the release date?

They were going for 16 October. They can't do that now, because I've shot so much stuff myself and paid for so much stuff – I own a lot of the negative that they can't get their hands on.

That must be a first – I've never heard of that situation.

I kind of knew that this might happen. I kept spending my money, knowing that I would own the stuff. But the problem is that I signed something saying that everything I do, even stuff that I've spent my own money on, is owned by them.

Why did you sign that?

Because, to be honest, I didn't care about anything this time. I just thought, 'I've got to do something and do it now, I can't be buggered with all the red tape.' Anyway, I've got all that neg in my lab, and they can't get their hands on it right now. They lost a court battle last week, due to a technical screw-up on their lawyer's behalf. So I've put their release date back two and a half weeks, because the new court date has to be set. They're going to allow me to take my name off the film, but they're not going to allow me to have it as 'An Alan Smithee Film'. And I've told them that if they're not going to let me have an honest-me film, I want it to be 'A Humpty-Dumpty Film'. I prefer the name 'Humpty-Dumpty' – 'Alan Smithee' is a bit dull. They told me there's no way they're going to allow me that. So I've now got a lawyer – who is under duress, I have to say – sorting out a battle to allow me to call it 'A Humpty-Dumpty Film'.

How much money have you spent?
I have no idea. A lot.

Where does Edward Norton come into all this? Are you two speaking?
What does that mean?

Are you friendly with each other?
I'm not friendly with anybody. Actually, that's not true, I'm friendly with everybody.

But is that amicable, your relationship with Norton? He did a cut, I hear.
Yes, he came into the editing room. Had I had final cut, I wouldn't have minded it, to be honest with you. I would have sent him the best editor I could find and said, 'Play to your heart's content and let me see what you come up with' – that would have been interesting to me, and I'm sure I would have got something, at least one teeny-weeny little thought that might have spun me into something else. My fear was of him doing stuff and them liking it just to keep him happy. He came into the cutting room, and was working with an assistant editor, and I just left them to it, because I was working with the editor at that time. When I saw what they were doing, at the end of the day, I was so worried – staggered – that I punched the wall and broke my hand. I was just petrified, and my fears were justified, in the sense that they did like what he had done, and I only wish they would release that. Then it really would be plain to see what I had to go through.

The idea that you'd bring in an actor . . .
New Line loved the first cut and it researched very well. Then they told me, 'Edward really wants to come in, because he's got problems with the stunts.' And I said, 'Yes, he just wants to come in to learn.' I thought that's really what he wanted to do – he obviously wants to make his own films at some point in time, and he wants to get the feel of what a cutting room is like, working with an editor and with footage. But the situation started to close in on me after that – it was a mistake for me to be open. Edward Norton doesn't even realize – or maybe he

does – but the only thing that he wants is for the film to be a performance. It is an excellent performance, and I think people are going to say so. It's not a fantastic film – but it's got its moments. And that's the tragedy. The moments are all from where I was going with it, and the other stuff – is the other stuff. I was good as gold for a long time, and it was only when they pushed me to a point where I just couldn't take any more that I had to change gear.

Tell me about the rabbi and the priest.
Oh, I had to go into a meeting to New Line to tell them that I wasn't finished. And, to be honest, I was frightened to go and tell them that. I thought, 'What can I do to make this meeting more relaxed, so they don't go nuts and start throwing tables around the room?' So I thought, 'I'll take some religious people in with me, and then they'll be more respectful in the way they deal with me.' I was also trying to make a film that did something else, that had a function in the world aside from being just a bit of entertainment or whatever. So I thought, 'I'll take as many religious people as I can find.' Three turned up, two more showed up in the lift as we were leaving.

How did you find them?
I just told my assistant, 'Get me this and this.' Also I told them before we went in there, 'Look, you're not here to be on my side, standing up for me. I want you to experience what's going on and to say things – say things to me as well, like tell me to shut up, "You're out of order here."' They didn't really understand it, they wanted it over with as quickly as possible. But when I left I couldn't stop thinking about it. And every time I thought about it, I smiled. So I told New Line that I wasn't finished, and I was smiling during it, and it was better than just telling them I wasn't finished.

How much more time did you want? Could you quantify it?
I didn't say then, but the next day I told them, 'In four or five days I can give you a specific time period.' It was about another four, five, six weeks. It wasn't that much longer. And the real reason why they shut the door was because they just got fed up. They had this power thing and they got worried that I was completely taking it over.

Do you think Hollywood has a sense of humour?
I think it has a fantastic sense of humour. But there's always that sense of, 'Well, this is the way to do it here.'

I find that it's a very conformist town. Yeah, they have a sense of humour and I'm sure they find you very amusing, and I'm sure the stories about you will entertain and brighten up their lives. It's not a common thing for people to do a performance. There is no history of performance art in this town.
Right. That's why I said to them, 'Look, I'm supposed to be doing this for a living. So if you're doing something for a living, you should be practising it all the

time. So if I'm having a meeting with you, why shouldn't we have a little bit of spirituality, of theatricality, a little bit of drama? It makes it a more memorable meeting.' That's really what it's about, isn't it?

People are very accepting of whatever the structure dishes to them. They will take the pain or the rejection in a very flat, philosophical way. There is no sense of the individual being able to transcend the problem through his own rage. It's like Mel Gibson said: there's this philosophical idea that if you just keep quiet and keep rising, in a year's time, hopefully, you'll be higher up the pyramid and you'll be able to get your revenge that way. But there's no history of trade unionism in this town and you understand that the whole point of capitalism is that it completely permeates everybody.

Mel Gibson is a pretty good actor. If you're a good actor you can pretend. But what if you're not? I don't really want to pretend – or rather I can't.

But you already had a flourishing career in film-making, albeit advertising. So you've been around the block, you're not a virgin. A lot of film directors are starlets when they come to this town. Most people come here because they want to get rich, and there's a lot of money to be made. And a director is no different from an actor or an actress who is prepared to sleep with someone, be humiliated, treated like shit for a long time – because you know the deal is that if you keep your mouth shut, eventually you might get lucky, you might get that job. So there is this pact. In any other industry, people would be being arrested, right, left and centre, for all kinds of abuse. You were working in a company that was exposed in a fairly high-profile article.

Yeah, and I thought that article was absurd because it was saying, 'Look at all this excess. Yet this company is a maverick film-maker, and they're pretty damn good at that. So is this the way to be successful?' I thought, 'That's not right, I don't know whether this company is so successful, I don't see it as a cutting-edge maverick.' You look at the three hundred films they've made over the last X years and tell me how many of them have got to that point above that line, and I don't think there are that many. The article should have said, 'Look, this company is spoken of in that light. Look at this list of films.' They're all going mad there, they're all going nuts. And it's highly indicative of the way the system is here. They're so used to going to these premières and having a couple of hours' sleep and waking up at the end and going on auto pilot, 'Marvellous, wonderful.' Now you've got a situation with this *Saving Private Ryan* shit where everyone's worshipping a guy for making this thing when he should be laughed out of the door. And when he was doing good things, no one was taking any notice of the guy. The system here is worse than it's ever been. I also think the system is amazing as well. I just think there's a way to play it, a certain key that fits the lock and opens the door. I'm just trying to struggle to find the right locksmith. But whatever anyone says about this place, it's still the best place on the planet for doing this kind of work.

Making films.
And it has to be dealt with. Because wherever you go to make films, you're always going to end up back here trying to do it.

Why, though? What makes it the best?
Because everything is here . . . Well, actually, that's not true.

It's not, is it?
The reason why I left England at the time I did – and I think it's changed a lot since I left –

I think so too.
But the reason why I left England and came to the United States of America, apart from the fact that I love this country, is that I thought Americans are better in front of the camera than the English. Because in England, in London, the theatre was God, the cinema was a lower art form, the acting talent were trained to project on a stage with no thought about how to behave in front of a camera. Also the whole English thing about fucking stiff upper lips and not showing your feelings doesn't work if you're making a film. There are exceptions to that rule. If you look at forties English stuff – we're in the David Lean building, and the way he used to do it was different, amazing. I just thought there'd be greater people to put in front of the camera here.

You find your team. Or you discover why other film-makers you know, once they've found their people, hang on to them like survivors on to a rock. So have you got another film cooking?
I've got this one going right now, the one I'm pointing the camera at you for.

It's pathetic, isn't it? We're both making little films on digital cameras. Now I'll ask you some simple questions that I ask everybody. Give me five pieces of music that make you have some kind of emotion.
Working Class Hero, All You Need Is Love – I can only think of those two.

Okay. Books?
Not that I'm that musically inclined, but I've only started reading very, very recently. So, books, I'm not qualified enough.

Give me five movies.
I haven't really had the chance to think about this for four or five years. But as I would have answered it in 1994 – *Lawrence of Arabia, One Flew Over The Cuckoo's Nest.* Can't think of any more.

Okay. Male actors that you admire?
I think once someone is 'an actor' – definitely Edward Norton is an actor, I think he's a great actor – I think they're not great, because I can fucking see it, I can see him work. I think it's all about being an awesome human being who you just

fucking want to watch and listen to. There are not many of those. Marlon Brando is definitely that. When he got it right, I don't think there's anyone who has ever got it as right as that on film.

Is there an actress of that stature?
Maybe Shirley Temple when she was a kid. Meryl Streep is a great person; the young Katharine Hepburn.

Do you go to the movies a lot?
I try and see pretty much everything. I've been a bit bad of late.

Have you seen anything decent? In the past couple of months?
In the past couple of months, no.

And what about telly?
I never watch the TV.

Do you spend time in England now at all?
I went back to England about three or four weeks ago, for two weeks. It's the first time I've been in England for two years, and I was horrified.

By?
I was horrified by, of all things, the class system.

It's a shock when you go back there.
I lived there all my life, I never even noticed it. I suddenly found myself trying to speak as well as I could, and try and be like those people that I thought were good, and I wasn't really like that. And it just horrified me, it was so transparent, and so impossible to play this game.

[*Interview resumes after a break.*]

I wanted to talk to you about the film specifically, because last time we spoke I hadn't seen your film. And now I have.
It's not my film.

Okay. But the film that was to be your film – have you seen it?
Well, I know the cut. And indeed I had the misfortune to work on that cut. But when I walked away, they then finished it up, so there was looping done and the music was inappropriately used. I have not seen the finished thing and I will not see it. I have no interest in seeing it.

I have to admit that I've never seen a finished cut of *Mr Jones*, on which I was replaced. And people have told me I'm foolish not to see it. But I went to see *American History X*, knowing all its problems that we had talked about. Clearly, what's there may have been stage-managed by someone else in its final stages.

But you prepared it, you shot that footage, you worked on those performances. And I really loved the feel of the film, and the experience of watching it. I could also see what it could have been, and I was fascinated enough to want to ask you specific things about what you would have changed in it, what your vision was.

I don't know if I can sit here and say, 'I would have done this, and that.' All I can tell you is that there are half a dozen to a dozen scenes in that film that are as I intended them to be. And it's the framework of those good scenes that needed to be built upon – the exposition needed to be got rid of, the flat ending needed to be got rid of . . . it's just such a long time ago now, and so many reviews have come out –

I've read all of them.

The critics' problems with it are all things that would have been cured, and I agreed with every single damn one of them – absolutely. There's a lot more I know about that they didn't even spot. And it was very annoying for me that these people just blamed me for the problems.

That's why I wanted to talk to you.

There were things I was going to reply to, but I thought, 'I can't be bothered.' I'm working on other things now. But I just get these images of the faces of these collaborators of mine – they're like clowns, porcelain wind-up clowns, and I see them all at the première, sliding around the room in their axle-grease, shaking hands with people and talking shit. And I'm just so happy that I wasn't there . . . You'd better ask me something else, quick . . .

I loved the cinematography, I thought it was gorgeous. I like the fact that it was a bit 'off' at times – the focus wasn't too clinical.

Well, God knows what they did to the grading.

It wasn't so bad. But going into the shoot, what were your feelings about the script you had?

It was a disaster. It was amateurish.

Had you worked on it yourself?

I'd spent about six months with the writer and the producer. But every time we did work on it, the script would then come back and there'd be four words that had been changed.

What were you trying to change in the script?

I have a method whereby I carry on working on something until it works properly. And don't ask me where I'm going, don't ask me what I'm trying to say, but I have a light-bulb that says –

'It's ready.'

It's ready, it's done, it's finished.

Obviously, one of the reasons you wanted to do this script was because it was fairly political, right? It seemed to me that it was very like a British film, in the sense that it had an interest in the left, in politics, in the way things are going.
I've never thought of myself as English, actually.

You stick out like a sore thumb, baby.
Well, I realize that, having this accent . . .

When we last spoke, you came across as having a political point of view, about class, for example. But the spin that seemed to have been put on the film I saw was something else.
Yeah. They were making *Romper Stomper 2* and I wasn't. You know, the infrastructure of film is as delicate as a house of cards. You take one card out and the whole thing caves in. And there's more than one card short of a pack in the current line-up of this film, because of what they did. Some of it is very watchable. But all of it should have been very watchable.

I was on the edge of my seat watching the entire film. You're a good film-maker and I think enough of it is still there to appreciate that. An hour and a half later, after a second cappuccino, I was able to deconstruct the script and say, 'This is complete nonsense.' But still, I'm grateful for having seen the film.
One problem is the heroism of the main character – so much of it is wordy and speechy. It's deemed as 'heroic redemption', which doesn't work because you can't actually see why the character's changed. And that is because the character is not actually believable. However brilliant Norton is on the screen – and there are certainly moments where he is absolutely brilliant – it's always a performance. It's never, ever real. I told the producer, 'I can provide an ambience and a stage, and I know that I can get the best work out of this guy. I know he'll get nominated for an Academy Award – he could even win it. But I'm telling you now, he ain't the character in the film. He ain't that person.' So at the end of the day, the best thing of the film is actually the worst thing of the film.

The lead performance . . .
The 'heroism' of that character should only have been in the eyes of the younger brother, the innocent one. Plus, there is no black voice in the whole film. The music – God knows what they did with it. Andovi is a brilliant composer, but when you smudge that stuff across the whole thing . . . you see, I would have laced it with rap. I would have had rappers coming on and off all the time, weaving their way through the film – going from smooth to rough, smooth to rough.

I was thinking when I was watching your film, 'You know, the way to fix this is not by naturalism.'
Yes, like what you did in *Leaving Las Vegas* when you see Elisabeth Shue just talking – it needed stuff like that in there.

I think you waste so much fucking fuel if you try to convince an audience that a character's having a major change of heart just by giving them some schematic dialogue. In plays four hundred years ago they solved all this just by having a guy come to the audience and say, 'Let me tell you what's happened.'
Absolutely. Maurice, the storyteller.

As I said, there was enough of your film there for me to see how elements could be reworked and the whole thing could work beautifully. And then you wouldn't get endless reviews saying, 'Well, the transition didn't work in jail. Where was his change of heart?'
None of the jail stuff was written. We invented it out on the fly. I just said, 'Give me five days in a prison.' And then I had the idea of the character of the black guy. Edward and the other actor went off, and they just worked on both scenes together. I just left them alone, I said, 'Do your stuff and when you're done I'll come in and we'll figure it out from there.'

And the ending?
Well, the ending is just really badly cut. It's really the wrong shots in there now. It should be – take the stuff down off the wall, get on the street, end of score, boom – finished, out. There's too much crying in each other's arms – eccch. Drives me around the bend.

So when you said to them, 'I need more time'?
I was working with Gary Woolcott at that point. He was giving me amazing stuff. He was giving me a text, words on paper for these characters, of a level I had not worked with. Actually I would probably have had the head-stump at the end of the film. I would have left the audience with that.

When you got to the stage where it became difficult with New Line, were you thinking, 'Okay, now I know how to fix this. It's to do with the relationship of one scene to another, and a few additions and a few subtractions, and having time to let this play out'?
No, it would have been a radical reinvention of the whole thing. I was becoming a more confident film-maker at that stage. I was getting into my stride, I was on a roll – enjoying the process. And when they told me, 'You can't go any further, it's clean-up time' – I had to make a decision. I could have cleaned up what is currently there – it would have made them happy and it would have been thirty per cent better than what it is now. Maybe I should have done that. But I got really angry, and when you get angry you lose your focus and you get emotional and you make mistakes. What you've got to do is keep up a focused aggression – which I didn't do.

That's not in your nature, is it?
Well, whatever – I didn't clean up what was there, because I saw something that

was a hundred per cent better. And I thought it was my job to fight for that. I've never made a movie before. So, as far as they're concerned, what qualifications do I have to say it isn't going to work? The only thing I have is my intuition. And actually my intuition was right. Critics, they slam things, and people like the Mike DeLucas of the world, and even Edward 'Ostrich Head' Norton – they just think, 'Those people are wrong and we're right.' They've made a mistake because there are a lot of people who like this film. It's not bad. There are a lot worse around.

This is why I have such a huge problem with critics. Couldn't any of them see a film like this, and come out and say, 'Okay, the script is flawed, and therefore the structure of the film ultimately doesn't make sense. But you're looking at the work of a real film-maker'? I didn't notice any of the reviews recognizing the talent of the film-maker, which is a real shame. You made all that fucking noise, and some of them mentioned it, but along the lines of 'Ha-ha, Tony Kaye's a bit of a nutter.' They didn't seem to understand why you were making that noise, or the problems that were within the film, which they then critiqued as 'your' film. I found that fascinating, and it made me very angry indeed . . . Just one other thing I wanted to say – I thought that the score did some damage to the film.
That was because it was directed by – nobody.

I was talking to Ray Cooper, an English guy from Virgin Records, now based here. We were discussing English music – Massive Attack and Portishead and the whole Bristol scene. The way those younger artists mix now is so beautiful and textured – their ears are very fine and subtle. And when you hear the use of score and the mixing in American films, it seems very antiquated and obvious and unsubtle. A film like yours really needed a more textured score.
Yes, it needed a lot more work. It started in one place, then it was taken somewhere else . . .

You've got other things cooking. How are you being received by the so-called community here?
I like to think of it the other way around, really.

How are they being received by you?
Yes.

Fair enough. It's important for you to make another film quickly, isn't it?
Oh, I've almost finished another one. I started to shoot another one about three weeks ago, and I've got a few others in mind.

Your own projects?
Yes, completely mine. I've become an industry. That's what this thing has done for me, if anything. I'm in the business now.

25   Bob Rafelson

Mike Figgis: What do you think of the idea of directors giving interviews?
Bob Rafelson: When I'm flipping around the channels and I see people talking about movies, I get off that channel very, very quickly. I'm embarrassed – even for somebody like Scorsese, when he talks about movies. There's something that comes out a bit pompous and a bit professorial and so knowing – all the while appearing to be modest, mind you – but so absolutely certain of his own education and his own enlightened point of view, and it annoys me. In the past couple of weeks I saw a little bit of this programme, about the hundred best films ever made or something like that. And now, when they play these movies, they are heralded by some interview – it might be somebody like Steven Spielberg or Martin Scorsese, talking about their admiration for the director of this particular film. There's something slightly self-congratulatory and incestuous about it that bothers me.

I agree. It seems to indicate that they think they've arrived at some plateau . . .
Well, it's as if you've achieved such status that the rest of the world is desperate to hear your views on Henry King, or David Lean, or whoever the director might be of the month, or the year – or the century, for that matter. But I think you have to be pretty careful about how you say these things, simply because – well, for example, so many young directors now are part of this choice of a hundred great films. But I wonder if they will be there fifty years from now, or twenty years from now. It's not that I resent that history has accorded them this absurd thing, that *Rocky* or *Rocky II* or whatever is considered one of the hundred greatest films – and Sturges doesn't get any points at all. Because if anybody drew up a list, there would be enormous disagreement and a certain amount of preciousness to the opinion. But more significantly, to me, it seems that you just have to recognize that time is the real arbiter of all this.

How do you feel about the way film is treated as an art form? In the bigger context of the culture, too. Do you feel that it's over-valued?
I think that it is over-valued aesthetically. I don't think that it's over-valued as a social phenomenon at all. I do think it's quite likely that if two people sit down anywhere, one of the first subjects they can discuss mutually and deservedly, as if they were entitled to have the opinion, is movies. It doesn't matter what job they have or where they come from – they can be hairdressers or they can be professors, or anything – but they do feel that their experience at the movies is just as valid as yours. And they get very highly charged, much more so than they might about international politics or any social issue that might be prevalent at the time. People come out of a movie theatre and they talk about the movie as validly as Roger Ebert might, or Steven Spielberg. And if they're admonished by their date – 'What the hell did you like that movie for, there was nothing in it' – they feel quite capable of arguing their case. Movies do that for people. You know, if somebody charges across Fifth Avenue in New York City, and it's raining out and

a cab comes by and spins the person around so they fall in the gutter, and they brush themselves off, unharmed – they might go down on their knees and say, 'Oh, God, thank you – I believe. I've been spared.' They've come to a total belief in God in that moment. Now, if a priest who has spent forty years of his life studying the most esoteric Christian documents, comes to a belief in God – his belief is no more valid than the guy who was just nearly whacked by a cab. And Steven Spielberg's opinion of what's good about a movie is no more valid than the hairdresser's. That's the point I'm trying to make.

You believe that no one has the right to a superior point of view?
I think everybody has the right. But because of that, for some reason or other, I'm rather bored with this opinion. I hear it altogether too much, from every source. I'm the kind of person who likes to talk about things that I don't know very much about, so that I get educated when I sit and listen. It's not that I think that I can't get educated about movies, but that I've heard enough talk about movies to last a lifetime.

Do you think films affect people, in a good way? We make films, people see them, they have an opinion. Do you think it changes them, one way or the other?
Well, I'm sure that certain films affect people in fairly enduring ways. But, do you know – there's such an onslaught of sensation and media in a Westerner's life today, that it's very difficult for him to be affected by anything for more than a few minutes. Because he's affected by so many things.

Do you think we make too many films?
That's another issue altogether. You know, I can watch one hundred and forty different channels on my television? I remember, when I started out, I was a story editor, working for Channel 13 in New York City. It was the last channel to join the spectrum – Channels 2, 4, 5, 7, 9, 11. So it had to find an identity for itself, and it chose more or less at the outset to become 'the cultural station'. Therefore, one was made to imagine, quite misleadingly, that if there were Channels 15, 17, 19, 22, 27, 30, then the level of programming was bound to go up. That hasn't turned out to be the case. Information is available to you, you can indeed watch Bravo or the Independent Film Channels or the local educational channel. But in proportion to what else is out there, the amount of quality programming hasn't increased one iota. In fact it's decreased. The more information we get, the more degenerate it becomes. Because in order for the programme makers to find their niche, to find the position popular enough to endure, concessions have to be made to the slightly more popular competitors. This is a total loss to the culture because it tends to homogenize things a bit.

For example, when I was growing up, I used to go to foreign movies much more than I went to American movies. It was by accident, because there just happened to be a theatre in the neighbourhood that I knew how to steal my way into more easily than the RKO or Loew's theatres. But in Los Angeles now, there are hardly any theatres that show foreign movies – far fewer being made as well. I deplore that fact. And when a French film is being made currently, it's not unlikely that somebody would favour the idea of having William Shatner in it. What if the character originally meant to be a French drug addict was now an American drug addict, who just happens to be living in Paris. Better for Shatner, no? Pretty soon the whole thing gets modulated down to, 'Well, why don't we all make the same films?' That's my point – somewhat labyrinthine, but . . .

When you started making films, did you ever think about being an actor?
No, I never thought about acting then. I'd like to now.

Seriously? You'd like a big role in a film?
Not necessarily a big role, but I would like to have the kind of latter-day prominence that John Huston had in films. I think of it as a very attractive and a very easy way to make money, if people want you to act. It's a very difficult way to make money if directors and producers and audiences are indifferent to your talent, but otherwise it's quite easy.

Why did you want to make films in the first place?
It was sort of an accident actually. I started off wanting to teach philosophy. So I studied philosophy, then – it's a long series of events in my life – I wound up being a disc jockey in Japan. Also writing about film for the Miniche *Times* to support myself. At the same time, there was a writer for *The Nippon Times* by the name of Donald Richie, who became an extraordinary interpreter and critic of Japanese film. And so I would go down and review Japanese movies. I even had a small job translating Japanese movies into English. It wasn't exact translation, somebody else had done that, and then I tried to make it a little bit smoother and more understandable. But occasionally I would just make up the movie, make it more interesting. So I single-handedly destroyed a number of really great movies, because the studio I was working for was Shochuku, and the primary director was Ozu. And I was advising Shochuku as to which films would come to the United States, whether the audience would be there for them or not. Now this is the fifties and there were some pretty fine directors coming into prominence in Japan, the best known of whom was of course Kurosawa. I was then going to do graduate work in philosophy at the University of Benares in India, studies in Hindu, theosophy . . .

What took you out of America in the first place?
Well, I'd already been around the world by the time I was seventeen.

Why?
I don't know.

Were your parents very hip?
No, quite the opposite. It was more of a defection than it was an urging. I grew up in New York. My folks were middle-class Jews. But they were very unlike even

their own friends, in that they were alcoholics – very unusual for a Jewish family. So, without making this too laboured and psychological, I wanted to get out of there. So I started travelling very early. I left my home, fundamentally, when I was fourteen.

Obviously you carried on your education, if you ended up doing philosophy?
Ah, well, I went to a boarding-school that only took Christian boys. It was in its first year, I read about it in the paper and went down for an interview. And I was the only Jewish kid, but since they had just opened, they needed the enrolment. So they admitted me, and that got me out of the city right off the bat. And then I was playing in a band in Mexico . . .

In other words, you sought that education as a way of getting out? Or did you actually think, 'I must educate myself'?
I wanted to get out, period. I suppose it came later, thinking that being smart was a good thing. In fact, they took anybody at this boarding-school – most of the kids were mentally or psychologically defective in some way. They were wards of the church, they were orphans, they were backward and tough and pretty twisted kids. So I got to thinking that I was bright simply because I was brighter than all of them. And I continued, even then, and all the way through college, to flunk almost every fucking course. Though I was smart in certain courses.

Were you interested in film at that point?
No. In college I began to get interested, a little bit, the way that anybody is now. But I didn't have any special feeling for it, or any notion that I wanted to be involved in it. I wrote a play when I was twenty-one, and it won some kind of a contest, and that was the first time that I even thought about theatre, film, anything seriously. Then I had this job in Japan and I got married there, and after that I didn't think that I could continue with this notion of being a philosopher – which a couple of professors had encouraged me to consider as a reasonable aspiration. So when I got back to America, I moved on to television, and finally worked up the courage to think that being the director was the right thing –

But you must have had a hell of a drive. People don't just fall into television. You've got to have some kind of confidence . . .
I suppose so. I certainly wasn't a shy fellow. But I looked at other people who got jobs directing, and I wondered how they got them. I wasn't that confident. I had to write and produce for a long time. I was working for David Susskind on a thing called *The Play of the Week* for Channel 13. Live.

And on Monday nights people stayed home in order to see the first night of the play, which played for six nights in a row. These plays were directed by famous Broadway and Off-Broadway directors, and they were being produced largely because nobody would make movies out of any of them. Once MGM or whoever had bought the rights to a play, you couldn't convince them to allow that play to be done free on live educational television. So our plays were Anouilh or Goethe or Shakespeare or Alexander Knox or Graham Greene – that's how I got my education. I read thousands of plays, because my job was to help pick them, and then make whatever very minor adaptations had to be made. Basically they were to be played authentically, but every now and then, when Shakespeare had neglected to introduce somebody properly at the door, I'd write a little introduction of my own, just a few lines, and see if I could get away with it.

I once met a curator of the Museum of Modern Art in Chicago, a complete pothead and a painter. And he and this other guy who worked there would get very stoned and go round the gallery adding trees to paintings. No one's noticed yet, because of his expertise.

That's their contribution. Anyway, a whole bunch of things happened to me; I had been an out-of-work musician in Mexico and had a lot of misadventures, which had nothing to do with music, playing at the Boom-Boom Club in Acapulco in 1953. Somehow that led to *The Monkees* television show – because of my own misadventures. I wrote it before The Beatles came along, and when they did, then people finally took interest in it. First time I wrote it, it was about a folk group like Peter, Paul and Mary. Then it became a rock group. The guys stayed the same because they were all my buddies, and what we did was what I had in mind. In the end, Paul Mazursky and Larry Tuckett wrote the pilot for the show.

Did Paul direct one of those?

No, I think we were too concerned that if Paul directed it, he wouldn't write, so we probably repressed his career. But he had never written for film before, and none of the directors on the show had ever directed before.

He made a funny point about *The Monkees*. He said, sadly, 'Maybe all that stuff that Rafelson and I did with *The Monkees* basically started the whole concept of MTV, that way of cutting and looking–'

I didn't think so, of course. But it has become so strangely articulated now that next week The Telluride Festival is making this very point, about *Head* – how, if you put on certain sequences, you'd for sure be thinking that the thing was made just last week for MTV. It had an insane amount of cuts in it. Because we didn't have any money to make most of the processes then, that kind of charged the film. We had to invent. It took me nine months to edit it.

Now I think people cut like that for a completely different reason – to be sexy in that rough scene or whatever. Why was it a challenging and interesting idea for you back then?

First of all, it was incredibly self-congratulatory. To show you how absurd this issue is for me, after *Head* I began to think that I would count the cuts in every film I made. And if they didn't decrease then I wasn't improving as a director. This is not entirely true – in case any film wackos are reading this – but it was a conceit that I had in mind. But there were fewer in *Five Easy Pieces*, and many, many fewer in *The King of Marvin Gardens*. But the main reason for the amount of cuts in *Head* was because nobody else had done it, so I decided I wanted to make it quick and fast. And the secondary thing was that I didn't have a great deal of faith in the talent. So I had to have some kind of stylistic triumph.

We do that, don't we? When we're unhappy with a performance, we go, 'Oh, let's cut around . . .'
It's a betrayal of talent, in a way. I love good dancing. Janet Jackson does an MTV video, or Madonna, or Michael Jackson – you never see them dance in a single shot for more than four seconds. How do I know whether they're good dancers? I can only tell if I see a sustained piece. But if somebody's going to twist them upside down, and divide them into a thousand parts, and then superimpose footage on top of that – you're not going to know. Now, in 1965, I knew I didn't have very talented people, so I had to make up something. By the time I got around to making the movie, everybody said to me, 'Don't do it, nobody wants to see a movie with The Monkees.' And I said, 'Well, I did the TV show for everybody else, I'm doing this movie for me.' And so Nicholson – who was an out-of-work actor at the time – and I decided to write it. He structured the whole thing on an acid trip. Well, just to start with, there's a lot of blink-blink-blink in the acid trip. It was almost impossible to make a one-frame cut in those days, two was the minimum – but we did it. We took black-and-white film, impacted it with colour, stuff you can now do in two seconds with a synthesizer. But, anyway, in those days I was trying to make myself look good, more than anything else.

It was appropriate to the time, wasn't it?
It's your first movie, too – it's playtime. But doing a picture with The Monkees – boy, that was discouraging. Everybody with a sensible point of view in life hated The Monkees, because they were a rip-off of the Beatles or the Stones or whatever. I quite liked all of them as individuals, by the way. And there was a measure of talent there. It's just that they weren't really actors – they weren't the Marx Brothers, they weren't The Three Stooges, and yet they were doing that kind of comedy.

Did *The Monkees* give you some financial security?
Well, more than I ever dreamed I was going to have. It didn't give me a lot, but it gave me enough to gamble.

What happened next?
Well, I always had an idea in my mind about what kind of film company could function in America – sort of a bit like the *nouvelle vague* or Windfall Films, who were making – I thought then and to this day – incredibly under-appreciated movies – tough, hard, working-men movies. And I thought that America had plenty of good directors, but that the system was not permitting them to come to the fore, since *Darling Lili* was kind of the popular movie fare of the time. So Bert

Schneider and I started up BBS, and the first film we made was *Head*. Then we used the money we made from *The Monkees* to finance *Easy Rider*. In other words, we bet it all on Dennis – that was our kind of film. After *Easy Rider* I began to feel the so-called ease of economic pressure. Actually, at the same time as *The Monkees* we had another film ready to go, from a novel called *Midnight Plus One*. When I first went to Cannes in 1969 for *Easy Rider* and *Head*, I learned that Orson Welles wanted to film the same novel – he'd read it, and found out that we had the rights. So Bert and I met with Orson, and he came and stayed in a suite at the Beverly Hills Hotel, for I think seven or eight months, writing what we thought was a script for *Midnight Plus One*. In fact, he was simply using the money we were furnishing him with to complete some project that he hadn't quite got round to for several years, and owed delivery on to a bunch of other people.

At that time – Dennis, Jack, and so on, were you like a gang hanging out together here?

I've never been too much of a gang person. But I'd known Dennis for a long time, I had met him in the fifties. Dennis was already a successful actor and already a drunk. And I was in this stripper's place in the East Village – Brandy Case, I'll never forget her name. It was a railroad flat, and I stepped on this guy, a body on the floor. 'My apologies.' Then I kind of recognized him, from Kraft Theatre or some Western movie. He was very young and very handsome, and a fantastic actor, I thought. During subsequent years, I came to California and Dennis was trying to work as an actor, but too often couldn't, and he was painting and taking pictures and was married to Brooke Hayward. We hung out quite a bit. His daughter and my son were best friends. My son was later to make a pornographic movie starring his daughter, at the age of sixteen or fifteen – great picture. Dennis wanted to direct, he said he wanted to do one of the *Monkees* episodes. And I said, 'No. Number one – you won't do it real well. Number two, let me get around to it in my own way, Dennis, I really do think that you can do something fantastic.' Then I brought him in with Michael McClure, and that was how *Easy Rider* got started.

Who else was around at that time? Clearly there were some very interesting and crazy people, and a lot of energy.

Well, the people I knew were people we sought out and asked to make pictures for the company, like Peter Bogdanovich. I saw his *Targets* – 16 mm, with Boris Karloff, and Peter playing the lead. And I thought the work was interesting, so I called him up. And so he joined us. But we hadn't known each other before that. Jack and Dennis knew each other, but as actors. Jack had been in a lot of failed motorcycle movies and was getting the B parts, Hopper had been in one or two of the same. There was Carol Eastman, the writer; Monte Hellman, more through Jack than anybody else; the Hungarian cameramen, Vilmos Zsigmond and Laszlo Kovacs. But most of my friends were writers, novelists and musicians. We had a very sequestered life, in fact. I had no agent, I didn't even have a lawyer. Bert did all the business, we had a building, and in that building there was madness going on all the time. A lot of political stuff – Bert was quite close to the Black Panther Party. There were a lot of religious fanatics. Everybody was trying to hang out in that building.

Lots of drugs?
Absolutely – a lot of dealers and a lot of drugs. A lot of acid; and grass. A lot of musicians, rock-and-roll musicians particularly.

Do you think there's anything like that now? Stupid question, because we always remember our own periods in certain ways. But what do you think about what's happening now?
Let me try to finish up one thought, Mike, because I'm not very good at this, at characterizing eras and stuff. You see, I didn't think we were all that special to start with. I never had this inflated vision of my work, or Dennis's work or whatever. I thought we were lucky, that's what I thought.

Define luck. Isn't luck about putting yourself in the right place at the right time, to an extent?
Yeah, but it's also . . . When I was in the army, I was court-martialled and sentenced to go to Korea. I had hit a sergeant in basic training, so they really wanted my ass – dead. And there was another kid from New York going with me, his name was Everjisto Remos, he and I were buddies. After a very arduous, difficult flight, we stopped in Tacoma, Washington, which was the shipping-off point. You either went to Okinawa or Korea. Now there was a line to stamp you for which boat you were getting on, what position you were being attached to. It was quite long, about five or six hundred people. And I said, 'Come on, Everjisto, let's take a walk.' He said, 'What, we're gonna walk around this fuckin' base, man?' I said, 'Well, Everjisto, we gotta create some luck. Otherwise, in a week, we're both gonna be dead in Korea.' So he said, 'How do you do that?', and I said, 'You widen the circumference of chance.' And that's what we did. I found out they needed a disc jockey – I had never been a disc jockey but now I was the best disc jockey in the world, and rather than be a clerk-typist in a tent in the 49th parallel, couldn't I serve my country more completely with my honed and practised and gifted voice? So they said, 'Put this motherfucker in there. We need him.' And I wound up being a disc jockey in Japan, and Everjisto became a typewriter mechanic, and a whole bunch of other motherfuckers got killed in Korea.

That wasn't simply being in the right place at the right time. In a way, there was a certain stark ambition, there was contrariness – the feeling that, 'Jesus Christ, do we have to do everything the way everybody has always told us to?' Now I had had that in my personality since day one. And at fourteen, I was already trying to figure out another way to do things. So when it came to movies, I figured the same thing. 'Isn't there another way to do things?' I met somebody who said, 'Yes, I think there is, we'll have to do it together.' And it was entirely his doing that it got done. I might have provided some of the energy, some of the ideas, a lot of the talent. But it took an absolute genius to create a system in which this could flourish. I mean – the first day of shooting on *Easy Rider*, Hopper got into an argument with the cameraman – snatched the camera out of his hand, hit him on the head with it, sent him to the hospital. He couldn't imagine that his eye wasn't going to be looking through the lens. The picture was going to be cancelled, right then and there. The point is, that for all of these talented and somewhat self-destructive, reckless temperaments that were around, it really required somebody who could identify with them, somebody they could look up to and somebody that they could talk to, to make them gel as a club, as a movement, as a bunch of guys. It wasn't simply real estate – it was the brains of Bert.

How long did your relationship with Bert last?
Well, I saw him last night at dinner. He's my best friend. We decided to quit the movie thing when we were ahead. At least, I did. I didn't like the idea of producing other people's films. Not that I needed to concentrate more on directing, but I had other things in my life that I wanted to concentrate on. And I didn't want to collect the rent any more in the building, and so on. The last thing we did that bore the imprint of BBS was the *Hearts and Minds* documentary, but I had very little to do with it. I had a hand in the choice of director and very little else. This was Bert's passion. He went off to continue with his passions, and I went off to try to discover what mine were – and how I'd do it without him, and so on. It was a very rude awakening, I must say, because I didn't know anything about the business, didn't have an agent. Nobody knew who I was. I was so little-known, in fact, that somebody actually posed as me, and raised an enormous amount of money to make films in Europe, using my name. I didn't even answer the phone, I didn't get any calls to speak of, so I didn't have any business, I had no life. I felt as if I was diseased, like being in a ward, completely protected. It was a good thing in one sense. But when you get ejected from the ward, or you run outside again, you're a little bit like that character in Ashby's movie, *Being There* – walking around with your pants too short, and a whole lot of the world has been reinvented while you were gone.

How do you feel now about making films? Still enthusiastic?
When I get around to doing it, I'm enthusiastic. I'm never enthusiastic in between – I rather hate it. The whole process of getting something made, that's a bit of an ordeal for somebody like me – it's never, never gone easily. Except during BBS. When I make a movie I become some kind of person that I don't particularly like – edgy and rude and caustic, as if this is the only thing that counts, the only thing that is worth breathing for. And you become very self-inflated – no matter how modestly you wish to behave on the set, still there are a hundred and fifty questions a minute being asked of you, and you're the only one who can give the answer. You know, these good times that everybody has while they're working –

for me it's hard work, I have a sense that I'm a labourer when I'm working on a movie. I think I'm only going to get the thing right if I do it a lot of times, and work at it hard, and get lucky a little bit. There's no inspiration that's coming to me.

The key thing is it's really hard work. A lot of time, I watch people and I think, 'They're not working hard enough.'
I think it's worse than that. I think that's true of about ninety per cent of the movies. I think that they shouldn't have got the job, or they should have worked a whole lot harder to get it. They don't know what the fuck they're doing. But I've had many people say the same thing about my pictures, so what can you say? I had an uncle who said the same things about my pictures all the time, hated them all. He gave me a good perspective, actually. He was a screenwriter, wrote a whole bunch of pictures for Hitchcock and Lubitsch. I met him through my wife's family, and very late in life. Occasionally he would like one of mine, and then he became my uncle. But I was a distant cousin when he didn't like the picture.

Do you read reviews?
I can't. I get them. I *want* to read them. But then I can't. They're on my desk, and I turn to the first one, and I say, 'What are you going to get out of this, Raf?' Look, the first picture I made was universally despised. The second picture I made got a lot of acclaim. But the same people who acclaimed *Five Easy Pieces* had written so degradingly about *Head*. When I first read that criticism, in order to stay sane I had to immediately make a declaration that they didn't know what they were talking about. So I wasn't about to credit them with brains and perception for the second picture because, number one, then I would have been a complete hypocrite. And number two, it would have meant that they were right about the first film – which I didn't think they were. They could have been right, but they could just as easily have been wrong about the second one – do you follow what I'm saying?

Yes. How do you judge the films you have made?
I think I just told you, Mike. I think the best way for me is – did I do as good a job as I could? And I kind of know which areas I put myself out on.

My experience is the same – let's hope we always do that, pretty much. Sometimes you can get – as you would say – lucky. And, you know, some of them work better than others.
Well, I look at it slightly differently. I think the whole process of arriving at what movie you decide to make begins that work. And right at that juncture there are people who don't work hard enough. They can't stand to be out of work. Their families are bleeding. Their egos are wanting in some horrible manner. They can't stand to be idle and they have no other pleasures in life. I could give you a list of hundreds of reasons why people work. For me, part of that hard work is deciding that I *will* work, in the first place. And quite often, I feel that I'm not working hard enough at that process. Do you really want to work now? Are you

in the mood to do this again? Are you in the mood to sit down and fucking talk about 'Fade-fucking-In'? Or would you rather go to Yemen? Now which would you rather do? I'd rather go do Yemen.

Absolutely.

And then, finally, I will have Yemened myself right the fuck out of consciousness, so I say, 'Well, I guess it's time to make a living. There are a few people bleeding now.' Or 'My ego needs that.' Or 'In fact maybe there's something that I want to say.' Whatever the thing is. And then I'll get around to working again. One of the horrors for me is that, at least in the past, that time was rather impulsive. It took me over a year to write about a certain character, in totally different places in the world, in different professions, drifting around my imagination and drifting around from place to place – in fact, the main character of *Five Easy Pieces*. But I couldn't even figure out what in the fuck I wanted to do, I just knew I was attached to the character. So I got Carol Eastman to write a script. But ten weeks later, I shot the movie – ripping the pages out, calling her and saying, 'This is the location, stick it in the script' – like the ferry from the mainland to the island where Bobby Dupea returns to his family. I feel I'm completely deprived of that impulse now. Or I've deprived myself of it. Betwixt the time that the original idea comes up – that, say, you want to do a character that's sort of drifting – and the time you make the film, four years can go by. And by the time you get to the fourth year and you've gone through so much effort to get the film made, you're wondering why in the hell you're making it. It doesn't seem very spontaneous any more. It seems rather shopworn. And then you have to go about almost destroying it, in order to make it fresh for yourself, in order to make it enduring for yourself.

Mike Figgis: How old are you?
Elizabeth Lowe: Twenty-seven, but I lie about it a lot.

Are you telling the truth today?
Yes. I am twenty-seven. I usually say I'm twenty-one.

Why?
Because I look younger, and I go out for a lot of parts where I have to play seventeen, eighteen, nineteen. And if you say you're twenty-seven, they're just not going to buy it.

Where are you from?
Massachusetts.

And how long have you been here?
Eight years. I came out for college, graduated in 1993, and then stayed.

What did you read at college?
I did a double major in Film Directing and Acting Theatre at Occidental College. We worked mostly in video and Super 8 and 16 mm.

What would you say your ambition was?
I was pretty naive. At the time I wanted to start off directing and then move into acting. I thought it would be easier that way. And then I gave that up.

At what age would you consider that you started thinking about film?
Probably when I was twelve – I saw the movie *The Outsiders* and I was obsessed with the movies after that. Plus, I hated the town I lived in, it was really small, and I wanted to get out of there more than anything – not that I didn't love my family, but I just didn't want to be a part of them any more. I thought they were very boring. Then I went to an all-girls boarding-school in Connecticut, because I thought it was closer to New York than Massachusetts. And then I came out to LA for college.

How do you feel about your town now?
The same – I don't like going back there, I feel stifled, like I'm missing something exciting. And I have sort of a resentment towards the town, like it's held me back or something.

Is that true?
I think that when I got into acting more seriously, I found that everyone was sort of tortured and had a great crazy past. And mine was very normal, which made me angry. I wanted terrible things to have happened to me as a child – which is a terrible thing to wish for. But I thought, that way, I'd have deeper stuff to pull on as an actress. There are certain people who walk into a room and there's just something that is broken about them. And you're fascinated by them. I didn't think I had that.

So now you've been here for eight years. And in that time, has enough weird stuff happened to you?
Oh yes, I think I've been broken, to a degree – definitely.

Are you pleased, in a sense?
No, it was a terrible thing to wish for. It was silly and self-indulgent to wish for bad things to happen.

Well, you didn't necessarily want bad things, you wanted interesting things.
Sure. But I definitely wanted to be more tortured. And I think, doing what I've been doing for five years now, I'm becoming more and more tortured.

What exactly do you do?
I'm a waitress three days of the week, and the rest of the time I'm trying to be an actress. I'm still trying to get established. I go on auditions, I've done a couple of low-budget movies, I go to class, I buy *Drama-Logue* every Thursday and submit to it. I go out on commercial castings in a bikini with thousands of other girls and try to get recognized and make money.

The other waitresses you work with – are they also actors?
Oh, everyone's an actress, and everyone's a little envious of someone else. 'Oh, you got a part. That's great. Great!' I know I'm very competitive, so sometimes I feign excitement. But I'm always looking for something new and different. And unfortunately it goes back to my childhood – I get bored with who I am and find it much more interesting to read a book or, if given the chance, to become some-one else in a scene or a commercial or a movie or a TV show.

Are there a lot of people like you in town?
Yes, I definitely think so.

So everybody comes here.
Yes, all looking for the same thing.

How many of you are there?
Every day I see thousands of people doing the same thing I am. Anywhere you go – you go to a bookstore and the person working behind the counter is probably an actor. I work with them, and a lot of my friends are actors. I go on auditions every day so I see them. There's a ton of very pretty girls who are out here trying to do the same thing. Sometimes you walk into an audition and you have to put up a wall because you think, 'Oh, my God, I would pick her, or her, or her, but not me.'

What would pretty be? You seem like a nice-looking person.
Thinner.

'Thinner'? You're thin . . .
I am considered thin but in this industry I don't consider myself as thin as I can

be. I've been told more than a handful of times to lose weight and get in better shape. It's like they think, 'Okay, you're an actress, so we can stomp on you a little. Because you need something from me.' So it's 'Hey, you should lose about five pounds. Why don't you go to the gym?'

Lose it – or put it somewhere else?
Either/or. I'm lucky in a way because I look innocent and young enough that I haven't been told to get a boob-job yet. But I know a lot of girls who have had them, and a lot of other things, for physical appearance. Because it is a physical business, it definitely is.

What else? What other choices?
Lip injections are very common. And you're told to go to the gym every day, get those little arm muscles, have a tight butt so you can go on commercial auditions in a bikini and get the job over the bombshell sitting next to you. I've stopped going on bikini calls though. I just couldn't handle it.

Are you a better person for that then?
I don't know, but I feel better about myself. I hated it. It was pretty degrading. I went in for one about two months ago, it was a Tampax ad, and you were standing there playing volleyball on a beach in a bikini, and talking about how you were such a better volleyball player than the guy, and nothing got in your way, not even your period. It's pretty embarrassing when you're in a bikini in front of ten men, hitting a ball and talking about your period.

What does it represent financially?
A lot of money. You could probably get seventy thousand for it, if it's a national commercial. Two years ago I quit waitressing because I had two national commercials running, and it was great. I made a vow to myself I'd never waitress again. Then the commercials stopped, and this TV show I was on stopped, and about three months ago I was broker than I've ever been in my life and I had to go back. I had to let go of that pride and realize that, yeah, it's a harder road than I ever thought it would be. I thought I'd graduate college and probably within a year I'd get a good job and move on up and already be well more established than I am.

Are you a good actress?
Yes, I am, very good.

How abusive is this scene for women?
I think that it is extremely abusive. Unfortunately everyone knows that when they go into it, and thinks they can handle it.

Did you know what you were in for?
I was a little naive going in, but I knew there were certain things that, as a woman, I was going to have to put up with.

Are you a feminist?
I definitely believe in complete equality, I believe that what is going on in this business is not fair and should change.

When you were younger, were you aware of feminist ideals?
I was much more hard-core when I was younger – hard-core feminist. I was sort of angry at my mom for being a housewife. And I was at an all-girls boarding-school so we took these ideals too.

You read.
Yes, and I realized that we were getting screwed, and I hated it.

So this is perverse, wanting to be in films – you know that?
Yes, I definitely know it.

What part does narcissism or ego play in wanting to be someone who's blown up to forty times life-size?
Oh, huge. You want people to think you're beautiful and talented. It's a basic need that I have. I could have stayed home, done theatre, and probably played a lot better parts. But I wanted to be big.

Yeah, fine – me too. But then, isn't that perverse?
Oh, God, yes. I get up every morning and make sure I look okay, and I'm very aware of my physical being, putting on make-up, buying nice clothes and feeling sexy. It's probably why I have very few female friends – because of the competition. Which is bad, considering that I just said I'm a feminist. But I'm in a business where I don't feel attractive a lot of the time, because of that competition.

Have you had any bad professional experiences of being manipulated?
There are a couple of instances in my career here where because I'm a woman I was manipulated into doing things that I definitely didn't want to do.

Do you want to tell me about that?
Well, the first part I ever got in a movie, I got it through an acting teacher, and I knew that I was going to be topless in it. I was playing a model, and I was sup-posed to be covered in a plaster cast. The teacher said, 'We're only going to see your chest after it's covered in the cast, and that's it.' I was twenty, and extremely stupid. So I'm lying down completely naked on this table, and I do the first take, which was rehearsal. Then I said, 'You know what? I really would feel more com-fortable if I could wear some panties. So they gave me a pair, I put them on, and she puts the stuff all over me. I thought they didn't start filming until the stuff was on me. So the movie comes out, and I see that I'm completely naked in it – I mean completely. They filmed the whole thing.

And, yeah, I should have known better but I was nervous and it was the first part I ever got – I got my SAG card out of it. But it was just one of those things that, if my parents ever saw it, I would die. It was an HBO movie. I turned on the TV and I saw it, and I almost died. It's just the most embarrassing thing. I saw it in the video store yesterday, and I was just, 'Ohhh – people are renting it?' I told people back home that I was in it. A bunch of boys who were old friends of mine all saw it, it's one of the only things they've seen of mine – and I'm naked in it. So it was a huge lesson learned there.

But you're still upset about it.
Oh, very. My dialogue's cut, I say maybe two lines. And that scene is just about a naked girl on a table. It was a bad experience.

You didn't have a no-nudity clause?
I didn't even have an agent.

Was it worth it?
Not at all. I booked a commercial a month later, I could have got my SAG card then. But at the time I was desperate.

That's an obvious example of what, in any other business, would be called sexual harassment.
I could sue them.

Did it cross your mind?
God, no.

Why?
Because at the time I thought, 'I'm not going to cross anybody, I'm a nobody and I'll get crushed. I don't want to seem like an ungrateful actress.' Now it's too far gone. I never even said anything to the person who got me the part, that's how weakly I handled the situation. I'm terrified of confrontation and that is not a good trait to have in this business. I have friends who are totally ballsy and would do anything to get what they wanted or get themselves out of a bad situation. But I sort of comply because I don't want to rock the boat.

In a way, auditions force you to act a certain role, in order to get a role.
Definitely. When I first started, I would walk into a room and be so scared. People said I looked like Bambi caught in the headlights. So I had to come up with a more confident persona to walk into the room. Nobody wants someone who walks in saying, 'Hi, don't want to bother you, but I'm here to audition, and I'll just be back here when you want me.' They want a strong person. I have friends who are cut-throat, and it works for them. Some people think they're bitches, but they get what they want.

I'm from Mars again, for the moment. Talk me through the casting process.
I have an agent. They will call me and say, 'You're going in tomorrow at noon for the part of Suzy on *Party of Five*. And they will fax me the sides.

And how will you be described?
Usually nineteen to twenty, girl next door, cute, perky, kind of loud – something like that. The sides will be three pages, and I'll work on them by myself, memorize them, and then I'll either go to my coach or go to a friend and rehearse . . .

Going to your coach, does that cost money?
Yes, a hundred bucks for an hour.

So you'll invest a hundred bucks?
Plus, you never know, you might buy a new outfit.

Which would cost how much?
Another hundred. Then I rehearse it as I plan to do it, to the point where I know that if I get nervous I can fall back on what I have in my head. And then the next day I get ready, wash my hair – which is a big thing. I make sure I have plenty of time to put on my make-up. I don't wear a lot but I'll put on lipstick, eye-shadow, mascara. And usually something under my eyes in case I look sleepy. Then I fix my hair, and go from the bathroom mirror to the bedroom mirror, which is taller. I stand in front of the mirror, naked, and say, 'You fat whatever, you should go to the gym.' And then I put my clothes on, walk past the mirror to see if my butt looks big while I walk.

Do you have a couple of mirrors?
Yes. Then I go to my roommate's room, he's a guy and will tell you anything about a woman's body. I'll say, 'Does this outfit look good?' He'll say, 'Fine' or 'No, try this', whatever. Then I make him read the scene with me one more time, which he hates. Then I go to the audition, sit in a room with usually about ten other girls, and we're all like, 'Hi!'

How many of the ten do you know?
I don't know any of them personally, but I recognize probably five of the ten.

Sometimes it sucks – I'll go in for a young part, a seventeen-year-old. And the girls are seventeen. I'm taller and I just don't have that pre-pubescent body. But anyway – they call you in and say, 'Do you have any questions?' And you think of some dumb-ass question to ask them, just so you can prolong it. Because that's another competitive thing – 'Who was in the room longest? Oh, they must really like her.' Then you do the scene. Sometimes you feel great about it, sometimes you suck. Then it's 'Thanks for coming in, nice to meet you.' Sometimes they talk some more to you, and you think, 'Oh, my God, they like me.' And then I go right to a pay phone and call my agents and tell them what happened. A few times I've said, 'I sucked, that was the worst audition of my life, please call them and tell them that I can do much better than that.' Then you hope you get a call-back, or sometimes a screen test, or sometimes you book it right off that.

And how do you feel about the way you're treated in these auditions?

In general, most casting directors are pretty nice. Sometimes you're bummed because you've got twenty pages of dialogue, five scenes, and you work on all five. Then you get in there completely pumped, and they say, 'Okay, choose a scene.' You think, 'Damn, I just spent all that time getting this character ready.' But I'd say generally casting has a cattle feel to it.

Who do you read with when you read?
The casting director.

And how good at acting are most casting directors?
There are about four who are awesome and the rest are, you know . . . I always make friends who read with me read it as dully as possible, because that's just what you usually get. But every once in a while, you go in and someone will be so good that it almost throws you. It's great when you get to work with other actors for auditions.

Would it make your life much happier if you always read with an actor?
I don't know. Sometimes I've been in with other actors and they've sucked. They're nervous, they can't get their lines, and so they pull you down. So it's debatable. You know who are the best at auditions? The soap operas.

I believe it. I'm a huge fan of television. They practise more.
Every time I go up for a soap, I read with another actor who's good, the casting directors are the best readers I've read with and they give you the most time. I don't know why.

How do you feel about TV? Would you be happy to be a TV actress?
I had someone tell me that the other day – which kind of shattered my heart, but – it was actually one of the guys from Farmer's Market saying, 'I think we need to take a new approach with your career. Maybe you're not a movie star. Maybe you're a TV star.' So in your heart you feel, 'I don't have what it takes to be a movie star.'

When I first came here ten years ago, there was such a stigma attached to TV that casting directors would say, 'Oh, you don't want to go with that person. She or he's a TV actor.' And I'd say, 'The problem is what?' If they're in regular work, they work quickly, they have to think on their feet, they don't get endless takes – all things which, to me, are huge pluses. And every TV-based actor I've ever worked with, I've been delighted with. They're just good team players.
One of the best jobs I ever had was a TV pilot. It wasn't picked up, but I loved it – there was a live audience, it was like doing theatre. Everyone's pumped, everyone's laughing. You go out and you get to do long scenes that aren't cut every two seconds. I love to do that kind of stuff. I would be very happy as a TV actor.

You've done some stuff for film students at the American Film Institute and at the University of Southern California. How were they?

I just wish I had been more prepared. I would rather do it now, because you get great stuff. If you act in one of the thesis projects the students do in their graduate programmes, it's something they've been working on for a year or two, and they treat you with a great deal of respect.

What's the sleaziest part of the film industry?
Waiting tables and having some executives come in and feed you a line like, 'If you go out with me, I'll take you to this première, I'll introduce you to the right people.' You just know it's going nowhere. But there is this underlying thing that if you give certain favours to a man, you get ahead in the industry.

As clichéd as that. So that still exists?
Definitely. I have two friends who used to be neighbours of mine; one used to be a dancer in Vegas, really pretty young girl, and the other was a stripper. They both fell into that. They're both being supported by men, but it didn't do anything for their careers. I once met a man who worked in some movie company and he gave me his card and he said he was going to take me to this big première. He calls me up on his car phone and says, 'Are you pierced anywhere?' I say, 'No.' 'Do you have tattoos anywhere kind of – interesting?' And then all of a sudden I hear this screaming, and he goes, 'Oh yeah, honey, I'm coming. Hang on, I'll call you back.' And he hung up. He was in his driveway, talking to me on his cellphone, trying to talk dirty to me. 'So you going to come tonight? What are you going to wear?' I just said, 'Oh, my God. Bye.' So, yeah, it's definitely as clichéd as that. But also, in the back of you mind, you're sick enough to think, 'I don't want to not play this game because you just don't know.' There's just a curiosity there.

It's a beautiful trap. If it were IBM, there are such clear-cut rules about conduct now, almost to the point of being stupid. But they're there for a reason. Because it's like the judge said: 'Hey, what do you expect if you go around wearing a short skirt? You're asking for it.' So, by that criterion, this town is full of people who are asking for it.
You go out and you're told to wear a sexy outfit. Two weeks ago, I was wearing this short dress and walking from my car to the office, which is a long walk, and I was just hating it – because you know you're asking for the catcalls. Like it's my fault that I wore this outfit, and I'm making you look at me or something.

How do you get rid of that feeling?
I don't know. Either you try to enjoy it in a way, and think, 'All right, I look good, but this is what I've got to wear, and if you want to look, look. Just don't talk to me.' Or else you don't go out for those parts. I had an argument like that with my agent, I said, 'I'm not that part, I can't do it.' Then I went and did it, and got the job. But I had already booked another job.

I always have the feeling when I come into the town that the atmosphere is full

of guilt and uneasiness – people uneasy in their skins about what they've done, whether it's people who behave badly to someone or people who feel that they invited a bad thing upon themselves.

Then there are times when you're just ignored – which is how I met the guys at Farmer's Market.

The guys on what I call the Cool Jew table – Paul Mazursky and fellow veterans . . .

They were always staring at me, then they'd all turn their heads, and make it very obvious that they thought I was cute or whatever. Finally they invited me over one day. And I was completely flattered. I don't know if it was because they're older and I wasn't threatened. But I enjoyed it, and we became friends. I see them doing it to other girls and I'm kind of doing it with them, like I'm one of the guys, which is weird. But I love it. Plus it's hard to have an intellectual discussion with a lot of actors. You bring up an article or a book you've read, and they don't respond. But with the guys at Farmer's, it's great. You can talk about anything. And a lot of the time we talk about silly stuff . . .

A lot of interesting people come and go from that table.

It's a great group. And they know that I don't expect anything from them. You don't bring business into it. It's more about humour, they're very funny. There's a lot of discussion of films, but it tends to be older films. Plus I think that they have a lot to teach me. There's always a book or a movie I don't know about.

Let me ask you some practical questions. How much rent do you pay?

Four-ninety a month.

What do you spend on food?

Probably about a hundred a week.

Car?

I have a car my parents bought me. I fill up with gas every three, four days, which is twenty bucks. I buy a lot of clothes. I drink, but I don't go out a lot. I go to parties more.

So really it doesn't cost that much to live here.

Not at all. It's the cheapest city I know.

And the weather's good. So really you can get by quite happily, not succeeding. What's the top limit before you've got to get out, if you haven't made it?

For me there isn't.

How many forty-five-year-old actresses do you know waitressing?

Not that many.

How many thirty-five-year-old actresses do you know waitressing?

A few.

How many forty-year-olds?
Not very many.

So it seems, somehow, between thirty-five and forty . . .?
Oh, no, you've got to figure out another career. Everyone's always thinking, 'Well, I could be a photographer.' Or, 'I really like clothes, so why don't I open a dress store?' You don't start thinking that until you're around my age. I'm constantly fighting with myself, just to get out there and create something on my own.

Tell me five movies that you like. Don't think about it. It could be that you've just seen them or you saw them ten years ago, it doesn't matter.
I watched *Pulp Fiction* yesterday, loved it; *Marathon Man* – loved it; *Ordinary People; Being There.*

You mentioned *The Outsiders* earlier . . .
Oh, *The Outsiders* changed my life. I don't know if I'd say it's one of my favourite movies. But I was obsessed with it.

Five books.
The Fountainhead, which I'm reading right now; *Anna Karenina;* Ted Hughes's *Birthday Letters* I love. Anything by Joyce Carol Oates; and Cormac McCarthy's *All The Pretty Horses.*

Five actors, male.
Anthony Hopkins, James Spader, Johnny Depp, Aidan Quinn, Gary Oldman.

Female actors.
Jodie Foster, Meryl Streep, Renee Zellweger, Katharine Hepburn, Grace Kelly.

Five directors.
Paul Mazursky, Robert Redford, Francis Coppola, Jay Pate, Amy Heckerling.

Five pieces of music, any style?
The Foo Fighters; jazz – Charlie Parker; Cajun zydeco music; hard-core rock like Rage Against The Machine. There's a Sunday night radio show called *The Open Road* which always plays blue grass and I just love it.

Mike Figgis: Can you pick out a point in your life when you really thought it would be interesting to be an actor?
Amy Graham: I've always done plays, since I was very young. In high school I was a little rebellious, so I strayed from it for a while. But by the time I graduated and left, I really wanted to pursue it – I took classes, did the agents, the whole bit.

Where was high school?
Agoura – it's thirty minutes west of Hollywood.

So you were raised in this area?
Pretty much. I was born in Wisconsin, lived there for a short time.

Any showbiz connections?
No. My mom is a poet, and she writes children's poems and does some photography. My dad was in the FBI.

And what age were you when you left high school?
I graduated when I was seventeen, and went to a little college in the vicinity of where I grew up. But I would always ditch my classes, and go off to watch movies.

So what was the first active step you made towards becoming an actress?
My sister was already an actress at the time. I think it was an agent of hers who said, 'We should bring your sister in.' And I met them and ended up working with them for a little bit, then moved elsewhere.

Did they send you to auditions?
Yes, for commercials. You got sides, you read for the casting directors, and you were either called back, or rejected – that happened a lot.

How long was it before you actually got a part in a film?
It took a while. I wasn't that committed to it when I was younger, then at some point it changed. When I was nineteen, I was tested for the lead in a film, and they ended up giving me a line to help me get my SAG card. Basically, to work, you have to be in SAG. And then it helps you to get jobs. Then I did a guest spot on a TV show.

So you were Taft-Hartleyed. My first time on an American set, someone asked, 'Would you Taft-Hartley me?' I said, 'I'd like to, but I don't know what the hell that means.' Then I realized – I needed one person to do a line, and among the extras there were twenty desperate people who would have done almost anything just to get this one line, and get their SAG card. So you got your line, and you got your card?
Actually, I waited until the next job, because it costs about a thousand dollars. And at that time, I was poor.

How did you support yourself? You'd moved to Hollywood?

Yeah, I did the whole restaurant thing, waitressing, catering. I did some work for my dad – I probably shouldn't say what. I was an extra a couple times in music videos. And I did promotions for Hemdale Film.

So how did you live when you first moved here?
I did a lot of house-sitting at first. I would stay at people's places when they were out of town. Then I sublet, then eventually I got my first part in a movie and I made a little money and I got my apartment. And from there on, I was paying for my rent.

What would be a typical week for you then? How many times would you go in and read for things?
Probably at least three or four. It depends – certain periods like Christmas are busier.

And the things you're going in for, are they a mix of television and film, or just film?
Well, it used to be commercials and television. Now it's pretty much just films, unless it's a really respectful television show, or a guest spot.

When I first came here, actors were really scared of being labelled as 'TV actors'. Casting directors would also say, 'She's a TV actress', and that would be a real put-down. I'd think, 'What's the problem? I like TV actors. They usually learn their lines quickly, they have more experience than most film actors.' I could never quite understand the snobbery.
I think there's much more of a crossover now. Soap actresses like Demi Moore and Robin Wright, they were able to go on into film. Sarah Michelle Geller, who's on *Buffy* – she's now making a lot of movies.

Did you see actors not making it who clearly were not going to make it?
I think maybe one per cent of the actors out there are actually working. So there's a huge fallout.

And what happens to the other ninety-nine per cent?
At some point, I guess you just have to say, 'Okay, this isn't working.' But people are different. Some people just keep plugging at it, and more power to them.

Okay – say you're eighteen, you're going to three auditions a week, you're meeting people for coffee, you go to parties, you hang out, right? Of the group of people you remember hanging out with then, what's happened to everybody? No need to name names, but in general . . .
A couple have left to explore other avenues; a couple are still struggling at it; a couple have become very successful at it. I think you just have to make a judgement from the responses you're getting when you're going out on auditions – you have to use that as a gauge as to whether or not to get out.

How many times have you changed agents?
I'm on my third.

Is that typical, do you think?
Yeah, it's very typical. People can move around more now.

Do you have a manager?
Not any more – just because I have really good agents.

When you had a manager, what percentage of your income did that involve?
Ten, but I think usually it's fifteen.

Ten for a manager, and ten for an agent.
Yes.

And you pay taxes obviously. So what percentage of what you earn do you take home? Fifty?
You see about a third of your cheque. But you save your receipts, and you go to the taxman and try to write things off.

What do you think is right about Hollywood, as a system?
I really enjoy working – the feeling on a set where it's a team effort, and you all have the same goal in mind, which is to do good work and put your heart into it and make it good.

Acting is a strange thing to do, isn't it? 'What do you do for a living?' 'Oh, I pretend to be someone I'm not.' And you work in a part of the industry that is very glamorous. Hollywood does focus a lot on beauty and attractiveness. You're a young actress, so in a sense you're in the middle of that. Do you sometimes resent that?
Yeah, sometimes you look and think, 'Why is she getting that job?' You can break it down into a couple of different things, and one of them is beauty. I've never really considered myself to be part of that glamour.

Why not?
I'm just not really interested in that side of it – in going to premières and so on. I'm interested in the work.

But say you go for a part, and you read a script that says, 'Mary is in her mid-twenties, a stunning blonde.' How do you prepare for that?
You think, 'Okay, I'm going to go in and do my best, and they'll probably give it to the hottest name around right now.'

Yes, but you've dodged the bullet there. How do you actually prepare? They're expecting someone to walk through the door. You want to act, you want to do good work. At the same time I imagine you're very often going in for parts described as 'glamorous'. Have you ever read a script that just said, 'Mary is an interesting woman'?

No – it bugs me, definitely.

Okay, so your agent says you have a meeting at eleven o'clock on Wednesday at Warners. How do you prepare?
Well, I go through a whole thing of 'I don't want to do this, I know what's going to happen.'

Is there a pressure to go in?
Yes. Because even if you don't get the job, maybe they will like you and remember you.

How are you going to make them like you and remember you?
Just by trying to do the part as best you can. Their stance is very much: 'Okay, prove to us that you can do this role.' You have to convince. I have to go in and put on a show: 'Oh, I can be this sexy, beautiful thing.'

What about the actual process of reading – of who you read with and how that reading is carried out – do you have any thoughts about that?
Sometimes you'll go in there and they'll just be goofing off with the sides. If you've put in three or four hours' work on the material, then that's irritating. But other people are more respectful – usually the people at a certain higher level of the business, who know how to treat people, who respect that it's a difficult process and try to help you.

What about going on tape for directors?
I'm fine with that – it's actually better sometimes, because then there aren't so many people in the room. With TV, you can get ten or twelve suits sitting there staring at you. Just the director and the casting person is the ideal situation, I think.

Outsiders tend to think of Hollywood as a sexual hot-pad, and there's much press mileage made out of it. I've never found it to be particularly that way myself, but I'm not an actress. Have you encountered that? Have you ever been harassed or made uncomfortable?
Never really in an office situation, where I've been reading for a role. Maybe if you go out on the town, it's different.

How important is money in your career?
Well, I like to be able to pay my bills.

Are there pressures from your agents, managers, and so on?
Well, people are obviously in this business to make money. I haven't come to that yet, but I know I have achieved a certain level. Going back to do a low-budget thing after achieving that was a little weird.

And when you chose to do the low-budget thing, what were the factors? How did you finally say, 'Okay, I'll do it'?

Because I liked the character. It was a lead role, and an interesting, complicated role for a woman.

Do you think women are valued in storytelling and film?
Some writers and directors treat them that way. The majority? Probably not.

Why are there so many stories about boys – about guys together?
You would have to look at who's running the show, who's making the decisions on what is being made and what isn't being made.

You read a lot of scripts. A lot of them are very violent, and often the women are called upon to be the objects of violence. Does that worry you?
Yes. There are so many crimes committed against women – rape, abuse, violence. It does get to me.

Does film endorse it? Or say, 'This is wrong'?
I think that sometimes film shows us the way something is, makes us look at it when we'd otherwise overlook it, and that's positive. I don't enjoy watching women being badly treated. In a lot of cases films just advocate it, saying over and over again that it's fine.

Even in some films that claim to be socially aware, there is the unfortunate possibility that you could be exciting a lot of men in the audience by showing violence. Have you ever been involved in a film like that?
I have. And yes, it did trouble me. It was hard to do.

What did you weigh up when you were deciding whether to do it or not?
I thought, 'Does this movie have anything good to say?' Sometimes you will compromise certain opinions that you might have, which you probably shouldn't do. Sometimes you need to work, and you need to do certain things to get your name out there. The instance I'm thinking about, the character starts out as a victim, and then throughout the story she becomes stronger, and she learns and she changes. That was important in deciding on the role. I don't think I could have taken it if she was simply a victim.

How do you feel about the depiction of sex in films?
It depends how it's done. I'm not against it, but I think women are exploited a lot through that. A lot of times, you see a movie where the woman didn't really need to be naked. They just thought, 'We need some nudity here, we need some sex, this will help sell it. Take your clothes off.'

Would you do that?
I've done nudity before, because it was realistic and necessary to the story.

It's now become accepted that you have to do it at some point in your career, right?

Yeah – 'When are you gonna get it over with?' I don't know how many actresses have gone through their career without getting naked.

I think it must be almost impossible.
It's embarrassing. I don't ordinarily get naked in front of strangers who I don't know and trust. But then there you are. So it's weird.

I did a Spanish film production, and they have a whole different attitude about sex in movies. It's supposed to be a closed set when you're doing nudity but all of a sudden the entire art department walks in while I'm sitting there. Then the still photographer took a picture of me, and I got up and left. You're not supposed to do it that way.

And then?
Then they fix it and you come back in and you do it. But you have to respect a person, make them feel comfortable, especially if it's about taking your clothes off. People have enough insecurities and hard times dealing with real life, let alone doing it for millions of people.

Some quick questions – just give really quick answers. Tell me some films that you've liked in your life; it needn't be in any particular order.
La Femme Nikita; A Woman Under The Influence; Opening Night; The Black Stallion; The Breakfast Club; Pretty In Pink – I liked all those silly John Hughes things.

Five pieces of music.
I like The Cocteau Twins; this new band, Air; Sly and the Family Stone; Al Green; Marvin Gaye.

Any books that you love?
I'm reading *Confederacy of Dunces* now. I like that. I'll try not to say *The Catcher in the Rye.*

Why not? Beautiful book. Five actors that have influenced you, male?
Brando, De Niro, Pacino, Paul Newman, Steve McQueen.

Actresses?
Gena Rowlands, Jessica Lange, Jodie Foster, Susan Sarandon.

Directors?
Jonathan Kaplan, I work with him a lot; Quentin Tarantino, I like him.

Mike Figgis: Let's start off by asking – and be as honest as you possibly can – why on earth did you choose to be an actress?

Julie Delpy: I started when I was fourteen, so I didn't really know at that time. Both my parents were actors. And I loved movies, more than I loved acting. It was a bit painful at the beginning – although the first person I worked with was Godard, and he was wonderful, amazing.

Which film?

Detective. It was a good movie, Jean-Pierre Léaud was in it. It was really inspiring, and I was so happy to work with him because he had been my hero, since I was eight or nine. But yes, the beginning was difficult. I didn't know until later that I really enjoyed acting. At first, I was just attracted to being part of the movies more than anything else.

What part did narcissism play in that?

Actually, not much at the beginning, because I hated myself so much. That was maybe what was painful. I was extremely insecure and scared. I learned to become more narcissistic, but not in the typical way where I look at myself in the mirror and I think, 'Oooh!' It's not that simple. It's more like torture than that. In fact, when I started acting, I was so nerdy, people didn't want to be around me. So for me, as a child at least, it became a weird kind of revenge – to be accepted by other people.

But I can remember at the time you did *Detective*, you were part of a little school of up-and-coming French actresses who were being photographed a lot. So suddenly you clearly weren't a nerd. You were being presented as a sexy young actress. How did that feel?

You know, that's really not how I saw the whole thing. I think I was lucky that my parents were actors, because I learned that it's all ups and downs, good times and bad times. I never expected too much. Some people say I'm a bit cynical because when good things happen to me, I say, 'Ahh, you know . . . I'm just waiting until something really bad happens.'

Is that maybe a typically European rather than American characteristic?

I don't think so. I just learned it from my parents.

I won't let you get away with that so quickly. How old were you when you made your first American film, as such?

I was eighteen. It was *Voyager* – almost ten years ago.

But you couldn't really describe it as an American film, could you? The director wasn't American.

Well, there were Americans in it – Sam Shepard. Really, I haven't done any truly American movies. *Killing Zoë* was a French production; *Three Musketeers* was shot in Europe. The people on set were mostly British, the actors were American.

But I live in Hollywood and I know how it works. Sometimes I'm horrified by it – the thing of what's hot right now, and who dates whom. But at the same time I just think, 'I don't care, all I want is to get on with my life and do the things I want to do.'

What would you say is good about Hollywood? Why are you here?
Because it attracts a lot of people, and in that mix there's a lot of bullshit, but there are also a few people with interesting projects.

But you're not from Los Angeles; you're not even American. So why are you here?
When I first moved here, I really was just planning on staying six months – I know a lot of people say that. But I moved into this little place and I met a bunch of good people, who want to work on good movies. And, as a woman, I find I express myself much more here. It's going to sound insane, but I felt there were more women in Hollywood who were accepted for what they are than there were in Paris. In Hollywood there are 'object women', but there are also strong, powerful women, with good minds. In France I felt there was a lot of the *Pygmalion* idea around – a lot of women who were empty and looking for someone else to fill them. That's not how I felt, and I couldn't deal with that in France. But sometimes I feel awful in Hollywood also. Right now I'm in a good mood, but if you catch me on a bad day I could say the most horrible things.

On a bad day, why is it bad?
Well, you find yourself at an audition, and it's truly unfair sometimes – the little time that's spent on the actors. If I was auditioning people, I would try to see a bit more than what they usually ask you for. Because how can you judge someone in half a second?

Describe a typical audition.
I know I'm going to sound cuckoo, but I'm very sensitive to vibes. Sometimes you go into a room and you feel they don't even care if you're there or not. They've already made up their mind on someone else. You feel, 'What am I doing there?' Sometimes you don't even want to be there because you're not sure you care about the movie. But you go to be professional, because your agent set you up, and you feel you have to do it.

Describe the process, for people who haven't a clue how it works.
They call you and say, 'Read this script tonight. You have a meeting tomorrow.' You maybe cancel the dinner you had planned. They send you the script by messenger, you start reading. By about page 35, you can tell if it's really, really bad. If it's mediocre, I go on. If it's very good I'm thinking, 'Yes! Finally! Oh, my God, a miracle is happening. A good script.'

What's a good script?

It's something you read from beginning to end, you want to read every description. And you enjoy it – you giggle, you're excited to be reading it. That's happened to me maybe ten, twenty times in my life. It's like reading a good book. You don't feel you're losing your day by reading it. Because otherwise it's very depressing to spend a whole day reading something that is of no value – it's like polluting your brain. So anyway, if I like the script I say, 'Okay, I'll have the meeting.'

What if you don't like the script, but it has an important director, or your agent's pushing it?
Well, if it's a really good director whom I like, I'm going to want to meet the director anyway. Usually my agent doesn't put pressure on me, I put pressure on myself because I feel that I can't be saying no too often. I don't go to every audition and every meeting my agent would like me to. So sometimes I just make an effort, I go. And sometimes it goes really well. Other times I go into the room and think, 'What am I doing here?' And I'm usually pretty quiet, and I just leave as soon as possible. I don't make a big deal out of it. I just make it something that I will forget as soon as possible.

Now, of the meetings that you go into, in what percentage do you actually meet the director and what percentage do you meet a casting director?
What if I tell you that half the time I don't even know who the director is? I can be saying hello to everyone and I have no idea. 'Oh, you're the director?' If I don't know the person's work too well, I don't necessarily know what they look like. So it's, 'Oh, it was the casting director? Very nice.'

Do you learn your lines?
Oh, yes. Learn by heart, no. But I learn them well enough. Sometimes you don't, but it doesn't matter – you go into a room and people are there for you, and you know it's going to go great. But the minute I go into a room and I don't want to do the audition, I'm not going to remember the lines. The audition process is very tricky, because your mind plays games with you. Whether you're nervous, or you don't care – it's all going to influence the audition tremendously. That's why I hate the idea of being judged by a one-time thing. If I feel I have only one chance, I'm going to fuck up – that's the way I am. If I feel I have more than one chance, I'll be totally fine. It depends on the director, whether people make you feel comfortable, if they make you rehearse a little bit.

Who do you read with normally?
Sometimes with the actors who are going to do the other parts. Other times, just with someone reading out the lines, who can be really good or really bad. And when they're really bad it's very hard – worse than acting alone.

What about going on tape for directors?
I really think, to judge actors, you first of all have to meet them. And the problem in Hollywood is that agents make people meet as many actors as possible. So

sometimes they don't have the time – everyone has about one minute each. But I don't mind going on tape. Once I actually felt that I didn't get a part because I wasn't on tape. The director insisted on reading with me, but he never looked at me. So I have no idea how he could judge me.

Would you say that he was just not a good enough actor?
No, he was doing fine. But he just wasn't judging me. He was busy reading the lines.

I've done that.
Oops.

No, it's interesting. I always read with actors. Sometimes I just take their photograph. But I love to hear their voices, and sometimes you don't listen hard enough if you're looking.
For me, it was a weird situation. He was hiding his face, too, that was very strange. I was talking to someone who was hiding.

Ah, well, you must understand. A lot of us are very frightened of you.
Actors can be very scary. But if more directors were aware that we're as scared of them as they are of us, things would be better.

How many meetings a week do you go on?
Maybe two. Not so many. That's good, for me; I could do more.

Would you like to appear in more mainstream American films? Would that be good for you? Financially, it would be nice.
Oh, financially, of course.

How important is money to you?
To me, it isn't. But I've done things for money. I read an article about Mastroianni after he died, and it quoted an interview where he was asked, 'So in the seventies you did a lot of movies that weren't so great?' And he said, 'Well, I knew I was in a terrible scene with terrible dialogue, but I was thinking, "I'm building my swimming pool here."' I might have done one or two movies because they helped me get through an entire year without having to do anything else, and they weren't such bad projects that I was totally horrified by them. And it was easy; you can make money easily. People forget. I see my parents, how much money they make in theatre, and what a struggle it has been. I just can't always say no to money – it's tempting. At the same time, you don't have to sell your soul to make money. You can keep your head on your shoulders.

Have you ever compromised yourself?
Sometimes. But I always keep the thought that it's not really compromise, as long as you're conscious of it. I think the real compromise is when you lose the sense of what you're doing and why you're doing it. A compromise is when you convince yourself you love someone because it's going to be helpful in your work or in your

life. Same with movies. A compromise is when you convince yourself you're doing good work when you're not, for money. If you don't give yourself an excuse for doing it, apart from the real reason you're doing it, I think you're fine.

Hollywood is a magnet for good-looking types who want to come and make something out of the way they look. The town is constantly being flooded by new arrivals, and as soon as someone gets older than twenty-five, there are plenty of eighteen-year-olds lining up to replace them. What's your view of this?
I've been very intrigued by lots of women who are pretty and smart. I ask them how they feel about what they do to actually succeed, what they're *ready* to do to succeed. And I know it's going to sound horrible, but I feel their souls are being diluted – as if they've lost touch with who they really are, and lost a bit of self-respect. I've been really trying to figure out this thing about plastic surgery – the lips, the tits . . . How can you lose touch with yourself so much? It hurts me when I talk about this because I find it so painful for a woman to observe other women in that situation.

Would you ever consider it?
Oh, never. Never. I'd rather quit acting, I'd rather move to the middle of the desert and stay there and meditate for the rest of my life, than do that.

Okay, carry on.
But I think it comes from slowly losing touch with themselves, with what the real priority is. And it's very easy in this town for this to happen because we are cut off from the rest of the world. So suddenly the priority is making it. So, if making it means looking better, having bigger tits, going to parties, taking coke with some big producer . . . you know, things don't happen from one day to the next. Slowly, people lose themselves.

Is part of it from an innate chauvinism in the town ?
But I think men do it as much as women. I mean – not as many men, but I think people lose themselves, in general. The world has been trying to show that it's true there is chauvinism, blah-blah-blah. But it's more about class. Women, men, black, white, it doesn't matter. It's about where you are at in life. And people with power can actually make those people – I was going to say, 'their slaves'. But they can to a certain extent take their souls away, and make them into whatever pleases them.

What is it about this town that makes that loss of priorities so easy?
Well, LA is so cut off from the rest of the world because all people talk about is movies and success, how people made it, what they're doing next, blah-blah. So you forget that elsewhere people have to fight for real, important, basic things, like food . . . People here are less and less able to communicate with other kinds of people. They communicate within their environment but they don't meet new

environments. You don't have unexpected things here, so your life is linear. And it probably has an influence on the rest of the world, because Hollywood has such a tremendous influence on the world. I don't know how bad it's going to get. But sometimes I joke around and with my American friends, I say, 'Oh, you were born in Disneyland.' But it's true. And Disney was a reactionary, racist homophobic . . . all the most horrible things you can say of someone.

Now he's frozen. I hope he doesn't wake up; he's going to be horrified.
He's going to be horrified, if he sees there's a Miramax making movies. I think he would die all over again, and be refrozen right away so that he could wake up again in another thousand years.

What do you think about French cinema right now?
I've seen a few films that look interesting. I saw *Western* last year and a few other movies that I thought were good. A few years ago I was feeling that some movies were pretentious just to be pretentious. I love stylized movies, but when there's just style and nothing else . . . It was as if they learned the lesson of the New Wave from the outside, in a superficial way, but they didn't get what a director such as Godard was really doing.

Sometimes you could be forgiven for not knowing that Godard had been an influence in French cinema, couldn't you? Or the Nouvelle Vague, even.
Yes. It's very strange what the Nouvelle Vague brought to French cinema. Because before that, there were people like Melville making really interesting movies. Then Godard and Truffaut came in and made great movies. But then what happened was like a downside – almost like what Warhol brought to art after the sixties. He did a good thing in breaking the rules of art, but afterwards people did it with no meaning. That's a bit like what happened with French cinema after the New Wave. Now I think it's good again, because people are going back to telling stories about people.

If I said, 'Okay, pick five pieces of art, and they are all you can have for the rest of your life', would you pick five movies or five books or five pieces of music, or what?
I would probably want a movie, a book, and a piece of music. To me, when movies work, they are the ultimate art because they can be a great mix. Think of certain Godard movies – they are literature, they are music, and they're also paintings. It took me years to watch a whole Tarkovsky movie because I found them hard to follow. Then, when I was finally able to watch one, I was blown away, because it's wonderful and deep, it makes you think as much as any book. It transports you somewhere else. Godard said how he thought cinema would evolve, and I think he's right – there will be huge commercial movies, not even close to art, and smaller movies about interesting topics, with styles of their own. And the two will become more and more separate. Already I see that happening

a little bit. Those big movies don't affect me too much, but they probably do affect some people – that's what's scary.

Without a doubt.
But I don't think you have such a big problem if you go and see a big commercial movie, as long as you go and see a really good independent movie, or you read a book, the day after. Have you seen the new Labute movie, *Your Friends and Neighbours*?

I haven't.
I'd like to know what you think of it. Some people hate it. It's about couples having affairs with each other, about people not loving each other – the death of love. I liked it, but it's very dark . . . I know, it is scary the way the studios think. The minute something makes money, that's all they want to do, and then they do it ten times over – like all those teenage horror movies. But people get over it. Unfortunately, you have very few producers who are able to look ahead and know what quality is. That's why you have to look towards independent people.

How often do you go to the cinema?
A few years ago I used to go almost every day. Now I think I go once a week. That's very little. Also I'm writing now, and the more I write, the less I go to the movies. Because each movie I see has a huge influence on me when I'm writing. It's very dangerous.

Charles Ives said he could never go and listen to music because only two things could happen. One is that he would think it was much better than anything he could write, and he would be depressed. The other was that if it was in any way close to what he was doing, he immediately became insecure about the path he was on. So it was much better never to see anything. I agree with him.
Me too. I have to be really careful of what I read, even. The process of writing is such that you jump from one idea that makes another idea grow. So the minute you read something it's going to influence your writing somehow, even if you're not at all inspired by it.

Would you ever consider being a critic?
And watch tons of movies, and judge them? I don't think I would like it.

I think critics are so important in terms of defining the cultural standard. And lately I think they've been helping in the dumbing-down of culture.
It is a conspiracy in a way, not only in the cinema, but the cinema is helping it tremendously. They've done it in America, but it's all over the rest of the world now. I remember being really shocked by the LA riots. I wrote a letter to Bill Clinton – I write letters to people all the time when I'm pissed at something, it makes me feel better. But in the riots – there was burning everywhere, blah blah. But

what people were doing was just stealing objects – couches, TVs. They weren't saying, 'We want better education for our children,' like in the sixties. It was all about, 'We want what wee see on TV.' I had a vision of these people watching themselves on TV stealing the couch and the TV. But actually a lot of young people now have a political consciousness. I see artists, singers, who are smart and want to raise the standard. But they have to fight against this whole system that is based on luring people into spending money and consuming things. I was raised by sixties' parents, and everything they were is the opposite of that.

Without thinking too much about it, give me five films, from any period of your life, that you thought were fine.
Repulsion; Bande Apart, Godard; *Minnie and Moskowitz; Fury.* There are two more I really like.

You can have six.
Okay, thank you: *Some Like It Hot* and *Some Came Running.*

Okay. Five pieces of music.
I like Mahler, *The Song of the Dead.* Nina Simone singing *Love Me –* I love all Nina Simone; Chet Baker, *A Touch of Your Lips;* I love Mozart's *Requiem –* the beginning is so beautiful I can't help it.

Five books.
Story of the Eye, Georges Bataille; *The Demon,* Hubert Selby Junior. I like a book called *Ask The Dust,* by John Fante. That's why I moved to America, to Los Angeles, that book made me love it so much. There's a book by Huysmans, *À Rebours,* about a man and the room he lives in.

Five actors that you admire.
Marlon Brando, Bette Davis, Peter Lorre, Charles Laughton . . .

Three painters.
Francis Bacon, Klimt and Munch.

Okay, so you're kind of obsessed with sex and death. Julie Delpy, thank you.
Thank you.

29 David Freeman
Plenty of Time

You can go a long way in Hollywood on charm. Careers have been built on it, though it's a coin best spent by the young. In the not so young, charm, which is the enemy of character, can be an excuse. The English director Robin Antonio, who amused himself parsing Hollywood's folkways, once told me, 'Charm is what lubricates Hollywood. "He's quite charming" means he's a good dinner guest but his accomplishments are in the future. "He can be very charming" means he's achieved a bit but is in danger of falling into the slag heap of the unperformed. "I don't quite see his charm" means he's utterly lost.'

'Surely there's more to it than that,' I said. 'What about talent?'

'Talent comes and goes with the jets at LAX, but if a fellow has the music of charm, the world will come dancing to him.'

When he was a young man, weary of England's rigid ways, Robin had longed for the classless kingdom of the cinema. He found Hollywood as stratified as Britain, but instead of family and school, what mattered was chance and the deal. Robin loved that. He was in the grip of America from the day he arrived. His pictures were psychologically astute, though Robin wasn't introspective and he was untroubled by other people's emotional burdens. He turned out movies that were the ones he wanted to make. That takes an act of great will. Capable directors are always in demand, but usually to do what the studios want done.

Robin was a romantic adventurer who thrived on the new; a pilgrim of pursuit. He had been single for years, though he remained close to Eva, his ex-wife, who lived in London with their son. Robin had long since decided dating was an activity for the young or the dim, preferring a succession of friends and lovers. He was fond of the polymorphous sex clubs of Silver Lake and West Hollywood. Club Fuck had been his favourite, but its name had gotten so much publicity that Robin said tour buses stopped there. 'Those Mexican boys with the maps send them.' When I doubted that, he said, 'No one cares where Lucille Ball lived. They want Club Fuck.' Robin's voice was slightly rhetorical, the syllables extended and given equal weight, as if he were speaking in translation from the French.

With my friend Martha Gunn, who was a painter and up for an adventure, we went to Sin-Opti-Con, a sort of sexual vaudeville in a warehouse in West Hollywood. Robin organized the visit in the spirit of a campy anthropological expedition, but I had still refused to go without a woman in tow. Robin mocked me, calling me a Rotarian coward. As we stepped into the dim and cavernous room, a young woman dressed as a forties cigarette girl, in fishnet stockings, offered condoms from her tray. Robin gave her money and said, 'Give some to the con-domless, in my name.'

Robin led the way, deeper into the fleshy crowd, amidst people in leather jock-straps and diapers with their nose- and nipple-rings. 'Fashion statements for the terminally libidinal,' he said, breezing past the merely heterosexual, stopping to watch two women on a shaky platform, dancing in a sinuous circle. Martha pointed out that the women had what must have been a double-ended dildo inserted in themselves. It kept them at a certain distance, but as Martha said, had a closeness all the same. We moved on, and watched an overweight man stapling his scrotum to a board. 'Interesting mischief,' Robin said. 'Think he's union?'

'IA,'I answered, meaning the stagehands.

Martha was occupied making sketches of a man attempting to descend on to a broomstick. When the guy realized Robin was also watching, he put more enthusiasm into his task. Everyone wanted to glow around directors, but it was also because Robin had an eccentric sexuality that was changeable and encom-passing. 'Robin,' Martha said, 'I think there's enough ambiguity here even for you.'

'*Très cher*,' he said, nodding to the gent on the broomstick in a lordly way, then lifting his arms in a sweeping gesture as if he were framing a panning shot.

After making movies, Robin's passion was his house in the Hollywood Hills. It was Spanish, with a courtyard and a cherub fountain. There was a tennis court and a pool house where one itinerant young actor or another was usually in resi-dence. The house looked out to the east. In the mornings, Robin watched the sun glint off the buildings downtown, making them look like a Deco movie set. It seemed fake but was real. He said it was perfect for Hollywood, a celestial joke. The house had an elaborate aviary with dozens of brightly coloured birds in stacked cages. Robin enjoyed naming them in what he called his feathered inven-tory: wren, grouse, grackle, oriole, cormorant, kestrel, toucan. Only the peacocks were allowed to roam, and they thought nothing of wandering into the house and crapping on the floor. Those strutting birds, always on display, seemed to be competing for Robin's attention with the self-absorbed actors sunning them-selves by the pool, or the writers and producers who were waiting nervously for Robin to approve their plans or just listen to their ideas.

The house was usually in some stage of remodelling. Robin never used blue-prints or an architect. He decided what he wanted, then hired carpenters and started directing them, knocking down walls or cutting new windows. It was the way he staged his pictures. Most directors work from storyboards with camera moves mapped out. Robin rarely planned his shots before the day's shooting. Oh, he made a shot list the night before, because if he didn't the studio production managers all but called the police. He decided the dynamics of the shots at the last moment, always trusting to the charged atmosphere of production to provide him with ideas. His movies could veer from drama to satire to sudden sex. It was as he was. Whatever interested him did so completely, for a few minutes. His personality was also reflected in his house. At first glance, it had a bourgeois calm about it that was wildly misleading. It was a place of sunlight and laughing gossip, of fanciful movie schemes and screeching-peacock afternoons.

Robin believed that spontaneity determined luck. He believed in luck. People in Hollywood all do, and why not? Who succeeds and who doesn't never seems to make any sense. In his pursuit of the new, Robin picked up and dropped colleagues without hesitation. I knew if the spirit moved him, Robin would fire me and hire another writer. He'd done it already – to me and to others. Later, he'd hire me back. There were no apologies. He'd say the situation was now different and the script still wasn't right and, after all, I knew it well having already done a draft. And I would come. I'd tell myself it was just business, so I should put irritation aside. The real reason I went back was I knew I'd do good work. That's a powerful draw. Robin had an instinct for the best, and he brought out the best in others, certainly in me. He said, 'Instinct is everything. A director must seize the true as it rushes by, pluck it from the air and pin it down.'

Robin's son Will, who was at Oxford, divided his holidays between California and his mother's house in Hampstead. When I knew Will, he was a gawky young man with his father's angular features, but not yet his father's wit or engaging style. Will's arrival for the summer was an occasion for Robin to give a Sunday lunch, the last of his English habits. Grand lunches that ignored California's food fashions were no longer as unlikely as people outside the movie business thought, because being thin was no longer the good business it had once been. Weight was now a sign of health.

When I arrived, Robin and Will were sitting by the pool discussing the menu. Will was asking if there were going to be vegetarians, as if he were inquiring about Hottentots. Robin must have been feeling mischievous because he ignored the question and asked Will to do his imitation of me. It embarrassed the boy terribly. 'I can't think I'd be anything but flattered,' I said, trying to get him to do it.

'It's the way the two of you argue,' he said. Then, in an irritated American accent, which I found nasal and unappealing, he muttered, 'Hollywood is a directocracy. Film directing is the most overrated occupation of our time.' Robin found it funnier than I did. Will had the family gift for mimicry with a touch of cruelty. Directors are always slightly at war with writers. I hadn't realized that this could extend to their children. It's not practical for either side to acknowledge the enmity, and in this case, I had genuine affection for Robin. We had feigned good will in order to make our work productive and it had become real. Still, Robin was the boss. Writers and directors talk about partnership, but it's mostly nonsense. They'd kill one another if they didn't need each other so much.

When Martha arrived, Robin asked her to explain the eating customs to Will.

Martha, who saw everything, said, 'The local motto is, "Use salt and die." What's the grub?'

'We've sent Jorgé down to the Chalet Gourmet with a detailed note,' Robin said. 'I've ordered a roast and a big salad. Someone will no doubt want white wine.'

'Do they really believe the whites have fewer calories?' Will asked.

'It's a fact,' Martha said. 'A Los Angeles fact, but still true.'

'There's a marvelous Napa cabernet in the cellar. We'll drink it if they don't,' Robin said. Perhaps when they were alone, Robin and Will had more private conversations, but I doubt it. I bet they always talked as if others were present. Robin often spoke in a rhetorical way. If something popped into his head, he might shout it from the roof whether there was anyone to hear it or not. When he talked about personal matters, he did it by allusion, like a puzzle.

'Vikram Ghosh is coming,' Robin said. It hadn't occurred to him to ask Will if he would like to invite any of his own Los Angeles friends.

'Isn't he your agent?' Will asked.

'No longer. He's still amusing. He calls this house El Raj.'

Vikram, who stubbornly hung on to his Bombay lilt despite ten years in Hollywood, arrived with Pam Riesel, an unsettlingly lean woman in her late twenties. She was a production executive at Paramount who had great swirls of blonde hair. When Robin greeted her, he said, ' "Only God could love you for yourself alone and not your yellow hair." '

'Yeats!' Pam fairly shouted, with the authority of an expensive education and glowing yellow hair. Pam's success depended on how many directors and writers she knew. This lunch was a business opportunity for her. When Pam arrived, I predicted that in the Paramount staff meeting on Monday, she would drop Robin's name. Vikram said if she played it right, she could also conjure with mine. He meant to flatter, but still I said, 'Do you know about the actress so stupid that she slept with the writer?' Only Will, who had never heard it, laughed. He seemed to be glancing at Pam. I saw Robin watching them. I knew Robin was wondering if it might be worth making a pass at her. The idea of being in a contest with his son for her attention interested him. 'Where's your water bottle?' he asked, because Pam usually had a litre of Evian water in a leather carrying case from Prada, as if she felt in danger of being stranded in a fashionable part of the desert.

'I thought you might be able to take care of my needs,' she answered, locking her eyes to his.

'The flirting lamp is now lit,' I said.

Robin and I were known for bantering and argument. It was a way of showing off, and that's probably how people regarded it but we also did it when there was no one around but ourselves. Over the salad, I challenged him by saying I had seen a compelling production of *Electra*.

'The Greeks?' Robin asked, sliding his glasses down his nose, as if he were Mr Chips in the sun. 'You? A proponent of the slash-and-burn school of dramaturgy?'

'This was hot. A storefront in Hollywood,' I said with a deprecating shrug, the way screenwriters always defer to directors. It irritated me when I did that, so I stepped up the argument, saying, 'It was vivid in a way only live performance can be.'

'I can't bear those plays,' Robin said, taking up the challenge and dismissing Euripides.

'Robin Antonio rejects the Greeks? Alert the media,' I said with more sarcasm than was entirely wise.

'They're so discursive. All that fuss about putting the action off stage. If there's action, is it asking too much that we all be let in on it?'

'Only in movies does action substitute for language.'

'Oh, but *Electra*? Really. The girl goes mad. She stays mad for years. Then the wretched brother turns up.'

'Perhaps you'd like a modern version? Set it in Malibu. Orestes returns, kills Clytemnestra, then he and Electra open a mental health and surfing clinic on the beach.'

'Wonderful,' Vikram said. 'Pam can put it in development.'

'And Robin can take credit as the *auteur*,' I said.

'People fuss endlessly about the importance of the script,' Robin said, no longer interested in *Electra*. 'Any interview with an executive, you can count on "It all starts with the page."'

'Because a studio executive says something does not necessarily make it false,' I said, still feeling reckless.

'The script is the most important element,' Pam said, trying to engage Robin and join the debate.

Vikram touched her arm and said, 'If the substance eludes you, pay attention to the form. When they're through, they may switch sides and do it all again.'

'Very Oxford Union,' Will said.

Robin ignored them and said, 'I can look at fifty feet of Hitchcock or Ford and know the director. I'm hardly alone in this skill.'

'The finest make their own rules,' I said. 'At your best, your pictures could only have been made by you. Not all your work is so particular. No one could say from fifty feet who made it. A few stars who can sell tickets to anything are more important than the director.'

'Now you're talking about commerce,' Robin said.

'Trade? Oh, dear. I've sullied the air.'

'Movie stars are children,' Pam said, still trying to take part.

'Yes,' Robin said, noticing her again. 'No studio trusts an actor with money. A director who can deliver picture after picture, no matter what, he's a man to follow.'

'Directors are father, lover and boss,' I said. 'You guys enjoy a droit de seigneur unknown since the Medici.'

'Seems only just,' Robin said.

I laughed and said, 'Directors are the true hustler-artists of the world.'

Robin bowed his head and conceded the point.

Vikram began telling a story about a parrot Robin had once kept in the kitchen. 'Pepé the screenwriting parrot. He could do rewrites. Dialogue polishes, actually. He had a great ear. He flew off one day.'

'He didn't fly off,' Robin said. 'He wouldn't do that. He was experimenting. It got out of hand.' As Robin was offering a toast to the disappeared parrot, Jorgé brought out the rest of the food. Pam was twitching her hair and glancing from son to father as Robin began to cut the roast. Perhaps if he hadn't been laughing at the tale of the parrot, or if he hadn't had quite so much of the cabernet, he would have been more careful. When the knife slipped, it went deep into the tip of his index finger. The cut created a little flap of flesh. It raised a tiny curtain. The message it revealed was clear to everyone. Robin's finger was pumping out the cankered rose that no trope could illuminate, no joke alleviate: ground zero for our time, pulsing rich and red on to the meat.

Robin had never acknowledged his condition, but he could see on our faces that it was no secret. He himself had said many times that in Hollywood if there's something about yourself that you'd prefer be kept private, that's as good as putting it on a billboard on the Sunset Strip. Each person was staring at the growing stain, unable to look away. As his finger leaked out the perfectly coloured red liquid, we were all doing quick mental tours of our bodies, trying to recall cuts and abrasions. Pam curled her fingers. Martha, who had been sketching us all, put down her pencil.

Will couldn't quite understand what had happened, but he knew that the tension was greater than a bad cut deserved. His father's romantic reputation wasn't something he had been able to think about, and even now, in the face of the fear around the table that could mean one thing only, it seemed to me that Will alone could not yet acknowledge the truth. Robin knew that appetites were gone. 'Excuse me,' he said, wrapping his finger in a napkin, stanching the blood.

'Maybe we should go down to Cedars,' I said. 'Get a stitch put in that. I'll drive you.'

'No,' Robin said, pressing the napkin against the cut, holding back the blood. 'Plenty of time for Cedars.'

'Are you sure, P'pa?' Will asked, reverting to a childhood name for his father.

'I'm positive,' Robin said. 'Why don't we get rid of this roast and open another bottle.'

'I'll do it,' Will said, about to clear the table.

'It's for me to do,' Robin said. Then, with his good hand, he picked up the soiled platter and sailed it into the pool. The meat hit the water first, turning it dark from the gravy and the blood. The platter floated for a moment before it too sank. In that moment of spontaneous nihilism, I could see the ache of understanding come over Will's face. Robin tilted his bandaged finger into the air at an optimistic angle and I knew he had seen it too. A message had been passed. Will bowed his head in a gesture that was his father's, then steadied himself and poured the last of the cabernet.

In the months that followed, Robin continued to work on scripts and to meet with actors until he began to lose weight and tire easily. Will took a leave from Oxford and came to stay with him. Robin wanted no part of hospitals, but to remain in the house that he loved. When his condition took its final turn, Eva came from London to say goodbye and to help their son who, everyone agreed, was handling the situation with great aplomb and even charm.

30 Getting Out of His Head: An Interview with Edward Norton

by Graham Fuller

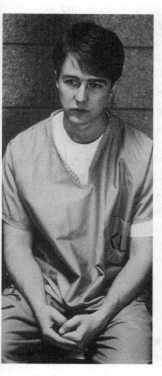

Edward Norton's emergence as one of the most powerful actors in American films has ironically coincided with one of those eras in movie culture when aesthetics have taken precedence over artistry. Brad Pitt, Johnny Depp, Leonardo DiCaprio, Matt Damon, and Ewan McGregor are all gifted actors whose popularity has much to do with their looks. But as dreamboats go, these are sloops and schooners, not destroyers. They are peculiarly passive idols – their non-threatening faces suitable for the walls of teenage girls – who represent the wholesale post-feminist eclipse of the Stallone–Schwarzenegger brand of cartoon machismo, and even of the manly types of the late eighties and early nineties, the Alec Baldwins and Kevin Costners. It says much for Tom Cruise's durability that he has been able to ride out the changes, Alpha-male aura intact.

Norton doesn't fit any of these moulds; rather he cracks them. Not blessed with cuteness, matinée-idol handsomeness, or obvious movie-star charisma, he possesses something far more interesting and troubling. That is, he is equally convincing playing a runt who jack-knifes into an evil little punk (*Primal Fear*, 1996, his astonishing début), straight-arrow suits with whimsy (*Everyone Says I Love You*, 1996) or ambition (*The People vs. Larry Flynt*, 1996), a pumped-up, bile-spewing neo-Nazi skinhead (*American History X*, 1998), or a sleazy, feckless high-stakes poker player (*Rounders*, 1998). Try to imagine another actor carrying off such diversity and you realize the extent of his achievement so far.

He is, then, one of those genius-touched chameleons like Alec Guinness or Daniel Day-Lewis who are unfashionable these days. We are impressed and unsettled in equal amounts by Norton for, if we are truthful, we yearn for fixed objects in the cinema – recognizability is the foundation of stardom – and he has pledged not to give us one, either in his career or within a role. His Derek, who stomps a black kid to death in *American History X*, uncannily metamorphoses into the prison-chastened figure who ministers tenderly to his mother and his siblings later in the film. We have followed the plot. We know screen characters have 'arcs'. We get that Derek's a better guy coming out of the can than he was going in. We are willing to suspend some disbelief . . . yet how does Norton do it without straining credibility? It's because, with a subtlety that goes beyond the signposts in the script, he imperceptibly lays the groundwork for emotional change. Few of his colleagues in the so-called Young Hollywood can manage that, or even get near it. (One who does is Jeremy Davies, but he, like Norton, is an anomaly.)

Norton was born into a well-to-do East Coast family in Columbia, Maryland, on 18 August 1969. In 1991, he graduated from Yale with a history degree, having also studied astronomy and Japanese and acted in student plays. After a spell in Japan, he moved to New York where he wrote for the Enterprise Foundation and acted in off-off-Broadway productions of such plays as Brian Friel's *Lovers* and John Patrick Shanley's *Italian-American Reconciliation*. In 1994, he played the lead part in the première of Edward Albee's *Fragments*, produced by the Signature Theater Company, and subsequently became a Signature board member.

Norton followed *Rounders* with a role opposite Brad Pitt and Helena Bon-ham-Carter in David Fincher's *The Fight Club* (set for release in the fall of 1999) about an underground club for young urban professionals who engage in brutal fistfights. He was, at the time of writing, scheduled to direct and co-produce a romantic comedy called *Keeping the Faith*, starring himself and Ben Stiller as, respectively, a priest and rabbi in love with the same woman, the three of them childhood friends.

The following conversation took place in a hotel room overlooking Central Park in Manhattan on 29 October 1998. Months after *American History X* had fin-ished production, Norton was happily back to his slender, pre-skinhead physique – and he articulated himself with erudition and no little ebullience.

Graham Fuller: What impels you to act?
Edward Norton: I have an almost intellectual or creative faith in the importance of storytelling through acting: it's a long-standing compulsion I've had since I was about five or six years old. I can literally identify the moment it struck me. I went to see a play [*If I Were a Princess*] in which a babysitter of mine [Betsy True, who later acted on Broadway] was performing. I was completely shell-shocked by the magic of this little community-theatre play; it just riveted me. My parents have said that I had a tendency towards mimicry prior to that anyway. I started taking acting classes but went away from it for a while when I was in high school because I had that teenage self-consciousness about the performance aspect of it, and it wasn't cool where I went to school. But when I was sixteen or seventeen, a teacher took some of us to the National Theater in Washington, DC, to see Ian McKellen do his one-man show *Acting Shakespeare*, and that reconnected me definitively with this compulsion. It was just him alone on the stage and it was a totally transporting experience for me. I remember sitting apart from my friends on the bus going home and being almost frightened by how intensely I had felt about it. Swirling around in my head was the realization that this kind of com-municating or representing was very profound – that it was valuable and not just frivolous – and that it was something I could do myself as an adult. After that, I was completely obsessed with it.

For a while I pursued other things because there's a panic that comes with deciding you're going to be an actor, especially if you think something else can bring a structure to your life, as well as a regular pay cheque. But once I started acting in plays, the more the obsession was confirmed. Even if I wasn't in a play, I'd catch myself following people on the streets of New York and imitating their walk or whatever. Or I'd just be walking along talking to myself and scripting scenarios in my head and playing them out, or doing voices. Finally, I just sur-rendered to it. I still have that compulsion, and it's the thing that grounds me against the hoopla that surrounds it at the Hollywood level.

Can you talk about the pyschological reasons behind your need to be an actor, or do you fear that deconstructing it in such a way might be detrimental to your process?
I was wary of deconstructing it for a long time, but I'm much less so now – I don't know why. I think I've come to grips with the fact that not intellectualizing it is actually a pose. There's a craft to it, just like there is to anything else, and that's something you should be proud of.

But beyond the excitement of acting, and your vocational drive, any neuroses urging you on?
[*laughs*] I'm sure a need for attention is a way of explaining it, and that some people who have little respect for acting would call it narcissistic. But I don't think or feel those things. I think my impulse is actually the furthest thing from narcissism because there's nothing that compels me more than getting away from myself and creating a character who lives distinctly and independently of me. I've almost never had an experience of working on a character or a piece of drama in which I've found that myself or my own experiences were a very colourful or useful resource. There *is* a certain addictive quality to acting, certainly in theatre, but that's not the case in film where you experience none of the energy that comes from interacting with an audience and performing a whole play seamlessly and live. There were times in the theater, when I was working in a good play or doing something that I really liked, when I'd feel myself in the zone. It's a difficult thing to describe, but it's a very floaty feeling that you can't wait to re-experience again, because you found something. You were transported to a different emotional place where you began to exist within the context of the character's motivations and responses to a degree that if something unexpected happened, you would completely respond as that person – and it's such a high. It's like in *Cat on a Hot Tin Roof*, when Brick is talking about drinking. He says he drinks until he gets that click. I think with acting, too, you go and go and go until you hit this click. And when you do, I think your pulse doesn't go up, it goes way down and suddenly the moment can't go on long enough, because you're so completely there that truly anything could happen – because you're out of your head. When I'm working with another actor and feel myself watching or analysing the process and I'm not living in that zone, I'll refer to it as 'I'm back in my head', or 'I can tell you're in your head'. Everything I do is to try to get out of my head, even when I'm working on a film. It's much harder in film because film-making is so fragmented. I used to read books between set-ups but I realized that books refocus you too much on other things, so now I play really mindless Yahtzee computer games. That way I can step back into a scene without having lost the thread of where I was.

Before I first interviewed you, towards the end of 1996, you gave me a tape of a test you'd made for *American History X*. It showed you as Derek, the LA skinhead you ended up playing in the film, gesticulating and ranting neo-Nazi

rhetoric. What was the key to finding Derek when you came to play him?
Whenever you approach a character it's as if you're supposed to enter a room that's completely boxed off, and you can walk all the way around it and there's no obvious door you're going to go through. There are lots of doors. On one door it might say 'clothes', on another it might say 'physique', on another 'accent'. Sometimes you have to go through all those doors, but you always have to start with one. With Derek, in particular, the physicality was a big part of it, not necessarily because I thought it was the most important part, but because when I started talking with the director, Tony Kaye, we were very confident about my ability to represent the intellectual ferocity and emotional intensity of this guy. But if you're honest as an actor, you sometimes have to say to yourself, 'I know this interests me emotionally and that I'd like to do it, but is there anything about the unchangeable package of me that means I won't be able to represent this?' Tony felt – and I agreed with him – that Derek needed to be as physically intimidating as he was on every other level. He needed to be larger that life, especially in his younger brother's memory. He needed to be the *über*-skinhead – the king of the skinheads. The physicality was the part I was the least sure of being able to pull off. But I shaved my head, grew a beard, bulked myself up, and we shot a test to see if it went over – that's the footage you saw. I wasn't nearly as large then as I would be when we came to do the film, but I think Tony and I were both satisfied that we were on the right track, that I'd be able to stretch my elasticity over the role and encompass it. I proceeded from there to get really large. I put on thirty or thirty-five pounds over the next couple of months.

What do you mean by elasticity?
This is something I've been talking about with Anthony Minghella. He said he thinks every actor has a certain elasticity and every role has a certain elasticity, and some actors have more elasticity than others and some roles have more elasticity than others. And if the elasticity of the actor overlaps the elasticity of the role, then you have a match, but sometimes they just don't and maybe it's because the role is not very elastic. It's not something that can be manifested in different ways.

Did changing your look prove to be the right approach to Derek?
Yes, it was a good entrance point because I started to feel different. Derek's physicality and how he carries himself is part of how he feels about himself, part of his intensity. I found you do carry yourself differently when you have that much power in your upper body; you start to feel that right away. One thing leads to another. I next started experimenting with tattoos, which is another way skinheads have of empowering themselves. That, in turn, led me into another type of research: which is, what does all this stuff mean? What are the specific ideas that these people are connecting with? So, yes, the door to this character was, for me, the physicality.

Derek, of course, goes through several stages in the film. There are two glimpses of him as a young, impressionable kid. There's his skinhead phase –
His nightmarish incarnation, I call it.

Then he experiences the catharsis in prison and finally there's the Derek who turns his back on violence and racism. So there's a real arc there. How did you go about effecting Derek's evolution, or did you break down the arc into segments?
That was directly impacted by the sequence in which we shot the film. I had hair on my head at the beginning of the shoot and I didn't want to wear a wig for the later scenes, so we shot the present-tense colour scenes first, which include all the redemptive, post-prison Derek stuff and go right to the end of the film. Then I cut my hair down halfway and we shot a few of the scenes in the prison where Derek's hair is growing back. Then I shaved it all the way and we shot all of the skinhead stuff in black and white. The last thing we shot was Derek as a kid and I did put a little wig on for that.

So you reversed the chronological sequence?
Literally. I worked hard at maintaining some consistency between Derek as a skinhead and Derek after he's renounced the skinhead movement. I didn't want there to be a total discrepancy between what he was like before he went into prison and what he was like afterwards because he's fundamentally the same person. Obviously he undergoes a change inside – his anger diminishes – but it was very important to me that this guy suddenly didn't become the Saint of Venice Beach. One of the things that's a thread is that he's intensely controlling; that's not something that changes in prison. He doesn't really start to let go of that until things really go to hell at the skinhead rally, where he finally says to his brother: 'I'm not even telling you what to do. I'm just telling you what happened to me.' In fact, he lets go of a lot at that point, but I think he's the same hard person in both halves of the film.

What about Derek's rage? I remember you telling me that you had no particular need to identify or explore any such rage in yourself, so how did you access it?
I usually don't find I can pull on my own emotions. Sometimes, obviously, some extension of things that you've felt can spin up, but it's much more of an imaginative process for me. Many people project on to actors the idea that they must be finding a particular emotion within themselves – from their own deep well – in the sense of the Method as taught by Lee Strasberg, or what's often very glibly *interpreted* as the Method. I've just never bought that or found it a very useful tool. I've always subscribed more to Stella Adler's maxim that an actor's greatest gift is his imagination. I find the most effective thing I can do is project myself into the given circumstances by using my instinct or empathic talent (though I hate to use that word) for understanding how other people express their emotions. It's an almost clinical ability to observe those emotions – to soak them up like a sponge and then turn around and represent them. I find that approach works best for me and is

more in sync with the kind of roles I want to pursue. It's certainly how I found my way into Derek because I've never experienced anything like the kind of frustration or rage or violent tendencies that he has. I've always been fascinated by anger anyway – how someone can hide it for a long time but it simmers away until it just explodes, making you realize how long that person has been holding it back. That can lead to extraordinary moments in drama. I enjoyed that disconcertingly intense conversation at the dinner table in *American History X* where you can almost feel Elliott Gould [who plays Derek's mother's boyfriend] getting caught in a trap. Elliott thinks he's having a heated but impersonal discussion about ideas and politics, but you can see in him this growing perception that there's an intensity in Derek that's out of sync with the conversation. And then, of course, it suddenly erupts into this out-of-control fury that targets the wrong people – Derek's own family. And when, in the middle of the wreckage Derek turns on Elliott's character and says, 'You don't think I see what's going on here? You think I'm going to sit here while some kike tries to fuck my mother?' you realize in a flash that the entire scene has been about none of the things that have been discussed.

You mean that Derek's rage is Oedipal rage?
Absolutely – it's *Hamlet*. It's about a young man simmering with rage because another man is sitting next to his mother in his dead father's chair at the dinner table. Elliott's face drops when I come out with that speech and it's such a wonderful reaction because it totally supports the revelation of the moment. Here's this poor guy suddenly realizing that he's walked into something that's not about politics, not about Rodney King, but about this boy who's projecting his anger at the death of his father on to other people. Those kinds of moments are very challenging because you have to connect with what's going on and then play the opposite almost. People have asked me in relation to this film, 'How do you find that level of intensity within you?' Part of my answer is that I don't really know why, but I have always felt a certain facility for those levels of emotion. And there are certain tricks of voice or the way you use your eyes in relation to the camera that can help you, as well as tricks of stillness and silence – pauses and stares – which I think are greatly underestimated in terms of the impact they can have. If there's one working actor who has a corner on the intensity of stillness on film, or who most profoundly understands how terrifying a stare can be, as opposed to what you might call generalized indications of anger through gestures or scowls, it's Robert De Niro. I think a lot of film acting is about coming to an understanding of those kinds of techniques.

You know, there's that famous story of Garbo being panicked about that last close-up she had to do in *Queen Christina*, and the director, Rouben Mamoulian, telling her: 'I want your face to be a blank sheet of paper. I want the writing to be done by every member of the audience.' What's implicit in that story was his understanding that, if he'd constructed his film well up to that point, there was no need for her to emote. The close-up is a completely artificial perspective provided by the camera, and that's why directors will often tell actors to do less, but good actors come to understand intuitively how tiny gestures have to be – if they're necessary at all – when the camera's in there. I've learned from some of the good actors I've worked with not to pay any attention to where a director is framing up a shot because you should always just know where the camera is instinctively; you should never have to look for it. But it's hard in something like the dinner-table scene in *American History X* because Tony shot it from many different angles and you had to stay aware of the framing. For example, if he was shooting a mid-sized shot from a wide angle I'd need to know that because my hands would become part of the visual language of what I could express. There was a moment in there where he did stay wide as the conversation broke up and the mother [Beverly D'Angelo] walked out, and Derek is tapping on the table with impatience – tap, tap, tap, tap, tap – and you know his anger is still simmering in him. He wants to go back into that conversation – he wants to let it out.

Would you have been saying to yourself at that moment, 'Keep tapping because it's building up the tension,' or would you have been unaware of it?
It happens intuitively. Once you're channelled into an emotion, all kinds of interesting things can happen and you learn to trust yourself in the moment. It's a broad generalization, but I would say that acting on film often has a lot to do with what happens off the lines, through non-verbal gesture. I find that, on stage, more gets communicated through the language.

How do you develop an awareness of what the director or director of photography will be seeing in the camera?
Well, it does become intuitive. You don't have to break out of character every time and say, 'Where are you framed up?' because you learn about the different lenses, or you might hear the director say, 'Let's go to a 35,' in which case you know you're wide. I still ask all the time, though, just to be sure. On *American History X*, Tony had a fondness for shooting the actors just below the hairline but just above the chin. You obviously can't express things in that proximity that you could in a medium shot, because it would just look ridiculous blown up to sixty feet by thirty feet. So you have to know how to scale things down. Ultimately, in terms of connecting with the intensity of a scene, I think it's something that's not deconstructible. It's just a facility I think I have.

There were a lot of rumours about what happened during the post-production of *American History X*. As I understand it, New Line invited you into the editing process. Tony Kaye, who wanted his name removed from the picture, subsequently criticized you in the press for getting involved, and he now has a lawsuit against New Line and the Directors' Guild. What's your version of events?

I have a background in writing and I write a lot – film scripts and other stuff. I've gotten very involved in the script development of a number of films I've been involved in, usually in close collaboration with the director or at the director's behest. I got very involved in the development of *The People vs. Larry Flynt*. After we'd filmed it, Milos [Forman] let me sit in on the editing and I gave him some notes. Sometimes people use what you suggest and sometimes they don't; it's just part of the collaborative dynamic. There's a moment near the end of *Larry Flynt* that I was particularly pleased with. It's where Alan [Isaacman, Norton's character] is sitting outside the courtroom and he calls Larry on his cellphone to tell him they've won the case, and Larry thanks him and Alan says, 'Don't mention it,' and hangs up the phone. Milos had cut away from Alan at that point, but I looked at the shot and said, 'Look, we have five more seconds. Why don't we use them?' And Milos looked at it and agreed to let it play. It shows you Alan when he looks up at the Supreme Court logo – which is above his head but out of the frame – and you can see that he has a moment of resolution where everything he'd worked for his entire life has been realized in the bizarrest of ways. And he sort of takes a deep breath, shakes his head, and laughs a little bit. So we got that in. And that's what I love about Milos. He has complete creative control from decades of great film-making, and yet he pro-actively seeks the collaboration of other people as part of his process. That is exactly how I want to work in films.

To come back to *American History X*, I got involved in it at a very early stage and said that my acting in it was contingent on my being able to work on the script with David McKenna, who wrote it, and my agreement about where we were going to try and head with it. And everybody was very thrilled about that because none of us felt the script was quite where it could be. David and I went away for just over three months and tore away at the script and kept beefing up the story until we had strengthened the central arc of the tragedy. Then Tony shot the film and we all went away while he edited it for about seven months. He did some experiments with restructuring it so that it was very different from the intentions we'd had when we filmed it. He'd skipped a step that a lot of people consider normal, which is to assemble the film as per the script, however long it ends up, and his first cut had been about ninety minutes whereas we'd figured it would be about three hours. And he wasn't satisfied with it and nor was anyone else. I think New Line said at that point, 'It's hard to know if this is the best cut because we've seen the dailies and we've got some very rich stuff. We feel that there's more here and we want to see it all.' They decided to bring in Jerry Greenberg, who'd edited *The French Connection, Apocalypse Now,* and *Kramer vs. Kramer,* to help Tony with the narrative, but he wasn't available immediately and in the meantime they asked Tony if he'd sit down with me and reassemble the film according to the script because I had worked so much on it and there wasn't a very good paper version of it available. There was no intention that what we ended up with at that stage would be a cut of the film because I'm not an editor. Tony and I did that in November and December of 1997 and we ended up with a version that was between two hours and thirty or forty minutes and it revealed a lot.

When Jerry Greenberg came in to start work on it, I went off to do *Rounders*. I believe he told Tony he was very glad we had done our reassemblage because it gave him the scope of what he had to work with before he and Tony started to sculpt it down during the spring of 1998. I had a break between *Rounders* and *The Fight Club* and came back in to provide notes about performance, because David and I had been vigilant about creating certain moments that were very disturbing and certain moments that would challenge the audience with the almost logical, well-articulated points that Derek had to make. We all wanted to make sure – I know Tony certainly did – that the end was an unequivocal conclusion about the tragic consequences and self-destructive reality of racism. Then I went away again and Tony and Jerry finished working on the film and delivered it to the studio, which was very happy with it, according to their notes. The response to the film was really terrific. At that point, I think Tony wanted more time and they gave him about two and a half more months. He came back, I believe, with essentially the same film, and then New Line moved forward. It was only at that point that Tony started getting frustrated. I think he had a tough time letting go of the film and dealing with the practical realities of a studio schedule. The studio had been far more involved in it than they normally are, and I believe to its benefit. I think it came out well.

Isn't it unusual for an actor to be so involved in post-production?

It's not the norm, I know, but it's also not a complete aberration. Every film has a different collaborative dynamic. *American History X* had a first-time writer, a first-time director, and a very low budget. The studio had decided to make the movie with me, and if a director didn't want me, they were going to get another director. As I said, contingent on my participation was my involvement in the development of the story, because the subject matter was too volatile to allow me to get involved with it casually. I was as upfront as I could possibly be about that at the beginning, and with great respect for everyone else involved. I needed to know my goals were in sync with the people in ultimate control of the film – New Line – in case it strayed very far from those goals. Because at the end of the day it was going to be me up there on the screen manifesting this guy and everything he stands for. I felt I had a responsibility to myself to make damn sure I knew why I was going into it, because the last thing I wanted was to have some gratuitously glamorizing effect on the skinhead aesthetic. I didn't feel like making a Calvin Klein ad for neo-Nazism.

For me – creatively and spiritually – one of the great things about the fervent argumentative process that emerges when you make a film is wiping off your brow, and going, 'Hey, look what we made.' And shaking hands with everybody involved because you have a permanent bond with those people. The only dismaying thing about *American History X*, which is one of the better experiences I've had, was that at a certain point, Tony's enthusiasm for that collaborative act broke down and he chose to see it as a negative instead of a positive. At the end of the day, in the long lens of history, those things are far less important than the film itself. And, I think, in his heart of hearts, he knows he made a stupendously dynamic film. There aren't many people who can point to a first film as good as this.

When you worked on *Everyone Says I Love You*, you obviously had a very different kind of experience, because although Woody Allen encourages improvisation from actors, he is not at all collaborative in the shaping of a film. Having been so involved in *American History X*, will you be content to stand back on other films?

Absolutely. I'm doing it right now on *The Fight Club*, which is being directed by David Fincher. You have to go into each project with a clear assessment of what your particular relationship with the director is. As an actor working on a Woody Allen film, you are a hired hand. You're working *for* him and, whatever happens, you're relieved of the responsibility of caring too intensely about it because it's going to be a Woody Allen film one way or the other. You come in and deliver whatever it was he felt he saw in you when he cast you. *On Everyone Says I Love You*, he would say after a run-through of a scene, 'I really like all the stuff you've thrown in there, so feel free to say whatever you want and if it's too much I'll pull you back.' So I improvised a lot, and a lot of it he left in and some of it he took out. That was the extent of my collaboration with him, and it was a thrill for me. I would do it again in a second.

Milos Forman is totally different. After he'd told me he'd like me to be in *Larry Flynt*, he invited the other actors and me to come down to the Cayman Islands for three weeks to work on the script with him. Working with Milos is an incredibly nervy, almost high-wire act, where you feel he doesn't know exactly what he wants at first. His approach is to say, 'Let's just go at it head on, and see what the hell we find.' He *demands* improvisation from his actors and the re-scripting of scenes, a constant wrestling until what he describes as unrepeatable moments emerge.

What prompted you to get involved in *Rounders*?

As much as any film I've been involved in, it was a simple decision: I read the script, loved it, talked to John Dahl once, said I'd love to do it, rehearsed it a week later, shot it three weeks after that. For me, it was about the theme of the film and the character's role in that. I don't know what John, or Brian [Koppelman] and David [Levien], who wrote the script, were thinking in any detail. You'd have to say that my character, Worm, fits in with the rogues' gallery of lovable losers, in which you could include Ratso Rizzo and the Artful Dodger, if you want to go way back.

Worm is an unrepentant sleaze, a bottom-feeder of the worst kind. But he neither carries the weight of the film as Derek does in *American History X*, nor does he have any particular social or political significance, so did that make him less of a risk to play than someone like Derek?

A couple of people said to me when I was doing press for *American History X*, 'Oh, you've chosen to do another anti-hero.' And I said, 'What do you mean? What anti-heroes have I done other than Worm?' My definition of an anti-hero is a character who represents the antithesis of heroic values and doesn't change – like Ratso Rizzo [in *Midnight Cowboy*], Travis Bickle [in *Taxi Driver*], or Rupert Pupkin[in *The King of Comedy*]. I see Derek as a tragic hero who goes through an enormous emotional transformation but ultimately falls, through the consequences of his actions, even after having come to an understanding of what his problem was. Worm, however, is an anti-hero because he represents a completely anarchic value system that he never sways from. I totally enjoyed playing him and I was comfortable playing him because I thought he was central to the overall theme of self-definition in the movie, something that I connected with a lot. It's about the importance of putting aside other people's notions of who you are and pursuing your passion and enduring risk to pursue your passion. Of all the people in the movie, I think Worm is the character who has the firmest grasp of that philosophy. He may be a nightmare if you get sucked into his world, as Mike [Matt Damon] discovers, but everything that happens to him happens to him because he chooses that lifestyle, not because he's desperate or out of control. As he says, 'The running, the hiding, the occasional beating: these are outgrowths of my choice to pursue the hustle, which I love. And I completely accept them.' Existentially, he's a completely pure character. Certainly he's the only person in Mike's life who says to him, 'You've got to get shot of other people's notions of how you ought to be living your life.' Ironically, it's only by Worm pursuing who he is so relentlessly and enthusiastically that Mike is ultimately forced to draw boundaries between himself and Worm, and between himself and Joey [John Turturro] and Jo [Gretchen Mol], so he can start pursuing who *he* is. Worm tells Mike that he, Mike, will thank him one day for that – and I think he's right. So I liked the fundamental message of all that but I also probably wanted to play Worm because I am *not* like that. It's thrilling to explore that idea of living free of the fear of consequence for a while and to try and move around in it, even if you're affecting a pose.

How did you decide on Worm's demeanour?
When you play poker at that level, there are all kinds of styles you can adopt. You can be the stone-faced killer, the chatty tourist, or you can be like Worm, a guy who relentlessly aggravates people to try and shake 'em up, and I tried to do that. I found it takes a lot of nerve to constantly step up and get in people's faces like that and sincerely not be afraid that someone's going to take you out back and beat you up.

You and Matt Damon took part in some off-limits poker games as part of your research, right?
Yes.

Is that when the acting actually started?
Sure, absolutely.

Generally, how will you prepare for a role?
I can't do a role with less than a couple of months to get ready for it; I'd be too pan-icked. If I plunged right into something without having had time to explore the particular world, I'd feel I was faking it. I don't think I can make a character distinct from myself if I don't take that time. Also, I want the personally satisfying experi-ence of the exploration and the research – that's a big part of the fun of it for me. If you're an actor, you can take the opportunity to be an experiential dilettante. You can live a certain way for a while and then get out of it without paying any of the consequences of choosing it as your natural lifestyle. I consider that a great treat.

Did you hang out with skinheads when you were preparing for *American History X*?
Yes, but not extensively because they were only valuable to me to a certain degree. It was more important to me to talk to people who had gone through the sort of transformation Derek goes through, which is what I did. The most important model for Derek was a terrific book called *Führer-Ex: Memoirs of a Former Neo-Nazi*. It's by a brilliant guy called Ingo Hasselbach [with co-author Tom Reiss], who was raised in terrible social circumstances and plugged himself into the skin-head world as an outlet for his frustration. Because he was so dynamic, he became one of the leaders, but that exposed him to a broader world and then his intelli-gence penetrated the holes in the whole thing and he had to leave it.

How do you assess a character you're thinking of playing without judging him?
I think you have to have both eyes open. You not only have to look at the piece as an actor, but also as if you were the dramatist as well. I always say to myself, 'What's the point of this? Why does this story need to get told? How am I hoping to affect people through this story?' First, you should identify with something in the piece in general and then with the role your character plays in shaping that message or that theme. If I don't connect with a piece overall, it won't matter to me what the dynamic of the character is. And by the same token, if I find the piece to have validity – if it's something I think I want to participate in putting out there – then I don't care if the character is an amoral character, because he's part of the structure of a drama that I believe in.

When I did *Primal Fear*, for example, I wasn't in the position of having a great deal of choice at that point in my career; having been offered it, I was obviously going to do it. But if I was to get a film like that right now, I would read it and say, 'This is a thriller – a piece of entertainment. That's my external assessment of it as a piece.' In the context of that piece, of course, my character, Aaron Stampler, is a completely amoral psychopath. But in terms of a story that has the goal of thrilling people, he's the key to the whole thing. And if you can scare people, that's a completely valid and worthwhile goal and one I have no problem with because I like thrillers, too. I like to get scared and I love the idea of giving people a great date movie to go and get scared at.

But doesn't that film have a semblance of a moral purpose, in that the Richard Gere character, who's a smug celebrity lawyer, needs a wake-up call – a reminder that he needs to serve justice and not simply feed his ego?
Yes. That's what makes it a better-than-average thriller. The element that thickens it up is that Richard's character thinks he's cornered the market on using illusion and manipulating people's perceptions of the truth. I think he likes the feeling that he controls the truth on some level. And so when he's taught this lesson, it's a real body slam. I was always thrilled that Greg Hoblit [director of *Primal Fear*] was completely committed to the idea of the last shot of the picture showing Richard standing there with his shoulders sagging as if he's just been kicked in the teeth. He gets to experience the deflation that he's inflicted on others.

I know if I'd judged Aaron externally, I'd never have been able to get away with the whole thing. In order to pull him off, you have to get inside him and celebrate his role in the piece. You have to adopt his perspective enthusiastically – and the sheer thrill of being him. And because he's not only the villain but also a kind of an actor perpetrating a deception on an audience, he's a character working on some kind of meta- level. It was interesting to step into those shoes.

That begs a question: When you were playing the meek, shaky, beaten-down Aaron, which was 99 per cent of the role, were you playing him exactly like that, or were you playing him as someone with deception going on in his mind?
I think for the most part I played him as that innocent kid, because that's what he himself is doing, even though he's a killer. He's playing those moments with completely sincere vulnerability. But if you go back and look at the film, there are some moments when, in the context of playing innocent, he comes close to getting busted and has to backpeddle. You can see him struggling around his own lie, but he retains his composure. This, for me, is where the medium of film is thrilling because you can make things happen in your eyeballs, literally, that can read a certain way and be very spooky. There was a moment when the psychiatrist played by Frances McDormand was interviewing me in the cell and, for her perspective on me, Greg and Michael Chapman [the cinematographer] cocked the camera just slightly higher than what would have been the normal position for it, and from that angle my eyes registered in a slightly alarming way.

Anything that involves a specific evolution of a character on film is tough because the shooting is broken up over many days. Having moved from stage to film, one of the things I've had to accept is that most days on the making of a film are not big acting days. There are days where you almost have to just go through the motions because if you don't all your moments would be too large. You have to trust minimalism through the bulk of the shooting process, and just pick the moments that need to be bigger. *Primal Fear*, of course, was the first large-scale film I'd worked on, and as soon as I looked at the schedule, I went, 'Holy shit! I have to shoot the ending of this before I shoot the middle of it.' I think they ended up adjusting the schedule so we did shoot more in sequence, but to make sure I built my character the right way – and I've done this on other films – I wrote on index cards the scene number of every scene that I was in and described for myself the point of the character's progression in that scene, or how much I felt he should be revealing. I tacked all these cards up in a big arc on the wall in my hotel room, leading up to the top at the end. Whenever we were shooting out of sequence, I would look at what we were doing that day and then go to the relevant card just to make sure I didn't overdo it or show too much.

The way you talk about acting implies to me that there's almost a triple consciousness that an actor has to have when he or she is making a film. One, you have to be in the moment; two, you have to be aware of the technical stuff that's going on; three, you have to have a sense of where you are inside the character's continuity. Is that about right?
Yes, I'd say it's double in a big sense, and then there's a little sub-challenge inside the working day. I have to say – and this is not to get snotty about it – that most actors probably don't do enough preparation. If you've done your homework properly, you'll have spent time breaking down the character on external levels and on those scene-by-scene levels. You'll have figured things out by working on bits of scenes so that you're not scrambling to do that on the day you start shooting. And since there are often no rehearsal periods on a film, it's usually up to you as an actor to do all this work. Sometimes you get an unexpected surprise. For example, we rehearsed *The Fight Club* for two months. It was [David] Fincher and Brad [Pitt] and me, and sometimes Helena [Bonham-Carter] and Andy Walker, the writer, in a room going through the script, talking about scenes, working on them, reading them, rewriting them if we didn't like them, putting things in, every single day. And since we started shooting, I literally haven't looked at the script once; we've done our work on it. We still talk about things, but we're talking off a base of preparation. So, one half of the job is creating that external consciousness, the other is being in the moment and that's the work of the day. And within that, there's a challenge, which is staying in the moment – or getting out of your head – in an extremely distracting environment.

What drew you to *The Fight Club*?
I felt it was the first script I'd read that struck a generational chord with me. As I said, I've worked on very few things that I've personally empathized with, but this one had that element. I feel that Hollywood studios have completely failed to make films that have touched my generation's nerve yet. Certainly the baby-boomer generation's spoon-fed vision of us as this low-energy, aimless, slacker generation has not resonated with me or anybody that I know, and I think that's been evidenced by the fact that we haven't gone to see those movies. Not to get

too specific right now, but my character's a true generational everyman whose experiences are depicted in a slightly heightened style. Although he's nothing like Ben in *The Graduate*, I think a lot of people will relate to him in the same way by identifying with the plight he's in and the negative choices he makes – the scramble he goes through to try to salvage a more positive option for himself.

You've been involved with the Signature Theater Company in New York City since 1994. Tell me about that group, and to what extent stage acting fits into your plans right now.
Our focus is that we select one playwright every year and ask them to become our playwright-in-residence. We devote an entire season to a retrospective and new presentation of that writer's work and invite them to participate in workshops. We give them readings and ask them if they want to rework any old plays that they felt they never got right, and we always ask them for one new one. We've had an astonishing list of writers: Romulus Linney, Lee Blessing, Edward Albee, Horton Foote, Adrienne Kennedy, Sam Shepard, Arthur Miller, and currently John Guare. I started out acting in the company during the Edward Albee season, although I haven't acted in a play with it since. Sometimes that's because there hasn't been a role for me to do but it's also because I've had these opportunities to work in films with people who are long-time idols of mine and on roles that were of enormous substance compared to what I could have done in theatre.

Will you act with the company again?
I would love to. I just haven't hit on the right character. There's nothing to compare with the experience of performing on stage. It's a much more 'adrenalized', intimate experience than working in film. Right now, though, I can't help feeling that although I believe in the ephemeral magic of stage acting, theatre has become a rarefied form, in that it plays to a limited audience, and in particular a very limited part of the socio-economic spectrum. It's not the people's art form for me these days – certainly not in New York – and I have some hesitancy about it. I've never been in a play that led to anyone other than a white person coming up to me on the street and saying they enjoyed my performance. The response to the work I've done in films has been completely across the board. So far, I would say the strongest emotional responses I've had to *American History X* have come from black people. That gives me more of a feeling as an actor who's playing to the times, and I value that aspect of it.

How do you balance your ambition with the day-to-day experience of being an actor focused on perfecting a role?
You have to avoid marginalizing your work on the project you're working on, because that can happen if you're worried about the next one. The most gratifying thing to me has been to hit a place in the business where people know me

enough that I have the freedom to choose to work on something for no other reason than my abiding interest in it. That kind of creative freedom is the Holy Grail for an actor, because acting is a profession which, because it's a collaborative medium, allows no other kind of creative freedom. It's particularly important to someone like me because I don't think I do particularly good work under any other circumstances. Also I've never really seen myself as someone with the potential to be the kind of actor who can represent a consistent persona that will be of any interest to people. I think all I really have to offer is the kind of work I've been doing, and that's good because it's what I like doing. I need to adhere to that as a modus operandi because there is a certain careerist pressure in Hollywood that puts a lot of value on commercial choices. A lot of people will tell you that it's a good idea to put something in the mix of characters you play that might have potential for later on, and sometimes it's hard not to let those bugs get in your brain. But I think you've got to fight them off because those kinds of choices are just as much a roll of the dice anyway. I've literally had some people say to me, 'Don't be a character actor,' and I've said, 'Well, what else am I going to be?'